The Life
of
ARETHA
FRANKLIN

"A rich, definitive portrait."
—*New York Times*

RESPECT

DAVID RITZ

Praise for David Ritz's

RESPECT

One of *Rolling Stone*'s Best Music Books of the Year

"*Respect* is a comprehensive, illuminating, and unfailingly solicitous account of a life that, whatever its tribulations, conflicts, and complications, has always somehow been redeemed by Franklin's musical calling.... Ritz has an exceptional capacity to listen with care and sympathy to what people tell him, and then render their words vividly and compassionately."　　　　—Gene Seymour, *USA Today*

"Clearly the book Ritz has been preparing to write his whole life. It's stuffed full with revealing interviews.... Knowing the details of Franklin's complicated, sometimes painful life...helps deepen an appreciation of the pain and passion that fueled her music."
　　　　　　　　　　　　　　　—Gavin Edwards, *Rolling Stone*

"You'll be in the nimble hands of a pro if you read *Respect*."
　　　　　　　　　　　— Janet Maslin, *New York Times*

"An honest and genuinely respectful portrait of a true diva by a writer who feels the power of her art."
　　　　　　　　　　　　　—*Kirkus Reviews* (starred review)

"David Ritz's *Respect* judiciously captures the conflicted life of the legendary Queen of Soul."　　　　　　　　—Lisa Shea, *Elle*

"A fascinating, delicious depiction of the life of a woman who'd rather not be depicted.... A book so juicy, it is dripping."
　　　　　　　　　　　　　　　—Rich Juzwiak, *Gawker*

"A remarkably complex portrait of Aretha Franklin's music and her tumultuous life."　　　　　　　　　　　　—*Rolling Stone*

"A candid, far less sanitized look at the enormously gifted but demanding diva."   — *People*

"*Respect* will stand as one of Ritz's greatest and most unusual achievements: a rich, definitive portrait set in motion by a bit of unfinished business."   —Nate Chinen, *New York Times*

"A compelling and much-needed redo on the career and complicated life of Aretha Franklin.... An unflinching portrait of a musical genius."   —Thor Christensen, *Dallas Morning News*

"Only someone who had the complete confidence and trust of Aretha's family and the elite of the Gospel and Rhythm and Blues communities could have gotten this story. An intimate and thorough account of this phenomenal woman's talent and life as only David Ritz could capture."
          —Tommy LiPuma, Grammy-winning producer

"Drawing on previous work and interviews with those close to Franklin, Ritz offers a portrait of a woman for whom faith and respect are essential."   —Vanessa Bush, *Booklist*

"The most comprehensive and accurate account of Franklin yet published."   —Christopher Loudon, *Macleans*

"Commendable for its depth...as well as Ritz's highly readable, captivating style. It's a compelling record of the life of a musical titan and a fascinating picture of the process of recording some of the seminal popular music of our time.... The king of cowriters provides the queen of soul with the definitive biography, along with a healthy dose of reverence, reflection, and, above all, R.E.S.P.E.C.T."   —Bill Baars, *Library Journal*

"The most revealing and well-rounded portrait of the Queen ever written."   —Jim Farber, *New York Daily News*

"Ritz's research—based on interviews with Franklin's siblings and departed legends from Ahmet Ertegun to Vandross—is solid, and he vividly expresses what made Aretha's voice and albums so monumental in the sixties."   —David Browne, *Rolling Stone*

"A major biography, and unauthorized in the extreme."
                    —Robert Christgau, *Barnes & Noble Review*

"The richest record of her friends' and family's words that we are likely to get....Reads like a series of inner-circle conversations held at the barbershop, beauty salon, or kitchen table."
                    —Emily J. Lord, *Los Angeles Review of Books*

"Ritz's intimate and elegant voice steps from behind the veil of the ghostwriter to tell a tale of genius, dysfunction, and blind ambition, describing a world of triumph and tragedy of near mythic proportions. A great read and a really heroic work of biography—honest, loving, no-holds-barred."
                    —Ben Sidran, author of *There Was a Fire*

"The monumental biography we've been waiting for of Lady Soul, our greatest soul singer, from the also very great David Ritz, confidant to an entire generation of soul stars—Ray, Smokey, B.B., Etta, Marvin, et cetera. He is The Man. This is The Book."
                    —Joel Selvin, author of *Here Comes the Night:*
                    The Dark Soul of Bert Berns and the
                    Dirty Business of Rhythm and Blues

"People will be reading *Respect* generations from now to understand our musical culture. David Ritz deserves a lifetime achievement award for 'Most Soul Full Account of America's Music.'"
                    — Charles Keil, author of *Urban Blues*

ALSO BY DAVID RITZ

Biography

Divided Soul: The Life of Marvin Gaye

Faith in Time: The Life of Jimmy Scott

Death of a King: The Real Story of Dr. Martin Luther King Jr.'s Final Year (cowritten with Tavis Smiley)

Autobiography

Brother Ray (cowritten with Ray Charles)

Inside My Life (cowritten with Smokey Robinson)

Blues All Around Me (cowritten with B.B. King)

Rage to Survive (cowritten with Etta James)

The Brothers (cowritten with the Neville Brothers)

Rhythm and the Blues (cowritten with Jerry Wexler)

Aretha: From These Roots (cowritten with Aretha Franklin)

Howling at the Moon (cowritten with Walter Yetnikoff)

Guillaume: A Life (cowritten with Robert Guillaume)

Reach! (cowritten with Laila Ali)

Inside Power (cowritten with Gary Sheffield)

Grace After Midnight (cowritten with Felicia "Snoop" Pearson)

Journey of a Thousand Miles (cowritten with Lang Lang)

Rickles' Book (cowritten with Don Rickles)

Rickles' Letters (cowritten with Don Rickles)

Hound Dog (cowritten with Jerry Leiber and Mike Stoller)

We'll Be Here for the Rest of Our Lives (cowritten with Paul Shaffer)

The Adventures of Grandmaster Flash (cowritten with Grandmaster Flash)

What I Know for Sure (cowritten with Tavis Smiley)

Brother West (cowritten with Cornel West)

I Was Born This Way (cowritten with Carl Bean)

Love Brought Me Back (cowritten with Natalie Cole)

True You (cowritten with Janet Jackson)

Not Dead and Not for Sale (cowritten with Scott Weiland)

A Moment in Time (cowritten with Ralph Branca)

Soulacoaster (cowritten with R. Kelly)

A Woman Like Me (cowritten with Bettye LaVette)

Sinner's Creed (cowritten with Scott Stapp)

When I Left Home (cowritten with Buddy Guy)

Balance (cowritten with Nik Wallenda)

Glow (cowritten with Rick James)

Rocks (cowritten with Joe Perry)

Fiction

Search for Happiness

The Man Who Brought the Dodgers Back to Brooklyn

Blues Notes Under a Green Felt Hat

Barbells and Saxophones

Family Blood

Take It Off! Take It All Off!

Passion Flowers

Sanctified Blues (cowritten with Mable John)

Stay Out of the Kitchen (cowritten with Mable John)

Love Tornado (cowritten with Mable John)

Power and Beauty (cowritten with T. I. Harris)

Trouble and Triumph (cowritten with T. I. Harris)

Inspirational

Messengers: African American Ministers and Gospel Singers Speak

RESPECT

The Life of Aretha Franklin

DAVID RITZ

BACK BAY BOOKS
Little, Brown and Company
New York   Boston   London

*In memory of Jerry Wexler and
Ruth Bowen, righteous mentors*

———————

Back Bay Books / Little, Brown and Company
Hachette Book Group
1290 Avenue of the Americas, New York, NY 10104
littlebrown.com

Originally published in hardcover by Little, Brown and Company, October 2014
First Back Bay paperback edition, November 2015

Back Bay Books is an imprint of Little, Brown and Company, a division of Hachette Book Group, Inc. The Back Bay Books name and logo are trademarks of Hachette Book Group, Inc.

The publisher is not responsible for websites (or their content) that are not owned by the publisher.

The Hachette Speakers Bureau provides a wide range of authors for speaking events. To find out more, go to hachettespeakersbureau.com or call (866) 376-6591.

Library of Congress Cataloging-in-Publication Data

Ritz, David.
    Respect : the life of Aretha Franklin / David Ritz.—First edition.
        pages cm
    Includes bibliographical references and index.
    ISBN 978-0-316-19683-3 (hc) / 978-0-316-19681-9 (pb)
        1. Franklin, Aretha. 2. Soul musicians—United States—Biography. 3. Singers—United States—Biography. I. Title.
    ML420.F778R57 2014
    782.421644092—dc23
[B]   2014018985

10 9 8 7 6 5 4 3

LSC-C

Printed in the United States of America

CONTENTS

Part Four
ARISTA

Part Five
THE LIONESS IN WINTER

RESPECT

MEETING THE QUEEN

In the mid-1970s, when I began my career as an author, there were three people I was determined to work with—Ray Charles, Aretha Franklin, and Marvin Gaye. These were the singers about whom I was most passionate. I simply had to meet them. I was certain that their lives were as intriguing as their music.

Ray came first. I pursued him unrelentingly. Blocked at every turn, I succeeded only when Western Union told me I could send him messages in Braille. I poured my heart into those telegrams. He agreed to meet me, we bonded and were off to the races—but not before I gave up my original plan of writing his biography in my voice and decided instead to write the story in Ray's own voice. That was the moment when I discovered the thrill and beauty of ghostwriting. The book that followed, *Brother Ray,* was well received and gave me the confidence to pursue my next project—collaborating with Aretha. But when Ray introduced me to her in his dressing room at the Dorothy Chandler Pavilion in Los Angeles, she said she wasn't interested—at least not then.

After writing a series of novels, I connected with Marvin Gaye, where the process was reversed. In the middle of our collaboration, Marvin was tragically murdered by his father. I had no choice but to turn our unfinished autobiography into a biography rendered in my voice. Writing *Divided Soul: The Life of Marvin Gaye* was a singular and riveting experience, but one filled with grief. I mourned for Marvin and wished, more than anything, that I could have written the book entirely from his point of view.

From that moment forward, I saw that, given the option, I'd much rather work as a ghostwriter than independent biographer. Not only did I cherish the personal connection with the artist, but I loved channeling the artist's voice. I felt like an actor playing a choice role. For the next twenty years, I ghosted books for, among others, Smokey Robinson, Etta James, B.B. King, and the Neville Brothers. After the publication of each book, I sent a copy to Aretha with a note expressing my hope that she and I would be collaborating one day soon.

After writing the autobiography of Jerry Wexler, Aretha's most important producer, I thought that day was imminent. In researching Wexler's life, I found myself researching a large portion of Aretha's life. Wexler had a long association with practically every major musician who had worked with Aretha and he put me in touch with all of them, including John Hammond, Aretha's original producer, whom I interviewed at length.

Working in the field of rhythm and blues for two decades, I had built up an enormous body of research on the life and work of Aretha. I had spent hundreds of hours speaking to her most knowledgeable colleagues—Luther Vandross, the producer of her comeback hit "Jump to It"; Arif Mardin, the orchestrator who had worked with her for over forty years; and Ruth Bowen, Aretha's booking agent and perhaps her closest business associate, who answered every one of my questions with unflinching candor.

Most significant, it was my relationship with Aretha's immediate family—her brothers, Cecil and Vaughn, and her sisters, Erma and Carolyn—that gave me access to the inner sanctum of the Franklin world before I began working with Aretha herself. Smokey Robinson, who had grown up in Detroit around the corner from the Franklins and was Cecil's closest friend, made many of those introductions. Aretha's siblings became my allies in convincing her to take me on as a collaborator. Over the years they provided me with invaluable and detailed information about their sister.

Every time I went to Detroit, which was often, I sent Aretha a postcard expressing my hope that we could meet. Then in 1994, it happened. On a Wednesday night at approximately eight o'clock, the phone rang in my room in the Atheneum Hotel.

"Mr. Ritz," she said. "This is Aretha Franklin."

A lifetime stutterer, I couldn't get out the first word. For a second I panicked. What if my two-decade pursuit resulted in my inability to utter a single sentence? What if the shock of her call rendered me mute? What if, right then and there, I blew the whole thing?

Perseverance overwhelmed fright, and, with considerable difficulty, I managed to say how happy I was that she called.

"I'm interviewing collaborators for my autobiography," she said, "and I wanted to speak with you."

"Thank you... Miss Franklin."

I wanted to call her Aretha but the formality of her tone—she would call me "Mr. Ritz" for several more weeks—let me know that would be unwise.

"I want to hear how you would go about working with me," she said.

"I'll be glad to come see you whenever it's convenient," I said.

"I'm not doing personal interviews. Just phone calls."

"So this is it?"

My question triggered her first laugh. "Yes, Mr. Ritz, this is it. Tell me your approach."

I explained in the most impassioned terms possible my view of this project—that it was her book I was interested in, not mine; that I was convinced hers was one of the great untold stories in modern American culture; that no one loved her music more than I; that no one listened to her records more obsessively or followed her career as studiously as I did; that no one would work harder to render her authentic voice authentically; that it was my lifetime dream to tell her story and tell it right.

She ended the call without saying when a decision would be

made. I couldn't sleep that night. Until the second call came, a week later, I was a mess.

When I learned that Miss Franklin had selected me, it was one of the happiest moments of my life. The first thing I did was pull out her glorious gospel album *Amazing Grace* and listen to it from start to finish.

I called my friend Billy Preston, whom I had met through Ray Charles decades earlier, to tell him the good news. Billy and Aretha shared a common mentor—Reverend James Cleveland, the gospel great and one of my most reliable sources of information regarding Aretha. Billy had traveled the same sacred-to-secular path as Aretha. They'd known each other since they were kids. They'd been in the same studios and on the same stages together dozens of times. For years, Billy had given me insights into Aretha's world.

He congratulated me and added a warning: "Keep your hopes high and your expectations low."

"Why do you say that, Billy?"

"Because I know her, and girlfriend ain't giving it up. *Ever.*"

I didn't want to believe him. I didn't want to believe other friends and associates of Aretha who told me that I'd never break through her armor and get the real story. I didn't want to believe Erma Franklin, who said, "I love my sister dearly and my prayers are with you. Nothing would make me happier than to see her purge all that pain she's been through. But honestly, I don't see her doing that. She's built a wall around herself that no one's been able to climb over."

Fueled by an inexhaustible enthusiasm, I saw myself scaling that wall, even if others said that was impossible. Nearly all Aretha's closest associates echoed Billy Preston and Erma. They said that Aretha had been increasingly difficult to work with—impatient, controlling, and quick to anger. I didn't care. I'd change all that. I'd be so patient, so uncontrolling, so sweet and mellow, that she'd have to come round. After all, at that point in my career, I knew how to handle stars. I was used to difficult personalities. For all his brilliance, Ray Charles could be cantankerous. I'd had to chase

Marvin Gaye from Hawaii to England to Belgium to get him to tell me his story while he dealt with debilitating depression. Etta James described herself as "schizophrenic to the bone" and thanked me in her book for "being able to stay in the lion cage" with her. Bring on Aretha. I'd reach deep down into my reservoir of good-will and find a way to charm her.

I did, but mostly I didn't. In spite of my determination to be a compassionate listener, someone whose gentle persistence would allow her to reveal all her sacred secrets, my technique ultimately did not work. In the end, I didn't make a dent in her armor. I left her the way I found her, untouched by what I considered my deeply sympathetic approach. In almost all other instances—Ray, Marvin, Etta, Smokey, B.B., the Neville Brothers, Jimmy Scott, Leiber and Stoller, Tavis Smiley, Cornel West, Buddy Guy, Bettye LaVette, Joe Perry—I got the book I wanted. In Aretha's case, I did not. At the same time, she got the book *she* wanted. To this day, Aretha considers her book an accurate portrait.

"When Aretha looks in the mirror," her sister Erma had told me years earlier, "she sees an entirely different woman than we do."

As a collaborator, I always aim for intimacy. I'm a surrogate for the reader, who wants to feel the star speaking directly and intimately to him or her. As I drove to Aretha's house for our initial interview, my plan was to create a relaxed conversational ambience that would promote intimacy.

I knew the exact location of her house in Bloomfield Hills, a woodsy suburb of Detroit, because the night before I had test-driven the route to make sure that on this, my first day on the job, I wouldn't get lost. I had no agenda, no list of questions or topics to cover. I thought it best to let Aretha lead the conversation in what I hoped would be an easygoing, let's-get-to-know-each-other encounter. My only plan was to start off with a prayer, thanking God for this opportunity to create a story that would reflect His love.

Since meeting Marvin Gaye in the late seventies, I had been

increasingly drawn to Christianity. Marvin spoke of Jesus in a way that made me want to believe. The process was slow—I wouldn't be formally baptized until 2004—but as a Jewish intellectual I had begun to see that my anthropological approach to black culture was changing into something else. I realized that at the very heart of that culture was an undying conviction that the God of love is a living spirit.

When Aretha opened the front door and invited me in, God was on my mind. Surely it was only through the grace of God that I was meeting this remarkable woman.

She invited me into the living room. She was still "Miss Franklin" and I was still "Mr. Ritz."

After we exchanged pleasantries, I asked if I might say a short prayer.

I had presumed that the preacher's daughter would be open to prayer anytime. But I quickly saw that my invitation to pray was far too intimate an act. I backed off, but I managed to get in a prayer anyway.

I said, "I just wanted to thank God for giving us the chance to work together."

We spent that day and the next several weeks speaking about music and music alone. When talking about music—especially the gospel world of the fifties from which she emerged—we were always on safe ground. I'd play her a contemporary gospel record she hadn't heard; she'd play me some traditional gospel record I didn't know. The give-and-take was great. Our talks in the living room moved to the kitchen, where she started making me lunch and an occasional dinner. I thought I was home free.

I wasn't. The sensitive questions—Aretha's mother leaving the family, Aretha having two babies while still in her teens, Aretha's being beaten by her first husband, Ted White, Aretha's dad beating his lady friend Clara Ward, the gospel superstar—were off-limits. So was the essential act of introspection. Self-confrontation was something Aretha neither understood nor welcomed. Idealizing her past was her way of hiding pain.

At times that pain, although not heard, could be seen in the tears that fell from her eyes when, in response to a question about some disappointment or loss, she remained silent. I knew that the answer was encased in those tears.

My challenge could not have been clearer. I had to go deeper. Maybe if I broke out the scores of interviews I'd done with her siblings, friends, and associates, their comments might provoke her to do a bit more self-reflection. Bad idea. The book Aretha wanted to write was, plain and simple, her book. I couldn't argue. And, in fact, the argument for the book that we crafted, *From These Roots,* is that, in spite of its enormous gaps and oversights, it remains an accurate view of Aretha's picture of herself. Students of culture and psychology who want to understand this defiantly inscrutable woman cannot afford to ignore her own carefully self-styled testimony.

I count myself among those students. But because my ghostly collaboration resulted in a story I found far-fetched in so many ways, I'm continuing my study. I'm writing the story as I see it.

In my view, my two years of working on *From These Roots* resulted in my failure to actualize the great potential in Aretha's narration. I didn't do what I set out to do. Since the publication of the book, some fifteen years ago, I have not rested easy. It took me a decade to recommit myself to the Aretha story, knowing that this time around, I would have to fly solo.

A few years ago, Aretha herself actually brought up the idea of another book—a follow-up to *From These Roots.* Although she had excluded me from the final revision process of her autobiography, our postpublication relationship remained cordial. She would call me from time to time. In the late nineties, I spent several pleasant evenings with Aretha and Jerry Wexler in East Hampton. I also visited her during her gospel extravaganzas in Detroit.

When I attended one of the several gospel concerts that she produced in Detroit, she took me aside and said, "I think it's time to do another book."

I was surprised and pleased that she wanted to collaborate again.

"I'd like to go back and review some of that earlier material," I said. "I'd like to do it more in depth."

"Oh, no," Aretha was quick to reply. *"From These Roots* is perfect the way it is. I'm talking about everything that has happened since. *Rolling Stone* magazine named me the number one singer of all time. And then there are any number of awards I've received in the past few years."

"I'm afraid that a new edition would have to include more than just a listing of new honors."

"I don't agree," she said. "These awards didn't get the publicity they deserve."

When I mentioned the possibility of my writing an independent biography, she said, "As long as I can approve it before it's published."

"Then it wouldn't be independent," I said.

"Why should it be independent?"

"So I can tell the story from my point of view."

"But it's not your story, it's mine."

"You're an important historical figure, Aretha. Others will inevitably come along to tell your story. That's the blessing and burden of being a public figure."

"More burden than blessing," she said.

When I renewed my research for this book, I did so without Aretha's blessing, but I did have the support of three of Aretha's closest relatives—her first cousin Brenda Corbett (who has also served as her background singer for two decades), her niece Sabrina (daughter of her sister Erma), and her sister-in-law Earline Franklin. They agreed that her story, from a perspective other than her own, needed to be told. They agreed to help me. "We trust you to write the *righteous* version," said Brenda.

I like the word *version*. For all my voluminous research, I do not view my first Aretha Franklin book as anything more than a version. I don't believe that there is such a thing as *the* Aretha story. I believe there are many. My Aretha story is not objective. After my years of working with her, I know her personally and I know her well. I have love and compassion for her as a sister and a believer. I stand in awe of her artistry. But I also come to this project—as Aretha came to *From These Roots*—with a deep bias. I bring the peculiar cultural mix that has informed me. I bring to the text a lifetime of attitudes about psychology and mythology. Because it was black music—not simply gospel, but jazz, blues, and R&B—that brought me to the church where God is worshipped and praised, praise and worship remain essential elements in my approach to art. At the same time, there is no righteousness—at least to my mind—without critical scrutiny. God is to be questioned as well as worshipped; probed as well as praised.

And I bring respect. That's why the book bears the name of her most famous hit. In the end, Aretha is all about respect—getting it and keeping it. There would be no *Respect* without *From These Roots*. I would not have written this book had I not cowritten hers. I see this second book as a companion piece to the first.

I had no choice but to begin it where all serious students of Aretha begin—with her sense of what is true. I honor that sense even as I challenge it. I respect her right to interpret her complex story even as I attempt to reinterpret and expand her interpretation. Most important, though, I thank Aretha for calling me that day at the Atheneum Hotel in Detroit. I thank her for entertaining my endless questions during the years we worked together. I thank her for feeding my spirit and responding to my enthusiasm. I thank her for her vanilla-wafer banana pudding and her lasagna à la Aretha.

Thirty-six years have passed since that fateful evening when Ray Charles introduced me to Aretha Franklin in his dressing room at the Dorothy Chandler Pavilion. Since then, the fact that I have been able to document her life from two radically different points of view—hers and mine—is a privilege for which I am deeply grateful.

Part One

SACRED
SOURCES

1. FATHER AND DAUGHTER

Though Nat Cole, Sam Cooke, and Marvin Gaye all had preacher fathers, none of those fathers were famous. None of them had national reputations or recording careers. Aretha's dad—the Reverend C. L. Franklin—had all that and then some. He was a towering figure in the history of black America, a social activist and progressive theologian who stood beside his close friend Martin Luther King Jr. as a national civil rights leader. His fame, though, came from a remarkable rhetorical talent married to the excitement of hot rhythmic music.

The great blues singer Bobby "Blue" Bland told me about his early memories of seeing C. L. Franklin preach at the New Salem Baptist Church in Memphis.

"Couldn't have been older than eleven or twelve when Mama and them took me to hear this new preacher man everyone was talking about. This was the early forties. We hadn't moved to Memphis yet but we'd go there on the weekend, one of the principal reasons being church. I liked church 'cause of the exciting spirit of the music, but when the preachers got to preaching, I'd get bored and fidgety. But here comes this man with a voice like a singer. In fact, he did sing before he started into preaching—and that got my attention right off. Can't tell you what hymn he sang, but his voice was strong. I sat right up and my mind didn't wander anywhere. He grabbed my attention and kept it. When he started into the preaching part, I stayed with him. Wasn't his words that got me—I couldn't tell you what he talked on that day, couldn't tell you what any of it meant, but it was the *way* he talked. He talked like he was singing. He talked music. The thing that really got me, though, was this squall-like sound he made to emphasize a certain word. He'd catch the word in his mouth, let it roll around and squeeze it with his tongue. When it popped on out, it exploded, and the ladies started waving and shouting. I liked all that. I started popping and shouting too. That next week I asked Mama when we were going back to Memphis to church.

"'Since when you so keen on church?' Mama asked.

"'I like that preacher,' I said.

"'Reverend Franklin?' she asked.

"'Well, if he's the one who sings when he preaches, that's the one I like.'

"'He's sure enough the one,' said Mama.

"Sometimes we'd go to East Trigg Missionary, where, according to Mama, the pastor W. Herbert Brewster was Reverend Franklin's teacher. There were two powerful voices in that church—Queen Anderson and J. Robert Bradley—who were about the baddest gospel singers you'd ever wanna hear. I know Reverend Franklin loved them because sometimes he'd show up at East Trigg for the late service after he was done preaching at New Salem. He'd sit there on the first row taking notes during Brewster's sermons. Then he'd be up on his feet shouting and waving when Queen Anderson and Bradley started into singing.

"Wasn't long after that when I started fooling with singing myself. I liked whatever was on the radio, especially those first things Nat Cole did with his trio. Naturally I liked the blues singers like Roy Brown, the jump singers like Louis Jordan, and the ballad singers like Billy Eckstine, but, brother, the man who really shaped me was Reverend Franklin.

"Years later, when I started driving for B.B. King, it turned out B. felt the same way about Reverend Franklin. By then, Reverend had gone from Memphis to Buffalo to Detroit, where me and B. would go to the New Bethel Church to see him."

"I sat under his sermons for many years," B.B. King told me. "I'd like to say that he was the bluesman's preacher because he'd come to the clubs to see us, but that wouldn't be fair. Frank—that's what his friends called him—was everyone's preacher. Because those sermons he recorded were selling in the same little stores as our blues records, we also looked at him as a fellow artist. He was one of us. Unlike other men of the cloth, he never called our music devilish—and we loved him for that. But he did more than that. He let us know that he admired what we were doing. He called us true artists and had no qualms about telling the world just how he felt. That made us feel like royalty."

The fact that Reverend was a liberal—even a radical—in the severely conservative black church culture shaped Aretha's story on every level. To take on that culture required an unusually strong character and conviction. Reverend had both.

"He possessed rhetorical genius," said Jesse Jackson, who preached at C.L.'s funeral in 1984. In the discussion I had with him in 2008, Jackson described his mentor as the model of the modern black preacher. "He not only infused his messages with great poetry and startling metaphors, but he imparted significant social meaning, pointing out that, as children of God, we were no more or less beloved than any other people. C.L. preached the say-it-loud-I'm-black-and-I'm-proud message generations before James Brown. Along with Dr. King, he was far ahead on the curve of civil rights. He was an assertive intellectual, not an apologist, a beacon of strength and hope for the millions of the transplants who'd come from the South in the forties and fifties to find work in the great industrial cities of the North."

"I saw Aretha's daddy as one of the few preachers powerful enough to dispel that old myth that says gospel and blues are mortal enemies," James Cleveland told me. "He had the courage to say that they actually go together as proud parts of our heritage as a people."

The creative tension between secular and sacred music is one of the enduring mysteries of African American culture. For those raised in the church, the bias against reconciling the spirit and the flesh runs deep. Singers praising God on a Sunday morning while using those same artistic passions—rhythms and riffs—to extol sensual pleasures on a Saturday night have faced angry rebuke.

In Jewish culture, a similar story is told in *The Jazz Singer,* the first talkie, a groundbreaking film released in 1927 in which Al Jolson plays Jakie Rabinowitz, son of a cantor—a singer of sacred songs. The boy defies his ultrareligious dad by singing popular songs and leaving the synagogue for the stage.

Ironically, Reverend C. L. Franklin was, along with his daughter Aretha, an Al Jolson enthusiast. And doubly ironic is the fact that it was Franklin, a pure product of the black church, who defied this strict separation of gospel and jazzy blues.

In the twentieth century, the sacred/secular split begins with Thomas A. Dorsey, the former barrelhouse pianist known as Georgia Tom, who invented modern black gospel music in the thirties by infusing blues into songs of worship. His first hit, "Precious Lord, Take My Hand," was sung by his student Mahalia Jackson at the funeral of Martin Luther King Jr. Aretha sang it countless times. Yet the black church community was slow to warm to Dorsey's music. They considered it too jazzy. Even when it was adopted into the repertory, old-timers complained that it was tainted with fleshly harmonies.

The Jazz Singer archetype—the singer caught between the church and the world—persisted in the black community throughout the forties and fifties. The Jazz Singer dramas vary but are linked by the same essential story line: a terrible tension between singing for God and singing for sex.

Superstition in the black community ran deep.

Remembering the death of Jesse Belvin in Arkansas in 1962,

Ray Charles told me, "Jesse used to talk about how he directed the choir in some church in LA. His people warned him about leaving the church. But, like most of us, Jesse had stars in his eyes. When he started singing R-and-B, you could hear the church in his voice. He was the cat who wrote 'Earth Angel.' That always felt like a religious song to me. Well, when Jesse and his old lady were killed in a car wreck, folks started talking much shit. They said he was dead because he'd left the church. They were sure that God was punishing him. A lot of church singers were plain scared to cross over to the pop side, including Mahalia. Not me. When I caught hell for turning gospel songs into R-and-B, I couldn't have cared less. I don't believe in no superstitions. Besides, I knew why Jesse was killed. His driver had been my driver first. I'd fired that guy for drinking and falling asleep at the wheel. He's the cat who killed Jesse and Jesse's wife. God didn't have shit to do with it."

The shooting death of Sam Cooke, murdered by a female hotel manager in Los Angeles in 1964, sent shock waves through the gospel/blues community.

"I remember my dad saying one word to me after we learned that Sam was shot," said Marvin Gaye. "He said, '*See?*'

"'See what?' I asked.

"'See what happens when you displease God.'

"I didn't argue," Marvin continued. "You couldn't argue with my father. But he was one of the ministers who thought if you sang the devil's music, you wound up going down with the devil himself. I like to tell myself that I don't have that attitude—that I'm liberated from the old way of thinking. In the deepest part of me, though, those thoughts are there. To survive this world, I'm pretty sure that one day I'll have to follow Saint Francis and devote myself to singing for the birds and the God who created them."

"One of the most astounding things about C.L.," said James Cleveland, "is that although his liberal attitudes about music seem like they should be coming from someone educated in the North, he was a farm boy from the Deep South."

Born January 22, 1915, in rural Mississippi to sharecroppers,

Franklin was raised by his mother, Rachel, who would, in turn, raise Aretha. Big Mama, as the family called her, was the prominent maternal figure in Aretha's life. C.L.'s dad disappeared when the boy was four.

"According to Big Mama," Aretha's baby sister, Carolyn, told me, "Daddy had the voice of a grown man when he was only ten. They saw him as prophetic. As a preteen, he was already delivering sermons."

"Big Mama worshipped her son," said Aretha's brother Cecil. "She used to talk about how he was years ahead of the other kids when it came to reading. She'd talk about how the nearest town with a library was thirty miles away, and how they had to ride a horse-drawn wagon to get there. By the time he was thirteen, he had read novels by Charles Dickens and Nathaniel Hawthorne and could name the books of the Bible from Genesis to Revelation—not only name them, but write commentaries on them. In deep backwoods Mississippi, he was considered a phenomenon, a wonder child."

At fourteen, C.L. experienced what he called "my born-again baptism" in the Sunflower River. Despite not completing grade school, at eighteen he was preaching on a circuit of churches from Cleveland to Clarksdale, Mississippi. Before turning twenty-one, he enrolled at Greenville Industrial College, an unaccredited Afro-Baptist school surrounded by sharecropper plantations.

"I had lived and worked in Greenville," said B.B. King. "That's part of the reason Frank and I got along so well. We knew the territory of each other's upbringings. We had both been treated like dogs and called dirty niggers. We had both witnessed lynchings. Yet our mamas taught us to believe in a God of justice.

"Frank told me that his college had taught him to believe every word of the Bible. You had to read it literally. He told me that when he challenged one of the teachers by mentioning the theories of Charles Darwin, the teacher slapped him across his face. But even then, Frank understood that, although there's deep truth in the Bible, there's also poetry, and that all poetry is open to interpretation."

"Daddy's college was all about Booker T. Washington's go-slow accommodation approach to the racial question," said C.L.'s son, Cecil. "Washington stressed technical colleges for blacks while W.E.B. DuBois, his adversary, argued for a liberal arts education that would increase our ability to think deeply and critically. Ironically, in spite of his fundamentalist indoctrination at Greenville Industrial, Daddy ultimately rejected fundamentalism. In sentiment and philosophy, he was closer to DuBois than Washington. His deep intellectual curiosity led him to read with not only his heart, but his head. He swam against the cultural tide of his times and, by the natural force of his native intelligence, became a progressive. Daddy loved the Lord as passionately as any fundamentalist, but he understood that God's word was often not self-explanatory. God's word required informed and loving explanation on the part of man."

By age nineteen, C.L. was married to Alene Gaines. By twenty-one, he had divorced Alene and married Barbara Siggers, who had a young son, Vaughn. When C.L. was twenty-three, Barbara gave birth to their first child, Erma Vernice. By then they were living in Memphis, where, at age twenty-four, Reverend preached his first sermon at the New Salem Baptist Church, where Bobby Bland first heard him. That was 1939. Barbara and C.L.'s son, Cecil, was born in 1940.

That same year Franklin fathered another child, not with Barbara but with Mildred Jennings, who was twelve years old when she became pregnant with C.L.'s daughter Carol Allan. The scandal was kept secret from his other children until he sat them down in 1958 and revealed the truth to them.

On March 25, 1942, Aretha Louise, named after his father's two sisters, was born in Memphis at 406 Lucy Avenue to C. L. Franklin and his wife, Barbara.

C.L. made his first foray into the media world in Memphis in the early forties. He hosted his own radio show, *The Shadow of the Cross,* whose mission, according to C.L., was "to offer hymns of inspiration, messages to unify the Negroes of the Mid-South, assuage racial animus, and acquaint white listeners with the Negro's loyalty and accomplishments." It was in Memphis where he began crafting his most famous sermon—"The Eagle Stirreth the Nest." Eighty years after Franklin employed the graphic and highly complex metaphor, the sermon is included in several academic anthologies of literature, is taught in colleges, and remains one of the essential texts of African American history.

In 1944, the family moved to Buffalo, New York, where C.L. preached at the Friendship Baptist Church. That same year, the last of the four Franklin/Siggers children—Carolyn Ann—was born.

As a media presence, C.L. grew increasingly comfortable. In Buffalo he became the first black preacher to utilize radio. According to his biographer Nick Salvatore, "Franklin's 'Voice of Friendship' program highlighted religious worship (including at times a brief sermon by C.L.), gospel music, and commentary on current events."

During the summer of 1945, when C.L. was thirty, his big moment arrived at the National Baptist Convention. The *Michigan Chronicle* reported that his thunderous sermon, taken from 2 Corinthians 5:1–2, "almost paralyzed the convention with logic and history and thought." The scripture itself—"For we know that if our earthly house, this tent, is destroyed, we have a building from God, a house not made with hands, eternal in the heavens"—proved ironic. The forcefulness of its message led to a new earthly church home for Franklin. His fiery delivery caught the attention of the elders of Detroit's New Bethel Baptist, who, when their pastor Horatio Coleman resigned, invited C.L. to lead their congregation. Starting in the summer of 1946, when Aretha was four, her family moved to Detroit, where, in the early fifties, Reverend C. L. Franklin became a national star.

Idealization is a fascinating phenomenon that I came to better understand when, while collaborating with Aretha on her autobiography, *From These Roots,* I saw *Minnelli on Minnelli,* the Broadway show where Liza sang songs associated with the movies of her dad, director Vincent Minnelli. She reminisced about how Vincent and her mother, Judy Garland, met on the set of *Meet Me in St. Louis*. Anyone remotely familiar with the Garland/Minnelli marriage knows that it was stormy from the start and ended in bitter divorce. But Liza didn't tell that story. She painted a portrait of an idyllic parental relationship that led to Liza's idyllic life. In reimagining her childhood as a privileged daughter of two deliriously happy people, Liza created a fairy tale that swept away the pain of a traumatic past.

In *From These Roots,* Aretha speaks of her two sisters, Erma and Carolyn, and her two brothers, Cecil and Vaughn. She does not disclose that Vaughn was her mom's son by another man. Neither does she mention Carol Allan, the daughter born to her father and the teenage Mildred Jennings. She clings to the myth that, while they were together, her parents enjoyed an idyllic relationship.

In the dedication of her book, Aretha wrote, "I dedicate my book to my parents, Reverend C. L. Franklin and Barbara Siggers, who came together in love and marital bliss and out of this union came I, Aretha."

Aretha was vague about the exact moment when her Mississippi-born mother took her son Vaughn and left her husband and four other children to move back to Buffalo in 1948.

Big sister Erma, ten years old at the time, remembered the event well. "We were devastated," she said. "Mother was an extraordinary woman, extremely beautiful and bright. Her singing voice was angelic. I believe she could have been a vocal star. She also played piano. She worked as a nurse's aide, and, even though Daddy had a good salary from the church, I felt that she wanted to be independent. Maybe that was the source of the problem. I really don't know. I do know that my parents' relationship was stormy and that my father had a violent temper. I never saw him strike her but we were all very conscious of not inciting Daddy's wrath. I'd also be lying if I didn't admit that we certainly knew about my father's reputation as a ladies' man. We saw how women in church literally threw themselves at him. After I became older, I saw for myself that he availed himself of many of those women. That didn't make us love him any less. That's just who he was.

"Mother moving to Buffalo might have been her idea or his— I'm not sure. She may well have been afraid of him or she may well have grown tired of sharing him with other ladies. I must say, though, that my parents handled the situation maturely. She assured us that she would always be our mother and we could visit her whenever we wanted. And we did. Buffalo is only two hundred miles from Detroit and we went to see Mother all the time."

In discussing her mother, Aretha railed against the notion that Barbara had, in fact, abandoned her family. She called that rumor a vicious lie. In discussing her mom, she remembered the woman as loving and caring in every way. In Aretha's view, her mother would be the last person in the world to desert her children.

And yet the myth of Barbara Siggers's desertion continued. As recently as 2012, Anthony Heilbut, a prominent scholar of gospel music, wrote in his otherwise brilliant *The Fan Who Knew Too Much,* "Barbara left home when Aretha was ten and died a few years later without seeing her children again." In fact, Aretha was six when her mother moved back to Buffalo in 1948, and, according to all four of the Franklin siblings I interviewed, they visited her on a regular basis.

"My father was a different kind of man," Aretha's big brother Cecil Franklin told me when we spoke in the mid-1980s. "His loyalty was essentially to God, his children, and his congregation. He was never going to be a one-woman man. In contrast, Mother was certainly a one-man woman. She was totally devoted to him and did not like sharing him with the world. During those visits to Buffalo, I know she wanted us to permanently move in with her, but that wasn't going to happen. Not only were we a handful, but she didn't have the funds to raise five children. Dad did. All sorts of women from church were more than willing to look after us— plus we had Big Mama, who ran our household with an iron fist. It was highly unconventional in those days for a father to assume custody of his children after a marital breakup, but C. L. Franklin was a highly unconventional man."

"Looking back at the whole situation," said Carolyn Franklin, Aretha's baby sister, "I think Mother's move impacted Aretha more than anyone. At the time I was barely four and less conscious of what was happening. Aretha was a severely shy and withdrawn child who was especially close to her mother. Erma, Cecil, and I were much more daring and independent. Aretha and I shared a room, and after Mother left I saw her cry her eyes out for days at a time. I remember comforting her, my big sister, by telling her how much fun it would be to visit Buffalo. Days before those trips to see Mother, Aretha would have her little bag packed and be ready to go. The highlight of the visits would be the toy nurse's kit Mother gave us."

Aretha had specific memories about modeling herself after a nurse's aide like her mother. She spoke about how her mom instructed her to care for patients and how she joyfully went to Buffalo General Hospital to watch her mother work. She remembered her mother as a faultlessly patient woman who neither scolded nor said a bad word about anyone, including the Reverend C. L. Franklin. In short, she saw her mother as a saint.

Her memories were also specific when it came to her mother's house in Buffalo on Lythe Street in a tree-lined neighborhood called Cold Springs. She recounted the furnishings: the blue-and-silver velvet chairs, the fancy couches, the upright piano. She and her mom sang together. Those were the times Aretha cherished most. Because the house was small, she and Erma slept next door at the home of Mr. and Mrs. Dan Pitman. Mrs. Pitman taught Aretha to crochet, a skill she cultivated throughout her life.

"During those trips to Buffalo," Erma remembered, "we were introduced to a gentleman, Trustee Young. I presumed he was Mother's boyfriend. We loved riding in his big car. Sometimes he'd take us to Niagara Falls."

"As much as Aretha adored our father," said Cecil, "she would have been thrilled to live with Mother. If she hadn't been so wary of displeasing our dad, I'm sure she would have asked him. But that question would never be posed. Dad made it clear that wasn't an option. So every time we had to leave Buffalo and return to Detroit, it broke Aretha's little heart. Dad did everything in his power to make Ree feel secure, but I know insecurity invaded her spirit at an early age. For all that she has achieved in her life, I think that basic insecurity has never left her. In fact, I believe it defines her—that and her soaring talent."

"Onstage and in the studio no one is more confident," Carolyn told me, "but offstage it's been a different story. She's changed a lot over the years, but if she acts extremely assertive now, I believe it's to overcompensate for her doubts. It sounds crazy that someone as gifted as my sister Aretha would harbor doubts, but she does. That came as a direct result of a challenging childhood."

The Aretha I began working with seemed anything *but* insecure. That's why I was surprised to reread the interviews I'd done with her siblings a decade earlier. Because Erma, Cecil, and Carolyn were all in agreement, I had no reason to doubt them. Aretha had been an insecure little girl.

Ruth Bowen, her booking agent, helped me understand.

"I've known Aretha ever since she was a little girl," she told me. "I met her through her daddy, whom I called Frank. Frank was great friends with Dinah Washington, my first major client. Dinah was not only her father's girlfriend for a minute, at one point she was also Ted White's girlfriend, the man who became Aretha's first husband. Ted and I were close. But don't let me get ahead of myself, honey. Let me tell you about the kind of child Aretha was. She was a traumatized child—that's who she was. It's one thing to have your mama move out of the house for reasons you don't understand. But it's another to have your mama die of a heart attack as a young woman. Aretha was ten when that happened. And it happened just like that—no preparation, no warning. Frank told me that he was afraid that Aretha wouldn't ever recover, that she was unable to talk for weeks. She crawled into a shell and didn't come out until many years later. What brought her, of course, was the music. Without the music I'm not sure Aretha would have ever found her way out of the shell."

In *From These Roots* Aretha devotes less than a page to the death of her mother. She simply recounts that her father called the four children into the kitchen and said that Barbara had died of a heart attack. She assures the reader that her father could not have been more understanding. In her account, there is no attempt to process the pain because, according to Aretha, pain is a most private concern.

2. INSTABILITY

The Franklins moved to Detroit in 1946, three years after the race riots that tore the city apart. "Hate strikes"—whites refusing to work alongside blacks in the auto industry—led to mounting tensions that exploded into full-scale rioting over two days and left thirty-five dead. Aretha remembered next-door neighbors Richard Ross and his family discussing the disturbances in dramatic detail.

"My brother Vaughn used to talk about the discrimination he had encountered in Buffalo," said Cecil, "but until Detroit we hadn't experienced any real racial animus. Detroit turned out to be a hotbed of political, social, and racial unrest. The stories we heard about the riots centered on the violent anger whites were feeling for blacks who'd moved from the South looking for work— looking, in the view of many whites, for *their* work. When I went to college at Morehouse, I did a paper on the riots that helped me understand what, at age six, I couldn't begin to grasp.

"Just before the riots, Packard had put a few black workers next to white men on the assembly line. Right after that, twenty-five thousand whites walked off the job. Remember, this was the middle of World War Two, when no patriotic American wanted to slow down production. Anyway, one of the protesters got on the PA system and screamed, 'I'd rather have Hitler win the war than work next to a nigger!'

"There was also the housing mess. Aside from the Brewster Projects—that's where Diana Ross grew up—public apartment buildings were white-only. Blacks were ripped off right and left, overcharged for filthy and unsafe living quarters. For a whole generation of blacks in cities like Chicago and Detroit, the Great Migration became the Great Nightmare.

"The spark that lit the fire happened on Belle Isle, a picnic spot in the middle of the Detroit River. The incident had sexual undertones. A white man said a black man made a pass at his girl. They began fighting and soon the fight spread. Rumors started racing. Blacks heard that a white man had thrown a black woman and her baby off Belle Isle Bridge. Whites and blacks went after each other for three days. Mobs attacked mobs. It ended only when President Roosevelt called in troops. By then thirty-five people were killed. Twenty-five of those were blacks. Of the twenty-five black deaths, seventeen died at the hands of the police. It was all-out racial warfare.

"As a college kid studying history, I asked Dad about how it felt back in the forties to move to a city where racial hatred ran so high.

"'I saw it as a challenge,' he told me. 'The NAACP was falsely being charged with instigating the trouble. And in the black community, the white establishment was being charged with neglecting our needs. My job was to tend to the spiritual needs of the black community, but I also saw the need to raise everyone's political consciousness. Back in Buffalo, I had invited A. Philip Randolph, the president of the Brotherhood of Sleeping Car Porters, to speak at church. Brother Randolph eloquently and unequivocally called for equal treatment of blacks in the workplace. He energized our congregants and me as well. I saw then that the life of a true Christian cannot be restricted to interpreting scripture. Moral justice and social justice cannot be separated.'"

★　　★　　★

Anna Gordy, sister of Berry Gordy and first wife of Marvin Gaye, knew C.L. well. When she and I spoke about him, she said, "Our relationship was far deeper than a mere friendship." She remembered meeting him in the late forties when she was twenty-five and he was thirty-three. She also remembered his preaching "The Eagle Stirreth Her Nest" and relating it to the race riots of 1943.

"I felt he was the most dynamic man in the city," said Anna. "His sheer brilliance attracted many people who were not regular churchgoers. The man was a poet and a healer. When I first heard him, we were still feeling the aftershocks of the riots. Everyone in Detroit was still on edge. Reverend Franklin helped take off the edge by explaining how God uses history for man's good. If I understood him correctly, God was the eagle, and history was the nest. Reverend pointed out how disturbances can lead to progress. That's the eagle stirring the nest. When the status quo is exploded, change is possible—change for the good. At a time when Detroit was filled with animosity and uncertainty, this minister reassured us that out of chaos can come a higher and more just order. Later, in the fifties and sixties, he would prove to be a great civil rights leader, but even as a young man we felt that Reverend was wise beyond his years."

Cecil, who heard the "Eagle Stirreth Her Nest" sermon countless times, said he never tired of the message.

"That was Dad's favorite metaphor," he said. "When he invoked that eagle, he really soared. If you look at the language closely, you'll understand that he's using it to show that, no matter how circumstances seem to be disrupting our lives, God is in control. And God is directing us to a better path. When we're moving in the direction that God wants us to move, when we're doing His will, we're flying high like the eagle. Dad's style was a combination of speaking, shouting—we called it *whopping*—and then singing. He'd go back and forth between those three modes until his message was hammered home and all the saints in church were up and praising God."

No doubt, after the loss of her mother, Aretha gravitated to the strength of her father.

"We all did," said Cecil. "And because Dad was a natural patriarch—both of his church and [of] our family—we were drawn to his side. He was our great protector. The difference between Aretha and the rest of his children, though, was this: Early on, she became his partner. She became part of his service and also part of his traveling ministry. Later on, I learned to preach, and I did preach in his church. Later on, Erma sang and sang beautifully in his church and on records. So did Carolyn and cousin Brenda. We realized we were all anointed with talent. We were blessed with the precious genes of our musical ancestors. But Aretha manifested that talent at an ungodly early age."

Smokey Robinson was another eyewitness. "Cecil and I were kids when we met," he told me. "We grew up on the same love of music—not just gospel, but jazz. The first great voice that influenced me was Sarah Vaughan. I don't think Cecil and I were ten when we started digging progressive jazz.

"Aretha was always around, a shy girl who came alive when we started playing records. I heard her singing along with Sarah in a way that scared me. Sarah's riffs are the most complex of any singer, yet Aretha shadowed them like it was the most natural thing in the world.

"The other thing that knocked us out about Aretha was her piano playing. There was a grand piano in the Franklin living room, and we all liked to mess around. We'd pick out little melodies with one finger. But when Aretha sat down, even as a seven-year-old, she started playing chords—big chords. Later I'd recognize them as complex church chords, the kind used to accompany the preacher and the solo singer. At the time, though, all I could do was view Aretha as a wonder child. Mind you, this was Detroit, where musical talent ran strong and free. Everyone was singing and harmonizing; everyone was playing piano and guitar. Aretha came out of this world, but she also came out of another far-off magical world none of us really understood. She came from a distant musical planet where children are born with their gifts fully formed."

★   ★   ★

Charlie Parker was blessed to be born in Kansas City when a variety of rich musical currents were converging. Dinah Washington came as a child to Chicago, a city whose impassioned gospel, jazz, and blues nourished her soul and informed her singular style. Aretha was a providential product of Detroit, a vibrant urban center, like Chicago, whose culture in the forties and fifties was shaped by the Great Migration of southern blacks looking to move up to greater income and status in a city largely hostile to their aspirations.

The tension caused by that hostility only intensified artistic expression. Blues singers—such as John Lee Hooker, who, like C. L. Franklin, had made the move from Mississippi to Detroit—were excited by the hope of social mobility. Down south, John Lee had sung on street corners and flatbed trucks. In Detroit, he sang in bars. It was also in Detroit that John Lee—as well as C.L.—started making records.

"When I first saw John Lee in Detroit," B.B. King told me, "he said that the white man had raised the rent on a couple of the bars where he'd been playing. When the bars closed down, John Lee went looking for nightclubs—which is how he wound up on Hastings Street."

Hastings Street is ground zero for the Aretha Franklin story. Her father's New Bethel Baptist Church was at 4210 Hastings, steps from the heart of the black entertainment district. It was the point where Saturday night merged into Sunday morning and sin met salvation at the crossroads of African American musical culture. High on the Holy Ghost, dancing in the aisles of New Bethel, the saints celebrated the love of Christ. High on wine and weed, the party people celebrated the love of the flesh. Was it the grinding grooves of the club that got into the church, or was it the sensuous beat of the church that got into the club? Did C. L. Franklin get his blues cry from Muddy Waters the same way Bobby Bland borrowed his blues cry from C.L.?

On Hastings Street, heavy commerce moved in both directions—saintly blues at night, bluesy gospel in the morning.

"When I first visited Detroit from Chicago," said Buddy Guy, "it was later in the fifties. I had to see two people. The first was Reverend C. L. Franklin, 'cause B.B. had told me he could preach better than Howlin' Wolf could sing. B. was right. Then I had to go to Hastings Street to see John Lee Hooker. The song that turned me into an aspiring bluesman was 'Boogie Chillen'.' It was the big hit in 1948 when I was still on the plantation in Louisiana. John Lee sang about 'walkin' down Hastings Street where everyone was talking about the Henry Swing Club.' In Louisiana, I imagined Hastings Street as something glamorous. I imagined big fancy cars and fine women, music blasting and couples grinding on each other to John Lee's sex blues. When I got to Hastings and saw it in person, though, it was even more amazing than what I'd imagined. The churches and the clubs were right next to each other. You'd see church singers singing in a jazzy style while jazz groups used the church organist in their rhythm sections. In both cases, the job was the same. Gospel music made folks happy. Blues made folks lose their blues. I didn't see that much difference between the two, even if preachers did claim it was the difference between Jesus and the devil. B.B. King loved C. L. Franklin because he didn't say that. He didn't pit one against the other. He said all good music came from God."

Aretha stressed that her father was interested in the good life and taught that goodness was not restricted to the church. In the late forties, C.L. also concluded that the good life required a grand house.

"Daddy's demand before moving to Detroit," said sister Erma, "was that the church construct a new sanctuary and buy him a parsonage. The old New Bethel, a reformed bowling alley, was a sight for sore eyes. The new one, built on the same plot on Hastings, was modern and attractive. Our parsonage, at six forty-nine East Boston Boulevard, was really a stately mansion. This was on the city's north end, a few miles from New Bethel but a different world altogether. The neighborhood was integrated, but there were more black families than whites. The blacks were mainly light-skinned professionals—doctors and lawyers and political leaders. If Daddy hadn't been an up-and-coming minister with a large congregation, his dark skin would have kept him off Boston Boulevard. But there was no denying Daddy. He knew his place was among the city's elite."

Describing the home on Boston Boulevard, Aretha said that she felt like a fairy-tale princess living in a castle. The house was situated on the corner of Boston and Oakland, the major street that divided the neighborhood into economic/social classes. The Boston class was the highest. Boston was a genuine *boulevard*, not a street, with an island in the center filled with beautiful plants and shrubs. She spoke proudly of her neighbors—Charles Diggs Sr., a congressman, and Dr. Harold Stitts, a physician. She remembered the color of the drapes in her living room (dark purple) and of the plush wall-to-wall carpeting (emerald green). The grand piano sat by the window. She was the first of her friends to have a television— a large Emerson on which she and her dad watched the boxing matches sponsored by Gillette razor blades.

"Our mother leaving and our mother dying were the two great traumas of our childhood," said Erma. "The third happened when we lost Lola Moore, our second mother."

Lola Moore moved in with C.L. and his children in the early fifties, shortly after Barbara Siggers died. Aretha saw her as a woman with a great flair for fashion, a wonderful sense of humor, and, to top it all off, extraordinary culinary skills. When Aretha and her siblings traveled to Chicago to meet Lola's family, she was certain that C.L. had every intention of marrying Lola. But it wasn't meant to be.

In *From These Roots*, Aretha narrates C.L. and Lola's breakup and Lola's subsequent departure from the Franklin household. She describes how Cecil was so devastated that he chased after Lola's cab and tried to stop her from leaving. But when Erma and Cecil told me the story, they both remembered that it was Aretha who nearly fell apart when Lola headed back to Chicago.

"I thought she was going to throw herself in front of that taxicab," said Erma. "She was inconsolable. We were all sad because we wanted a mother to replace the one we had just lost. I cried, Carolyn cried, and Cecil cried, but Aretha was inconsolable. It took her days to come out of her room and face the reality that we had lost Lola."

"The difficult part," Cecil explained, "was that we all wanted to plead our case to Daddy. We wanted to tell him that Lola was perfect, that he should marry her and complete our incomplete family. I recall Aretha coming and asking me to intervene on our behalf. 'Tell him we need a mom,' she said. 'Tell him we want Lola.' 'I can't do that, Ree,' I said. 'Daddy won't listen.' 'He'll listen to you, Cecil.' 'No, he won't. I'm not saying a word.' And I didn't.

"Even after Lola had left for Chicago, Aretha wanted to ask Daddy to bring her back to Detroit. But she knew better. Erma might challenge Daddy or question his decisions—Erma was a very strong young woman—but Aretha would do nothing to displease him."

"None of us knew why Lola left," said Carolyn, "but looking back at the situation and putting together certain dates, it seems clear that while Lola was living with us, Daddy had also started his romantic relationship with Clara Ward. I'm sure that Lola couldn't have been too happy about that."

Clara Ward's entrance into C.L.'s life rewired the emotional circuitry of the Franklin household. The romance began as early as 1949 and, despite many breakups and makeups, didn't abate until Clara's death, in 1973, with C.L. by her bedside.

"We saw Clara and Frank," said Reverend James Cleveland, referring to Reverend Franklin, "as the church's version of Ike and Tina. Of course, we didn't say that out loud, but among ourselves we knew what was happening. They didn't even try to hide it. And there was no reason they should have. They were our royalty—he our greatest preacher, she our greatest singer—a couple beyond reproach."

Aretha never admitted that her dad and Clara were lovers. She preferred to view them strictly as friends. She praised Clara's full-throated gospel style, her extravagant manner of dressing, and her sky-high coifs. She praised her hats. She even praised the way she ate chicken. She described how Clara had taught her to eat a chicken leg. It was a matter of taking dainty, baby-size bites. She called Clara a great lady and spoke of how she wished Clara had married her dad.

"Every little girl needs a mother," Carolyn Franklin told me, "and we were no different. Big Mama, of course, was a major presence in our lives. She was a force to be reckoned with. She was a loving, no-nonsense, dipping snuff–loving lady who spared no rod and took no prisoners. Big Mama was wonderful, but she was Daddy's mom. Her son was the center of her world. We were on the margins of that world. We all desperately needed a woman—a mother—to hold us to her heart and call us her babies. Aretha had this need in the worst way because of her introverted nature. When our mother left and then died, Ree became even more introverted. But then she suffered the loss of another mother when Lola left. That's when she told me that Clara was going to be our mother. Every winter she'd predict that Daddy and Clara would marry in June. She'd fantasize about their storybook wedding. When it didn't happen—and continued not to happen—Aretha was crushed.

"Daddy tried his best to reassure her but, given his gifts and obligations, he was distracted. When Aretha began singing in church, she caught his attention, but that only covered up her insecurities. It actually buried them. In truth, they never went away."

3. MOTHERS AND FATHERS

Aretha is a heartfelt fan of the great voices, and in that respect too she is her father's daughter. She freely expresses her admiration for all types of singers, from obscure gospel vocalists, like Jackie Verdell, to Peggy Lee—"one of the all-time hippest singers"—and she lavishly praises Leontyne Price. Among her favorite male singers is Little Jimmy Scott, a deeply soulful jazz artist who, back in the fifties, was close to both Billie Holiday and Dinah Washington and who sang a haunting version of a song dear to Aretha's heart: "Sometimes I Feel Like a Motherless Child."

"Everyone wanted to mother Aretha," said Ruth Bowen. "When I first saw her in her father's church, she looked like a lost child. Her eyes were filled with sadness. She looked afraid. Then when she got up to sing, this sound came out. It was gospel filled with blues. I mean, frighteningly strong blues, beautifully mature blues. After she sang, she sat back down and withdrew into her own little world. I know all the church ladies—especially those looking to get next to her father—were looking to mother her. I had this feeling she had dozens of mothers, but she really didn't have any at all."

At the very time of her life when she was dealing with maternal loss and searching for comfort, she had begun to sing in public.

She remembered singing her first solo in church at age ten, the year her mother died.

"She was going to do 'Jesus Be a Fence Around Me,'" Erma told me. "She learned it from the Sam Cooke and the Soul Stirrers version. She stood behind the piano and looked out into the big church—there might have been a couple of thousand people in attendance that day—and paused before starting. I wondered if she could do it. We all knew she had a beautiful voice, but we also knew she had been an emotional mess all week, crying her eyes out. It took her a minute to get it together, but when she did, it all came pouring out. The transition was incredible. She transformed her extreme pain to extreme beauty. That's my sister's gift. She had it as a child and has never lost it, not for a second."

The pattern was set: the most traumatic parts of Aretha's life would produce her most moving music. Misery would breed miraculous creativity. Introversion would blossom into extroversion. An insecure little girl would turn into a remarkably confident artist. As the turmoil troubling Aretha's heart grew over the years to increasingly dramatic degrees, so did her adamant refusal to articulate it. The pain stayed silent in all areas except music, where, magnificently, it formed a voice that said it all. Music was the sole area where the truth could be told.

"Give the church some of the credit," Billy Preston told me when we discussed Aretha's early years. "The black church is about truth-telling. The black church is the most loving, encouraging audience in the world. Ain't no shame in crying in church. Ain't no shame in moaning low and shouting high. If you have the least amount of fear, those saints sitting up in church will make the fear go away with shouts of praise. That was my introduction to playing piano and singing, same as Aretha. After that kind of baptism as a performer, no audience ever scared me because, no matter where I was, I'd close my eyes and pretend to be in church. Did that my whole life. And I know for a fact that Aretha did the same. She was singing for the approval of the church, and that approval came unconditionally."

But she was also singing for the approval of her father, her sole protector, and for the women who loved him and whose love she sought for herself.

"No doubt," said Erma, "that when Aretha learned that Clara was interested in Dad and vice versa, Aretha became more interested in Clara. We all did. It was perfectly natural. She was a powerful and charismatic woman. She was a star. And even if she hadn't been one of our father's love interests, she would have influenced all three Franklin sisters as a singer. Her style was fabulous in every way."

If Mahalia Jackson, adorned in a somber black or lily-white church robe, represented the dignity of gospel singing, Clara Ward, dressed in gowns of silver and gold, represented the dazzle. They were both extravagantly gifted vocalists whose baroque embellishments and unrestrained emotionality set the standard for decades to come. But while Mahalia stood flat-footed in the pulpit and belted out her prayers of praise, Clara worked the room. She moved while she shouted. She was also the first of the gospel stars to work the jazz and dinner clubs. Although Mahalia's repertoire included the blues-inflected work of Thomas A. Dorsey, she sang in churches and concert halls, making a rare exception with her celebrated appearance at the 1958 Newport Jazz Festival. Clara would go almost anywhere to spread her gospel, even to Vegas and Broadway. Like C.L., Clara wanted the widest possible exposure.

God was in the center of this formulation, but money was also in the mix. Clara's mother, the formidable Gertrude Ward, was gospel music's version of Mama Rose, Gypsy Rose Lee's unstoppable stage mom. The original group, the Ward Trio, began in the early forties when Clara was a teenager. The other members, Mother Gertrude and big sis Willa, were soon augmented by more powerful voices, notably the great Marion Williams, whose piercing soprano made a mighty impression on Aretha and both complemented and rivaled Clara's commanding lead.

According to Willa, her mother ran the operation with an

iron hand, displaying strong entrepreneurial gifts in establishing her own management firm, booking agency, and publishing company. During an era when promoters cheated gospel artists unmercifully, Gertrude held her own. She also kept a tight hold on Clara.

"Everyone has a Mother Gertrude story," James Cleveland told me. "Her take-no-prisoners personality was legendary. When I was playing piano for the Caravans, I saw [Clara] performing in one church with Reverend Franklin. After the services, the two of them began to leave together. When Mother Gertrude saw that, she called out, 'Frank, return my daughter to me this very minute!' Now, Frank was not a retiring man. He was not accustomed to being ordered around. But when Gertrude gave commands, even Reverend obeyed. He led Clara back to her mother. Later that night at the hotel, after Gertrude had gone to sleep, I did notice a couple walking out of the lobby that looked suspiciously like Clara and Frank."

Ruth Bowen, who knew Clara well, said, "It's so touching to me that Aretha picked Clara as a role model. I say that not because Clara wasn't a lovely person—she was—but she was, like Aretha, a troubled and insecure soul. Aretha's father was the love of Clara's life. And the man would never commit to her, another reason Clara suffered so deeply. I'm not saying Frank didn't love her, but he was hardly the marrying kind. His sexual appetite required a large variety of women. That fact tortured Clara, who wanted him and him alone."

In *How I Got Over*, Willa's autobiography, Willa wrote that Clara had become pregnant at seventeen, got married, and, due to the burden of rough travel and countless performances, lost the child. She divorced at eighteen and never married again. Willa believed that because their mother chased off Clara's male suitors, Clara found safety in several sexual relationships with women. In the gay gospel world, homosexual encounters were commonplace. According to Willa, Clara was fragile. She was plagued with health issues and suffered serious breakdowns. "Her glamorous gospel image was part of the role model Aretha embraced," said Ruth Bowen, "but so was Clara's struggle to find happiness and her fruit-less attempt to escape a domineering parent."

"There's only one man who could have taken on Gertrude and won," said Billy Preston, who worked the gospel circuit as a wonder-boy singer and organist. "That was C. L. Franklin. Gertrude scared all the others away. Clara was her cash cow, and she wasn't about to lose control. I think that's why Clara clung so tightly to Frank. She saw him as the knight on the white horse who could help her escape her mama. When Frank failed at that task, Clara was crushed. She never gave up on him, but at the same time, he never came through for her."

"Reverend Franklin was my man," B.B. King told me. "He was a great storyteller and a proud black man at a time when pride was a rare commodity in our community. He made us prouder people. But I also have to say that he took me by surprise one night in the fifties when he showed up at a club in Chicago with Clara Ward. I wasn't surprised that he came to hear the blues and I wasn't surprised that he was dating Miss Ward. They'd been going together some time. But back in my dressing room when she said something Reverend didn't like, he hauled off and whacked her so hard across the face she fell to her knees. I was too shocked to say a word."

"Frank and Clara had a strange thing going," said James Cleveland. "She adored the man, and the man adored her. But their mutual-admiration society broke down on a regular basis, and when it did, Clara bore the brunt. Given the times, it wasn't all that unusual for a man to brutalize a woman. In that sense, Frank was a man of his times. I saw him lose it with Clara on several occasions. She was surprisingly passive about it all. Usually she just took it, but sometimes she'd get mad and say she was through with him. Then he'd send her flowers and candy and they'd start up all over again. She never got over Frank. *Ever.*"

"My father may have deserted other women," Erma explained, "but we never had to worry that he would desert us. He did give us that security. I know that Carolyn and I felt that security strongly. Cecil certainly did. He never made us feel that we had to earn his approval. And yet my sister Aretha worked harder than anyone for that approval. Maybe that's what made her so great."

"I can't remember at what age Aretha saw Clara Ward play piano in our living room," brother Cecil told me, "but I was probably ten and Aretha eight. Of course, Daddy had lots of artists come out to the house for his parties. Probably the most amazing was Art Tatum. He had one eye and played like he had four hands. Aretha and I sat on the landing on top of the staircase and looked down in amazement. We'd never heard anyone play these kind of arpeggios and flourishes. Sometimes during Daddy's parties there was just drinking and dancing with music in the background, but when someone like Art Tatum played, it turned into a concert. Everyone stopped and listened in rapture.

"I remember on another night when Arthur Prysock sang while his brother Red played sax. Oscar Peterson came by with his bass player Ray Brown. That's when Ray was married to Ella Fitzgerald and she was over that night as well. All us Franklin kids got to hear Arthur and Ella accompanied by Oscar Peterson. Talk about a treat! After they'd been playing for more than an hour, Oscar said to Daddy, 'Reverend Franklin, I never expected to ever play a jazz set in the home of a minister.' In turn, Daddy said, 'Oscar, I never expected the Lord to gift me with such beautiful music in my very own living room.'

"That was just one evening among dozens. Royalty came to visit on a regular basis. Duke Ellington once stopped by to meet with my father and wound up playing a beautiful piece on the piano. Like my dad, Ellington was a modern man who looked to the future, not the past. When I told him how much I loved jazz, he told me, 'Well, son, you'll want to be listening to a cat named

Monk. He's doing it differently.' Monk soon became one of my heroes.

"Aretha took a different path. She spent hours in my room listening to my growing jazz collection. But her magical moment came the night Clara Ward got happy on our grand piano. Miss Ward did a solo concert of all her hits, like 'Surely He's Able' and 'Packin' Up.' But she also improvised like a jazz musician. Aretha didn't miss a note, and the next day she was on the piano playing everything she'd heard Clara play. It wasn't long after that Aretha learned Avery Parrish's 'After Hours,' a popular blues song from Daddy's day. Daddy loved it. Sometimes during his parties, Daddy came up upstairs and woke up Ree. It might have been three or four a.m., but he wanted his friends to hear her play 'After Hours.'

"Everyone who'd gone to our church knew Ree could sing 'cause she started so young. But her piano playing was a whole separate talent. Later on in the fifties, when Eddie Heywood had his instrumental hit 'Canadian Sunset,' not an easy piece to play, Aretha's version became another favorite at Daddy's parties.

"Here's how it worked—Aretha heard a song once and played it back immediately, note for note. If it was an instrumental, she duplicated it perfectly. If it was a vocal, she duplicated it just as perfectly. She got all the inflections right, voice and keyboard. Her ear was infallible. We always knew that she possessed a different kind of talent. That's the talent they call genius. You can't learn it. You just have it."

I once asked Reverend Cleveland if he thought C. L. Franklin had exploited Aretha's genius.

"Depends what you mean by *exploit*. If you write a song, you want it exploited. That simply means you want it sung and recorded. If you have a child with genius, you want that genius exploited as well. You want your child heard. You want her potential fulfilled. Frank was an ambitious man. He wanted to enlarge his audience at every turn. A singer himself, he realized the power of music to carry God's message. He wanted to surround himself with the most powerful singers. That his own daughter turned out to be the most powerful of all was something that brought him immense pride. He saw it as his obligation to turn Aretha into a star. Anything else would have been a travesty.

"After Frank hired me as minister of music, in the fifties, I moved into the Franklin home. I got a bird's-eye view of that father-daughter relationship. And yes, there were times when Frank got her out of the bed in the middle of night to show off her singing and playing in front of his famous guests like Nat Cole or Billy Eckstine. I'm not sure any eleven-year-old girl wants to be awoken in the middle of the night to play for a crowd of heavy-drinking partygoers. And yes, maybe that didn't make her feel especially good. But at the same time, she shared her father's drive. She inherited that drive.

"If I was in the living room working out a new arrangement for the choir on piano, Aretha would slide on over and sit on the bench beside me. She'd watch me put together the chorus. She'd hear how I was going to voice the tenors against the sopranos. She saw how octaves worked. She saw how melody worked with harmony and how harmony worked with rhythm. She saw it all, and, just like that, she could do it all. They call me one of her teachers, but I taught the young Aretha Franklin very little. She simply watched, and then she did.

"Was she exploited? If she hadn't been, she would have been furious. She would have seen that as a betrayal on the part of her father. After her talent was manifest, she wanted to be with Frank every minute of her life—in church, on the road, and finally at those parties where he presented her to the best entertainers in the world. It was her living room where she met Dinah Washington."

In 1954, Dinah Washington was a huge star, and Aretha, a pre-teen, was sitting at the top of the staircase watching the party below. That's when she first saw Ted White. He was the man who would, in the sixties, become Aretha's first husband, her first important manager, and a figure strong enough to whisk her away from her father's domain. White had the reputation of a gentleman pimp. That night, Aretha watched him scoop up and carry off an inebriated Dinah Washington, whose musical path from gospel to blues to jazz to rhythm-and-blues to pop was the very route Aretha would soon seek to travel.

4. THE SEX CIRCUS

Ray Charles and Billy Preston used the same expression to describe the gospel circuit in the fifties. They called it "a sex circus."

Ray told me that when he started out on the R&B circuit in the early fifties, he'd often run into the gospel groups that were playing in the same city.

"Because hotels wouldn't take blacks, we'd wind up in rooming houses run by some local lady," said Ray. "Cats like the Blind Boys of Alabama and the Dixie Hummingbirds would be there, along with bluesmen like T-Bone Walker or Lowell Fulson. I loved the church singers 'cause of their harmonies and rhythms. I'd come out of a country church and could relate to the excitement of their music. Sometimes late at night we'd jam on some old hymn that brought me all the way back home. When it came to pure heart singing, they were motherfuckers. When it came to pure sex, they were wilder than me — and that's saying something. In those days I had a thing for orgies, but I had to be the only cat in a room with two or three chicks. The gospel people didn't think that way. The cats liked it with the cats and the chicks liked it with the chicks and no one minded mixing it up this way or that. I wasn't judging no one, and I got a kick outta seeing how God's people were going for it hard and heavy every which way. I was just surprised to see how loose they were. Someone told me that the ministers in the churches where they were singing didn't know about those going-ons, but, hell, more than one time I heard about a minister showing up at the rooming house 'cause he wanted in on the action."

"It wasn't the R-and-B crowd that turned me out," said Billy Preston when we were discussing his autobiography. (Unfortunately, Preston died before we had a chance to complete the work.) "It was the church crowd where the vibe was wide open. It was anything goes. Many times the 'anything' involved men-and-men and women-and-women hookups. That almost seemed the norm. In the community outside the church, gay men were called sissies. There was zero tolerance. But inside the church, a lot of the music was created by gay men. It was almost a tradition. Everyone knew that my mentor James Cleveland, who became the King of Gospel, was gay. He wasn't just a great singer, piano player, choir arranger, and writer—he really invented big-choir modern gospel. James had his own church and a national following. So many of the other major figures—like Professor J. Earle Hines out of Los Angeles and Professor Alex Bradford out of Chicago—were gay. Mahalia surrounded herself with gay men her entire life. In the neighborhood, they made you ashamed of being gay, but in the church you were almost proud to be part of the gay elite of musicians. Along with the preachers, we were the people who kept the church going. The people came for the sermons and the music. In black churches, the word is always musical. God is in the grooves."

Aretha's father was an established star on the gospel circuit in 1954, when she went on the road with him at twelve years old. A year before, C.L. had begun recording his sermons for Joe Von Battle, the black owner of Joe's Record Shop at 3530 Hastings Street, close to the New Bethel Baptist Church. A man who understood both sides of Hastings Street, Von Battle also released records by bluesman John Lee Hooker. C.L.'s sermons sold briskly in Detroit, and then, after Von Battle acquired distribution, they found an audience in Chicago and New York. The sermons were also played on a powerful radio station in Gallatin, Tennessee, WLAC-AM. The gospel program was sponsored by Randy's Record Store, whose mail-order business helped boost C.L.'s sales. Music markets opened—before long Los Angeles was in the mix—and by the mid-1950s Franklin had a national audience. He put together a "traveling religious service," as Aretha called it, to both earn additional income—ministers at the churches where he performed solicited a "love offering" from the assembled congregants—and sell records of his sermons.

C.L. had three opening performers—Sammy Brant, a female little person with an enormous voice; Lucy Branch, another powerhouse vocalist; and Aretha herself, who would sing a solo either with the choir or while accompanying herself on piano. The centerpiece of the program was, of course, Reverend's fiery sermon. As he spoke, Aretha punctuated his remarks with pianistic flourishes.

Never a passionate student, she was happy to leave school for these tours. She not only loved being with her father but was thrilled to be part of C.L.'s spreading popularity. She was equally thrilled to skip from childhood to adulthood.

"Aretha couldn't wait to become a woman," said Ruth Bowen. "She didn't like being a little girl. She wanted to be a lady—and her talent let her make that leap before she was a teenager."

Interviewers have always found Aretha reluctant to discuss the fact that she was pregnant at thirteen. Neither has she been willing to talk about the sexual component to the gospel circuit.

"I can understand Aretha not wanting to talk about that," said Etta James when I asked her about her early road experience. "Who wants to admit that you're praising the Lord at the eight p.m. service and servicing some drop-dead gorgeous hunk of a singer an hour later? Both Aretha and I started out before we were teenagers. We were out of our homes for the first time, and we wanted to experience it all. I wouldn't use the expression *sexually active*. I'd say *sexually overactive*. We couldn't wait to give it up 'cause that's what it meant to be grown. Aretha was as anxious as anyone. I know for a fact that Aretha gave it up often and easily. In that respect, she was just like most of us young singers out there. The fact that she was the daughter of a famous preacher made no difference. In truth, PKs—preachers' kids—were known for promiscuity. Because they were expected to act one way, they rebelled and acted another."

"You're wanting to know if Aretha was promiscuous?" asked Ruth Bowen. "Well, it was a promiscuous culture. She was a product of that culture. She was a child prodigy of that culture. Prodigies tend to feel big-time entitlement. I think that's true of everyone from Mickey Rooney to Judy Garland to Elizabeth Taylor to Dinah Washington. Their gifts are so big they feel as though they have the right to do what they want, especially in the sexual arena. Beginning at a young age, they also have to work very hard. That distinguishes them from other kids. They know they're special. All that rigorous traveling, all those performances, all that money they're making for their parents or their sponsors—it all makes them feel that they deserve any treat that comes their way."

"I know I didn't develop in no natural way like no average kid," said Etta James. "I didn't go through the usual growing-up stages. One day I was a child, the next day a grown woman. It was strange, and it no doubt fucked me up. I'm sure it fucked up Aretha too. We were thrown into a world of too much excitement where we were overstimulated way too soon."

Jerry Wexler, a scholar of African American music as well as a celebrated producer, had his own analysis of gospel music and the gospel singers' lifestyle. He and I had a running dialogue on this subject for decades.

"It's all suppressed sexuality," said Wexler, a committed atheist. "They call it Holy Spirit, but it's really libidinous. Gospel music isn't simply more animated and emotional than secular, it's sexier."

I disagreed with Jerry—and still do.

Archbishop Carl Bean, with whom I cowrote *I Was Born This Way*, his autobiography, is the product of the gospel circuit. A protégé of Professor Alex Bradford, Bean is founder and prelate of the national Unity Fellowship of Christ Church.

"The truth of gospel music is in the moment," he explained. "The extraordinary energy of that moment is the manifestation of God. The nature of the moment—its overwhelming power—is too great to be attributed to man. Man is the vehicle. God is the fuel. If you listen carefully to the singing and the music, if you open your heart to what is being said, you realize that no human being could conjure forth such spirit. It matters not if, after the service, the singers celebrate in a worldly fashion. For in the moment—in the service, in the praise and worship of a mighty God—there is complete and absolute sincerity. I know for a fact that Reverend C. L. Franklin loved the Lord with all his heart. I can say the same about Reverend James Cleveland and sister Aretha Franklin. That all these people—like you, like me, like everyone— displayed human frailties has nothing to do with the authenticity of their witness. Their art form, whether in a sermon or a song, are testimonies to the everlasting glory of God."

When I asked Aretha's siblings whether they had ever gone through a crisis of faith, they all had the same answer: "Never."

"As a family," said Erma, "we faced many challenges. We fought and fell out among ourselves many times. But faith was never an issue. Each of us have an abiding faith in the living God."

As far as I'm concerned, Archbishop Bean put the matter to rest when he said, "Does the rampant promiscuity associated with the gospel circuit undercut the authenticity of our holy message? Of course not. If that were the case, then virtually every holy message expressed through human beings would be invalidated, since every human is a deeply flawed vessel. Men far wiser than I have said, 'You can trust the message without trusting the messenger.' God speaks through man, and man, in virtually every cultural setting, is a mess."

"Aretha is a mess," said Reverend James Cleveland, using the colloquial expression in a positive light. He laughed when he said it.

"When she was starting out on the road with her daddy, he tried his best to rein her in. But she was pretty and quietly flirtatious and possessed a voice that everyone loved, especially the men. Given the circumstances, Frank was a good father. I know he tried his best. He certainly took care of his children. But he was an unorthodox man on every level, and you'd have to believe that his children would be unorthodox as well. Parents often say, 'Do what I say, not what I do.' But children wind up imitating their folks' actions, not their words. In the case of Reverend C. L. Franklin and his talented children—and especially Aretha, the most talented of all—they did just that."

In *From These Roots*, Aretha was not reluctant to discuss her first crushes. They were many. She freely listed her puppy loves—starting with Gordon Blasingame in Buffalo—in extremely romantic terms. Aretha always became most explicit when she was discussing the physical beauty of men and the lure of certain foods. She described her introduction to the bacon, lettuce, and tomato sandwich, for instance, in ecstatic terms.

When the subject of Sam Cooke came up, though, the terms changed. Her voice grew excited. She described seeing him when his gospel group sang at New Bethel—and how he drove the church girls crazy. She also proudly stated that Sam and her dad were close friends.

Aretha was twelve and Sam was twenty-three when, in her own account, she went to his motel room in Atlanta. When her father learned they were together, he banged on the door. When the Staple Singers passed by, he asked them whether his daughter was in there with Sam. They played dumb. Aretha claimed nothing happened that day. And even though she admitted to visiting him in his hotel room in New York some time later, she also insisted that their relationship remained platonic.

"That's not what Sam told me," said Johnnie Taylor, the great soul singer who performed in the Highway QC's, the gospel group begun by Sam. "Sam said that he enjoyed a lot more than Aretha's voice. But I didn't need to hear that from Sam. When I was on the gospel circuit and played the same cities as Reverend Franklin and Aretha, I saw it for myself. She looked to be very shy and she didn't talk all that much. But when it came to partying, she was ready to go."

"We were precocious children," said Erma, who joined the gospel circuit with her sister and dad when she was fifteen and Aretha was twelve. "We did things far ahead of other people our age. Living in an adult world let us break through the boundaries of childhood at an early age. Our father disapproved—he was a strict parent—but our father could not exert total control over us. In the cities where he traveled, his schedule was hectic. In addition to preparing for the service, he was speaking to newspaper and magazine reporters. If there was a gospel radio station in town, he was interviewed. Then he was always reading his books—politics, poetry, theology. Keeping track of his energetic and curious daughters was next to impossible. We got away with a lot."

The subjects of sex and sibling rivalry are intricately related in Aretha's life. Carolyn, whose preference was for women, told me how Aretha and Erma would often fight over the same man.

"I remember them coming off the road and squabbling over some guy," said Carolyn. "Aretha was convinced he had a crush on her, and Erma was convinced Aretha was trying to steal him. Both my sisters are strong personalities with strong attitude. They can be headstrong and arrogant. And neither likes to back down. Intellectually, Erma might be sharper, but Ree is no slouch. Musically, no one can touch Aretha, but Erma is a fine singer. Erma is much more the extrovert. Socially she was ahead of Ree. She was far more comfortable speaking with people. Aretha had a fear of people she didn't know."

From the observations of her siblings and of witnesses like James Cleveland, Ruth Bowen, and Etta James, the picture of the prepubescent comes into focus: Traumatized by the departure and sudden death of her mother, devastated by the departure of Lola

Moore, heartbroken that her father refused to make Clara Ward her mother, she found herself in the spiritually charged, sexually overcharged culture of Holy Ghost music-making where, night after night, the excitement reached fever pitch. That she probably became sexually active at twelve or thirteen is neither surprising nor unusual. Preteens and teens act out in a variety of ways. Aretha's way was sex. The sexually permissive atmosphere in which she grew up did nothing to discourage her. Yet at the very moment she was discovering grown-up sex, she was also being recorded as a grown-up singer of sacred song.

In those first examples of her voice, we hear something more than a child transforming into a woman. We hear a miracle.

5. THE BLOOD

There were a score of fine trumpet players who came up in the 1920s with Louis Armstrong. But the quality of his sound— the piercing beauty of his tone, the deep humanity of his voice—profoundly altered American music. The same is true of the saxophone playing of Lester Young, Charlie Parker, and John Coltrane. These were men who had the cry. Billie Holiday was a woman who had the cry, as did Mahalia Jackson and Dinah Washington.

You hear Aretha's cry when, as a young teenager, she steps into the spotlight at the Oakland Auditorium and sings "Take My Hand, Precious Lord." By then Reverend Franklin and his gospel service were drawing crowds up and down California. Thomas A. Dorsey wrote the song in the thirties based on a nineteenth-century melody. His lyrics are a prayer for faith—that God will transform the raw pain Dorsey suffered by the death of his wife and infant son into fresh hope. Knowing that he can't make it alone, he asks Jesus to take his hand and lead him on. He prays for the trans-formation of darkness into light. The message is among the deepest and most beloved in all black gospel, and for Aretha to approach the sacred hymn signals a readiness—even an eagerness—to stand beside the magnificent Mahalia, who performed it countless times.

Barely a teenager, Aretha embraces the most grown-up of spiritual moments—the declaration of despair before the reality of death. "'When my life is almost gone,'" she cries, "'hear my cry.'" The cry for a connection to the unseen source of creation is chilling. This is not a child singing, but a woman. She is singing outside the rhythm of time—there is no set groove for the song—making her way through life's tragic maze. She stands in darkness. She sings, "'As the night draws near and the day is past and gone, at the river I stand.'" The river is the Jordan and the river Styx, the river between life and death, sorrow and renewal. After the lyrics are sung a single time, they are no longer adequate to express the depth of her feelings. "Ain't no harm to moan," says Aretha, who word-lessly renders the melody. Her voice is ageless. Her art is fully formed and wholly realized. She is much more than a child prodigy or a surprisingly good singer. She is already a great artist.

"Remember Venus coming out of the sea in Botticelli's paint-ing?" Jerry Wexler asked me when we listened to the song together. "That's Aretha—a goddess whose maturity and beauty cannot be explained."

At the same time, singing before the adoring crowd at the Oak-land Arena, she is also a fifteen-year-old girl who has given birth to one baby and is pregnant with another.

Listen to her sing "Never Grow Old," also recorded live in this initial grouping of her first documented performances, and you hear her soaring even higher. The text is heaven, the subtext the movement from the finite to the infinite. The tone is serious.

The couplet she sings in "While the Blood Runs Warm"—"he bought the pain of death/while he rocked you on his breast"—is astoundingly complex. The song comes alive when Aretha explo-sively punctuates the word *rock* in gutbucket R&B fashion, lending the text a sensual/sexual flavor.

According to Erma, this was the period when Aretha began singing "Precious Lord" because she associated the hymn with Billy Kyles, whose Thompson Community Choir performed it often. Erma conjectured that her sister had a crush on Kyles, eight years her senior—the same Kyles who became a leader in the civil rights movement and was standing next to Dr. King on the balcony of the Lorraine Motel in Memphis on that fateful April day in 1968.

"My three favorites of Aretha's early recordings are the ones she sang to show Daddy she could compete with Clara Ward," said Erma. "Those songs—'There Is a Fountain Filled with Blood,' 'While the Blood Runs Warm,' and 'The Day Is Past and Gone'— were often performed by Clara during the services that featured Daddy's sermons and the Ward Sisters. Daddy raised all of us to be our best and not shy away from competition, and Aretha was especially competitive. I learned that early on, when, right around this time, I formed a gospel quartet and asked Aretha to join. The idea was that we'd take turns singing lead. But Aretha wanted *all* the leads. Our group lasted about two weeks. Aretha's competitive drive—the same drive that later enabled her to survive so long as a star—was not conducive to group harmony."

Carolyn looked at it somewhat differently. "I'm not saying that Ree isn't competitive," she said, "but something else deeper happens when she sings. She goes somewhere else. She slips into the zone. That's her gift. The zone is where she's connected to the spirit. Doesn't matter what she's singing—a gospel song or a worldly song—the minute she opens her mouth, she's off into the zone. She can't explain the zone. Erma can't explain the zone. I can't explain the zone. No one can. Not even Daddy. It's where great artists go to channel what I call the blood. I'm talking about the artistic blood that flows through certain people and has them expressing all the emotions of the world."

Cecil agreed with Carolyn. "When you listen to the early things that Aretha recorded," he said, "you realize that it's all there—all her musical intelligence. Since we were all raised in the same household by the same dad, it makes sense that we'd all have that same intelligence, but we don't. She was born with it. Later on, musicologists can try to analyze how she came to it. They can say that she practiced harder than the rest of us, or paid more attention to the music around her, or was more motivated to learn, but I'm here to tell you that none of that is true. She didn't practice. She didn't pay any more attention to the music around her than Erma, Carolyn, or myself. As a child, Ree was never motivated to learn to read or write music because she didn't need to. She had it all on her fingertips. She absorbed it and then replayed it better than the original. That's what you're hearing when you hear her sing the Clara Ward songs. If you hear a thirteen-year-old girl sounding older and wiser than a thirty-one-year-old woman, it isn't because Aretha was trying to outshine Clara. It's just what happened when my sister got up to sing."

In 1955, the same year Aretha made these early recordings, Clara Ward found herself in the middle of a controversy that had nothing to do with her romance with Reverend Franklin. It had everything to do with the bridge that both separated and joined sacred and secular music — the same bridge over which Aretha would soon travel.

The *Chicago Defender,* a prominent black newspaper, reported Ward's response to sharp criticism from rhythm-and-blues star LaVern Baker, who had started out as Little Miss Sharecropper and didn't find fame until she changed record labels and cut "Tweedle Dee" for Jerry Wexler and Ahmet Ertegun at Atlantic Records. LaVern had accused Clara of stealing her grooves. Clara fired back. "If anyone is guilty of taking a beat, it's the current R&B artists because most of them are former choir singers, including LaVern. Where else did they copy their style from except church groups?" Clara went on to say that she had turned down $2,500 to "jazz up 'Swing Low Sweet Chariot' with her group under an assumed name."

The dialogue between Clara and LaVern is basically about which came first, the chicken or the egg. After Al Green, newly a pastor in the service of the Lord, performed at James Cleveland's Cornerstone Institutional Baptist Church in Los Angeles in the early eighties, I posed that question to Cleveland. Which came first—the spirituals or the blues?

"Aretha's father would laugh at that question," said Reverend Cleveland, "because he knew there was no answer. It's a riddle that can't be solved. You could say that the spirituals came first, but if you broke it down further you could also say that the field shouts came before the spirituals. How do we know whether someone out there picking cotton didn't first start moaning about how tired he was, or about how much he wanted a woman? Then maybe a God-fearing woman heard that song and switched it up to where she was praying for God to save *her.* The fleshly needs and the godly needs are very close. We're likely to use music to call out both those needs because they're both so basic. Which comes first? You tell me."

In the mid-1950s, things were happening fast in Aretha's world. Her father's prominence was growing exponentially. His sermons were a hot item in black record stores across the country. Chess, in Chicago, began distributing his records, which over the years have gone through every format—from 45s to LPs to cassettes to CDs to MP3s—and are still available today. In 1956 alone, the *Chicago Defender* reported, C.L.'s sales exceeded a half a million copies.

The Chess brothers, Phil and Leonard, were contemporaries of Jerry Wexler, white Jewish businessmen with an instinctual feel for black music in all genres. Theirs was the first national label to list Aretha Franklin as a recording artist.

That same year—1956—Aretha faced a daunting challenge: how to balance a burgeoning career in gospel music with the responsibilities of motherhood and school. A year earlier, two months before her thirteenth birthday, she had given birth to her first child, whom she named Clarence, after her dad. By then the Franklins had moved to an even larger mansion. The home at 7414 LaSalle Boulevard on Detroit's West Side was, according to Erma, "the most magnificent I had ever seen. It was a showplace created by European craftsmen, the same artisans who had built palaces in Italy and France. Because of his popularity, my father's financial fortunes had turned from good to superb. He deserved all the material rewards of a great man and a great leader. He had a study worthy of the great theologian that he had become. He had also become the voice of his people in Detroit."

I was reluctant to ask Aretha about a rumor that had circulated through the black community and entertainment industry for decades—that C. L. Franklin was the father of Aretha's first child. I first heard about it through John Hammond, who had also told Jerry Wexler. When I questioned Hammond about his source, he simply said, "It was a well-established fact in the black community," and pointed to the scandal of C.L. impregnating twelve-year-old Mildred Jennings in Memphis as evidence of his predilection for young girls. Wexler often quoted Hammond and, with little discretion, spread the incest story for years. The rumor was prominent enough to be addressed by C.L.'s biographer Nick Salvatore, who found it completely unsubstantiated.

When I mentioned the rumor to Erma, she was quick to say, "It's an ugly and utterly false statement."

Carolyn and Cecil had told me the same thing, and given their extreme candor in discussing their father and sister, I saw no reason to doubt them. My own research, like Salvatore's, had not produced a shred of evidence.

In *From These Roots,* Aretha characterizes her pregnancy as noneventful. Her father was understanding, not scolding. She was grateful for the presence of Big Mama, who mothered everyone—her son, his children, and his children's children. Erma, for instance, was sixteen when she gave birth to her son, Thomas. Thus Big Mama was already busy raising babies.

Aretha refused to name the father of her baby, referring to him only as Romeo.

According to Brenda Corbett, who moved into the Franklin home when her mother, Louise, C.L.'s sister, died in 1954, Donald Burk was the father of Aretha's first child. There was no talk of marriage.

"He was just a guy Ree knew from school," said Cecil. "She wasn't at all that interested in him and I don't think he had any deep interest in her. Ree told me before she told Daddy, and I thought he'd explode. But he didn't. He understood that these things happen. He did, however, call us all together to discuss the consequences of having kids at a young age. He took me aside and mentioned birth control and the importance of condoms. Back then in the fifties, I'm not sure many other fathers had that kind of discussion with their sons. He said that daughters were more difficult. They were harder to speak to about sex. He worried a lot about his girls."

"Daddy was a prince of his people," said Carolyn, "and we were certainly his princesses. Because we had cooks and housekeepers and many ladies from the church eager to help our household run smoothly, we couldn't help but be a little spoiled. Daddy was aware of this, and that's why he made sure we did our share of sweeping and mopping. His children were going to know the meaning of hard work. And his children were also going to be educated. From the time we were small, it was understood that college was part of our future. Given my father's insistence that we all have a broad intellectual outlook, it could be no other way. I think that's what worried Daddy most about Aretha's pregnancy— how it would impact her education. Would she have to leave school? And if she left, would she return?"

"Aretha went right back to school after having Clarence," said Erma. "She was an excellent student who did well in all her classes. After school, she'd fly over to the Arcadia, our local roller-skating rink. The Arcadia is where she first ran into Donald Burk. Aretha could skate up a storm."

Aretha's first memory of indulging herself with money earned from her gospel appearances was the purchase of Raybestos skates, the Cadillac of wheels.

After the birth of Clarence, she was on her feet in no time, back on the road with Daddy and back at the Arcadia on weekends. If there was heartbreak, she brushed it off as the lessons of life learned by young girls everywhere. Aretha's picture of herself as a normal youth could not be shattered, not even by her own facts.

In her book, she calls the father of her second child, born two months short of her fifteenth birthday, Casanova. She says only that her son Eddie was named after him. Brenda Corbett identified him as Edward Jordan. Cecil called him a player, as did Aretha. Like Clarence, Eddie would bear the Franklin family name and be raised in the Franklin compound principally by Big Mama and the army of women eager to fulfill the family's needs.

Aretha described her father's reaction to this second teen pregnancy as one of complete acceptance. According to Aretha, he was not upset or scolding.

"I don't want to go into graphic details about what happened when Ree told Daddy that she was expecting another child from still another man," said Cecil. "It's enough to say that he wasn't at all happy and he made his unhappiness quite clear."

"Babies are blessings," Erma explained. "That was always Big Mama's attitude. The idea of an abortion was unthinkable. The circumstances of our pregnancies made no difference. It was understood that our babies would be welcomed into the world and cared for with limitless love. It was also understood that our future as women—our education and our career—would not be compromised because of these early births. Daddy recognized our ambition as a psychological force we had inherited from him. He did everything in his power to encourage that ambition. He did not see his daughters as housewives. He saw us as stars, and that's how we saw ourselves."

"Ree dropped out of school after the birth of her second son," said Erma. "At the same time, he didn't want her to stop doing his out-of-town services. She was one of his main attractions. Word got round that Reverend Franklin had a daughter who could sing. He told her that she could continue her formal education at a later time, but that never happened. The business got hold of Aretha and never let go."

"One of the reasons I believe Aretha has this insecurity," said Cecil, "is that she's the only one of us who didn't pursue her education. Erma, Carolyn, and I all wound up in college at some point in our lives and Ree never did. The reason is obvious. All concentration was on her career. But I think being a high-school dropout, combined with having super-smart, super-educated siblings, did nothing for her confidence. I don't think there was any rivalry between me and Ree — I was her biggest supporter — but between her and her sisters, it got a little loony."

"I'd been singing in my father's choir since I was seven," said Erma. "I didn't have what I consider the high art and dramatic delivery of Aretha, but I was certainly an effective and emotional performer. My father encouraged me, as he encouraged all his children. I don't think I had reached age thirteen when I formed a girl group called the Cleo-Patrettes. They came about because the Four Tops, who lived in our neighborhood, encouraged me to get out there with an act of my own. Levi Stubbs, Obie Benson, Duke Fakir, and Lawrence Payton have always been close to the Franklins — including my dad, my sisters, and my brother — and are beautiful guys. Back then they were called the Four Aims and had a deal on Chess Records. They wanted to take me to Chess but Daddy was already connected to Joe Von Battle. In 1953, when I was fourteen, JVB Records put out a single — 'No Other Love' on one side and 'Say Would You Baby' on the other. I was ready to quit school and go on the road. This was before the appearance of the Chantels and the Shirelles. This was a chance for me to be a pioneer in the field of girl groups.

"I was ready but my father wasn't. He had no intention of allowing me to leave school. He was insistent that I not only complete high school but eventually get a college degree as well. So that's what happened. I put education first, finished high school with honors, and went to Clark College in Atlanta, where I majored in business. That served me well for the rest of my life. But music would never leave my heart. I had many more musical adventures ahead of me."

6. MOVING ON UP

The last half of the 1950s, the years when Aretha grew from a thirteen-year-old girl to an eighteen-year-old woman, was intense for working-class blacks struggling for a piece of America's Cold War prosperity. For members of Reverend Franklin's New Bethel Baptist Church, the majority of whom had come to Detroit from the rural South, the goal was economic betterment—better jobs, better housing, better education. The goal was to move up the social ladder. The bottom rung was no longer acceptable.

African Americans looked to leaders like Walter White, who headed the NAACP during the *Brown v. Board of Education* decision in 1954, and Adam Clayton Powell, the first black congressman from New York State, as avatars of the new middle class. In Detroit, Reverend C. L. Franklin embodied the qualities his people admired most: he was articulate, forward-thinking, grounded in God, proud of his ethnicity, and successful as a promoter of his own spiritual talents. The fact that women found him attractive only added to his aura.

"When you have a congregation comprised of former sharecroppers from the South," said James Cleveland, speaking of New Bethel, "and their pastor is a former sharecropper himself, his improvement in life becomes your improvement. Maybe you can't live in a fine mansion, but your pastor—a man you can relate to—well, he can. And you can be proud of belonging to a church with a pastor smart enough to make his way into the wider world with style, dignity, and intellect. Even if you don't ever make enough to move into the middle class, he has. And part of you goes along with him."

C. L. Franklin rode the wave of upward mobility. Along with his friends Clara Ward and Sam Cooke, he had passionate ambitions that drove him to break through barriers. Prompted by Mother Gertrude, Clara took gospel into nightclubs while Sam transformed gospel into pop. From C.L.'s point of view, all this was done without sacrificing his artistic integrity. He envisioned ever-expanding markets for his ministry and his daughter's music. Every day was a new opportunity for progress and self-betterment.

At the same time, the musical vehicles used by the minority culture to capture a majority audience were changing. Following Billy Eckstine, Nat Cole represented the great black crossover dream of the era. When Cole's national TV show debuted on NBC in the spring of 1956, it was one of the first for an African American. Hazel Scott and Billy Daniels had hosted smaller shows earlier in the decade but they were short-lived. Unlike Nat, Scott and Daniels lacked the status to host major white stars. As a consummate jazz pianist and, more to the point, a masterly pop vocalist, Nat stood apart. His rendering of ballads like "Mona Lisa," "Nature Boy," "Too Young," and "Unforgettable" endeared him to white audiences. His enunciation, while idiosyncratic, was exemplary. He spoke as he sang, with subtle refinement and infallible taste. He became a touchstone for generations to follow. From Johnny Mathis to Clyde McPhatter to Marvin Gaye to Aaron Neville, the most gifted singers viewed Nat as the highest expression of vocal art.

One of Cole's most ardent admirers, a man who began his career as a Nat imitator, would radically change the crossover equation, thus paving the way for Aretha's eventual breakthrough. In the late forties, Ray Charles left Florida's state school for the blind, worked local clubs, moved to Seattle, and finally settled in Los Angeles, all the while making his way with a Nat Cole–inspired trio that sang Nat Cole–sounding songs.

"I might have done it forever," Ray told me, "if it hadn't been for a record-company owner who said, 'The world already has one Nat Cole. Maybe people in the clubs get a kick outta hearing someone who sounds so close to Nat, but you're never gonna sell any records or make any real money until you find your own sound.'"

The sound that Ray found was backwoods country, raw, and unapologetically black. Its roots were field hollers, spirituals, gospel, and deep blues. Because, like Nat, Ray was an accomplished jazz pianist, he could adapt his voice to the jazz medium. In fact, while retaining the coarse cry of his people, he could adapt his voice to any medium. Thus in 1956, the same year that the Franklins watched Nat Cole singing with Peggy Lee and Julius La Rosa on their Emerson television, they were also listening to Ray Charles's "This Little Girl of Mine," a gospel song—"This Little Light of Mine"—that he had reworked into hot rhythm and blues. In less than three years, "What'd I Say" would move Ray's style of church-rooted call-and-response sexy dance grooves to the top of the pop charts.

"Jazz is the intellectual expression of the black musical expression," Oscar Peterson, the great jazz pianist, told me in discussing Nat Cole and Ray Charles. Peterson idolized Nat and, in fact, had unsuccessfully tried to follow Cole's pop vocal success. "Jazz is also visceral and emotional, and of course jazz is based on the blues. But in the fifties, when Ray came along, jazz had been moving away from its blues base. Ray's down-home honesty changed that. If you talk about jazz's return to soul in the fifties, if you listen to what Charles Mingus and Art Blakey and Horace Silver were doing, you hear Ray's direct influence. Nat Cole was a giant in terms of pianistic virtuosity and vocal perfection, but he was more an interpreter than innovator. Ray changed the game for everyone."

While 1956 was also the year of "Please, Please, Please" by

James Brown—the same singer who two years earlier had abandoned his Ever Ready Gospel Singers—Brown's enormous cultural influence would not be felt until the sixties.

Aretha's own upwardly mobile dreams, inherited from her father—the dream of triumphing, like Nat Cole, in the white world as well as the black—would paradoxically stall Aretha's triumph for many long and difficult years. There was great confusion about how to sell black music to the majority market. Motown would cloud the issue, as would Ray Charles's country-and-western hits. But as the fifties wound down and Aretha prepared to leave gospel and enter the pop arena, one thing was clear—she would go for the gold, the big, broad crossover market.

"C.L. wanted everything for his daughter," said James Cleveland. "He wanted megasuccess on every level. He knew all these people—Mahalia Jackson, Sarah Vaughan, Dinah Washington, Della Reese—and he felt like Aretha could outsing all of them. So there was no material she couldn't handle, and the idea was to get her to handle it all."

"We loved Ray Charles," said Erma, "and we knew he was making church songs sexy. We saw nothing wrong with that and we played his music all the time. But we were young girls with stars in our eyes. We couldn't help but fall in love with Sam Cooke. He was irresistible. When 'You Send Me' came out in the winter of 1957, I was eighteen and Ree was fifteen. We were already mothers. We were already professional singers. We had been on the road and seen something of life. We were hardly giddy groupies—that is, until we heard that song. When it came on the radio, we were on the road and made our driver pull over so we could catch our breath. Then we told him to speed to the nearest record store so we could buy it. We played nothing else for a week. Daddy liked the song but said if he heard it again he'd come at the forty-five with a hammer. Didn't matter. We kept playing it. Just before Christmas, Sam came on *Ed Sullivan*. That's all we needed to know. I went out and bought an evening gown for his appearance. Mind you, I didn't wear the dress to the theater in New York but to the little lobby of our hotel in Atlanta—that's how seriously I took the occasion. Watching Sam on TV, I couldn't wear just anything. I imagined him looking through the screen and seeing how I had dressed up just for him."

"You Send Me," Cooke's own composition, topped not only the R&B charts but the pop charts, and it stayed number one for three weeks. This was the ultimate crossover dream: black gospel's matinee idol became an American matinee idol. As the Nat Cole TV show was winding down due to weak ratings and nervous sponsors, Sam Cooke was revving up. In his perfect blend of gospel fire and silk-smooth cool, he would turn out a string of classic hits and eventually start his own record empire that included a label, a publishing firm, and a roster of singers, among whom were his protégés Bobby Womack and Johnnie Taylor.

"Sam was the cat who got Aretha to hurry up and make the switch," Johnnie Taylor told me in his office in Dallas, Texas, in the late seventies. "When I took Sam's place in the Soul Stirrers—that was in '57—we appeared on the same bill as her dad and Clara Ward and the Ward Singers. Her daddy had gone off somewhere with Clara and we were all just sitting around the lobby. The topic was Sam. The topic was always Sam. Aretha was a different kind of chick. You wouldn't call her a church girl, even with her daddy being who he was. She was more a party girl—a shy one, but a fox nonetheless. I didn't even know she had two babies back then until years later. She didn't act like no mother. Like her papa, she wanted to hang out with the stars. And why not? She was the best singer I'd heard since Jackie Verdell. Jackie, who was in the Davis Sisters, sang so hard she'd go around saying that she'd peed on her robe. I thought Jackie was gonna be the next big thing after Dinah. Don't know why that never happened, except that Aretha caught Jackie's thunder the way I caught Sam's. Turned out that we peed harder than anyone. Took me and Aretha a while to switch tracks and catch on, but soon as we heard 'You Send Me,' we knew we weren't long for the gospel world. Wherever Sam was going, we was following."

Brother Cecil backed up Johnnie Taylor when he told me, "When Aretha came off tour with Daddy, all she talked about was Sam's crossover. I remember the night Sam came to sing at the Flame Show Bar in Detroit. Erma and Ree said they weren't going because they were so heartbroken that Sam had recently married. I didn't believe them. And I knew I was right when they started getting dressed about noon for the nine o'clock show. Because they were underage, they put on a ton of makeup to look older. It didn't matter 'cause Berry Gordy's sisters, Anna and Gwen, worked the photo concession down there, taking pictures of the party people. Anna was tight with Daddy and was sure to let my sisters in. She did, and they came home with stars in their eyes."

In 1958, at age sixteen, Aretha traveled back out to California with her father. At the Watkins Hotel, she ran into Nat Cole, whose dark skin and handsome demeanor reminded her of her dad. On that same trip, Sam Cooke invited her to his home, where he gave her a fringed suede jacket he had once worn. She said she wore it to sleep that night and was dismayed when several weeks later it went missing.

She and her father's troupe went home by way of Florida, where she filled in for the Caravans' new lead singer, Shirley Caesar, and, for a night, became a Caravan herself. Given her love for all the Caravans, especially Albertina Walker and Inez Andrews, she called this "one of the great highlights of my gospel career." She also saw it as something of a finale. "Once I sang with the Caravans," she said, "I knew I had reached the top of the mountain. There were other super-talented gospel ladies—Dorothy Love, Edna Gallmon Cooke, Bessie Griffin, Gloria Griffin, Delois Barrett—the list goes on and on. I admired them all. They are the equivalent—and then some—of grand-opera divas. But the Caravans, like the Ward Singers, have their own special place. They were more than stupendous individual singers. They were harmonizers. They were church wreckers. And, to me, they were among the greatest artists of our time."

For all Aretha's genuine admiration of her gospel idols, both she and her father knew that, in light of Sam Cooke's triumph, it was time to move past them. If Sam could win the hearts of black R&B fans and top the white charts as well, why not Aretha?

While Aretha was preparing to fulfill her crossover dream, Berry Gordy had dreams of his own. He had gone from Golden Gloves boxer to assembly-line worker to jazz-record-store owner to composer of Jackie Wilson hits—"To Be Loved," "Lonely Teardrops," "Reet Petite." Gordy was the son of energetic entrepreneurs—his father was a contractor; his mom owned her own insurance agency—and his talents were matched by his ambition. When he turned thirty, in 1959, he began a record label that would soon become Motown. Before that, though, his concentration had been songwriting. One tune in particular—"All I Could Do Was Cry"—composed with his sister Gwen, fell into the hands of Erma Franklin.

"Everyone knew Berry Gordy," said Erma. "He was smart and many levels above your average street hustler. Not that he wasn't hustling himself—in those days, the music business was nothing but a hustle. Berry hustled with class and verve. I liked him. I started singing demos for him in the little house where he was living with his lady at the time, Raynoma Singleton. He had one song that was especially good, 'All I Could Do Was Cry.' The story was about a gal who watched her man marry another woman. That wasn't my story, but I could sure relate to the crying part, since my own marriage had fallen apart. I loved helping out Daddy when he went on tour, and in Detroit I was working as a nurse's aide, but my heart was in music. So I was tempted to make this demo for Berry. At that point, though, I saw myself as a jazz singer in the Sarah Vaughan/ Ella Fitzgerald style. I wasn't willing to do R-and-B. Well, Berry took the song to Chess Records, where Etta James sang it and had the hit. I realized then that I had made a mistake."

"It's difficult when everyone in the family has talent," said Cecil. "Daddy had raised us all to achieve on the highest level. We all wanted to confirm his faith in us. Had Erma recorded 'All I Could Do Was Cry,' she would have had the first hit in the family. I'm not sure Aretha would have liked that. But Erma didn't live her life to please Aretha or her father. She lived her life according to her own lights.

"Erma was no shrinking violet. She was as determined as any of us. When Aretha was younger, she was unwilling to challenge Daddy. Aretha worked in Daddy's shadow until she finally stepped out of the shadow into her own. Not so with Erma and not so with Carolyn. They were feisty girls and independent thinkers. Erma had a brilliant mind and read all the time. Daddy got to calling her Madame Queen because of her self-assurance. It's a quality we all admired, but Erma's assertiveness concerned Aretha. She worried she might steal her thunder. Later Aretha had the same problem with Carolyn. When it counted, the sisters were there for each other. But that didn't mean Aretha didn't feel them nipping at her heels. She didn't like that. Aretha had to be out front—and also first. That's the quality that helped make her a star."

Another quality was artistic curiosity.

"During the late fifties when everyone was R-and-B crazy, I took another route," Cecil further explained. "While Erma and Ree went running off to the Warfield Theater to see Little Willie John, I kicked back and listened to Thelonious Monk. Monk was my man. I was deep into modern jazz.

"My pal Pete Moore, who'd later join the Miracles with Smokey Robinson, showed me how to process hair. He and I ran a little barbershop out of the first-floor bathroom of our house. Some people complained that a preacher shouldn't have a son doing up 'dos in his house, but Daddy thought I showed initiative and encouraged me. In addition to our serious hairstyling chops, what made our shop different was the music. We played the coolest jazz out there — Charlie Mingus, Miles Davis, Sonny Rollins, Betty Carter. We'd sculpt those super-bad finger waves to the sound of Sonny Stitt.

"Aretha liked to hang out around our 'shop' — not only because she was crazy, but because of the music. She also spent a lot of time in my room — I had a separate apartment-like setup in the mansion — where she'd sit in front of the hi-fi for hours on end. That's where she first heard Sarah Vaughan, Smokey's favorite. But she didn't stop with Sarah. She studied Ella Fitzgerald, Billie Holiday, Carmen McRae, Anita O'Day, June Christy, Dakota Staton — anyone I had on the box. She got to a point where she could imitate these singers, lick for lick. Years later, she made vocal imitations part of her act. She'd do Diana Ross, Gladys Knight, and Mavis Staples. But those were her contemporaries. It was in my bedroom where she met her jazz masters, on my Magnavox stereo. It wasn't a conscious thing with Aretha. I don't think she listened to harmonically complex jazz in order to enhance her style. Jazz did enhance her style — not out of design, but because she absorbed everything she heard. The same was true for blues and gospel. In her mind and heart, they all mixed and mingled together. You can't separate them out. Call Aretha a great blues singer and you're telling the truth. Call her a great gospel singer and no one will argue. Call her a great jazz singer and the greatest jazz artists will agree. Bottom line — she's all three at once. And in the language of the jazzman, that's what's called a motherfucker."

In 1959, C. L. Franklin thought his daughter was ready.

Aretha often spoke about being nervous when she performed anywhere but church. She considered believers the best audiences. She liked saying that they weren't critics but worshippers. She saw nightclubs as places populated by cynics who came to see you fail, not succeed. She viewed critics as people who looked for mistakes. She realized that she required support, and if she was going to move into show business, she wanted not only her father by her side but her brother as well.

"I was ready," Cecil told me, "but Daddy had other ideas. Just as he had insisted that Erma go to Clark College in Atlanta, he wanted me at Morehouse in that same city. I told him I didn't want to go to college. 'Son,' he said, 'there's nothing more important than education. You have no choice. What's more, it's a black college, where you'll be able to learn about the history of your own people. Martin Luther King is a Morehouse man. And you're going to be one as well.' I still didn't want to go, so I put up all sorts of objections. But Daddy showed me the plane ticket he bought me and the receipt for tuition—all paid. 'When you get there,' he said, 'and you decide you don't want to stay, fine. You're on your own. Just don't come back here.' I went, and I stayed, and it turned out fine. Changed my life for the better. But I still wanted to be with Ree and watch her move into the big time."

At the conclusion of the fifties, with Aretha about to turn eighteen, she had been a professional for some five years. Her father paid her a modest salary, and her gospel work was recorded and distributed nationally. As a single mother, she retained custody of her two sons. She was not romantically attached, a situation that would soon change.

For all practical purposes, her father was her manager. He would select those advisers he felt were needed to educate both himself and his daughter about the wider world of popular entertainment.

"Daddy knew dozens of famous singers and musicians," said Carolyn, "but he didn't know the music business. He knew the church business. But because he was always a man who knew what he didn't know—that was a big part of his intelligence—he was ready to rely on others. As Ree prepared to try this new thing, there were a lot of uncertainties out there. One thing, though, was for sure: Daddy had stars in his eyes, and so did Aretha. The plan was to make her a star—and make it happen quickly."

That it didn't happen quickly enough would be the source of dramatic frustration for years to come.

Part Two

COLUMBIA

7. THE BIGGEST AND BEST

In 1960, the year Aretha sought her first secular recording contract, Cecil Franklin's best friend, Smokey Robinson, released the newly formed Motown Records' first million-selling single, "Shop Around." Because Berry Gordy was actively recruiting Detroit's local musical talent, it made perfect sense that he'd want Aretha.

"He did," said Cecil. "I was studying at Morehouse at the time, but Smokey and I never lost touch. Nothing would have been easier than getting Ree signed to Motown. And of course Daddy was close to Anna Gordy, Berry's sister, who knew all about Aretha. It made sense, but not to Daddy. He wanted Ree on Columbia, the label that recorded Mahalia Jackson, Duke Ellington, Johnny Mathis, Tony Bennett, Percy Faith, and Doris Day. Daddy said that Columbia was the biggest and best record company in the world. Leonard Bernstein recorded for Columbia.

"Berry Gordy was cool, Berry Gordy had written some good songs, Berry Gordy had signed Smokey, and Smokey and his Miracles were great, but you couldn't begin to compare Berry to Columbia. Berry was Detroit, and Daddy was convinced that Aretha's career couldn't be launched from Detroit. Look at Della Reese. Della grew up in Detroit, but her career didn't take off until she left town with the Erskine Hawkins big band. So it came down to Aretha moving to either Los Angeles or New York. California was too far away. Aretha wanted to be closer to home. Given her insecurities, she also wanted protection. Daddy would handpick her chaperones and her managers. Daddy was the general in charge of the whole operation."

The general had to hire a sergeant—an agent/manager. In Aretha's book, the only time she mentioned her father's violence concerned this process. She didn't like the man he had picked to manage her. When she refused to go along with C.L.'s plan, he slapped her across the face. But she remained adamant and got her way.

This was a critical omen of things to come. The first fissure between father and daughter would grow in the next few years. The issue would continue to be management, especially with a major break not far off, causing a seismic change in Aretha's relationship to men, power, and control. Who would be in charge of Aretha and her career?

For the time being, she and her father compromised on a female manager, Jo King, who worked out of New York and had contacts with the major labels. It was during this trip to New York in early 1960 that C.L. took Aretha to meet the great Phil Moore.

When Aretha and her dad walked into Moore's small For Singers Only studio in Manhattan in 1960, Moore was a forty-two-year-old piano player/arranger/coach whose vast experience spanned Hollywood film scores, cabarets, and jazz clubs. He had written arrangements for Tommy Dorsey and Harry James. He had composed dozens of movie soundtracks for MGM and Paramount. He had engineered Dorothy Dandridge's enormous crossover success and coached Lena Horne.

"When Reverend Franklin came to see me," Moore told me, "the singers he was most interested in were Dorothy and Lena. That's the kind of future he saw for his daughter. He wanted to break her in New York and then have me move her out to Hollywood and get her in the movies. I sat down at the piano and asked her what she wanted to sing. She said 'Navajo Trail.' That surprised me, but I played it anyway. What surprised me even more was the gospel flavor she gave the song. I suggested several standards, and she knew them all. She stuck to the melody, her pitch was perfect, but she transformed every mood—even a tune like 'Ac-Cent-Tchu-Ate the Positive'—to something very serious. I decided immediately that this was a serious singer. Her father kept discussing stage presentation. He wanted to know how I might help her find the kind of audience Lena Horne had found. How could I refine her style?

"I said, 'Reverend Franklin, my years in this business have not made me shy about speaking my mind. Singers come to me who, unfortunately, will never realize professional success. I consider it my duty to tell them just that. And I do. Other singers come to me with potential but require vigorous training. They must work diligently at their craft for years. I have several such students. Your daughter, however, fits into neither of these categories. She does not require my services. Her style has already been developed. Her style is in place. It is a unique style that, in my professional opinion, requires no alteration. It simply requires the right material. Her stage presentation is not of immediate concern. All that will come later. The immediate concern is the material that will suit her best. And the reason that concern will not be easily addressed is because I can't imagine any material that will not suit her.'

"Reverend Franklin took in everything I said. He had arrived prepared to pay me a considerable fee to help his daughter, and yet I was telling him that, in good conscience, I could not accept his money. That won his respect. Because I was being absolutely candid with him, he wanted to know whether his notion of placing her with Columbia Records was a good idea. I thought it was. I also thought that John Hammond, whom I had known through the years, would be an ideal producer. Hammond worked at Columbia. I considered him a great man. He had recorded Benny Carter, Fletcher Henderson, and Benny Goodman. He was the first one to bring Billie Holiday into a recording studio. He had produced

Count Basie. He was the most serious music man I knew. I felt strongly that he would immediately understand Aretha's talent. He would bring out her musicality and protect her artistic integrity. Additionally, he was a genuine aristocrat, the son of a Vanderbilt, and his position at Columbia would guarantee that Aretha would receive all the proper promotional effort required. I also suggested that Reverend Franklin contact Major Holley, a premier bass player, to produce a demo for Mr. Hammond to hear. Major hails from Detroit. He and the reverend had met on several occasions and held one another in the highest esteem. With such stellar participants in place, I was convinced that her career would blossom."

Like Phil Moore, Major Holley was a seasoned pro, a brilliant jazz artist who had backed a remarkable number of jazz greats, from Coleman Hawkins to Charlie Parker. When we spoke, he had a distinct memory of performing in the Franklin living room with Oscar Peterson. He also recalled C.L. waking his daughter to have her come downstairs and do her rendition of "Canadian Sunset."

"She didn't sing that night," said Major, "and she didn't stay long. She was terribly shy but she did play beautifully. Later, friends who had heard her sing at a revival meeting raved about her voice. I suppose I shouldn't have been surprised that her father, a minister, wanted me to produce jazz demos for her. After all, some musicians in Detroit called him the Jazz Preacher. He wasn't exactly sure which songs he wanted her to sing and was open to my suggestions. I opted for familiar tunes. I can't recall how many songs we did, but it was very straight-ahead. I put together a trio that I knew would give her rock-solid accompaniment. She came one afternoon around one, we rehearsed for an hour, and by three we had what we wanted on tape. She was a natural. The song she liked best, I recall, was 'Today I Sing the Blues.' We were all struck by how an eighteen-year-old girl sang that blues ballad with the authority of a grown woman.

"My hope was that, if she did attract a record contract, I'd be called to the studio to play on her first album. But I wasn't. When I listened to that album, though, I was struck by the fact that the song that made the greatest impact was the same 'Today I Sing the Blues.' I know I'm prejudiced, but I felt that the raw demo was a lot stronger than the version they released. I told Reverend Franklin the same thing as Phil Moore—the less you produce her, the better she'll be. Lesser artists require greater production. The greatest require very little."

John Hammond, who heard the demo, immediately signed her to Columbia, and he produced the first record.

I first spoke with John Hammond in the early eighties when he was in the process of bringing Stevie Ray Vaughan to Columbia. This was to be Hammond's last hurrah, his final significant signing. Jerry Wexler had introduced me. Wexler looked up to Hammond, who was seven years his senior, and Jerry had enormous respect for the man's commitment to not only quality jazz but civil rights. At the same time, their friendly rivalry was evident. Hammond was the first to sign Aretha, but his recordings with her were not commercial successes. Out of Hammond's presence, Wexler told me, "John has unfaltering taste for talent but is not good in the studio. He seeks to document music, but a producer must do more than that. A producer must sculpt a sound. John doesn't know how to do that."

For his part, Hammond was defensive about his years with Aretha. He claimed that he never got to produce her the way he had envisioned.

"Those first sessions," he told me, "were put together in haste. It was Curtis Lewis, writer of 'Today I Sing the Blues,' who brought me the demo of that song sung by Aretha. I was knocked out. I wanted to sign her immediately. Funny, but years later, Helen Humes, a great singer who I brought to Count Basie, reminded me that I had recorded the song with her on Mercury in 1947. Helen claimed that she had cowritten it with Curtis, who never put his name on it. She never received any royalties.

"My vision for Aretha had nothing to do with rhythm and blues. It was a market that neither I nor, for that matter, Columbia

Records cared to cultivate. I saw her as a jazz/blues artist. For the first Aretha sessions, I immediately hired the best jazz musicians in town, but I wanted more time to work up the arrangements. Reverend Franklin was in a great hurry to get something out there. He felt as though they had waited a very long time for this moment. They were looking to book her in jazz clubs and needed product. I didn't see the rush. Aretha had just turned eighteen. At the same time, I learned that Sam Cooke had told RCA to pursue Aretha. If I didn't have a signed contract and assure her father that we would have a record out that very year—1960—I feared we'd lose her."

Columbia didn't lose her. Contracts were signed, and in May the label placed an ad in *Ebony*, the national black magazine, for both Aretha's debut album and a new record by Oscar Brown Jr., *Sin and Soul*. The media selection indicates that the record company was aiming primarily for the African American market.

In her book, Aretha offers at least two different versions of the person she was when she first stepped into a professional recording studio. One was a young ingénue who had moved from Detroit to New York and required chaperones. She mentioned two—Sue Dodds Banks, a friend of C.L.'s who drove for a funeral home in Detroit, and Elizabeth Thornton, former secretary to Mahalia Jackson. She spoke of living at the YMCA, at the Bryant Hotel in midtown, at the Chelsea Hotel—where she was evicted because C.L. forgot to pay the weekly rent—and at a small hotel in Greenwich Village. In describing her sequestered New York life where her every move was supervised by an older woman, she hardly sounded like a mother of two boys.

Aretha's other self-portrait was of a woman on the hunt for men. Both she and Erma were interested in the Flamingos. They had met them through Harvey Fuqua, the doo-wop master who mentored Marvin Gaye and brought him to Motown. Sisterly rivalry ensued, and Aretha wound up dating Flamingo Nate Nelson. She also went out with Paul Owens, a singer for the Swan Silvertones, one of the great gospel groups. She explained that the affair lasted until she caught him with another woman.

"I still had the Moonglows," said Harvey Fuqua, "when I met Aretha. Like most of the teenage girls, she was doo-wop crazy because doo-wop was such a romantic music. It was all about worshipping women and promising them eternal love. The harmonies were geared to get the ladies.

"Aretha was an unusual young girl because when you first met her, you'd think she was the shyest young creature ever invented. She'd be in a room with other people for hours and not say a word. The cat always had her tongue. But when the room emptied, she sure wasn't shy about coming up to me and asking for an introduction to this guy or that guy. Once she was introduced, she pursued him—and I mean pursued him hard. The girl was relentless."

Of all the Franklin children, Carolyn, the baby, had perhaps the most objective view of what was happening in 1960.

"I was sixteen and still in high school," she said. "I was the last child left at home. Aretha was in New York. She'd come home often to visit her babies, but it was Big Mama who was raising her boys. There was never any doubt—not for a second—that having two babies would interfere with Aretha's career. Erma was also pursuing her career. She was on the road with Lloyd Price. Cecil was off at college. So Daddy decided that it would be better for me to move in with another family in our neighborhood. That decision crushed me. I argued and cried but couldn't change his mind. I understand now that, after raising four children as a single father, he wanted the run of his household. I also suspected he wanted more freedom to bring in his lady friends without his prying kids around. Whatever he wanted, though, I resented being thrown out. For years I was angry at my siblings for not coming to my defense and convincing our father to let me stay. I knew their arguments wouldn't make any difference—once our father made up his mind, that was it—but I felt deserted by everyone. I was the odd duck. Cecil was the brilliant student. Erma and Aretha were the brilliant singers. They were also chasing after boys when I was discovering that my romantic preference went in an entirely different direction. In a family of stars—and in the case of Aretha, a superstar—it took me a long time to find my own identity and voice. Looking back, I see that we were all searching. Even Aretha wouldn't find her true voice for years to come."

Jerry Wexler agreed with Carolyn's assessment—Aretha's six years at Columbia were essentially an attempt to discover her real voice.

"In those early recordings," said Wexler, "she sounds uncertain and unharnessed. She's trying to figure out who she is, and I don't think John was really helping her."

Hammond had another version of the eighteen-year-old Aretha. "She needed little direction. Her style was intact. Anyone with decent ears could hear that she was a gospel-trained singer extremely comfortable with jazz and blues. I hired Ray Bryant, a jazz-blues pianist rooted in gospel. He understood Aretha and she adored his playing. In fact, the first thing we recorded—'Today I Sing the Blues'—became a classic and remained in her repertoire even when she changed labels. If you listen to it, you aren't hearing a singer in search of a style. She's found it."

No doubt, "Today I Sing the Blues" captured the real Aretha. When she signed with Atlantic later in the decade and recorded the *Soul '69* album, she refashioned it to fit in the "Dr. Feelgood" mode, but the alteration was slight. The original was right to begin with. What wasn't right, though, was the rest of Aretha's first record. The material is uneven, the arrangements weak. Only when Aretha settles in on piano and belts blues variations like "Right Now" and "Maybe I'm a Fool" does she take command.

"Those are the songs," said Hammond, "that worked the best for me. My original notion was to do an entire record of such songs. Aretha and her dad said they were excited to work with me because I had worked with Count Basie and Billie Holiday. I saw her in that great timeless tradition. But when we got into the planning stage, they started saying how important it was that the record get airplay. They wanted singles—and they wanted a hit. That's how we wound up doing 'Sweet Lover,' an innocuous tune they thought would hit with the teen market. The same thing applied to 'Love Is the Only Thing.' The musicians I hired for the session—Ray Bryant, Osie Johnson, and Milton Hinton—were among the most experienced in New York and could adapt to any style. At our studio on Thirtieth Street, they did their best coping with the inferior material. At first, Aretha and her dad thought adding a trombone—the wonderful Tyree Glenn—on certain tracks would sound too old-fashioned, but I finally convinced them otherwise. I also didn't think that including 'Over the Rainbow' was appropriate. But the Franklins were adamant. They said they wanted to reach a wider audience and thought paying tribute to Judy Garland was the way to do it. I capitulated.

"I suggested 'It Ain't Necessarily So' from Gershwin's masterful *Porgy and Bess*. George Gershwin deeply understood the blues idiom and, together with his brother Ira's witty lyrics, wrote sterling vehicles for black voices. I was a bit worried that the story, which questioned the literal truth of the Bible with a wink and a nod, might be problematical. But Reverend Franklin had not the least concern. He told me how much he admired the Gershwins. He also said that, when it came to scriptural analysis, he opposed literalism. I was most impressed with the reverend's erudition and liberal theology.

"We had disagreements, though, when it came to his strong suggestion that we include a gospel song. I'm a passionate fan of gospel. I brought Sister Rosetta Tharpe and the Golden Gate Quartet to Carnegie Hall back in 1938. There's no music for which I have greater appreciation. At the same time, I didn't feel that sticking in a single gospel number would help the cohesiveness of this first record. Reverend Franklin disagreed. We discussed it at length and he and Aretha came up with what they considered a compromise—a song called 'Are You Sure' from the Broadway musical *The Unsinkable Molly Brown*. The song had somewhat of a spiritual message. Reverend Franklin saw it as white-friendly. I thought it was anemic. I wanted something much closer to what Aretha had been singing in church, but, again, I was outvoted.

"When we were through recording and listened to the playbacks in the studio, Aretha and her father could not have been more pleased. Their goal was to cover all the bases. My goal was to capture the essence of this remarkable young talent. With the exception of a few songs, I'm afraid I didn't do that. Yet the reviews were generally excellent, and 'Today I Sing the Blues' and 'Won't Be Long' reached the top ten of the rhythm-and-blues *Billboard* chart. They didn't enjoy tremendous sales, but they did garner airplay. In that regard, the record, for all my reservations, was seen as a semi-success."

The recording sessions began in August of 1960 and continued, off and on, for six months. Hammond explained that was due to the dispute over material.

"The company wanted to release two singles before the album was complete," he said. "'Love Is the Only Thing' came out and didn't perform. Then we released 'Today I Sing the Blues.'"

Billboard gave each of the singles three stars. The reviewer called the first "a smartly styled blues by the gal in dual track. Fine gospel-type piano is heard in the backing. She can catch some spins with jazz-oriented effort." Of the second, *Billboard* wrote, "A slow rhythm blues chant with gal backed in okay style by guitar, piano and bass. The artist has talent and should be watched."

For the third and fourth singles, "Won't Be Long" and "Right Now," released in time for Christmas 1960, *Billboard* was equally generous: "Young blues thrush Aretha Franklin comes through in solid style on her second outing for the label. She handles the swinging 'Won't Be Long' with a sure vocal touch and does a fine job on the flip as well. Strong wax."

According to Dunstan Prial, Hammond's biographer, the producer wrote Aretha's manager that "Won't Be Long" had sold forty thousand copies and was on its way to becoming a major hit. But that prediction didn't prove true. It peaked at number seven on the

R&B charts and did not cross over into pop territory. At best, it was a minor hit.

"It languished because Aretha did not show up for several interviews and press events," Hammond told me. "She refused to promote it properly. I don't know what her problems were, but she had a habit of missing important dates. I suspect she withdrew into a kind of depressive state. I think she had real challenges in the area of mood management."

Before the album was released, in February of 1961, Jo King had already booked Aretha into the Village Vanguard, perhaps the most hallowed of all New York jazz clubs.

Aretha has told interviewers about her initial opportunity to play the Apollo. She said she chose the Vanguard instead because of the jazz venue's enormous prestige.

Hammond had a different memory. He told me that Aretha simply didn't show up for her appearance at the Apollo. She also missed several studio and club dates, all without explanation.

"Sometimes she'd say she had a sore throat," said Hammond, "but most of the time she offered no excuses."

Dunstan Prial quoted from a letter that Hammond sent to Aretha after she had missed the date at the Apollo as well as an engagement at New York's Village Gate: "If you don't straighten up soon you will be a legend in the business and not one of the nice ones."

In her book, Aretha does not discuss any friction with Hammond. Her attention seemed to be on the development of a jazz base before R&B. As Ray Charles once said, "Prove yourself as a real jazz artist, and everything else will follow. Jazz is the hardest thing we do. Sing jazz right and the critics gotta respect you."

And yet, according to three eyewitness reports, Aretha didn't perform a true jazz set.

In October 1960, *Billboard* wrote, "When Aretha Franklin sat at the piano and sang the blues, the audience at the Village Vanguard in Greenwich Village erupted into applause. The gal singer, who has had one single disk so far on the Columbia label, has a fine strong voice that bears emotional fruit when it is channeled into the material she knows and feels best. Miss Franklin's New York singing debut was a marked success when she relaxed and sang such blues material as 'Love Is the Only Thing' and 'Won't Be Long.'

"Aretha Franklin was accompanied by a fine trio under the direction of pianist Ellis Larkin, with Floyd William Jr. on drums and Major Holley on bass."

Major Holley told me, "We were surprised how she kept mixing the material. She wanted Ray Bryant to play the gig but he wasn't available, so I suggested Ellis Larkin. There's no better jazz piano player. For years he worked with Ella. When I told that to Aretha, she grew excited and during rehearsals had us work standards that Ella had sung—'I Thought About You,' 'A Foggy Day,' 'I've Got a Crush on You.' Aretha sang them magnificently. But a day or so before we opened, she decided to sing the songs she'd been working on for her album. The blues tunes were great, but the novelty songs—I guess she thought they'd be hits—seemed beneath her. She also insisted on including Broadway songs. It all felt sort of disconnected to me."

"The first time I caught Aretha," said Carmen McRae, the great jazz singer, "was at the Vanguard in the early sixties. My knowledge of gospel is limited so I hadn't heard of her or her father. But Max Gordon, who owns the Vanguard, pulled my coat to her. He said she was gonna be the next Dinah.

"She blew me away—I'll say that for starters. I leaned over to Max and said, 'You're right. She does have Dinah Washington chops.' She sang the shit outta some blues and put a hurting on 'Ain't Necessarily So' that I thought was just perfect. The one thing she lacked, though, was taste in material. She sang some seriously stupid shit. Maybe she was looking for a teen hit, but she did at least four or five songs that were crap. At the same time, she took a corny song like 'Hello, Young Lovers' and turned it inside out. It had been a long time since I'd heard a singer express so much emotion in her voice. After her first set, Max introduced me, and, given how emotionally she sang, I expected her to have a super-charged emotional personality like Dinah. Instead, she was the shyest thing I've ever met. Would hardly look me in the eye. Didn't say more than two words. I mean, this bitch gave *bashful* a new meaning. Anyway, I didn't give her any advice because she didn't ask for any, but I knew goddamn well that, no matter how good she was—and she was absolutely wonderful—she'd have to make up her mind whether she wanted to be Della Reese, Dinah Washington, or Sarah Vaughan. I also had a feeling she wouldn't have minded being Leslie Uggams or Diahann Carroll. I remember thinking that if she didn't figure out who she was—and quick— she was gonna get lost in the weeds of the music biz. And I can testify that those weeds are awfully fuckin' dense."

Carmen saw the situation accurately. Excited to be in New York, excited by the jazz scene, the Broadway scene, the R&B scene, and the pop-music scene, Aretha went in different directions at once.

"If, in the beginning, she had hit big as a mainstream artist, she and I would have never worked together," said Jerry Wexler. "She would have been thrilled to have a Nancy Wilson–style career."

Wilson, discovered in Ohio by Cannonball Adderley, came to New York and signed with Capitol Records in 1960, the same year Aretha signed with Columbia. Her first single, "Guess Who I Saw Today," an exquisitely articulated musical short story, was a huge hit and catapulted Nancy into the front ranks of cabaret/nightclub/ concert-hall jazz chanteuses.

On the other side of the ledger, Mary Wells signed with Motown that very same year—1960—and took off shortly after with hits like "Bye Bye Baby." Ironically, it was Aretha's onetime neighbor and her brother's best friend Smokey Robinson whose productions and songs—"Two Lovers," "You Beat Me to the Punch," "My Guy"— formed the foundation of Motown's unprecedented success. They were teen ditties, comparable to Aretha's "Sweet Lover" and "Love Is the Only Thing" from her debut Columbia album.

When you listen to early Aretha side by side with early Mary Wells and early Nancy Wilson, the differences are obvious. Nancy's "Guess Who I Saw Today" is an exercise in the high art of jazz storytelling; the arrangement is a paragon of understatement. Mary was working with brilliant material, and her sound, with Smokey's help, was sculpted with great subtlety.

Unlike Wilson's work with Smokey, Aretha's work with Hammond resulted in poor sales. Aretha was understandably frustrated. She expected major crossover play and was disappointed when that didn't happen. She was convinced that Columbia had failed to promote her properly. They had stressed her R&B material like "Today I Sing the Blues" at the expense of her pop material. She didn't see herself in a position to challenge the marketing department. That was her manager's job. It was especially frustrating because everywhere she looked, she saw black singers crossing over to the white market.

It was 1960, the year of Chubby Checker's "Twist" and Ray Charles's "Georgia on My Mind." Sam Cooke hit with "Chain Gang," Jackie Wilson with "Doggin' Around," and Dinah Washington and Brook Benton with "A Rockin' Good Way." The Shirelles had "Tonight's the Night," and the Drifters "Save the Last Dance for Me."

Aretha was correct; left and right, black music was crossing over. When I asked her whether she thought that the production and material might have been impediments to that crossover, she replied adamantly, "Not in the least. I have never compromised my material. Even then, I knew a good song from a bad one. And if Hammond, one of the legends of the business, didn't know how to produce a record, who does? No, the fault was with promotion. The head of Columbia was a famous executive named Goddard Lieberson. He was the big boss and supposedly very close to Mahalia. He was the executive who could approve the ad budgets and make sure you received the media attention required to sell records. But in all my years at his label, I never as much as met the man. He never bothered to come to the studio when I was recording or even call me to say that he liked what I was doing. I was simply neglected in favor of bigger Columbia stars, like Percy Faith and Guy Mitchell. Soon after I signed, Andy Williams and Barbra Streisand came to the label. They were given major marketing budgets. I wasn't."

Hammond disputed that. "When Aretha signed with us," he said, "we saw her as an across-the-board star. I don't believe she ever suffered from neglect in any area. In my long career, I've known few artists who, having failed to achieve commercial success, didn't blame it on the record company. It's the oldest story in the music business."

In February of 1961, as John F. Kennedy settled in at the White House, Aretha's debut album was released. Despite the introduction of one of the most compelling voices of modern times, Aretha made only a small splash. Her secular career had begun with uncertainty.

Her personal life was also less than sanguine. She was dating several men in New York but missed her babies, who were being raised by Big Mama.

"Aretha was committed to New York," said Carolyn, "but I think the fact that Daddy would always be anchored in Detroit bothered her. She would have greatly preferred that he find a church in New York and move there so she could have him nearby. Aretha's one of those women who needed and wanted a strong man. She's changed over the years, but in those first years, when she was aiming at stardom, it was very important for her to have a man by her side and help her choose the right direction."

Aretha found that direction from a surprising source, combining her professional and personal life in a move that would infuriate Reverend Franklin and, for the first time, rupture the sacred father/daughter relationship.

8. GENTLEMAN PIMP

In May of 1961, *Jet* magazine, the magazine with which Aretha would enjoy a warm and close relationship over the next fifty years, reported in its New York Beat column that "Marv Johnson and Aretha Franklin, the Detroit preacher's daughter, are not telling friends of their hot romance, which could lead to the altar."

"Ree didn't go with Marv Johnson for more than a minute, but it was an important minute," said Erma. "Marv had the first hit on Motown, 'Come to Me,' and was a good-looking guy with a Jackie Wilson/Sam Cooke voice. Marv, like Aretha, was on his way up."

"My sister didn't need a man who was involved in his own career," said Carolyn. "She was looking for a career herself. Marv was way deep into cutting hits of his own. He didn't give Aretha the kind of attention she required. On the other hand, Ted White gave her all the attention she required. He saw her potential. And he came out of the Detroit culture of music hustlers Aretha could relate to. He might not have been Berry Gordy, but in some ways he was cooler than that. He was more composed and confident than Berry, who was always a nervous little guy. There was nothing nervous 'bout Ted."

"You can't understand the music culture of Detroit in the early sixties," said R&B singer Bettye LaVette, who emerged from that culture, "without understanding the role of the pimp. Pimps and producers were often the same people. The sensibility was the same—get women working for you; get women to make you money. We demonize pimps now, but back then they were looked up to by men and sought out by women. They had power. They knew how to survive the ghetto and go beyond the ghetto. Some of my best men friends were pimps. Some of the women I admired most were working for them—classy, sophisticated, beautifully dressed women. I didn't have what it took to be a high-class prostitute of the kind that the best pimps like to parade, but as a singer, I was certainly pimped by certain producers—and glad to be.

"Back then, women were powerless. If we wanted to get ahead in show business, we had to operate in the system. The greatest example of that system was probably Motown, where Berry Gordy's first wife, Raynoma Singleton, claimed that Berry himself had pimped women. He wasn't good with whores, but he was great with singers. The parallel is strong."

Bettye LaVette was also close to Ted White, the man who, in 1961, would become Aretha's first husband.

"I'd call Ted a gentleman pimp," she said. "He was a cut above. The older generation of Detroit's famous pimps who came before Ted—like Jimmy Joy, another friend of mine—were charismatic men, but they had flashy ghetto style. Ted upgraded that style. He dressed like a successful businessman—tailored suits, suede coats, custom-made suits imported from England. He was also highly educated and well read. He was well bred. Ted was the first man to take me to fancy French restaurants. He knew his wines. He knew which perfumes suited me best. When we'd be dining in some posh dining room, he'd tell me to lower my voice and act like a lady. He helped me become a lady. Beyond that, he was always there when I needed him. When I got stuck out of town because a promoter didn't pay me for a gig, Ted would send me plane fare to come home. I had great respect for him.

"I met him in 1963 after he was married to Aretha, but that didn't keep him from wooing me. I wasn't physically attracted to him. I was socially attracted to him. He represented a higher class. He always had lots of women—women who were lovers, women who were whores, and women who were singers. I was flattered that he wanted me. I was seventeen and Aretha was twenty-one. She didn't have a lot to say back then. Those were her pre-Queen days."

"Ted White was famous even before he got with Aretha," Etta James told me. "My boyfriend at the time, Harvey Fuqua, used to talk about him. Ted was supposed to be the slickest pimp in Detroit. When I learned that Aretha married him, I wasn't surprised. A lot of the big-time singers who we idolized as girls—like Billie Holiday and Sarah Vaughan—had pimps for boyfriends and managers. That was standard operating procedure. My own mother had made a living turning tricks. When we were getting started, that way of life was part of the music business. It was in our genes. Part of the lure of pimps was that they got us paid. They protected us. They also beat us up. Lots of chicks felt like if her man didn't beat her, he didn't love her. I remember my mom playing me Billie Holiday's record where she sang, 'I'd rather for my man to hit me than jump and quit me.' She was saying if her pimp didn't have no money and she said, 'Take mine, honey,' wasn't no one's fuckin' business but her own. I think a lot of us felt that way—until the beating got so bad that we couldn't take no more. Naturally, women's lib came along and changed all that. I'm glad for women's lib. I'm a women's libber myself. But back in the fifties and early sixties, it was a different world. We were young girls looking to make it at any cost. We wanted men who could carry us to where we wanted to go."

How did Aretha meet the man who she hoped could carry her where she wanted to go, the same man whom, as a child, she'd watched carry a drunk Dinah Washington out of her father's living room?

Aretha claimed the introduction was made by her sister.

"I knew Ted White," said Erma, "as did most entertainers in Detroit. He was a fixture at the clubs. He was a handsome man with a smooth manner and excellent taste. He had been to our house during several parties. I didn't need to introduce him to Aretha. She already knew him."

"There had been tension between Aretha and my dad over her management even before she signed with Columbia," Carolyn told me. "She knew that Daddy understood the gospel world, but she questioned his knowledge of the world of popular music. The break didn't come, though, until Ted White. Ted changed the entire emotional dynamic. Daddy didn't want her to have anything to do with him."

"All children go through rebellious periods," said Cecil. "Aretha's rebellion started when she was around eighteen or so. She wanted to make it as a pop singer in the worst way. She wanted to lose her identification as a church singer. Her full ambition took hold of her, and, although our father wanted nothing more than for her to succeed, he still thought he knew best. He prided himself in being a good judge of character. In that regard, he did not have a high regard for Ted White's character. He knew Ted was something of a shady character—and he thought the association would hurt Aretha."

In Aretha's book, there is not a hint of White's shady activities.

"Anyone who didn't see Ted White as straight-up pimp had to be deaf, dumb, and blind," said Harvey Fuqua. "He made no effort to hide it. He was proud of it. He was proud to be one of the slickest operators in Detroit. It took someone that slick to get a great talent like Aretha in his stable."

Before Ted White, the notion of anyone wresting control of Aretha's career from C. L. Franklin seemed outlandish. Of all his children, she was closest to him. He had encouraged her every step of the way. When she was seventeen, he told her she was ready. When she was eighteen, he assembled the supporting cast to take to New York and lead her into the big time.

"In those years," said Erma, "Aretha's story was pretty much a struggle over her career by two men—our dad and Ted. Ted won because Ted could concentrate completely on Aretha while Daddy couldn't. He was not only the preacher of a huge Detroit church but he continued to travel. Beyond that, these were the years when the civil rights movement was gathering steam. Our father would prove to be a national leader in that movement. He and Dr. King were not only close friends but spiritual allies. They thought alike. They were both intellectuals, both liberals, and both proponents of nonviolence. There was no disagreement between them on any issues whatsoever. All this meant that, more than any time in his life, Daddy was engaged politically. He no longer had time to watch over Aretha's career. That didn't mean he approved of Ted taking over. He didn't. He tried to convince Aretha to continue with Jo King or find other management, but by then Ted had made his move. In short order, he went from being her lover to her husband as well as her manager."

"People forget," said Cecil, "but in those first years, Aretha struggled financially. Columbia didn't give her much of an advance. Her records were all respected but they never sold well. I'm not sure she ever saw a royalty check from Columbia.

"Ted was a diligent manager," said Cecil. "He was responsible for getting her on a short tour with Jackie Wilson and another with Sam Cooke."

"I think Ted White was the man who Aretha really needed," said Bettye LaVette. "Ted had everything—sophistication, taste, and savoir faire. If she was talking too loud in a restaurant or making the wrong remarks to a booking agent, Ted would let her know in a hurry. Ted was older and knew how to mold her into a lady. He also had some money that he could put into her career. One of his working girls—a gorgeous gal—was an especially good earner. Ted told me that he used her earnings to help finance Aretha's early career. Aretha had every reason to be grateful to Ted—and for a long while she was."

"You could compare the Aretha/Ted situation," said Etta James, "with Ike and Tina. Ike made Tina, no doubt about it. He developed her talent. He showed her what it meant to be a performer. He got her famous. Of course, Ted White was not a performer, but he was savvy about the world. When Harvey Fuqua introduced me to him—this was the fifties, before he was with Aretha—I saw him as a super-hip extra-smooth cat. I liked him. He knew music. He knew songwriters who were writing hit songs. He had manners. Later, when I ran into him and Aretha—this was the sixties—I saw that she wasn't as shy as she used to be. He brought her out. He had her dressing with more pizzazz. She'd become a hipper chick, smoking a little reefer, sipping a little wine. I'm not sure that was so bad for her, since she wanted to make it in the big bad world of show biz. Ted gave her an edge she needed. And if things went bad for Aretha later on, welcome to the party. That was the story of how it went with most of us and our men. They came on to promote us at a time when we wanted help in the worst way. They hooked us up with other slick promoters and producers. They dressed us and trotted us out to the stage. At the time—and this is the part no one gets—we didn't mind it. We fuckin' liked it! We were hoping these cats would choose us and sell us and show us how to get over. That was the good side. The bad side was when the devil popped outta them and they thought they could control us forever. That's when the violence started. Just like Billie and Sarah, I experienced that. Just like me, Aretha experienced that. In the meantime, though, we became stars. Could we have had one without the other—a career without the pimps selling us? Who the fuck knows?"

Two press items from August 1961 indicate Aretha's state of mind at the time of White's courtship. The first is the announcement in *Down Beat* magazine that she had won the new-star female vocalist award in the magazine's ninth international jazz critics poll. She had thirty votes to Abbey Lincoln's twenty-five. The rest of the list included LaVern Baker, Helen Humes, Nina Simone, Marjorie Hendricks (Ray Charles's fiery backup singer), Gloria Lynne, Nancy Wilson, Etta Jones, and Carol Sloane. That was stiff competition for nineteen-year-old Aretha and an indication that Hammond's argument—that she was a critical hit, if not a commercial one—was undeniably true.

Shortly after the August *Down Beat* issue hit the stands, Aretha wrote a guest column for the *New York Amsterdam News,* a prominent African American publication, entitled "From Gospel to Jazz Is Not Disrespect for the Lord."

"I don't think that in any matter I did the Lord a disservice when I made up my mind two years ago to switch over," she wrote. "After all, the blues is a music born out of the slavery day sufferings of my people."

Her position mirrors the one long held by her dad—that black music at its very root, no matter how it might branch out, contains a divine spirit.

What's interesting, though, is that the first single released from her second album, *The Electrifying Aretha Franklin,* is far more show-biz pizzazz than jazz. The arrangement for "Rock-a-Bye Your Baby with a Dixie Melody" was written by Bob Mersey, soon to be an important figure in Aretha's career at Columbia. He was the label's musical director and a staff writer for CBS television. At the same time he began producing Aretha, he arranged "Moon River" for Andy Williams. A year later, in 1963, he would produce Barbra Streisand's debut record, also on the Columbia label.

Al Jolson had sung "Rock-a-Bye" in blackface in the twenties. Later, it was recorded by Sammy Davis Jr., Judy Garland, and Jerry Lewis. Though an essential American song, it seemed a strange choice for Aretha, especially at the start of the civil rights movement.

Cecil explained to me C. L. Franklin's love of Al Jolson and his reason for urging Aretha to include the tune.

"My father told me how Jolson harbored great affection for black people," said Cecil. "His entire blackface act was a way of paying tribute to our musical genius. Dad knew the history of American entertainment and had read how Jolson had hired black writers and helped bolster the career of Cab Calloway. We forget now, but back in the day, Al Jolson and black people had a mutual-admiration society."

In spite of Cecil's spirited defense of Aretha's inclusion of the song, it's difficult for me to listen to her version without cringing. Although her vocal is enthusiastic, the strings feel anemic, the horn chart cheesy, and the rock-'em-sock-'em finale forced and false. A more generous reading would appreciate the soul piano introduction, rendered by Aretha herself, and the slightly ironic big-band flourish at the song's grand conclusion.

Aretha liked "Rock-a-Bye" so much that she sang it on her network television debut. On October 30, 1961, she appeared on *American Bandstand,* where the teen crowd seemed bewildered by her choice of a song associated with their fathers' or grandfathers' generation. Aretha's selection might have seemed wildly inappropriate, but such choices would be part of her pattern in the years to come.

"I thought the Jolson song was a mistake," John Hammond told me. "It had no business on an Aretha Franklin album. The idea was to present her as a great jazz/blues artist, not a revisionist of show-business lore. I thought it was outrageous, but what I thought no longer mattered since I had been told Aretha was peeved at me. While I was in Europe vacationing, an A-and-R man at Epic, a Columbia subsidiary, offered a contract to Aretha's sister Erma. Apparently there was intense sibling rivalry, and Aretha was not at all pleased. She presumed that I was the man behind the move, even though I wasn't. I tried to explain, but by then she had withdrawn into stony silence and was not interested in hearing any explanations."

"It was Daddy who suggested to Columbia that they listen to me sing," Erma told me. "One of their executives heard me at a club. At the time, I was with Lloyd Price. Actually, Lloyd had asked me to go on the road with him a year earlier, but Daddy, always protective, didn't think I was ready. Then in 1961 I joined Lloyd for what would be nearly a five-year professional relationship. My mother-in-law, Ollie Patterson, was caring for my children, Thomas and Sabrina, back in Detroit.

"The Columbia A-and-R man was impressed enough with my singing that he told my dad that he thought he could get me a deal. The man also said that I would be on Epic, which was a different brand than Columbia. They were part of the same company but I'd have my own producers and an identity separate from Aretha. I thought she would be thrilled. She wasn't. She threw a fit. She told Daddy that she didn't want me on Epic, that it would hurt her career and that people would be confused by too many singing Franklin sisters. By then she and Daddy were having their problems because of her relationship with Ted. I wasn't privy to their conversation, but I do know that my father took up my part and told Ree that she wasn't the only one in this family who wanted—and deserved—a career in music. Later, when Carolyn went out there to do her own thing, she'd get the same grief from Aretha."

While the hubbub with Erma continued, Aretha worked in the studio on her sophomore effort. *The Electrifying Aretha Franklin,* the first time we hear her with strings and a big band, lists John Hammond as its producer, but Hammond claims that was in name only. His work with Aretha was essentially over.

"I was told that I could do album cuts with her," he said, "but the company's producers were taking over. It was thought that they, not I, were in a better position to produce hits. They took the budget allotments that had accumulated from my sessions, which were extremely low cost, and applied them to larger productions. I found those productions vapid. I was still interested in documenting her prowess as a jazz and blues artist. The last songs I remember producing with Aretha were in the winter of 1961. They were both Ray Charles–related. The first was an instrumental written by Ray Charles called 'Hard Times (No One Knows Better than I)' that she played on piano and added a great vocal flourish at the end, in which she sings, 'Ray Charles says it was hard times but I feel all right.' It was a splendid piece of bluesy spontaneity. The company deemed it unworthy for release. The second did appear on the *Electrifying* record. This was 'Lucky Old Sun.' Frankie Laine, of course, had the hit on Mercury back in the forties. Louis Armstrong and Sinatra had also recorded it, but it was Sam Cooke's version that Aretha remembered. I heard it as basically a haunting blues ballad, and she interpreted it with great feeling and intelligence. I was told by my friend Sid Feller, then producing Ray Charles, that Ray heard Aretha's version and then decided to sing it himself on his

Ingredients in a Recipe for Soul album that appeared a year after Aretha's *Electrifying.* By then, the word *soul* was beginning to replace *rhythm and blues* as a code word for popular black music."

The big soul ballad on the rhythm-and-blues charts in 1961 was Etta James's "At Last," the Mack Gordon/Harry Warren song that hit for Glenn Miller in 1942. While working with Etta on her book, I asked her why she thought her string-heavy jazzy standard had turned into a smash while, in that same year, Aretha couldn't hit with a bluesy standard like "That Lucky Old Sun."

"The answer's easy," said Etta. "Aretha sang the shit outta those standards—just as good if not better than me. But Columbia didn't know how to reach black listeners, and my company, Chess, did. Leonard Chess had a genius for feeling out the black community. Jerry Wexler was the same. They were white Jews who would never use the word *nigga,* but they knew us niggas better than we knew ourselves. Columbia didn't have no one like that. They had John Hammond, but he was like a college professor up there in the ivory tower. He wasn't street like Chess or Wexler. If you wanna have black hits, you gotta understand the black streets, you gotta work those streets and work those DJs to get airplay on black stations. Wasn't true of everything she did on Columbia, but in general, Aretha's Columbia shit wasn't black enough for blacks and too black for whites. Or looking at it another way, in those days you had to get the black audience to love the hell outta you and then hope the love would cross over to the white side. Columbia didn't know nothing 'bout crossing over."

As a purely musical package, *Electrifying* is mystifying, alternating between brilliant and banal. Leslie McFarland, a journeyman writer who contributed five songs to Aretha's first album, has four more on her second, among them "It's So Heartbreakin'," a slight teen-oriented vehicle with Aretha on piano; "I Told You So," an even thinner blues ditty with big-band backing; and the shocking "Rough Lover," whose story seems to mirror the very relationship Aretha had entered into with Ted White. She envisions someone who will take charge, and, if she gets sassy, "be a man who dares shut me up." She doesn't want a meek man; she wants a "boss," "a devil when he's crossed." There is conviction in her voice.

There is also greatness in her reading of McFarland's fourth song, "Just for You," a poignant ballad that benefits not only from a subtle string chart but also from the sensitive accompaniment of Tommy Flanagan, the great jazz artist who would go on to spend a dozen years as Ella Fitzgerald's pianist. Here Aretha, at twenty, expresses the emotional richness of a woman decades older. Like Ray Charles, who claimed teen material never fit his aesthetic, Aretha requires the deepest dramatic material.

That material arrives in the form of two songs on *Electrifying*. One is "Blue Holiday," by Luther Dixon, writer of "Sixteen Candles" by the Crests. Dixon's songs for Perry Como, Bobby Darin, and Elvis Presley brought him to the attention of Florence Greenberg, the boss at Scepter Records, the label that soon would explode with Dixon-produced hits for the Shirelles.

"Blue Holiday" was, in fact, recorded by the Shirelles, who cut it in 1961. When Aretha interpreted it in New York during the Christmas season of that year, she remembered being especially homesick for her family in Detroit. She was also nearly eight months pregnant with her third son, Ted White's child. The Shirelles' version of the song features Doris Coley offering a heartfelt reading of a teenager longing for lost love. In contrast, Aretha renders the song as a straight-ahead jazz classic. It helps enormously that she is surrounded by sterling accompaniment—Miles Davis bandmates pianist Wynton Kelly and drummer Jimmy Cobb; Count Basie's trumpeter Joe Newman and his trombonist Al Grey; veteran guitarist Mundell Lowe; and saxophonist/arranger Oliver Nelson.

"I didn't really know who she was," Joe Newman told me. "I think it was John Hammond who hired me for the session. I don't even remember if he was in the studio that day. I was just so glad to play the date, especially because Wynton and Jimmy were on it. They'd done *Kind of Blue* with Miles for Columbia and were the hottest cats in New York. I figured Aretha Franklin was one of those up-and-coming chicks, like Dakota Staton, who wanted to be Dinah Washington. Man, was I wrong! Aretha was the real fuckin' deal! I mean, she cleaned our clocks. Wynton set the grooves and she floated over it like vintage Sarah Vaughan. Only— at least to my ears—she had more soul than Sarah, more church, more funk, more hurt. I remember 'Blue Holiday' and I remember another killer song called 'Nobody Like You.' It was a beautiful bluesy ballad where she played piano. I was sure it was written by someone like Ray Charles. When I asked her about the writer, she said it was James Cleveland, the gospel cat who had led her dad's choir in Detroit. 'You're kidding,' I said. 'A churchman wrote that?' Aretha didn't say much in the studio—she was a shy thing who kept to herself and just focused on her music—but when I said that, she looked up to me and said, 'Joe, it's all church.' That shut me up."

"Blue Holiday" and "Nobody Like You" represent Hammond's last and most effective effort to bring out the beauty of Aretha Franklin. She hits the sweet spot where jazz, blues, and rhythm and blues meet. As Quincy Jones—who produced Aretha in the seventies—told me, "All the greats bring the streams together. Ray Charles was as much jazz as R-and-B. Marvin Gaye had a tremendous jazz feel. Listen to his feeling for phrasing. The same is true of Stevie Wonder. Aretha fits into this category."

9. WATER, WATER
EVERYWHERE

I had moved to New York," said Erma Franklin, "when my first single on Epic — 'Hello Again' — came out. There was a flurry of activity, a good review in *Billboard*, and some prestigious gigs, including Small's Paradise Lounge in Harlem, where I often enjoyed the company of Bettye LaVette, a wonderful singer from Detroit, and Esther Phillips, who was going through her heavy drug period. Drugs, of course, was part of those times, especially in the world of rhythm and blues. I indulged. In fact, all the Franklin children indulged. But, as a problem, that didn't really enter the picture till later in the sixties.

"It was still the early sixties when Aretha was downtown while I was playing uptown. That's maybe only ten miles but it might have been ten thousand. We would see each other, but when we did, there was a bit of a chill. Some of our friends — like Mary Wells or Smokey — had enjoyed big hits. And because Aretha still had not put out what could be considered a smash, she worried that I might have one before her."

On February 20, 1962, Aretha appeared at the Village Gate, a jazz club, where she shared the bill with fellow Columbia artist

Thelonious Monk. According to Robin D. G. Kelley, Monk's superb biographer, almost five hundred people crowded into the small club. Monk's young nieces and nephews were there, as excited to see Aretha as they were to see their uncle.

"I was there," said Erma. "Cecil also came into the city that night because Monk was one of his heroes. In the company of the great master, Aretha more than held her own."

"I'm a jazz freak," Cecil told me, "and if I had to name my three favorite pianists they'd be Erroll Garner, Oscar Peterson, and Thelonious Monk. I wasn't gonna miss seeing Monk on the same bill as Ree. It was an amazing night. Monk had just signed with Columbia—I guess that's why he and Ree were costarring—and he had his man Charlie Rouse on tenor. I don't know if he had started recording that first album he did for Columbia—*Monk's Dream*—but I know he played 'Body and Soul' and 'Just a Gigolo,' songs that turned up on that record—a record I listened to over a hundred times.

" 'You seem more interested in hearing Monk than me,' Ree said before the show.

" 'I'm excited to see you both, sis. Excited to see you with him.'

"Because of Monk's presence, I think Aretha directed more of her show toward jazz. She wanted to show the jazz crowd that she was one of them—and she was. I believe that's one of the first times she sang 'Skylark,' a song she'd soon cut for Columbia. Same thing for 'Just for a Thrill' and 'God Bless the Child.' We all heard Ray Charles do 'Just for a Thrill' on his *Genius* album, and we'd been hearing Billie Holiday's 'Child' ever since we were children. She smashed them both. Monk had his fans, and Monk got his respect that night. But Sister Ree, who had learned how to tear down a church, tore down that club. We knew she was on the verge of having that monster breakthrough hit we'd all been waiting for."

The monster hit didn't arrive then—and wouldn't for five more years. Meanwhile, Bob Mersey took over Aretha's recording career.

"Mersey was a pure product of the Columbia culture," said Bobby Scott, who, in another year, would become a major music figure in Aretha's life. "I worked with Bob a long time. We were both producers and arrangers, but with much different backgrounds. Goddard Lieberson, who ran the company, saw Mersey as the Pasha of Pop. The great pasha before him was Mitch Miller, the man who defined fifties pop music, and he made a fortune for the label and set the tone for Columbia for years to follow. Mitch was a first-class musician and superb oboist—he played oboe on the famous *Charlie Parker with Strings* session—but his thing was sales. If you wanna sell music, dumb it down. He was all about Rosemary Clooney doing 'Come On-a My House' and Sinatra singing 'Mama Will Bark' with Dagmar. Lieberson had made a fortune for the label with the soundtrack of *My Fair Lady,* and Lieberson had put Bob Mersey with Andy Williams, another moneymaking move. When it became clear that Aretha was not happy with Hammond, Mersey was Lieberson's logical go-to guy. If she wouldn't sell as an R-and-B artist, turn her pop. But because she had established some solid credentials as a jazz artist, the label felt she couldn't abandon jazz entirely. That's where I came in. I'm a jazz piano player. I was Lester Young's piano when I was still a teenager. I can also play gospel and blues when I wanna. I'm also a writer—the Beatles covered my 'A Taste of Honey' and the Hollies and Neil Diamond had hits with my 'He Ain't Heavy, He's My Brother.' For years I worked as Bobby Darin's musical director. Back when I first met Aretha, though, I was seen as a jazzy auxiliary to Mersey. Mersey became her main man. I was on the set, but, metaphorically speaking, I was an intermission pianist. Goddard pinned all his hopes on Mersey, and if you listen to those albums he did with her, you'd have to think that Goddard had the right idea."

Mersey contributed three seminal albums to the Franklin oeuvre: *The Tender, the Moving, the Swinging Aretha Franklin,* from 1962; *Laughing on the Outside,* from 1963; and *Unforgettable: A Tribute to Dinah Washington,* in 1964. Each has moments of singular grace and even immortality.

For Aretha, the highlight of her Mersey association came on *The Tender* with "Without the One You Love," her own song. It was the first time she had fashioned a melody, written a lyric, and watched it all transform into a huge string orchestration.

The blues ballad, modeled after "The Masquerade Is Over," was a harbinger of even bolder Aretha compositions to come. There was no doubt that she had the compositional gift. (A string-less and far more moving version of the song would be recorded live, with Aretha herself on piano, on her 1965 *Yeah!!!* album.)

There are missteps on *The Tender*—a mediocre Berry Gordy song, "I'm Wandering"; a heavy-handed cover of Billy Eckstine's 1949 hit "I Apologize"; a cheesy chart of "Look for the Silver Lining"—but Aretha redeems it all with her otherworldly reading of three songs: "God Bless the Child," "Just for a Thrill," and "Try a Little Tenderness." According to Jerry Wexler, Aretha's version of "Tenderness" inspired Otis Redding to record it in his singular style. (Redding's biographer Scott Freeman suggests it was Phil Walden, Otis's manager, who urged him to sing it, but when I spoke with Walden in the nineties, he confirmed Wexler's story.)

"Otis had Aretha's Columbia album where she sings 'Tenderness' and 'God Bless the Child,'" Walden told me. "No doubt that Otis's take on 'Tenderness' became iconic because of the double-time transition. But I know he was trying to channel Aretha. He also wanted to cut 'God Bless the Child' but never got the chance. It was Aretha, along with Sam Cooke, that got Otis Redding into standards, which is ironic since it was Aretha's redo of his 'Respect' that turned his little R-and-B tune into an enduring standard."

The Tender, the Moving, the Swinging Aretha Franklin was recorded in April and May of 1962. In July, she appeared at the Newport Jazz Festival on the same bill as her father's friends Clara Ward and Oscar Peterson. The lineup also included Sonny Rollins, Count Basie, Basie's former blues belter Jimmy Rushing, Thelonious Monk, and Duke Ellington.

Jazz critic Jack Maher wrote the *Billboard* review: "During the Ellington time on stand, Thelonious Monk showed off his unique abilities as composer and soloist in a performance of 'Monk's Dream,' especially written for the band. Duke conducted. Also a show stopper with Ellington was the appearance of Aretha Franklin, whose gospel-like vocals brought screams of 'more' from the crowd."

Later that same month Dr. Martin Luther King Jr. was jailed for participating in an Albany, Georgia, demonstration.

"I remember Daddy telling me about how he and Martin were talking about working up a demonstration in Detroit," said Cecil. "They spoke often, and Dr. King knew he could count on my father. I'd say they were twin souls with the same mission."

In August, *Billboard* reviewed "Just for a Thrill" and "Try a Little Tenderness," saying, "Here are a pair of the best sides that Aretha ever cut and that's saying a lot. She shows off some of her best vocal work yet on the two standards, and either or both could turn into her biggest seller to date."

On August 2, Aretha appeared on *American Bandstand* for the second time. She sang "Don't Cry, Baby" as well as "Try a Little Tenderness." But neither song made the charts.

"We all were listening to Barbara Lynn's 'You'll Lose a Good Thing,'" said Erma. "It was a hit, and we loved it. We loved Little Eva's 'Locomotion' and Gene Chandler's 'Duke of Earl' and Ray Charles's 'Unchain My Heart.' They were all hits, they were all great, but were they any greater than the songs Aretha was singing at Columbia? I don't think so. Ree felt like there was water, water everywhere, but not a drop to drink."

On September 27, the United States Department of Justice filed suit to end public segregation. Three days later, Mississippi governor Ross Barnett blocked James Meredith from enrolling at the state university.

In mid-October, the Cuban missile crisis traumatized the nation for two weeks. Aretha had little memory of the crisis but specific memories of the comics who opened for her. She spoke about Buddy Hackett and his Chinese-waiter routine, and Professor Irwin Corey, with his frizzled hair and crazy expertise on everything and nothing. She had special regard for the intellectual Dick Gregory, with whom she worked at the Playboy Club in Chicago.

The gigs got bigger, to the point where Aretha was ready to make a management change. In November, *Jet* reported that "Aretha Franklin's split with her manager, Jo King, may end up in court because the rising young star wants out of their contract and the manager wants to settle for $9,000."

"When Ted took over," said Erma, "the man *took over.* He had a scorched-earth policy. Jo King was history. Anyone in Jo's circle was history. Anyone who had previously been involved with Aretha's career—including her own father—was marginalized. Ted demanded and got total control."

"Why would Aretha permit that?" I asked Erma.

"I think she was more frightened of the outside world than the rest of us," Erma answered. "I think she felt the need for protection. Our father had been extremely protective of Aretha. Maybe even overprotective. He led her to the world of show business, but then he had to return to his church world. He could no longer play the role he had been playing since she had begun traveling with him. He could no longer be her day-to-day protector. When that became clear, she looked for a substitute protector. I know it sounds far-fetched, but Ted White had many of our father's attributes— he was self-assured, he was charismatic, definitely a woman's man, highly intelligent, highly organized, and able to deal with the cold cruel world effectively. Daddy helped Aretha attain fame in sacred music. Aretha looked to Ted to do exactly that in secular music. You don't need a PhD in psychology to realize that there's a reason why we gals often call our lovers and husbands 'Daddy.' "

For Aretha's biological daddy, 1963 was a milestone. Reverend C. L. Franklin had watched as, a few years earlier, an urban renewal project had torn down Hastings Street—the bars, the clubs, and the New Bethel Baptist Church—for what would become the Chrysler Freeway. Franklin's congregation found temporary quarters elsewhere, while the minister spent increased time on the road. According to his biographer Nick Salvatore, this was a period when Los Angeles became his home away from home. His guest sermons in churches around the country increased, along with his involvement in local Detroit politics. C.L. became founding president of the Metropolitan Civic League for Legal Action. As a progressive politician, his time had come. His sermons stressing ethnic pride and self-worth, long his signature message, had become touchstones as the national civil rights movement gained strength and wider exposure.

On March 10, he gained a new and more prominent pulpit when the *new* New Bethel opened its doors on Linwood and Philadelphia. Once a theater, the building had been transformed into a twenty-five-hundred-seat sanctuary by—as C.L. was quick to tell people—an all-black construction company. The minister pointed out that this was not reverse racism. He said it was proof of what "as a race we can do for ourselves if we take advantage of opportunities to qualify ourselves."

By May, Franklin was in the final stages of formulating his plan to hold a massive freedom march in Detroit with his close friend Dr. King as the main speaker. The conservative/establishment Baptist Ministerial Alliance opposed the march—or at least a march led by Franklin. C.L.'s national stature had excited jealousy among many of his peers. When he came to the Alliance meeting to argue his case and was told by the organization's president that he couldn't speak because his Alliance fees were in arrears, C.L. exploded and went after his adversary. Franklin's colleagues held him back, and the physical fight was averted. In the end, C.L. prevailed because of his close relationship to Dr. King. If Franklin could get King to lead a Detroit freedom march, that march would go forward, no matter how vehement the opposition to Franklin's involvement.

On May 27, Mahalia Jackson sponsored a fund-raising rally for Dr. King's Southern Christian Leadership Conference at McCormick Place in Chicago. The Freedom Fund Festival featured Al

Hibbler, Mayor Richard Daley, Dick Gregory, Eartha Kitt, and Aretha Franklin. *Jet* reported that "gospel-turned-blues singer Aretha Franklin came on last in a tough spot after all the preachers and big stars at Mahalia Jackson's benefit for Martin Luther King and literally broke up the show by sending the crowd home shouting when she closed with a back home rendition of 'Precious Lord.' The daughter of Detroit's Rev. C.L. Franklin, Aretha then plunked down four $100 bills in Mahalia's hands for being on the show."

"The other area where Daddy still held sway over Aretha," said Cecil, "was performing her civic duty. He drummed that into all of us. Ted White had complete sway over her when it came to what engagements to accept and what songs to sing. But if Daddy called and said, 'Ree, I want you to sing for Dr. King,' she'd drop everything and do just that. I don't think Ted had objections to her support of Dr. King's cause, and he realized it would raise her visibility. But I do remember the time that there was a conflict between a big club gig and doing a benefit for Dr. King. Ted said, 'Take the club gig. We need the money.' But Ree said, 'Dr. King needs me more.' She defied her husband. Maybe that was the start of their marital trouble. Their thing was always troubled because it was based on each of them using the other. Whatever the case, my sister proved to be a strong soldier in the civil rights fight. That made me proud of her and it kept her relationship with Daddy from collapsing entirely."

Shortly after returning from Chicago, Aretha went into the studio and recorded what could be considered her greatest performance on Columbia.

"I'd say it was her best performance ever," said Etta James. "Everyone loves her shit on Atlantic, and no doubt they're classics, but when I heard her sing 'Skylark,' I told Esther Phillips, my running buddy back then, 'That girl pissed all over that song.' It came at a time when we were all looking to cross over by singing standards. I had 'Sunday Kind of Love' and 'Trust in Me,' and Sam Cooke was doing 'Tennessee Waltz' and 'When I Fall in Love' at the Copa. We were all trying to be so middle class. It was the beginning of the bougie black thing. I truly believe Aretha had a head start on us since she was the daughter of a rich preacher and grew up bougie. But, hell, the reasons don't matter. She took 'Skylark' to a whole 'nother place. When she goes back and sings the chorus the second time and jumps an octave—I mean, she's *screaming*—I had to scratch my head and ask myself, *How the fuck did that bitch do that?* I remember running into Sarah Vaughan, who always intimidated me. Sarah said, 'Have you heard of this Aretha Franklin girl?' I said, 'You heard her do "Skylark," didn't you?' Sarah said, 'Yes, I did, and I'm never singing that song again.'"

The record on which "Skylark" appears, *Laughing on the Outside,* was recorded during the spring and summer of 1963 and is the most consistent and satisfying of the Robert Mersey/Aretha Franklin albums. It is among her most memorable interpretations of any song in any genre.

"When I heard 'Skylark,'" said Jerry Wexler, "I called John Hammond to congratulate him. I thought he was still her main producer. It was stunningly good. But John told me he had nothing to do with it. Aretha was angry at him because she thought he had signed Erma, and Columbia was looking to put her with Bob Mersey, a mainstream pop guy. Say what you want about those guys, but sometimes even the corniest of them—like my good friend Mitch Miller—can do brilliant things. When it came to Aretha, Mersey served her well. Give the guy credit. His charts were gorgeous.

"Later in the sixties when I met Donny Hathaway and he started talking about singing standards, he pointed to that *Laughing on the Outside* album. He had it memorized. He wanted to do 'For All We Know' in the Aretha vein. If you listen to his version, which is bone-chillingly beautiful, you'll hear him channeling Aretha."

Aretha spoke often of her regard for Frank Sinatra and favorably compared her version of "Where Are You?" from her *Laughing* album to his.

"There are two sides to my sister," said Cecil when I mentioned to him her bold comparison of herself to Sinatra. "She's always been confident about her singing. She always knew she had the gift—a gift that big can't be denied, even by an insecure person. She'd been told by every blood-washed believer who'd heard her sing in church that she was phenomenal. But even though she knew just how good she was—that at age twenty-one, she could sing a ballad with the depth of a Frank Sinatra or a Billie Holiday—another part of her was super-insecure. Her insecurity wasn't about her talent but about her ability to get over and be a star in show business. That's why she was willing to try anything to get over—pop, blues, ballads, R-and-B, you name it. That's also why she was willing to let a tough guy like Ted White lead the way. She thought she needed a bull to break down the doors for her. She never thought she could do it herself—and she was right."

The songs say as much—Duke Ellington's lonely "Solitude," Lerner and Loewe's "If Ever I Would Leave You," Johnny Mercer's "I Wanna Be Around." The title track, "Laughing on the Outside," makes the same point—that beneath the veneer, behind the klieg lights of the cover shot and the glamour of Aretha's glittering gown, there is a reservoir of deep feelings that transcend time and space. She laughs on the outside and weeps on the inside.

She also sang a song Ray Charles had recorded in Los Angeles only months before. Aretha's New York session took place on June 12. The song—Rodgers and Hammerstein's "Ol' Man River"—is one of the great warhorses of American music. It contains an essential metaphor: time is a river, time keeps rolling along, time is indifferent to pain, if only we could disappear into the anonymity of time and leave the burdens of this world behind. It is also a dramatic vehicle written by white men, designed to be sung by blacks. Paul Robeson's version is perhaps the most iconic. Ray Charles sang it at the height of his addiction to heroin. His producer Sid Feller told me, "Ray nodded out at the keyboard. At first I was afraid he'd died of a heart attack but I soon saw it was the effects of drugs. When he awoke, as if nothing had happened, he began singing the most stirring version of the song that I have ever heard. It's hard to fathom how deep he gets. He's literally crying."

Aretha took the song in another direction—lighthearted and whimsical, with a jazz rhythm section swinging behind her. She declined to seek out the dark suffering but instead kept it on the surface.

"They said it was supposed to be sung by a man," she said, "but I sang it anyway. It was written for a Broadway musical and I wanted to give it a jazzy Broadway feeling."

Not so with Irving Berlin's "Say It Isn't So."

"That's the other item I remember from that record," said Etta James. "My mother used to play the tune by Billie and Dinah, but it wasn't until I heard Aretha sing 'Say It Isn't So' that I understood it as a sure-enough soul song. After she's sung it through once, she comes back and bites the song in the ass. She spits out that 'Say everything is still okay' in a way that you know she's been listening to Ray. We were all listening to Ray, but Aretha was every bit as bad as he was. She could fuck up a standard so completely, with such funk and fire, you'd never want to hear it straight again. It took me forty years to approach that song—that's how much I revered Aretha's version. And when I finally did do it, on an album called *Heart of a Woman*, I put a Latin beat behind it and sped up the tempo and damned if I wasn't still singing those same Aretha licks that had been buried inside my head for all those years."

On Sunday, June 23, 1963, ten days after Aretha's final session for *Laughing on the Outside,* over a hundred thousand people took to the streets of Detroit in the freedom march led by Reverends C. L. Franklin and Martin Luther King. The start time was 4:00 p.m., but as soon as the church services ended, the crowd began to swell. C.L. was certain two hundred thousand people participated; more conservative estimates said one hundred and twenty-five thousand. Either way, it would prove to be a landmark event in the history of the great industrial city, and it would never have happened were it not for the tenacity and power of C. L. Franklin. A reporter for the *Michigan Chronicle* wrote, "Negroes of all classes—street walkers,

doctors, senior citizens, drunks, clergymen and their congrega-
tions, etc.—came from near and far to 'walk for freedom.'" Biographer Nick Salvatore wrote, "The joyous marchers took possession
of the streets in the city's main shopping and entertainment district
where, until recently, they had been denied equal service. Signifi-
cantly, the march was a black affair. White marchers never appeared
in appreciable numbers...Some black unionists expressed disappointment at the noticeable absence of most of their white
coworkers."

The march ended at Cobo Hall, where C.L. had arranged for
Dr. King to speak. Before the address, though, there was
entertainment—jazz pianist Ramsey Lewis; C.L.'s close friend and
Queen of the Blues, Dinah Washington; jazz organist Jimmy
McGriff; the Four Tops; and Erma Franklin. Aretha did not attend.

"I believe I sang a gospel song," said Erma, "but I can't say for
sure. What I do remember is the excitement. It was one of those
moments when, as Daddy would say, 'The presence of God was
everywhere.' There was a unity among our people I had never felt
before—a pride, and a sense of purpose. Given the open-minded
attitude of my dad and Dr. King, it was perfectly appropriate that
there were jazz artists and blues artists along with a mass choir that
sang 'Lift Every Voice and Sing.' President Kennedy sent his con-
gratulations and so did Walter Reuther, the union leader. I can't
tell you how proud I was of my father and what he had accomplished. Dr. King called him 'his good friend' and gave a stirring
speech. We left Cobo Hall believing that the tide had turned and
that a brighter new world was around the bend. For me it was the
brightest moment of the sixties."

The occasion is also notable for Dr. King's famous line in his
address: "This afternoon I have a dream. It is a dream deeply rooted
in the American dream." King was, in fact, previewing the speech
that two months later he would deliver at the Lincoln Memorial, a
seminal moment in the long fight for civil rights. Berry Gordy
issued the speech in LP form and called it *The Great March to
Freedom.*

★   ★   ★

In September, Aretha went back into the Columbia studios in New York, where she met Bobby Scott, the brilliant pianist/arranger/composer who had been hired by Bob Mersey to do a number of jazz-oriented sessions.

"My first memory of Aretha is that she wouldn't look at me when I spoke," Scott told me. "She withdrew from the encounter in a way that intrigued me. At first I thought she was just shy—and she was—but I also felt her reading me. I wasn't shy about telling her my accomplishments, and it wasn't until I rattled off my credits that I felt like I had caught her attention. What knocked me out the most, though, was when I told her I'd been Lester Young's accompanist. 'You play for the President?' Only the hippest jazz aficionados knew that Lester was nicknamed 'Pres,' for President. That told me that she was much more than a church girl. Of course, I'd heard the stuff she'd done with Mersey. 'Skylark' floored me. Having done that, Mersey looked to me to put her more in a jazz bag. The truth, though, is that Aretha's musicality knew no boundaries. The only other singer I worked with who had her feeling was Marvin Gaye."

Later in the sixties, Scott did a remarkable ballad session with Marvin, released posthumously, titled *Vulnerable*. I asked Bobby what he saw as the common link between Marvin and Aretha.

"They each sculpted and improved any song they sang. They each came out of that holy place that breeds genius. Strange, but when I started working with Marvin, he had enjoyed a string of hits and didn't care about commerce. He was going for art. But in that first meeting in which she called me Mr. Scott and asked that I call her Miss Franklin, Aretha did say something I'll never forget. For all her deference to my experience and her reluctance to speak up, when she did look me in the eye, she did so with a quiet intensity before saying, 'I like all your ideas, Mr. Scott, but please remember I do want hits.'"

The Aretha/Scott sessions took place over three days in October 1963. Instead of the jazz-oriented sessions that Mersey had originally envisioned, the final repertoire, like most everything Aretha sang on Columbia, seemed to be moving in many directions at once. "Aretha wanted to sing 'Harbor Lights,' a song she knew from the Platters," said Scott. "She said she thought that, in the post-doo-wop era of the early sixties, it could be a hit again. I'd been listening to the song ever since I was a kid. Everyone from Guy Lombardo to Bing Crosby had covered it. I saw the possibility of its reinvention, especially in the hands of a great blues balladeer. So we went all out. Aretha helped me arrange the female backup vocal arrangements—she was great at that—I worked up a horn chart, found a righteous groove, and thought we'd hit the charts. We didn't.

"As a songwriter, I'm always hustling singers to do my stuff, and I was no different with Aretha. I presented her with a lot of jazz tunes, but she wasn't partial to any of them. Instead she was drawn to ballads—'Tiny Sparrow,' one of the more spiritual-metaphorical things I wrote. She said it reminded her of church. She sang my 'Johnny,' a motif I wrote in a Rodgers and Hammerstein vein. When I played her 'Looking Through a Tear,' something I also wrote in a Broadway bag, she went for it. Suddenly the notion of a jazz album went out the window. She brought in something by Sam Cooke's brother L.C. called 'Once in a While.' She thought it could be an R-and-B hit; I didn't; we cut it, and it wasn't. Felt lame to me. I had the same reaction to 'Bill Bailey, Won't You Please Come Home.' I love Jimmy Durante doing it, but Aretha Franklin? 'I hear it with a Count Basie big-band sound behind it,' she told me. 'I can do that,' I said. 'I can write an Ernie Wilkins–Count Basie chart.' I do admit that she sang it soulfully, but it felt like a nightclub routine to me, not suitable for an artist of Aretha's caliber.

"By then, in terms of theme or cohesion of style, we had lost our way. But Aretha and her husband, Ted, didn't seem concerned.

They were both so knocked out by her singing that they were certain that every song we cut—even 'Moon River' or 'I May Never Get to Heaven'—was gonna be a hit. I understood their enthusiasm, and I shared it, but there was no communication between the studio and sales forces. When the sales guys heard what we'd done, they said, 'What are we supposed to do with this stuff?' It was great, but it was neither fish nor fowl. Listening to it decades later, it still sounds strong. Aretha is always Aretha. She got on top of the chart I wrote for 'I Won't Cry Anymore' and absolutely crushed it. Tony Bennett had sung it. So had Charles Brown and Big Maybelle and Dinah Washington and Joe Williams. But Aretha owned it in a way I never thought anyone could approach it again. It wasn't until I rewrote the chart, added strings, and gave it to Marvin Gaye that I saw I was wrong. When it came to melodic reinvention and fearless interpretation, Marvin and Aretha were locked in a dead heat. It killed me that they never sang together."

On November 22, 1963, Aretha was seven months pregnant with her third son and in the Broadway Market in Detroit, a gourmet-food outlet, when she heard news of the assassination of John F. Kennedy. In her book, she recalls that among her strongest memories of that day were the powerful smells of hanging hams, salamis, and cheeses. On other occasions, she reflected that, in the aftermath of the president's death, she found comfort in the presence of her father.

"My father was a rock," Erma said. "Especially in the sixties, when changes were happening so quickly and great leaders began to fall, he held steadfast. He taught us all to stay the course. He believed in a future where wrong would be righted and the love of almighty God would prevail. He raised us, he nurtured us, and he comforted us in times of trouble.

"Ted White was a highly possessive husband and could be a scary character. But when the world felt shaky and fears were unloosed, Aretha lost her fear of him and went home to Daddy. No matter how deep our past disagreements, we always reconciled with our father. Our bond with him was stronger than our bond with anyone else."

A month later, another sudden death had a more immediate impact on the Franklin family. On December 14, Detroiters, along with the rest of the country, were shocked to learn that in their city Dinah Washington had died of a toxic combination of drugs—secobarbital and amobarbital—at age thirty-nine. Married to her seventh husband, Detroit Lions All-Pro defensive back Dick "Night Train" Lane, Dinah had appeared to be at the top of her game; in the words of her biographer Nadine Cohodas, "It was as though Dinah had been snatched from [her friends] in the fullness of life."

"Ted and Aretha were in New York and rushed home to Detroit," Cecil remembered. "More than anyone, Daddy was distraught. He and Dinah had been tight for years. I remember Aretha looking afraid—as though death was coming too close to all of us. Ted's attitude was 'The Queen is dead. Long live the Queen. Aretha is the new queen.'"

10. WHAT A DIFFERENCE A DAY MAKES

I got a Dinah Washington story," Etta James told me. "I was a young thing with a couple of jive-ass hits under my belt. I was playing a small club in Providence while Dinah was booked into the big Loew's State Theater. When someone said she'd come to see my midnight show, I nearly fell out. Dinah was in the house! With that in mind, I decided to open with her big hit, 'Unforgettable.' I didn't even get to the chorus when I heard this earth-shattering crash. Dinah had got up off her chair, swept all the glasses and plates off her table, and was pointing at me, screaming, 'Bitch, don't you ever sing the Queen's songs when the Queen is right there in front of you!'

"I ran off the stage crying. Didn't even do my set. No one could console me. Didn't wanna see no one. But it was Dinah herself who came back to my dressing room and said, 'Sorry, I lost it for a minute, but look, girl, you learned a valuable lesson. If a star's around, you don't ever sing the star's songs. *Ever.*' 'Yes, ma'am' was all I could say. She invited me to her show at the Loew's the next day. I went and we tightened up. I loved me some Dinah, but, man, that lady was something else."

The Dinah encounter that Aretha remembered in *From These Roots* also involved a dressing-room encounter. After her show at a Detroit club, Aretha was visited in her dressing room by Dinah Washington. Dinah criticized Aretha for the disorder—clothes and shoes were scattered everywhere. Aretha deeply resented the remarks and thought Dinah was acting like a diva.

At the time of Dinah's death, Aretha was twenty-one and clearly not a diva. She was working jazz clubs, with occasional stints at venues like the Apollo, and building a reputation. The money was minimal. There were no royalties, and the advances from Columbia were small. Her gigs, though, were steady. She traveled with the trio put together by Ted White—Teddy Harris on piano, drummer Hindel Butts, and bassist Roderick Hicks. When Harris wasn't available, Earl Van Dyke often took his place. They were splendid musicians. For those who listened carefully—John Hammond, Carmen McRae, Bobby Scott, Jerry Wexler—there was no doubt that Aretha's greatness was already established. Her potential was unlimited. At the same time, her public demeanor remained almost painfully timid.

"She would talk to me," said Ruth Bowen, the woman who, at various times, booked both Dinah and Aretha, "but never at length. I didn't become her agent and confidante until a few years later. Before that, though, I would see her from time to time and knew she had great fears about asserting herself. She spoke through Ted— and it was Ted who suggested that she go in the studio and quickly record a tribute album to Dinah. Ted always saw Aretha as the new Dinah, and he didn't waste a minute trying to make that happen."

There were two memorial services for Dinah—the first in Detroit at New Bethel, where C.L. presided and Aretha sang. The second was in Dinah's hometown of Chicago.

"I attended both," said Ruth. "It was in Detroit, right after the service, when I saw Ted, who said something about Aretha singing a tribute record. That hardly seemed the right place to mention it, but I suppose it was because Ted knew how close I was to Dinah— she and I began the Queen Booking Agency together—and he

wanted my approval. He also wanted me to pay the kind of attention to Aretha that I had paid to Dinah. I wanted to say, *Ted, her
body's still warm. Can't we wait to talk about business for a few weeks?*
But I didn't say anything. I was in so much pain. Losing Dinah was
like losing a sister."

Columbia was as eager as Ted to record the tribute. They saw it
as a big opportunity and went for a big production. Bob Mersey
and Aretha selected the songs, Mersey quickly wrote charts for
horns and strings, and on February 7, 1964, eight weeks after
Dinah's death—and just a month after Aretha gave birth to Ted
White Jr.—the first session kicked off at the label's studio at 799
Seventh Avenue in New York.

"Aretha's dedication to her career and her craft is something
people underestimate," said Erma. "No matter what she's going
through—whether it's giving birth or mourning a death—she
gets right back to work because her work, her ability to express
deep, deep feelings in song, is what gets her through."

Aretha sounds both vulnerable and powerful. The album is
sweet, sassy, and sad, a fitting—and at times soaring—musical
tribute to the fallen queen by the aspiring one. By any measure, it's
a classic.

"Ted wanted to call it *What a Difference a Day Makes,*" said
Ruth Bowen, "but I didn't like that. I took that to mean that in the
difference of a day, Dinah's reign was over and Aretha's had begun.
I was relieved when they changed it to *Unforgettable.* That was more
like it."

The title track is a marvel of understatement and sincerity.
Aretha comes to this tribute with great respect for Dinah's mystique. While Dinah sang Hank Williams's "Cold Cold Heart" in a
jazz vein, Aretha puts a heavy gospel-blues spin on the song, a fore-
shadowing of her Atlantic material. As would be the case with
Atlantic, Aretha also served in the role as uncredited coproducer.
The chart is built around her concept.

In her early church days, Aretha reflected the sensibility of

Clara Ward and Jackie Verdell, but her singular style was there from the get-go. Extravagant runs are an essential part of the grammar of gospel singing, yet Aretha's trademark runs, in which she jumps octaves and forges flourishes both simple and complex, are wholly her own.

Aretha's reading of "What a Diff'rence a Day Makes" is especially sensitive and respectful of the original. Aretha does not try to reinvent the song. She doesn't want to forget Dinah. Dinah is on her mind. You feel Dinah's spirit in her heart. She doesn't attack the song; she approaches it with gentle but firm confidence. She sings it straight for the first few bars, telling a slow-moving story of the discovery of love. It isn't until she comes to the line "My yesterdays were blue, dear" that she starts caressing the lyrics. She elongates and exaggerates the *blue* to let you know that, though this is a tribute to Dinah, she intends to make this song her own.

All the songs on *Unforgettable* are made her own. And listening to it, one has no doubt that—in spirit, technique, imagination, creativity, and pure soul—Aretha measures up to Dinah. But the album made little impact on the music world, which was caught up in two huge phenomena.

In 1964, the Beatles arrived in America, hitting pop culture harder than anyone since Elvis. Meanwhile, Motown exploded. The Supremes broke out with a string of number-one hits, starting with "Where Did Our Love Go"; Mary Wells had "My Guy"; Martha and the Vandellas had "Dancing in the Streets"; and the Temptations and the Four Tops both crossed over to top-ten pop.

Just when Ted White and the executives at Columbia wanted the world to measure Aretha by the past—by Dinah, one of the most enduring artists of the previous decade—fans were looking to the future. Black pop, geared to a white audience, was finally coming into its own, and Aretha had nothing to do with that. She was presented as a mature adult. Although Aretha was only twenty-one, the marketing men targeted her to a much older demographic.

"*Unforgettable* is probably the best thing she did on Columbia,"

John Hammond told me. "Mersey found a solid jazz footing for the project. On 'Evil Gal Blues' and 'Soulville,' he employed a Hammond B-3 organ that created a wonderfully authentic blues feeling. 'Drinking Again' is a marvelous evocation of a late-night bar. Dinah sang it beautifully, but Aretha put it in the Sinatra category. It's reminiscent of his 'One for My Baby.' I believe it's that good. The problem wasn't the material or the vocals. The material was perfect and the vocals were astounding. I remember thinking that if Aretha never does another album she will be remembered for this one. No, the problem was timing. Dinah had died, and, outside the black community, interest in her had waned dramatically. Popular music was in a radical and revolutionary moment, and that moment had nothing to do with Dinah Washington, great as she was and will always be."

"If I'm not mistaken," said Clyde Otis, who would be the next major figure in Aretha's musical life, "*Unforgettable* was the first time Aretha had sung one of my songs. I'm talking about 'This Bitter Earth.' I was on staff at Mercury when I brought it to Dinah, who recorded it in 1960. It was one of her biggest hits. I'd also been producing hits on Brook Benton, and, of course, I'd done hit duets with Brook and Dinah—'Baby (You Got What It Takes)' and 'It's a Rocking Good Way (to Mess Around and Fall in Love).' When Bob Mersey, my neighbor in Englewood, New Jersey, mentioned that Aretha was doing a Dinah tribute, I said that I thought 'This Bitter Earth' would be a natural. Aretha wanted to do it before I even suggested it. I would have loved to produce it, but Bob was running the sessions for that album. When I heard what Aretha did to it, I realized there was nothing I could have added. No one loved and admired Dinah more than me. But Aretha took the song to the heavens. After her version, I knew that, from that day forward, my composition would be considered a standard. She created the standard. She set the standard. Other versions are superb—I especially love the way Nancy Wilson did it. But Aretha...that girl tore the song apart and put it back together again in a way that had me shaking my head in wonder. I consider it her song and no one else's."

Aretha felt the composition's intrinsic drama. One of the finest of all blues ballads, "This Bitter Earth" goes from despair to hope. Just as the truest blues are transformational—the very act of singing or hearing the blues lets you lose the blues—"This Bitter Earth" takes us on a journey out of the depths of depression. It is the crowning achievement of *Unforgettable,* the most forgotten and underrated of Aretha's many grand achievements.

When the record was released in February, the initial single was "Soulville," an up-tempo romp aimed at the R&B market. For the first time Aretha provides self-styled backups; she overdubs her vocals with her own harmonies, a technique that, at the end of the decade, Marvin Gaye would perfect in his *What's Going On.*

"I thought putting out 'Soulville' was a mistake," said Hammond. "Bob Mersey had produced a classic album for the ages. Why not promote it as such? Instead, Columbia went for the youth market, when, in fact, it wasn't a youth-oriented project. Sam Cooke had done a marvelous tribute album to Billie Holiday, and in the same spirit Aretha was evoking the spirit of Dinah. In a desperate attempt for a hit, they misrepresented the album. Ironically, while the sales force was trying to break her on the R-and-B charts, the publicists were also booking her on Steve Allen's TV show, where she sang the more adult material, like 'Skylark.' A week later, I looked up and saw they had also booked her on *Shindig!* singing 'Soulville.' It was amazing how much demographic confusion surrounded her promotion."

In March, *Ebony* ran its first feature on Aretha. The article began by mentioning that "she has become the top female interpreter of a gospel-tinged blues idiom pioneered by the old 'blues preacher' himself, Ray Charles." It went on to say that she had "several fast-selling single records and four Columbia albums behind her…a number of TV guest spots, and a tight schedule of night club and theater dates that ought to net her at least $100,000 this year." Elsewhere the article stated that John Hammond "signed her as one of Columbia's 'five-percent artists'—a choice deal which guaranteed the then 18-year-old singer high royalties for five years." The writer concluded with a litany of Aretha's complaints: that her former personal manager disrespected her; that her booking agents didn't attend to her needs; and that Columbia didn't give her the "same big build-up" that they gave Robert Goulet or Barbra Streisand.

In response to the booking-agent disputes, Ruth Bowen said, "I can't tell you how many times over the course of several decades that I have been fired and rehired by Aretha. That's simply her way. If something didn't go right at a gig, her first reaction is to blame the booking agent. The circumstances didn't matter. A sudden snowstorm might result in a small audience, but it was my fault for booking her at a club who didn't really appreciate her style of singing. I was used to moody artists because, after all, I had worked with Dinah. But Aretha was moodier than most. After a while I stopped taking it personally. When a gig went well, as many of them did, I was praised to the sky. When a piano was slightly out of tune or the dressing room was too small, I got hell. I simply shrugged my shoulders and took it in stride. This was what it meant to be working with genius."

Aretha's genius is evident on her appearances on Steve Allen's TV show, first in March, then again in May. Each time, Allen calls her "one of the most exciting young singers in the business today" and holds up the just-released *Unforgettable* album. Oddly enough, only one of the four songs she sings during her several appearances is from the Dinah album. She rips through a ferocious "Lover, Come Back to Me," goes to the piano and bangs out a "Rock-a-Bye Your Baby with a Dixie Melody," stays at the keyboard for a down-and-dirty "Won't Be Long," eviscerates "Skylark," and returns to the piano to knock out a gutbucket "Evil Gal Blues," a Dinah favorite. On camera, Aretha looks fabulous—svelte and sexy. Her gowns are elegant. As a performer, she's on fire.

Twenty-five years after she appeared on his show, Steve Allen told me, "A jazz pianist myself, I recognized her jazz chops. They were tremendous. But I also saw that she had enough poise and experience to sing standards. My motivation to have her on the show was simply to introduce her great talent, but I wanted to get her to sing some of my songs. Fortunately, she did. With the help of my friend Clyde Otis, a year later I was able to convince her to record two of my songs, thus bolstering their status as standards—'This Could Be the Start of Something Big' and 'Impossible.'"

In spite of good reviews, *Unforgettable* languished on the shelves, and, once again, Columbia executives tried to figure out a way to sell Aretha to a wider audience.

"That's when they turned her over to me," said Clyde Otis. "Goddard Lieberson himself called and said, 'We know she's every bit the singer that Barbra Streisand is, but we can't sell her to an adult market. We can't cross her over. You know the R-and-B market, Otis. You've had hits. Cut an R-and-B hit on her and we'll take our cue from Motown and cross her over to pop.' I had no problem with that except for one thing—Ted White didn't agree with Goddard. He saw how Barbra Streisand was selling to the masses and that's the market he wanted for Aretha. He wanted to go after a white market. I'm a strong-minded fellow, but Ted was a lot stronger. He also had Aretha on his side. The two of them had been listening to Sinatra's 'Only the Lonely.' They'd been listening to Pat Boone and Johnny Mathis singing 'Friendly Persuasion.' Hell, they even wanted me to do an arrangement of 'That's Entertainment.' I tried to tell them that they were heading in the wrong direction, but I was outvoted. That was okay because, in the mainstream mode, I had a song of my own I wanted recorded. I knew that Aretha could do it perfectly.

"I called Goddard and told him the situation. I said, 'They wanna go white.' He said, 'Well, maybe she can have a crossover hit if you write it. So write her a crossover hit, Clyde, and just keep the budget low.'

"The budget was high and I did come up with a crossover hit. I called it 'Take a Look.' Aretha called it a hit. So did Ted. I ran over and played it for Goddard. He even said it was going to be her breakthrough song. It was pop, but deeper than pop. It had soul and it had a message. It was going to let her leap ahead of Streisand. It just couldn't miss."

11. FOOLS

The big pop hits in 1964 ran an astounding gamut. Ethereal Brazilian jazz made it on the charts in the form of Stan Getz and Astrud Gilberto's exquisite reading of Antonio Carlos Jobim's "The Girl from Ipanema." For the first time in his storied career, jazz giant Louis Armstrong had a number-one pop hit with "Hello, Dolly." Beyond the initial successes of the Beatles and the Supremes, there were also hits from the Four Seasons ("Rag Doll"), the Dixie Cups ("The Chapel of Love"), the Beach Boys ("I Get Around"), the Shangri-Las ("Leader of the Pack"), Dean Martin ("Everybody Loves Somebody"), and Roy Orbison ("Pretty Woman").

The pop landscape was, and I suspect always will be, littered with an eclectic mix of music, a smattering of jewels and junk. Aretha was right to think that she had crafted a jewel in singing Clyde Otis's masterly "Take a Look," the song that he and Lieberson were certain would raise Aretha to a higher commercial level. The melody soared. The lyrics, a self-confrontational examination into the dark heart of mankind, mirror "This Bitter Earth." The movement is from despair to hope. Otis asks what has become of the precious dream. He sees it floating away in "bloody bloody stream." We're told that there's no winner when the prize is hate; only love can change our fate.

Aretha attacks the first six words—"Take a look in the mirror"—with startling immediacy. It's an order you can't ignore. She wrings out the soul of the song with the kind of intensity that would convince the most skeptical record executive that the single would have to sell. It didn't.

"I was miffed," said Clyde Otis. "If you listen to something like Bobby Vinton's 'Mr. Lonely,' a number-one hit that came out the same year as 'Take a Look,' you'll hear a song about the solitude of war seen through the point of view of a soldier. There's nothing wrong with the melody or the story. But I'd have to say it's a cliché, a clichéd melody and clichéd lyrics. At the same time, it was a smash. Compare it to 'Take a Look,' though, and it's night and day. Aretha is no cliché. She's singing for all humanity. She's singing about the deepest mystery out there—why evil is so strong. Remember—we were cutting this album during what they were calling the Freedom Summer. We were all shocked all those three young volunteers—Michael Schwerner, Andrew Goodman, and James Chaney—had been shot to death in cold blood by the Klan down in Mississippi. Their only crime was trying to register black voters. So when Aretha was singing 'Take a look,' that's what we wanted people to look at.

"Aretha sang it so strong that we cut it two ways—with strings and then again with a close-harmony horns and girl backup singers. One version was better than the other, but we still didn't get any chart action.

"Maybe we were ahead of our time. Maybe if I had waited a few years I would have been in sync with the Curtis Mayfields and the Marvin Gayes who had great success with message songs. There are record men who say they can read the tea leaves. They say they can predict hits. I was one of them—and I knew this was my biggest hit, until the marketplace told me otherwise. Aretha, though, couldn't be deterred from her determination to beat Barbra Streisand at Barbra's own game. I kept saying, 'Ree, you can outsing Streisand any day of the week. That's not the point. The point is to find a hit.' But that summer she just wanted straight-up ballads. She insisted that she do 'People,' Streisand's smash. Aretha sang the hell out of it, but no one's gonna beat Barbra at her own game. She also insisted on singing 'My Coloring Book,' another song Streisand had cut. Bob Mersey had written a beautiful chart for Barbra. 'Write a more beautiful chart,' Aretha told my arranger Sinky Hendricks. I told Ted White that I thought it was a mistake to go head-to-head with Streisand. 'She wants the world to hear that whatever material Streisand is handling, she can handle with even more polish,' said Ted. 'It's more important for Aretha to mark out her own territory,' I argued. The argument did no good. She and Ted also demanded that we include a bluesy thing that they wrote, called 'I'll Keep On Smiling.' I considered it a throw-away. Of course I couldn't tell her that. I couldn't tell her that I thought the inclusion of 'Jim'—an extremely subtle jazz ballad done by Sarah Vaughan she had heard on her brother's phono when they were kids in Detroit—was not going to break the bank. The truth is that Aretha could and did sing all these things quite easily and quite wonderfully. But where was the continuity? My feeling was that she wanted to be all these people—Sarah and Streisand and Sinatra—but still didn't know who she was. 'She's a hit maker,' Ted White would tell me, 'get her hits.' 'Then why are you making her sing standards?' I asked. 'She's singing everything because she can sing everything,' Ted said. 'We throw it all against the wall and see what sticks. The more variety, the better.'

"Ted was giving the marching orders, so I reached out to other writers. I called Van McCoy, a bright up-and-coming composer. I knew Van had written 'Abracadabra' that Aretha's sister Erma had recorded on Epic. I liked the song and I liked Van. I asked him if he had anything for Aretha. He gave me 'Sweet Bitter Love,' and I thought it was a perfect Aretha vehicle. She fractured it. She loved it so well that she kept singing it, even when she left Columbia. She was devoted to this song. She attached herself to the tune so closely, I believe, because it ran true. She and Ted were starting to have their problems. She was tired of taking his orders. She was living through a 'Sweet Bitter Love.' When she got to the bridge and sang, 'My magic dreams have lost their spell,' she turns it into grand opera. Was it a masterpiece? Hell, yes. Was it a hit? Hell, no.

"And talking about masterpieces, how about her version of 'But Beautiful,' cut during those same sessions? She had Nat Cole's version in mind, but I told Sinky to listen to the orchestration Ray Ellis had written for Billie Holiday. I challenged him to improve upon that. That's the only album that Billie had cut for Columbia, just before she died in the late fifties. I thought Billie's 'But Beautiful' was the benchmark, but I didn't play it for Aretha because she didn't require inspiration or motivation. Every time Aretha sang, she was motivated to outdo every version that came before her. Sinky's chart was gorgeous, and Aretha brought home the bacon. She's not Billie, but Billie's not Aretha. Billie bleeds. In every song she dies a slow death. She's like the dying swan in that ballet. Aretha works through the pain and comes out on top of it. Billie died young. Working with Aretha, I knew that, no matter what, she wasn't gonna die young. She was introverted on the outside but the lady had inner toughness. She had inner steel. For all her uncertainties about this or that, she had what it takes to survive this tough bloody music business."

Otis understood Aretha on both a deeply personal and a creative level. Yet in spite of their rapport, their initial work together was far from a commercial success. When the summer sessions of 1964 failed to yield a single hit, Clyde Otis received word that it was time to change course entirely.

"Lieberson and Mersey got together and decided it was time to quit fooling around and go right at the teen market," Otis told me. "By then, Ted and Aretha were frustrated enough to go along with the program. They knew they had to drop the throw-everything-against-the-wall-and-see-what-sticks shtick. And they were ready. Forget the standards. No more 'That's Entertainment,' no more Judy Garland songs. We were going for the kids. I'd found her a song called 'Runnin' Out of Fools' that I thought might get us some airplay. It was a little ditty that I worked up in an R-and-B vein. Ted didn't like that. By then, Ted and I were practically at each other's throats. He was sure I was the wrong producer and I was sure he was the wrong manager. Aretha was stuck with me because her contract with Columbia ran through 1966 and Columbia saw me as the guy to get her over. I was stuck with Ted because Aretha saw him as the guy to get her over. Anyway, we put out 'Fools,' and while you couldn't call it a smash, they started playing it on the radio and you heard it all over Harlem. Turned out to be the only semi-hit she ever had on Columbia. To this day, people still remember it.

"Aretha had a thing for covers. Occasionally she and Ted would bring me a song that they wrote, but it usually didn't measure up. Later she told me she was the one who wrote it. He just put his name on it. Anyway, she was not what you call a prolific writer, but, as an interpreter, she always felt she could outdo the original. She usually did. On the *Runnin' Out of Fools* album, she covered a couple of Motown things. She was always talking about her good friend Smokey Robinson and so she recorded the big hit he had on Mary Wells, 'My Guy.' We even followed the original Smokey chart. I thought the vibe was too kicked-back for Aretha, but Aretha did it anyway. She redid the other big Motown hit that season, Brenda Holloway's 'Every Little Bit Hurts.' If she was going cover crazy, she might as well cover a song of mine. I could use the royalties. So I got her to do 'It's Just a Matter of Time,' a tune Sinky and I had written with Brook Benton back in the fifties. Inez and Charlie Foxx had done 'Mockingbird' the year before and Ree wanted to do it again. Same goes for other teen-style hits, like 'The Shoop Shoop Song.' Dionne Warwick had started singing those Burt Bacharach/Hal David songs. Practically all of them went top ten. That's why Aretha sang 'Walk On By.' She thought she could have a hit right behind Dionne's. I didn't. I said, 'Dionne had this soft, subtler thing that works with Burt's melodies. You're too strong for his stuff.' She sang it anyway. Later she proved me wrong on another Bacharach/Dionne combination — 'Say a Little

Prayer'—but by then she had established her own identity on Atlantic and practically anything she did sold. This was years earlier, during her last days on Columbia, where, to my mind, she was sounding desperate. To me, *Runnin' Out of Fools* is not prime-time Aretha. It's Aretha and Ted feeling like they're running out of time. I said they were fools to be chasing all these teeny hits. If they had given me more time, Sinky and I could have written her original hits in the R-and-B style, just like we'd done for Dinah Washington and Brook Benton. But Ted and Aretha, man, they were in a hurry. They thought the train was leaving without them."

"The sad thing," said Jerry Wexler, who would be the savior in the next chapter of Aretha's musical story, "is that Clyde, for all his talent, was behind the curve. His string sessions and jazz sessions with Aretha were fine, but when he put her in an R-and-B bag, the bag was at least five years old. There just weren't any hits in that bag. The sound he gave Dinah in the early sixties was fine, but it was passé. R-and-B is very street, very right-now, very immediate. His grooves were tired."

"I had two distinct disadvantages," Otis explained. "First, my relationship with Ted was going nowhere fast. We didn't like each other. He thought I was old hat. He thought I took too long in the studio. I saw him as just another amateur throwing his weight around because he happened to be the artist's husband. He kept telling me how for years he had supported Aretha's career with his own money. He was saying that if it weren't for his financial backing, she'd never have gotten this far. But I knew he was exaggerating like crazy. Ever since she came to Columbia, she had worked steadily—R-and-B shows, nightclubs, jazz festivals. I'm not saying she was getting rich, but she was booking good money—and I suspect he was living off her. Which brings me to my second disadvantage. Ted and Aretha were often at odds with each other. They did not present a united front. I think she was coming to the same conclusion as me—that Ted was living off her. She had problems with Ted but she also had problems of her own. She missed many sessions without ever telling me why. Just didn't show. Some people said she was drinking, but I didn't see any of that. I saw that she'd get down in the dumps sometimes and didn't want to work. I saw how Ted would force her to work—and maybe she needed that push. But I also saw that sometimes that push became a shove. He didn't hesitate slapping her around and didn't care who saw him do it.

"Things got crazier when I got word from the boss upstairs, Goddard Lieberson, that she probably wouldn't re-sign with Columbia when her contract ran out in a year or so. So they were eager to get as much inventory on her as possible before her commitment ran out. Because I had seen her live in the jazz clubs and knew how good she was in that setting, I suggested a live album. But in those days, portable equipment was expensive and sometimes unreliable so I was told to do a studio album with her jazz trio, the one led by Teddy Harris, and then sweet it with applause to make it sound like a club. We called the record *Yeah!!! In Person with Her Quartet,* and I thought it was one of her best. If you want to hear exactly who Aretha Franklin was at the period in her life—just before she switched labels—listen to *Yeah!!!*

"I got Kenny Burrell, the jazz guitarist from Detroit who's one of the best who's ever played, to sit in with the trio. Kenny added so much subtlety and class. Her regular guys—Beans Richardson was on bass and Hindel Butts on drums—they swing from start to finish. The sessions went smoothly. I don't even remember Ted being there. I do remember, though, that Steve Allen dropped by to hear her sing two of his songs—'This Could Be the Start of Something Big' and 'Impossible,' the tune Nat Cole had recorded in the fifties. He was knocked out. I was knocked out how she did Erroll Garner's 'Misty.' Erroll was a friend of mine, and a few months later I played him Aretha's version. Sarah had sung 'Misty'— *everyone* had sung 'Misty'—but Erroll actually had tears in his eyes after hearing Aretha. 'Goddamn,' he said, 'she makes it seem like *she* wrote it.'

"She also sang a song she'd written and Mersey had orchestrated a few years earlier, 'Without the One You Love.' I'm keenly competitive with other writers and don't give out compliments easily, but I was certain she had written a standard. If you listen to the record, it's her, not Teddy Harris, who's on piano. When she anchors herself at the keyboard, you get an entirely different Aretha. She's more centered and more powerful.

"The folk scene had started up and Aretha, who always wanted to be up-to-date, talked about singing 'Puff the Magic Dragon' by Peter, Paul, and Mary. I thought that was not a good idea. Instead I played her Sam Cooke's version of Pete Seeger's 'If I Had a Hammer,' another Peter, Paul, and Mary hit. Sam had done it on his live Copa date and that's all Aretha needed to know. She was crazy for Sam. In fact, we were in the studio on some session when word came down that Sam had been killed by some woman in Los Angeles. Aretha got up and left and didn't come back for a week. I certainly understood."

At the end of January 1965, Aretha appeared on *Shindig!* promoting "Can't You Just See Me," another attempt at the teen market by the soon-to-be twenty-three-year-old.

"Sinky wrote the song," Clyde Otis told me, "a little dance ditty that we thought might work. By then, though, nothing was working, at least not commercially. On the B side we did something called 'Miss Raggedy Ann,' a song about a doll. Aretha thought it was cute. She said it reminded her of her childhood. I thought it was beneath her, but my marching orders was to cut as many tunes on her as possible—so that's what I did. Our last year in the studio together was the craziest. Ted wasn't really talking to me and I was happy not to talk to him. Aretha was as remote as she could be. I felt like she needed counseling 'cause she kept missing gigs and kept taking all kinds of abuse from Ted. But no one appointed me her counselor and I simply shut up and supervised the session. It got bizarre.

"I was friends with Neal Hefti, the marvelous writer who did such fabulous songs and charts for Count Basie. Neal wrote a movie theme for a Jack Lemmon flick, *How to Murder Your Wife*. It wasn't one of Neal's best, but Columbia wanted me to produce it on Aretha. Turned out to be another snoozer. You can sum it all up with the opening lines of a tune she wanted to cut, called 'A Little Bit of Soul.' It talks about how she's struggling to compose a song and, to quote the lyrics, 'if I don't get me a hit soon I won't be here long.' Well, it wasn't long before Columbia and Aretha both decided they had had enough of each other."

In March, a month after the assassination of Malcolm X at the Audubon Ballroom in New York City, Aretha appeared on *Shindig!* and sang "Can't You Just See Me." The tune entered the pop charts at number ninety-five and rose no higher. Meanwhile, Marvin Gaye's "How Sweet It Is," the Temptations' "My Girl," the Righteous Brothers' "You've Lost that Lovin' Feeling," and Petula Clark's "Downtown" became not only blockbuster hits but classics that would be played for decades to come.

In April, President Lyndon Johnson ordered ground troops into Vietnam.

In May, Aretha's "One Step Ahead," yet another single, was released, and while it never crossed, it did climb into the R&B top twenty.

"It was our answer to the Dionne Warwick phenomenon," said Clyde. "It wasn't a cover or a Bacharach song, but it tried to create that refined and relaxed feel. Of course, Aretha is twice the singer Dionne will ever be, but Dionne had this defined personality— this very appealing musical persona—and it's my contention that Aretha still lacked an identity."

On May 29, *Billboard* reported that Columbia had recruited one of their A&R men, Bob Johnston, to bring Aretha to Nashville "with the hope of duplicating his Patti Page 'Hush, Hush, Sweet Charlotte' success." Those sessions, in May and October of 1965, actually took place in New York and proved to be Aretha's last for the label.

"Was I hurt that I was being dumped as Ree's producer?" said Clyde Otis. "Well, I wasn't thrilled. I still saw myself as the guy who could turn her into a superstar. Deep in my heart I did believe she was as great as Dinah. No other woman out there could touch her, and yet I also had to admit that our work together had really gone nowhere. Aside from five or six superb cuts, I hadn't captured her greatness. I hadn't been able to give her an identity. Sure, I could say that desperation did us in. Both she and Ted were so desperate to have hits they lost their judgment and were going in five different directions at the same time. The big brass at Columbia was also desperate to recoup the advances they gave her. But lots of great music has been created in a mood of desperation. In our case, the stars simply weren't aligned.

"I'd known Bob Johnston for years. In fact, I produced Bob back in the fifties when he wanted to be a singer. I cut one of his songs—'Born to Love One Woman'—and brought him from Texas to New York. I knew Bob was a real talent. I wished him good luck with Aretha but also told him that he'd be lucky if she showed up half the time. From what I understand, my predictions turned out to be optimistic. For a long time she went into a cocoon and no one knew where to find her, not even her husband. Strange woman. Brilliant woman. A woman blessed with inordinate talent. And yet, for all our time together, a woman I never really understood or even got to know. I saw her as a woman holding in secret pain—and I wasn't let in on those secrets."

The first Bob Johnston/Aretha session, on May 25 at Columbia Studios, produced four songs, including a misguided, string-laden, horn-heavy attempt to reinvent Jerome Kern and Oscar Hammerstein's "Why Was I Born" as a gospel lament. The second session, at first scheduled for later in the summer, was postponed till October.

"I was asked to locate Aretha," said Clyde Otis, "who was said to have disappeared. But I had no more knowledge of her whereabouts than the CBS brass. I wished them luck and went my merry way. My hope was that the 'live' quartet session I produced—*Yeah!!!*—that came out that summer would do some business.

When it bombed, I knew I was permanently out of the Aretha Franklin business."

In a parallel universe, on June 15 and 16, 1965, Aretha's label mate Bob Dylan entered the same Seventh Avenue Columbia Studios and cut the first session for what would become his landmark *Highway 61 Revisited*. His producer was Tom Wilson. In July, Dylan shook up the folk world by going electric at Newport. Days afterward, he was back in the studio, this time with a new producer— the same Bob Johnston who had been working with Aretha. It was Johnston who supervised the recording of, among other songs, "Desolation Row."

Two months later, Johnston was back with Aretha, who, after an extended stay in Detroit, finally showed up at the midtown studio, where she cut her last three Columbia sides. It seems fitting that two of them—"Swanee" and "You Made Me Love You"— represented a return to the mainstream showbiz style she had adopted four years earlier with "Rock-a-Bye Your Baby with a Dixie Melody."

"It was disheartening," said John Hammond. "Bob Johnston is a great producer. Look at what he did with Dylan. He also did great work with Simon and Garfunkel, Johnny Cash, and Leonard Cohen. Don't fault Bob. At that point, the confusion surrounding Aretha and her camp was enough to undermine any project."

That same summer of 1965, between the two Johnston sessions, Aretha had flown home to Detroit to help her brother and sister celebrate C.L.'s nineteenth year as pastor at New Bethel.

"I don't remember Ted being at the event," said Carolyn. "I do remember feeling relieved that we wouldn't have to deal with the tension that was always there between Ted and Daddy. We wanted to have Aretha to ourselves—back in the bosom of her family. I had just turned twenty-one and had begun feeling my oats. Like Erma, I had my own R-and-B record out and was determined to have my own career as a writer and a singer. One of the beautiful things about singing for our father was that—at least for a night—we could put behind whatever little jealousies that had been brewing with Ree. Erma had always encouraged my career and later Aretha did too. But during that time when she still hadn't broken through to the big time, I think she secretly worried that we'd get there before her. Personally, I didn't have that worry. Erma and I were good—very good—but Aretha was great."

"In some ways," Erma told me, "you could compare us to the Jacksons. Jermaine could sing, Jackie could sing, and so could Marlon. All the brothers have tremendous talent. But then here comes Michael, a once-in-a-generation talent. He took it to another level—the genius level. I think that's how we viewed Aretha. Her ability was not of this world. At the same time, Carolyn and I knew that our strengths were not inconsiderable. We also shared Aretha's drive to be noticed, appreciated, and paid. By that time I had cut a couple of dozen songs for Epic—not hits, but all solid stuff. I felt that Ree continued to resent my presence in the business. I only wish that we all could have sat down and discussed these issues—Carolyn and I were certainly eager to do just that—but Aretha was not one to verbally express her feelings. She kept everything inside until it was time to sing. Then she put her every last emotion smack in your face. This served her art but it did not serve our sisterhood. Except for these wonderful occasions when our focus was on our beloved father, we tended to fall into misunderstanding. This sisterly strain, together with the sisterly love and concern, went on forever."

After her father's anniversary celebration, Aretha went into hiding. Erma remembered visiting her once or twice in the midtown apartment that she and Ted shared. Carolyn recalled her visiting Detroit every few weeks to check in on her three sons. Cecil looked back on it as a time when Aretha and Ted were often separated.

"He had different women and she knew it," said Cecil. "Everyone knew it. She was not only frustrated with that, but also the fact that Columbia had not marketed her correctly. She was seriously thinking about leaving Ted, leaving Columbia, and making a fresh start."

For the rest of 1965 and all of 1966, Aretha would not make another record.

"I know many of the producers did lots of things to try and lure her back into the studio," Hammond told me, "but she stopped answering anyone's call. I had an idea that she might want to go back to our original plan of five years earlier and record a pure blues album. Someone else had the notion of having her do a Mahalia-style gospel album with modern orchestrations of sacred hymns. At that point, though, she had closed the door. I assumed she was simply waiting for our contract to run out. I assumed her management was shopping her to other labels."

Years later Aretha looked back at her Columbia experience in a positive light. She had been introduced to the world as a major artist. She had proven she could sing jazz, pop, blues, and rhythm and blues with uncanny emotional strength. Her vocal technique was beyond reproach. From "Today I Sing the Blues" to "That Lucky Old Sun" to "Just for a Thrill" to "Skylark" to "This Bitter Earth" to "Take a Look" to "Impossible," she had recorded a series of masterpieces. For all her missed recording and performing dates, she had nonetheless demonstrated that, year in and year out, she was capable of showing up and turning out a steady flow of brilliant performances. In five years, she had cut some eight albums. She appeared on television as a well-groomed figure, an appealing singer whose interpretations of songs in any number of genres were, more often than not, thrilling.

And yet no one was thrilled—not Aretha, not her husband, Ted, and certainly not the executives at Columbia Records. Everyone wanted more. Everyone wanted hits. After all, Aretha had not crossed over from gospel to pop for mere critical acclaim. She had crossed over in search of the American dreams—glory and gold.

"She definitely fell into a depression," said Erma. "I remember being in her New York apartment watching her looking out her window at the gray sky and falling snow. 'What are you thinking about, Ree?' I asked her. 'I'm not thinking,' she said. 'I'm just dreaming.' 'Dreaming about what?' 'That things will get better.'"

Some things did get better—spectacularly better—but some things got spectacularly worse.

Part Three

ATLANTIC

12. NEVER LOVED

In 1966, Jerry Wexler, age forty-nine, was a hungry man — hungry for even greater success in a field where he had already proven himself. The field — root righteous rhythm and blues — was his lifelong passion.

"I was born hungry," he told me. "The hunger never went away. In fact, I believe that gnawing hunger is the driving force behind every great record man. And more than anything, I wanted to be a great record man."

Wexler was a dynamo — personable, charismatic, opinionated, confident to the point of being cocky. Along with Ahmet and Nesuhi Ertegun, he was one of the owners of Atlantic Records. Children of the Turkish ambassador to the United States, the Erteguns were renegade and highly educated aristocrats who, like Wexler, had been consumed with black music since their childhood. This fanaticism for funk had driven the company since 1949, when, with its first hit, Stick McGhee's "Drinkin' Wine, Spo-Dee-O-Dee," the label was established as a gutsy independent willing to go where the mainstreams were not. Corporate Columbia and mom-and-pop Atlantic were at opposite poles of the music business.

"When I came on board in the fifties," said Wexler, "Ahmet had already signed Ray Charles. Before him, Ruth Brown was the big hit maker. I didn't really earn my stripes in the studio until the sixties, when I hit with Solomon Burke and Wilson Pickett. While Motown specialized in soothing soul—which, by the way, was beautiful—I was more attracted to screaming soul. I like it raw. Fortunately, I signed on early to what was becoming the golden age of soul. At the same time the British Invasion was in full swing. But that attracted Ahmet, who is a natural-born internationalist, far more than me. While he was signing Cream, King Crimson, and the Bee Gees, I found myself deep in the Memphis–Muscle Shoals axis where a small army of blues-minded white boys were writing brilliant head charts—basically made-up-on-the-spot-in-the-studio arrangements. Their spontaneous methodology became one of the great epiphanies of my life.

"The more traditional way, of course, were orchestrations notated well in advance of the studio. In short, written music for the musicians to read. But the southern boys just liked to jam—and God, did they ever! Visionaries like Chips Moman, Tommy Cogbill, Roger Hawkins, Spooner Oldham, Jimmy Johnson, and David Hood might have looked like hillbillies, but they were secret geniuses of the good groove. They laid it down with neither preparation nor forethought. The shit just happened.

"Not only was the music magnificent, it sold like hotcakes. Pickett was burning up the charts. What's more, I had cut a favorable distribution deal with Jim Stewart at Stax, where Sam and Dave and Otis Redding, backed by one of the most ferocious rhythm sections of all time—Booker T. Jones, Al Jackson, Steve Cropper, and Duck Dunn—had taken off like a rocket. The soul world was exploding around me. So while Ahmet had begun combing the Continent for rock talent, I was mining Memphis and Muscle Shoals, where, relatively late in life, I was getting a whole education about how to run a recording session."

"We saw Wexler as a savior," said Jimmy Johnson, the guitarist who would play on many Aretha records. "He said he was charmed by our easygoing southern ways, but, man, he was the one who charmed us. He had the thickest New York accent I'd ever heard.

He had more energy than a hound dog chasing a rabbit. He was a hustler in the best sense of the word—a go-getter—and, best of all, he was big-time and we sure weren't. Whatever he had—his connections, his promotional skills, his ability to get songs on the radio—we wanted. Plus he had the ears of a wolf. He wanted it down and dirty. He had all the best stories about Ray Charles and Professor Longhair and Clyde McPhatter and anyone else you could think of."

"My history with Aretha began in the fall of 1966 when I was at Muscle Shoals recording Wilson Pickett," Wexler told me. "Percy Sledge, another of our soul-singing artists, came by the studio and started giving Pickett a hard time, telling him he was sounding like Otis or James Brown. Well, Wilson hated James—they had once fought over a woman—and now Pickett, pissed as hell, went after Sledge. Literally. To protect my label's interest—after all, both these singers were making us serious money—I stepped in between them. Pickett flung me out of the way and was ready to do battle with Percy, a former boxer, when suddenly the phone rang. 'Calm the fuck down!' I exhorted. The men backed off as I picked up the receiver. 'Jerry,' said a female voice. 'It's Louise Bishop. Aretha's ready for you.'

"I'd been waiting to hear those words for a long time. Louise Bishop was a gospel DJ out of Philly. Back then, the best way to get to Aretha was through the gospel world. More than a year earlier, when I had learned Aretha was unhappy at Columbia, I'd tell Louise and others that I'd love to talk with her. The person who answered my call, though, wasn't Aretha. It was Ted White. From John Hammond and Clyde Otis, I had heard Ted White stories—how he not only ran the show but wanted to run her recording sessions. From friends in Detroit, though, I also knew that White represented serious songwriters and had a sharp sense of music. From the first moment we spoke, I realized he was a slick cat.

" 'Mr. Wexler,' he said.

" 'Call me Jerry.'

" 'Call me Ted.'

" 'I heard your artist is available, Ted.'

" 'I heard you were interested in my artist, Jerry.'

" 'Very interested. Intensely interested.'

" 'Then we should meet.'

" 'Right away,' I said.

" 'Name the time and place.'

" 'Monday in New York. My office at noon.'

" 'We're there.'

"And they were. Right on time. I was delighted to see that they came with neither a lawyer nor an agent. In our first meeting, Aretha dressed in a conservative brown suit. She gave me little eye contact and was closed-mouth in the extreme. I couldn't get her to call me Jerry. It was 'Mr. Wexler.' Though it was against my nature, I had to reciprocate and call her 'Miss Franklin.' I couldn't get her to say anything about the kind of music she wanted to make, other than 'I want hits.' When I asked her to discuss her experience at Columbia, all she said was 'It was nice. I did some nice things. But now I want hits.'

" 'And money,' added Ted.

" 'I can advance you twenty-five thousand dollars for your first album,' I said. 'The second we sign, you'll have the check.' I expected the arm wrestling to start. I was sure that Ted would ask for fifty thousand. Much to my shock, though, he didn't.

" 'We're going to accept the twenty-five,' he said. 'As important as front money is, what's more important is that Atlantic establish Aretha as a superstar. No reason she shouldn't be selling as many records as Otis and Sam and Dave.'

" 'Couldn't agree with you more, Ted. That's why I want to turn her over to Jim Stewart at Stax. We do their distribution and promotion. We're their selling arm and they're one of our production arms. She'll love Jim.'

" 'Stax has had a lot of hits,' said Aretha, not objecting to my suggestion.

" 'And they're just getting warmed up.' "

When Wexler told me that he'd initially chosen not to produce

Aretha himself, I was surprised. He said he had tracked her career from the start and considered her a major talent. Why would he want to hand her over to Jim Stewart?

"Aretha's voice was always there, no doubt," he said. "And I definitely saw her as part of our stable. At that point, though, I was into delegation. I was looking to free up my time. I had my eyes on winters in Florida. Because of our success, I started thinking of what it would mean to sell the company and cash out. Ahmet and Nesuhi were initially not enamored of the idea, but—because persistence is my middle name—I kept at them. Along with Motown, we were the indie label stars of the midsixties. The early sixties—especially after Ray Charles had left us for ABC Paramount—had not been easy for us. Now that we had a strong string of hits, who knew how long it would last? I didn't want to take any chances. So at the very moment Aretha arrived, my mind wasn't focused on producing; it was on finding a buyer. Besides, the Stax machine turned a raw rhythm-and-blues singer like Otis Redding into an international sensation. There's no reason why they couldn't do the same with Aretha. So you can imagine how surprised I was when Jim Stewart turned her down.

" 'You sure you want to pass on Aretha Franklin?' I asked Jim.

" 'She's great,' said Jim. 'I just don't see her recording in this environment.'

"I couldn't have disagreed more, but Jim was his own man. He didn't sign her—I did—so now it was up to me to put my time and money where my mouth was. Looking back, I see that turning her over to Stewart would have been a colossal mistake. My atheism does not allow me to thank God for Jim's decision to reject her. Instead I thank the good angels of R-and-B who were protecting Aretha and, by extension, me, her humble servant."

As Wexler was firming up the contract with Aretha, word got back to Columbia.

"An internal memo came down from the top indicating that Aretha was talking to Atlantic and that their deal was all but consummated," John Hammond told me. "Of course I was not pleased, but what could I do? She had been out of my hands for several years. And even though I admired the more recent material that Clyde Otis had developed for her, I realized that, with all Columbia's enormous resources, we had not served her well. Of course, Ted White and Aretha didn't always help. They had their own ideas that often conflicted with the Columbia producers'. The results were often confused. Our promotion and salespeople were also confused about how to sell Aretha. All this is a great pity because, at least on paper, a great record company like Columbia should have been able to make her an international star. At the same time, I was hopeful that Atlantic might provide her with the kind of culture that suited her personality. Atlantic was not a corporation but a small label specializing in R-and-B where the owners—Jerry, Ahmet, and Nesuhi—actually produced the artist themselves. They were passionate and highly skilled record men. Wexler was especially adept at promoting. When he had a product he liked, he'd go to the ends of the earth to make sure the right people heard it and played it on the radio."

The *Billboard* article on December 3, 1966, made it official. Under a photo, the caption read: "Jerry Wexler, vice-president of Atlantic Records, signs blues singer Aretha Franklin to an exclusive contract while her manager, Ted White, looks on from above. Her first release with Atlantic is slated for January."

"When I explained to Ted and Aretha that I, and not Jim Stewart, would be producing her," said Wexler, "they had no objections and even seemed somewhat relieved. They liked the idea that one of the Atlantic bosses was going in the studio with them. Then came discussion about the studio. They wanted to record in New York. I argued long and hard for Muscle Shoals. I cited the fact that Percy Sledge had cut his monster hit 'When a Man Loves a Woman' at Fame—the studio I wanted to use—and that I had enjoyed several smashes with Pickett, all done at Fame. Ted said he had apprehensions about the South and had heard that Rick Hall, the Fame owner, was overbearing. I joked and said the only overbearing personality was me—and that I'd be running the sessions. Rick's role would be minimal. He would not be producing. Ted said that Aretha was used to recording in New York. New York was her comfort zone. I argued that Muscle Shoals would be an even greater comfort zone because we were going to record in an entirely different way. We weren't going to have prepared charts like they had at Columbia. Nothing would be written down. 'That's good,' said Ted, 'because she can't read or write music.' I told Ted my theory of preliterate geniuses—musicians who bypass mere notations because they hear it all in their heads. They can call out the parts. They can sing out the parts. They don't need to write down notes. They just play them by ear. 'That's Aretha,' said Ted. 'She has the complete picture before she starts. We've been trying to tell producers that for years.' 'You don't have to convince me,' I said. 'I'm sold.'

"At that point Ted said he had a few songs he wanted to sell me, songs by writers in his publishing company that were custom-composed for Aretha. I was all ears. The first was 'I Never Loved a Man (the Way I Love You)' written by Ronnie Shannon, one of Ted's guys in Detroit. I loved it. 'Good,' said Ted, 'she's already figuring out how she wants to cut it.' 'Fine,' I replied. 'The boys in Muscle Shoals could not be more flexible. Flexibility is what this thing's all about.'

"He had a tape recording of something he said Aretha had written, called 'Dr. Feelgood.' Just her and the piano. All I could do was smile and wave my hand like I was in church. 'Fabulous,' I said. I saw it straight in the Bessie Smith–Dinah tradition of a woman demanding her sexual satisfaction. 'Don't put it to Aretha like that,' Ted said. 'She doesn't like to think she writes sexy songs.' I suggested two covers—Henry Glover's 'Drown in My Own Tears' that Ray Charles had made famous and Sam Cooke's 'A Change Is Gonna Come.' 'She loves both,' said Ted. 'We're all on the same page. She has another cover she's been doing live—Otis Redding's 'Respect.' 'Long as she changes it up from the original,' I said. 'You don't gotta worry about that, Wex,' said White. 'She changes it up all right.'"

"Jerry Wexler deserves a ton of credit for producing Aretha right," said Ruth Bowen, "but I think it should be clear that she was developing her own sound and style without anyone's help before she met Wexler. I actually heard her do that version of 'Respect' live, the one that became the signature song of her career. She was singing 'Respect' before she ever signed with Atlantic. Jerry definitely put her with the right musicians, but she came to the party full prepared. She came with the goods."

As the musical elements of Aretha's life were brought into harmony, the personal elements became more dissonant than ever.

"If Ted hadn't helped put together that Atlantic deal," said Erma, "I'm not sure their marriage would have lasted. Their relationship was on its last legs. Changing record companies only postponed the inevitable. It was the beginning of a strange but beautiful period in Aretha's life when she leaned on her family more. She was putting together her sound—in her own way—and she realized that no one could augment that sound better than me and Carolyn. I don't care what you say, but siblings who sing—especially siblings who began singing in church—have a certain built-in harmony you can't find anywhere else. Think of the Clark Sisters and the Winans. Aretha knew that, and when she started envisioning churchier-sounding backgrounds to highlight her lead vocals, she turned to us. We were there with open arms. Whatever the past friction—and the past friction was serious—we remained sisters in Christ. Our father taught us that."

"It took Aretha a while to leave Columbia for Atlantic," said Carolyn, "because Columbia was the most prestigious label. I think she felt like she'd be giving up status. But Aretha was also aware of the current market, and she decided that Columbia wasn't. Ironically, when she gave up the idea of 'crossing over' into the mainstream with jazzy standards à la Ella or Sarah and Dinah, that's when she crossed over the most. That's because she became more fully herself."

As far as studios went, Wexler prevailed, convincing Ted and Aretha that Muscle Shoals was the place where magic was being made. They were set to meet there at the end of January 1967. Hopes, confidence, and expectations were all high.

"I didn't see how anything could go wrong," said Wexler.

And then everything did.

"Before we got to Muscle Shoals, Aretha had worked out the pattern for the songs on her Fender Rhodes at home," Wexler explained. "She and her sisters worked out the background parts. The plan was to have her come into the studio, show that bad Muscle Shoals rhythm section her outline, and let them jam around her. I thought it was important not to have an all-Caucasian band so I made sure to get the Memphis Horns and Bowlegs Miller. I loved all the material Ted and Aretha brought—Sam Cooke's 'A Change Is Gonna Come' and 'Good Times,' Otis's 'Respect,' and the three Aretha tunes—'Dr. Feelgood,' 'Don't Let Me Lose This Dream,' and 'Baby, Baby, Baby,' written with Carolyn."

Wexler loved King Curtis, who, along with Motown's Junior Walker, was the reigning king of R&B tenor saxophonists. Beyond his instrumental prowess, King was a prolific writer and arranger. He'd soon become Aretha's musical director. For this first record, Wexler gave Aretha one of King's best, "Soul Serenade," a song Curtis had written with Luther Dixon, whose "Blue Holiday" Aretha had sung on Columbia.

"The first day started off fine," Wexler remembered. "We had Chips Moman and Jimmy Johnson on guitar, Roger Hawkins on drums, and Tommy Cogbill on bass. Spooner Oldham knocked everyone out—including Aretha—with those opening chords on electric piano. Those were some mournfully funky riffs that became a permanent part of the song. Aretha was on acoustic piano, and because she had walked in the door with the groove in hand, it happened quickly."

"She was a very shy and withdrawn woman," Roger Hawkins told me. "She called everyone 'Mister' and we called her 'Miss Franklin.' There was no small talk. She was all business. That made me nervous because mostly we'd done sessions with singers who picked up our relaxed manner right away. Not Aretha. She stayed to herself. But when she sat down at the piano and began to hit those chords and that sound came out of her mouth, nothing mattered. I've heard a lot of soul singing in my time, but nothing like that."

"Aretha sang it with the conviction of a saint," said Dan Penn, who was at the session, where, on the spot, he and Chips Moman wrote "Do Right Woman—Do Right Man," a song that would eventually be included on the record.

"Before she started playing we were worried she might have qualms about playing with a white rhythm section," said Jimmy Johnson, "but when we all got to grooving, it was nothing but a party. She didn't like the support we gave her—she *loved* it. She knew that, color be damned, we were all coming from the same place. The woman just sang—and sang—and sang some more. We were hysterically happy, giddy happy, like schoolchildren, running into the studio to hear the playback. To the last man, we realized we were watching the birth of a superstar. The experience gave joy new meaning."

Until the joy stopped and the heavy drama started.

"My plan was to do everything live," said Wexler. "Have Aretha and the musicians playing together in real time. Of course, Rick Hall was there because we were using his studio. There had been tension between me and Rick earlier about Clarence Carter, a big-selling R-and-B artist with hits like 'Slip Away' and 'Patches.' Hall stole him from us. But I put that aside for the sake of having a smooth Aretha session. The euphoria of these first takes of 'I Never Loved a Man' led to some celebratory drinking that night. I had left the studio before it got bad, but apparently it got ugly between Ted and Rick Hall."

"I confess that I'd been doing some drinking," Hall told me, "but so had Ted. And so had Aretha. No one was in his or her right mind. It began when one of the white horn players, who had also been drinking, got into some argument with Ted. Whether the racial stuff started with Ted or the trumpet player, I don't know. But it was there. So Ted stormed out of the session and took Aretha with him. That was a crying shame 'cause the session had gone so well. I knew Wexler, who was my client, would be pissed out of his mind. So I went to Ted and Aretha's room to try and make it right. I made it worse. Ted didn't wanna hear any explanations but I gave 'em anyway. That just led to a bunch more yelling with Ted telling me how he never should have brought his wife down to Alabama to play with these rednecks.

" 'Who you calling a redneck?' I said.

" 'Who you calling a nigger?'

" 'I'd never use that word.'

" 'But you were thinking it, weren't you?'

" 'I was just thinking that you should go fuck yourself.' That led to Ted taking a swing at me and I swung back and we both landed a couple of good blows and before I knew it, I was in a full-blown fistfight with Ted White."

"The very thing I had worked so hard to avoid was racial animus," said Wexler, "and that's exactly what the night session had excited. Everyone was playing the race card. At the motel there was screaming and yelling and doors slamming. At six in the morning I was in Ted and Aretha's room trying to undo what Rick had done. Ted, though, could not be consoled. 'You were the one who said Muscle Shoals was soul paradise,' he said. 'Far as I can see, Muscle Shoals is soul shit. These honkies down here are some nasty motherfuckers. I will never submit my wife to circumstances like these. We're outta here.'

" 'But what about the schedule?' I asked. 'We were going to do all her vocals this week and the sweetening next week. All we have in the can is one completed song — "I Never Loved" — and the beginning of "Do Right Man." That's all I got.'

" 'What you really got, Wexler,' said Ted, 'is one big fuckin' mess on your hands. I'm not sure this lady is ever gonna record for Atlantic again.' And with that, he showed me the door."

When Aretha wrote about the incident, it was entirely different. She said she couldn't recall any details and wasn't in the room where Hall and White came to blows. She knew there had been discord and arguments intense enough to make her want to leave. But in Aretha's account, she left on her own, not with Ted. She packed up and headed out to the airport.

"I've never been so frustrated in my life," said Wexler. "In all my years in the record business, I had never experienced a better session. I knew we had a goddamn smash and now it looked like it was all in vain. The singer's husband/manager gave indications that he wanted out of the deal. He had physically fought the studio owner. He and Aretha had run out of Muscle Shoals after the very first day. I was crushed.

"When I got back to New York, Ahmet said I looked like I was on the verge of a nervous breakdown. I said I was on the verge of what I was convinced could be one of the most important and successful records in Atlantic history and suddenly it had all fallen apart. I couldn't let that happen. I called Ted but couldn't get through. Through the grapevine I'd heard that [Aretha] was back in Detroit—without Ted. I got a number. Carolyn answered. She said she couldn't tell me anything—that her sister needed some time alone."

"After that Muscle Shoals incident," said Carolyn, "I was sure that Aretha and Ted were splitsville. She felt that he had undermined the session. She said he was drunk half the time and belligerent as hell. She said she didn't want to see him again."

"I was going crazy," said Wexler. "I had disc jockeys calling her, I had preachers calling her, I was on the verge of calling out the FBI and Canadian Mounties. At the same time, I had a completed song—'I Never Loved a Man'—but only half of another. We'd only begun to cut the song that Dan and Chips wrote in the studio, 'Do Right Woman—Do Right Man.' There was no vocal. Where was my artist? Where was her manager? Were they really leaving the label before we even got started?

"I finally got Ted White on the phone. He was still mad as a motherfucker. I wanted to know what was happening. He had nothing but scorn. He was still seething about Rick Hall and Muscle

Shoals and my insistence that we record there. I apologized for Hall for the twentieth time but that made no difference. I told him that the past was the past and we had a hit on our hands but I needed Aretha back in the studio. He said something that surprised me: 'I'm not even sure I'm her manager. I can't control her. No one can.'

"So with the artist missing and management in doubt, what was I supposed to do? I decided, in my typical way, to leap before looking. I decided to act. I had this one song that I knew was cooking. I made a couple of dozen acetate copies of 'I Never Loved a Man' for DJs in key markets. These were guys I could count on. They'd let me know if I had a smash or whether I was simply jerking off. Within hours, I got the response I needed—they loved it, their listeners loved it, the phone lines started burning up. Airplay was immediate, but what about sales?

"Well, there are two sides on a forty-five single, and I had only one. I needed another song. Our distributors, who had heard 'I Never Loved' on the radio, started screaming for product. They knew me as an aggressive marketer and wanted to know what the fuck was wrong. I wasn't about to tell them that I had lost control of my artist. All I could say was 'Stand by.' Meanwhile, every minute the record was being played on the radio but was unavailable in stores, we were losing money. To be perfectly honest, the other thought I had was this—if I could get Aretha Franklin on the pop charts and establish her as a bestselling act, the value of Atlantic would jump considerably and my own dream of selling more easily realized. In every possible way, I was motivated.

"Ten days passed, ten of the most difficult days of my life, before I finally got the call.

"'Mr. Wexler, it's Miss Franklin calling. I'm ready to record. However, I won't be recording in Muscle Shoals. I will be recording in New York. I know you have studios in New York.'

"'Yes, we do. What about the band?'

"'Bring up the boys from Muscle Shoals. They understood me. As far as the backgrounds go, I'll be with my sisters.'

" 'Beautiful.' "

"I remember arriving in New York with Aretha," said Carolyn, "and feeling like we were all on a mission. We realized that our sister was on the brink of letting the world know what we had always known—that she was hands-down the scariest singer in the world. When she was in her element, no one could touch her. Well, we were her element. We arrived in New York as a family united, realizing that her problems with Ted had her on edge. Both in and out of the studio, she needed our support."

"I think of Aretha as Our Lady of Mysterious Sorrows," Wexler wrote in his memoir, *Rhythm and the Blues*. "Her eyes are incredible, luminous eyes covering inexplicable pain. Her depressions could be as deep as the dark sea. I don't pretend to know the sources of her anguish, but anguish surrounds Aretha as surely as the glory of her musical aura."

According to Wexler, when Aretha resurfaced and showed up at the Atlantic studios at 1841 Broadway in midtown Manhattan, Ted was not with her, only her sisters. She gave no apologies or explanations about where she had been.

"She came loaded for bear," said Tommy Dowd, the Atlantic engineer who was at the controls. "She went right for the piano, where, without a word, she played piano over the existing 'Do Right' track. She and Erma and Carolyn laid down the vocal harmonies, an arrangement from heaven. All that was left was Aretha's vocal. She ran it down once. Thank God I had pressed that Record button, because the rundown was unworldly. There was a calmness about her delivery, an attitude that said, *Brother, I own this song, I'm gonna take my time, and I'm gonna drill it into your soul.* When she was through, there was nothing to do but shake your head in wonder."

"When it came to producing Aretha's vocals," said Wexler, "it was the same as Ray Charles. I didn't say a word. She didn't need my critique. She didn't need anyone's critique. Her taste in vocal riffs and licks was absolutely flawless. She was only twenty-four and yet had the poise, authority, and confidence of someone who had been singing for sixty years. Her voice was young and vital, but it also came from a place of ancient secret wisdom."

"The method she'd begun in Muscle Shoals was continued in New York," Dowd explained. "She played the instrumentals with the band while singing a scratch vocal to help the musicians understand exactly how she was going to tell the story. We'd then throw away the scratch vocal, and, with an instrumental take that was acceptable to her, she went into the studio to sing the lead to track. That was the moment of truth. She was out there alone on the other side of the glass; I was behind the board in the control booth with Wexler hovering over me and all the musicians gathered around. After a couple of takes, she nailed 'Do Right' for all time. We were speechless. We were stunned. We knew we were in the presence of rare and immortal greatness."

"Do Right Woman—Do Right Man" was cut on February 8, 1967. Two days later Wexler released it as the B side to "I Never Loved a Man (the Way I Love You)." The response was immediate. "I Never Loved" flew to the top of the R&B charts and quickly crossed over, where it went top-ten pop and competed successfully with the Beatles' "Penny Lane," the Supremes' "Love Is Here and Now You're Gone," the Rolling Stones' "Ruby Tuesday," and the Turtles' "Happy Together." It took Atlantic two weeks to do what Columbia had not been able to do in five years—turn Aretha Franklin into a superstar. "I Never Loved" became the first million-seller record of her career.

Cecil thought that the success of the first single helped heal Ted and Aretha's marriage. "After all, it was Ted's writer, Ronnie Shannon, who wrote the song, and it was Ted who brought the song to Aretha. That was the song that blew open the door. Aretha was always cognizant of that fact. It made her think that maybe, despite everything, she needed Ted to get where she was going. But that was just the beginning. That first single—'I Never Loved' and 'Do Right'—was nothing compared to the next one with 'Respect' and 'Dr. Feelgood.' The second single put her into orbit. Things went crazy after those songs hit. Everyone in the world wanted her, and she required help."

"Atlantic was very different than Motown," said Wexler, "where the record company also managed and booked their acts. We were careful to make sure our artists had outside management, outside advisers, and outside booking agents. Aretha was not an especially trustful person—and with good reason—and it was important for her to have her own counsel. I saw that her relationship with White was rough, to say the least, and I could have tried to influence her to leave him. I could have persuaded her to hire management more sympathetic to Atlantic, but I knew that'd be a mistake. I had to separate church and state. The producer/record exec is one animal. The manager/agent is quite another. Plus, her manager/agent was also her husband."

According to Aretha's siblings, White was not only a savvy manager, but someone who recognized her talents as a composer.

"For all you might say about Ted," said Cecil, "it was Ted who got Aretha to write. That was partly because he had a thriving song-publishing concern and wanted to build up his inventory of copyrights, but it was also because he saw that her talent as a writer rivaled her talent as a singer."

In 1990, discussing Aretha's first Atlantic album, Luther Vandross commented first on her writing, not her singing. "I'm not saying that the lady didn't sing her behind off," Luther explained. "She did. She turned it out, but what impressed me even more was that she wrote or cowrote the four best songs on the record—'Don't Let Me Lose This Dream,' 'Baby, Baby, Baby,' 'Dr. Feelgood,' and 'Save Me.' As much as I adore Diana Ross and Dionne Warwick, the same can't be said of them. Beautiful singers, but hardly writers.

"When I produced Aretha in the eighties, the first thing I told her was how much I loved 'Don't Let Me Lose This Dream.' It had this bossa nova–ish silky groove that was pure heaven. I asked her where the song came from. She said she'd been listening to Astrud Gilberto, the girl who sang with Stan Getz, and she wanted to write something with the feeling of Latin soul. You go from there to 'Dr. Feelgood,' which is basically nothing more than a twelve-bar blues. But the lyrics! And her piano playing! It's like something my mama's mama listened to—one of those original ladies, like Bessie Smith or Ma Rainey. I believe it's one of the greatest blues ever written. Same is true of 'Baby, Baby, Baby' that she wrote with her sister Carolyn, another major talent. It's another brilliant blues variation with a line that I wish I had written myself—'I'm bewildered, I'm lonely, and I'm loveless.'"

Aretha wrote about composing "Save Me" with King Curtis. She called him a gentleman because, even though she described the musical contribution by her and Carolyn as minor, King gave them full credit as collaborators. She also sang King's blistering "Soul Serenade," another testimony to the great horn man's pivotal role in helping Aretha become Aretha.

The centerpiece of the first Aretha album is, of course, her cover of Otis Redding's "Respect." Wexler told me that he personally played her version for Otis. "He broke out into this wide smile," Wexler remembered, "and said, 'The girl has taken that song from me. Ain't no longer my song. From now on, it belongs to her.' And then he asked me [to] play it again, and then a third time. The smile never left his face.

"If you listen to Otis's original and then Aretha's cover, the first thing you notice is that her groove is more dramatic. That stop-and-stutter syncopation was something she invented. She showed the rhythm section I had shipped up from Alabama—Jimmy Johnson, Tommy Cogbill, and Roger Hawkins—how to do it. I knew she'd been intrigued with the song for a couple of years and had tried it out onstage. She had already come up with this new beat. But the creation of the background vocals and ingenious wordplay was done on the spot in the studio. The backgrounds were more than wonderful aural augmentations. They gave the song a strong sexual flavor. The call for respect went from a request to a demand. And then, given the civil rights and feminist fervor that was building in the sixties, respect—especially as Aretha articulated it with such force—took on new meaning. 'Respect' started off as a soul song and wound up as a kind of national anthem. It virtually defined American culture at that moment in history."

"The sock-it-to-me line helped shape the song for sure," said Carolyn. "I had heard the expression on the streets and thought it might work in a call-and-response call with 'Respect.' Obviously, Otis wrote the song from a man's point of view, but when Erma and Aretha and I worked it over, we had to rearrange the perspective. We saw it as something earthier, a woman having no problem discussing her needs. It turned out that it was interpreted in many different ways—having to do with sexual or racial politics. Far as I'm concerned, all those interpretations are correct because everyone needs respect on every level."

The sock-it-to-me line gained further fame as a running gag on *Laugh-In*, the television comedy show that hit the airwaves the following year. Even Richard Nixon had a cameo in which he weirdly demanded, "Sock it to me."

Spelling out the title—"R-E-S-P-E-C-T"—and juxtaposing it with the demands "Find out what it means to me" and "take care of TCB" were additional lyrical augmentations. "TCB" echoed Aretha's own lyrics from "Dr. Feelgood," in which she proclaimed that "taking care of business is really this man's game." In the fade of the song, she also referred to her recent past by singing, "I get tired, keep on trying, runnin' out of fools and I ain't lying." "Runnin' Out of Fools" was her biggest R&B single on Columbia. By calling out its title, she honored the soul-music tradition of self-referencing previous successes. She also sealed the deal on personalizing the song so that, in its composer's own words, "it belongs to her."

"I also heard 'Respect' as part of her ongoing fight with Ted," said Cecil. "He might have respected her talent, but he didn't respect her as a human being. He was a violent cat whose violence only got worse. I felt like Aretha was singing 'Respect' to Ted, but it hardly made any difference. He kept slapping her around and didn't care who saw him do it."

In April, in the first cover story on Aretha in a national magazine, *Jet* quoted White about his wife's success: "We are getting calls from all over the country for her appearances...the European scene is throbbing for her. We have had to cancel a scheduled May European tour until fall because we can't fit it into the present schedule." He went on to say that he expected his wife to jump from making a hundred thousand in 1966 to a quarter million in 1967.

"Respect" hit the pop charts on April 29, 1967, a day after Muhammad Ali was stripped of his heavyweight-champion title for refusing to be drafted into the United States Army. It would go to number one on both the R&B and pop charts and become the song that would both define and forever change Aretha's career. As a result of it, a few months later at the start of her show at Chicago's Regal Theater, she would be crowned Queen of Soul by DJ Pervis "the Blues Man" Spann. Aretha took the ceremony seriously, noting the beauty of the "bejeweled crown" placed on her head, where it would remain, metaphorically, for the next five decades.

There was Bessie, there was Dinah, and now there was Aretha.

Her dream was coming true — the fairy-tale dream of a little girl whose father had promised her the moon. The dream, though, was rooted in a storybook sensibility where everyone lives happily ever after. Aretha bought into that fairy tale as a child and clung to that fairy tale despite harsh reality. In 1967, the year of her dazzling breakthrough, she was in the throes of emotional chaos. Even though it was her husband/manager who was controlling a career that, in a matter of a few months, had taken off like a rocket, her marriage had officially become a misery.

13. KEEP ROLLING

The blues is a motherfucker," said Carmen McRae, "and not everyone can sing 'em. It's more than chops. You have to live 'em. If you ask me, Billie Holiday's greatest album was *Lady in Satin,* done just before she died. Her voice was rough around the edges, but her blues were deepest. In Aretha's case, her greatest album is that first one on Atlantic, when her voice was the strongest, but, from what I heard, her blues was also the deepest."

"America had the blues," said Jerry Wexler, "and Aretha's blues reflected that. Antigovernment feeling was fermenting. The civil rights movement was fermenting. The bullshit Vietnam War was building. But this was a different kind of blues. It was blues with an attitude—a black attitude. In the first part of the sixties, Motown reflected less militant middle-class desires. Motown was beautiful, but Motown, at least in its early configurations, was mild. Aretha was anything but mild. Her voice carried the assertiveness of a new class of not only blacks no longer content to get-along-and-go-along but also young whites whose discontent with the status quo was deep. The seeds of the soul revolution had been planted by artists like Ray Charles and Solomon Burke and Sam and Dave. But it didn't come to full fruition until Aretha. Aretha's 'Respect' happened in 1967. James Brown's 'Say It Loud (I'm Black and I'm Proud),' great as it was, didn't come along till 1968."

"Funny," Ray Charles told me, "but the first Aretha song I remember loving wasn't 'Respect' or any of those first hits, but Sam Cooke's 'Change Is Gonna Come.' I thought that was the one that explained who she was and how she was changing up the shit. When I heard that, I realized Aretha was my one and only true soul sista."

She also proved to be a devoted sister: she took time from her hectic schedule to attend the wedding of her brother Cecil to his bride, Earline, on April 30 at the New Bethel Baptist Church with Reverend C. L. Franklin presiding. Two thousand people were in attendance.

"Aretha could not have been sweeter," Earline told me. "She even helped design my dress. At the beginning, my sister-in-law gave me every indication that I'd be a welcome member of her family. She was loving and supportive, at least for the first two or three years. But as her personal life began to unravel, so did our relationship. As much as she loved and came to depend upon Cecil, that's as much as she'd come to resent and distance herself from me."

In the spring of 1967, Aretha was moving at a frenetic pace. The demand for her concerts shot up overnight. Her performance fees quadrupled.

"Ted was eager to make money," said Cecil. "His attitude was that he'd been hanging tough, waiting for this very moment—and he wasn't about to be denied. So, using Ruth Bowen, he was booking her everywhere he could. It was especially crazy because both Ted and Aretha were drinking more than usual. Neither of them did well when they were high on liquor. It brought out the worst in them."

"I had booked Erma and Carolyn before Aretha came to me to officially ask me to become her agent," said Ruth Bowen. "The timing was perfect. I was there for the birth of a star and happy to help her and Ted. I liked Ted. He was smart, well spoken, and hardworking. He agreed with Aretha that I was the right agent to figure out how to maximize her earnings. I could book her into bigger and more prestigious venues. The days of the Village Vanguard and Village Gate were over.

"One of the first big gigs I got her was at a nightclub Gene Chandler was opening in Chicago. I went out there to make sure everything went like clockwork. It didn't. Aretha came out looking grand, but when she sat down, the piano stool collapsed. She landed on her rear. But being the complete professional, she made a joke of it, got back up, and played standing up until a sturdier stool was brought. I wanted to kill Gene. This was my first date for my new client and he couldn't even provide a decent seat! I was sure she'd never work with me again. But I have to say that she was very understanding. She went on to give a stirring performance and thanked me for what was a big payday.

"What I didn't realize when I started working with Aretha, though, was that she was not only a heavy smoker but a heavy drinker. She had a habit of getting loaded before a performance. In no way did that help her singing. When it comes to singing, Aretha needs no help of any kind. Everyone knows that she possesses natural genius. But she'd been using booze to numb the pain of her lousy marriage. It had become a crutch. That's the word I used—a *crutch*—when I mentioned the problem. From day one I was honest with her. I also told her that she wasn't doing herself any favors by smoking like a chimney—she was up to three packs a day. She said that smoking and drinking calmed her nerves. I said that was bull. Liquor didn't calm her nerves at all. Liquor was just making her sloppy. I told her that in plain English. She didn't like hearing it. Well, that was tough because I had raised her rate from about seven hundred fifty dollars a performance to five thousand and, before long, ten thousand.

"Now, I wasn't in Columbus, Georgia, for the next incident. That's when she fell off the stage and broke her arm. She said it was because the stage lights had blinded her. Maybe so. Her assistant told me it was because she was tipsy. Whatever it was, I hoped she had learned her lesson. Unfortunately, she hadn't."

The May 18, 1967, edition of *Jet* has a photo of Aretha at the Ford Hospital in Detroit, her arm in a cast. The story states that the break required surgery.

By June 20, she was back in the Atlantic studios.

"That first album put us on a roll," said Wexler. "Everything in me said, *Keep rolling, keep recording, keep the hits coming.* She was red hot and I had no reason to believe that the streak wouldn't continue. I knew that it would be foolish—and even irresponsible—not to strike when the iron was hot. I also had personal motivation. A Wall Street financier had agreed to see what we could get for Atlantic Records. While Ahmet and Nesuhi had not agreed on a selling price, they had gone along with my plan to let the financier test our worth on the open market. I was always eager to pump out hits, but at this moment I was on overdrive. In this instance, I had a good partner in Ted White, who felt the same. He wanted as much product out there as possible.

"The news that Aretha had been injured in concert was alarming, but Ted reassured me that she'd soon be back in the studio. She didn't show up for the first few dates. That turned out to be standard operating procedure for Aretha. I didn't ask why. She wasn't the first emotionally fragile artist I'd worked with and she wouldn't be the last. I saw my job as making her as comfortable as possible. I knew that once she did show up, it'd be more than worth the wait.

"Turned out the reason she was a no-show, though, didn't have to do with her injury. She wouldn't tell me directly—direct address is not Aretha's style—but I finally got it out of Ted. Aretha was pissed at me over the fact that her sister Erma had gotten a deal. She thought I had set it up. Nothing could be further from the truth."

Erma told me the backstory. "I was still living in New York," she said, "and no longer singing with Lloyd Price. After five years I hadn't gotten a single raise and decided I had had enough. I was grateful for the music I'd made for Epic, but the songs, as good as they were, never charted. I found work at IBM and was quite content. It wasn't that I had given up singing — singing would always be my passion — but practicality required that I go to work. I was also happy to help Aretha on those first sessions. Then came 'Respect.' Well, that opened the floodgates. Aretha had given the Franklin name a new shine. I got several calls from producers. The most interesting was from Bert Berns, who said he had once been partners with Jerry Wexler and Ahmet Ertegun. He said he had his own label, Shout, and that he had written 'Twist and Shout,' a hit for the Isley Brothers and the Beatles. Now he had written another song he thought would be even bigger. He and a gentleman named Jerry Ragovoy had composed 'Piece of My Heart' and did I want to hear it? I did. I liked it, although I thought the calypso beat was wrong for my style. At the recording session, they let me change it into a soul groove. Everyone thought the result was great, including me. Bert was so excited he immediately signed me to an album deal. We got almost immediate airplay. I was thrilled when it went into the top ten on the R-and-B chart. I'm not sure how Aretha felt about that."

"I pleaded with Ted to tell Aretha the truth about me and Bert Berns," said Wexler. "Bert and I had suffered a bad falling-out, even though I had enormous respect for him. After all, he was the guy who brought over guitarist Jimmy Page from England to play on our sessions. Bert, Ahmet, Nesuhi, and I had started a label together — Bang! — where Bert produced Van Morrison's first album. But Bert also had a penchant for trouble. He courted the wise guys. He wanted total control over every last aspect of our business dealings. Finally it was too much, and the Erteguns and I let him go. He sued us for breach of contract and suddenly we were enemies. I felt that he signed Erma, an excellent singer, not merely for her talent but as a way to get back at me. If I could make a hit with Aretha, he'd show me up by making an even bigger hit on Erma. Because there was always an undercurrent of rivalry between the sisters, this only added to the tension."

Aretha saw history repeating itself. She still believed that John

Hammond had gone behind her back to sign Erma at Columbia. Now Wexler was doing the same, using Bert Berns as his proxy.

"I don't know if Ted White was able to set her straight on the story," said Wexler, "but she finally did show. There was a chill in the air. Even though we were 'Jerry' and 'Aretha' after the first album, she reverted to calling me 'Mr. Wexler,' and I had to go back to calling her 'Miss Franklin.' She was also still having mobility problems with her elbow. Yet when she sat down at the piano, she elbowed her way into the deepest grooves imaginable. I remember thinking, *Man, when Aretha arrives, all superfluous problems disappear.* That's when I knew we had to call this second album *Aretha Arrives*."

On four of the songs on that album, Aretha employed her sisters, Erma and Carolyn, on background vocals. They can be heard most effectively on the album's big hit, "Baby, I Love You," by Ronnie Shannon, the writer of "I Never Loved a Man."

"But sometime while we were making that record, Aretha's mood turned," said Carolyn. "She didn't like the idea of Erma working with Bert Berns and me going out on my own. That's when she took up Jerry Wexler's decision to use the Sweet Inspirations."

Cissy Houston, head Inspiration, had already sung on two of the songs on *I Never Loved a Man*. She and Aretha shared a church background. The other Inspirations—Estelle Brown, Sylvia Shemwell, and Myrna Smith—were equally adept at creating close harmonies in the gritty gospel mode. Wexler called them "one of the pillars of the Atlantic Church of Sixties Soul." They proved solid replacements for Aretha's sisters and in the future would become a semipermanent part of Aretha's studio sound.

Key players from Muscle Shoals—Spooner Oldham, Tommy Cogbill, and Roger Hawkins—were brought back in. From Atlanta, Wexler also recruited Joe South, the great guitarist/composer.

"When I saw Aretha in that studio in New York City," South told me, "I was awestruck. I'd heard the first record she'd done and considered her a goddamn saint. I'd written 'Hush' that became a hit for Deep Purple but I hadn't yet written 'Games People Play' and I wasn't all that confident. I'd always felt that soul music was my heart, but hell, this was the big time. Besides, I was white and I was about to play behind the blackest genius since Ray Charles. 'It ain't about color,' said Wex. 'Aretha's color-blind. She's already gotten a taste of how funky those Muscle Shoals boys can be. She'll love you.' Well, Wex was right. She did. I remember standing there while she was singing that old blues 'Going Down Slow,' the one that had been done by everyone from Guitar Slim to B.B. King. I mean, she was wailing in a way where I had goose bumps. She nodded at me to play a couple of licks. I gave it all I had and suddenly she smiled. The woman smiled! Brother, that smile has carried me through life. That smile was the only validation I needed to let me know that I belonged in the same room as her. Aretha Franklin smiled!"

Wexler invited critic Nat Hentoff to the sessions. In his liner notes Hentoff wrote, "She still didn't have complete mobility with her elbow but nonetheless, in several of the slow numbers, she provided bedrock accompaniment on the piano. For the faster numbers, she couldn't play with her right hand, but on 'You Are My Sunshine,' undaunted, she used only her left, and the resultant rhythmic drive is a witness to the extent of spirit within her."

When I spoke with Hentoff some thirty years after the session, his memory of it was still vivid. "You have to put it in context," he said. "This was the late sixties, when free jazz was dominating the New York scene. I was hungry for something more accessible. I was eager for sound that reaffirmed the roots of the music I loved best. I saw Aretha as the living embodiment of that reaffirmation. Like most jazz critics, I had a prejudice against pop songs and pop sensibilities. But Aretha broke down that prejudice. Her songs had great pop appeal. In fact, she became one of the dominant pop artists of our time. But in doing so, she never compromised an iota of her authenticity as an artist schooled in the deepest and most creative tradition of blues, gospel, and jazz."

At the same session, she covered "It Was You," a James Brown song from the late fifties. "Aretha wanted to release it as the first single," said Wexler. "She sang it beautifully but I thought the chart was a little stiff. So we held it back, along with a strong Van McCoy song, 'So Soon.' Listening to it years later, I can't believe it was not released back then. But there was so much great Aretha product and she was cutting it so fast and furiously that, at any given moment, we really had more than we could use. For years to come we'd put out two Aretha albums a year but had enough material to put out even more. Sales-wise, we were doing fabulously."

"Atlantic Smashes Own Sales Records," *Billboard* reported. "The Atlantic-Atco combine's gross volume for the first three months of this year was up almost 100 percent over the similar period in 1966."

Time magazine also ran an article about Atlantic's hot streak. In Wexler's mind, more than ever, it was time to sell. He convinced the Ertegun brothers to accept $17.5 million from Warner Brothers–Seven Arts.

"A poor boy from Washington Heights," said Wexler, "I was suddenly a millionaire, the first in my old neighborhood. I was thrilled. But I was also foolish. I was convinced that, due to Aretha, Atlantic Records had reached the height of our success. I was ridiculously wrong. As years went on, the industry looked at our deal as a joke. Had we waited a few years, we could have gotten ten times as much. At the time, I saw the sale as a triumph. Later I saw it as a disaster."

The other disaster came on the final day of the sessions for *Aretha Arrives*—Sunday, July 23—when the Twelfth Street riot broke out in Detroit.

"I've never been so frightened in my life," said Earline. "Cecil had gone to New York because Ree was fighting so bad with Ted. Carolyn and Erma were also out of town. I was home alone and as soon as I saw the burning and looting I called Cecil, who told me to go to Reverend's. I figured that would be the safest place. When I got there the phone was ringing off the wall—Erma and Carolyn and Aretha calling to make sure their daddy was safe. Their daddy was everything in life to them. Reverend was cool. Reverend was always cool. Nothing bothered him. I think he felt like he had special protection from God. I was hoping I could borrow some of his protection. That day it felt like the end of the world."

"I was shocked but I wasn't shocked," said Cecil. "It was started by a police raid, but it was so much more than that. Police brutality had plagued the city for decades. Civil unrest was everywhere. My father had been working for years to find solutions to uncaring city policy that ignored our people's basic rights. It didn't take much of a spark to ignite the fire. The police raided a club and that was it. My first thought, of course, was for Daddy and Earline. When I learned they were okay, I attended to Aretha, who, due to the friction with Ted, wasn't in good shape. She'd been drinking, and the news freaked her out. She started talking about hiring private detectives to go in the city and rescue Daddy. I told her that Daddy was fine, that no one was more respected by his own people than Reverend. I spoke to several of the deacons at New Bethel and they made sure that his house was being protected. But Aretha was inconsolable. She was sure something terrible would happen to Daddy. That thought had her beside herself."

Aretha had been worried about her father for other reasons. In 1966, he had been indicted on four counts of tax evasion. The government claimed that he failed to report over $75,000 in income in the years 1959 through 1962. Both he—and later his daughter—would claim that a disgruntled congregant had undermined him by going to the IRS. C.L. actually wrote President Lyndon Johnson, arguing that he didn't realize that cash gifts from his congregation were considered income. The president didn't respond. In 1967, Franklin pleaded no contest; he was fined $2,500 and put on probation.

"He told all of us," said Cecil, "that he was convinced that it was his role as a civil rights leader and fellow traveler with Dr. King that got the IRS on his back.

"We made it back to Detroit when the riots were over, and the city looked like a war zone. Over forty people had been killed, nearly two thousand injured, something like seven thousand arrests. They were calling it one of the worst riots in American history. Governor Romney had called in the National Guard, and then President Johnson called up the Eighty-Second Airborne. Detroit had gone absolutely crazy. Aretha begged Daddy to move out of the city entirely. She wanted him to find another congregation in California, where he was especially popular—or at least move out to the suburbs. But he wouldn't budge. He said that, more than ever, he was needed to point out the root causes of the riots—the economic inequality, the pervasive racism in civic institutions, the woefully inadequate schools in inner-city Detroit, and the whole-sale destruction of our neighborhoods by urban renewal. Some ministers fled the city, but not our father. The horror of what happened only recommitted him. He would not abandon his political agenda. I remember someone saying, 'Reverend, aren't you afraid to stay?' He liked that question because it gave him a chance to quote the scripture that says, 'A perfect love casts out all fear.' Daddy had very little fear."

By summer's end, "Baby, I Love You" was certified gold, Aretha's third million-seller single, while she was performing for Dr. King at the annual banquet of the Southern Christian Leadership Conference in Atlanta. King asked if she would join other artists—including Joan Baez, Sammy Davis Jr., Harry Belafonte, and Sidney Poitier—in appearing at a half a dozen benefit concerts for his organization in October. Aretha readily agreed. From Atlanta, she flew to California, where, according to her booking agent Ruth Bowen, she grossed a combined $100,000 for concerts in San Diego, Long Beach, and Oakland.

"I was worried about her," said Ruth, "because of all the drinking. I think the excitement of so much success happening so suddenly—together with the anxiety caused by the riots—got to her. I spoke to Ted White about it, but his drinking was worse than hers. For a while she separated herself from him—but then she went back because she was afraid her career would collapse without him. Cecil and I talked a lot. I said, 'Listen, at some point she's gonna decide she can't take anymore and when that happens you're gonna have to step in.' 'That'll be my father's role,' Cecil said. 'He managed her before and he'll manage her again.' 'Don't be ridiculous,' I told Cecil. 'A famous minister like him has neither the time nor the knowledge to manage a superstar like Aretha.' 'Well, I don't have the knowledge either,' said Cecil. 'I do,' I told him, 'and I'll teach you everything you need to know.'"

The marital discord, though, was not something Aretha discussed.

"Everyone knew it," said sister-in-law Earline, "everyone knew that Ted White was a brutal man. But Aretha...well, she's always clung to this fairy-tale story line. She wanted the world to think she had a storybook marriage. She hates to admit being wrong—that she'd chosen the wrong man to share her life and manage her career. Rather than admit that, she'll go on living with the mistake longer than she needs to. Which is actually what happened with her and White. It took her at least two years longer to get rid of him than it should have. His sorry ass should have been out of there a long time ago. But she was having all those hits and making all that money. She was scared of rocking the boat, until one day the boat capsized and she nearly drowned."

14. NATURAL

The pace was frenetic. As Aretha entered her midtwenties, she was trapped by a manager/husband who, along with her producer Jerry Wexler, successfully engineered a career that was moving at lightning speed. Just as Wexler wanted her to quickly record as many songs as possible, Ted White wanted her to headline all the major venues eager to book her. Ambitious since childhood, Aretha wanted to respond to these demands—and she did, but at a cost.

"Sometimes she'd call me at night," said Wexler, "and, in that barely audible little-girl voice of hers, she'd tell me that she wasn't sure she could go on. She always spoke in generalities. She never mentioned her husband, never gave me specifics of who was doing what to whom. And of course I knew better than to ask. She just said that she was tired of dealing with so much. My heart went out to her. She was a woman who suffered silently. She held so much in. I'd tell her to take as much time off as she needed. We had a lot of songs in the can that we could release without new material. 'Oh, no, Jerry,' she'd say. 'I can't stop recording. I've written some new songs, Carolyn's written some new songs. We gotta get in there and cut 'em.' 'Are you sure?' I'd ask. 'Positive,' she'd say. I'd set up the dates and typically she wouldn't show up for the first or second sessions. Carolyn or Erma would call me to say, 'Ree's under the weather.' That was tough because we'd have asked people like Joe South and Bobby Womack to play on the sessions. Then I'd reschedule in the hopes she'd show. Any way you look at it, the work she did during 1967, her first year at Atlantic, will go down in the history books as some of the strongest rhythm and blues that the soul nation has ever produced."

The album titled *Lady Soul,* recorded in '67 and released in early '68, is notable for four smashes—"Chain of Fools," "A Natural Woman," "Since You've Been Gone," and "Ain't No Way."

Before the final sessions began in December 1967, Aretha rode in the Macy's Thanksgiving Day parade.

A week later, *Jet* ran a picture of Aretha "taking a call from a fan" while the "injury-prone" star was attended by a nurse in Detroit's Daly Hospital. The result of an "eye injury suffered in a fall" was a series of canceled dates.

"She showed up at our sessions looking like she had literally taken a beating," said Wexler. "But I didn't ask any questions. I gave her a big hug and told her we were overjoyed to see her. Look, when Aretha showed up, whether two hours or two weeks later, it didn't matter. We knew that she was ready to do some serious singing.

"Besides, whatever agony she was going through, there was another downer that none of us could ignore. Only a few days before Aretha showed up in New York, Otis Redding, along with members of the Bar-Kays, had been killed in a plane wreck in Wisconsin. That happened on December tenth, 1967, when my wife, Shirley, and I were returning from a music-business conference where I had been awarded music exec of the year for the third straight time. My ego was flying high. But the tragic news put my soaring ego in place. I was destroyed. Otis was only twenty-six. I was asked to give the eulogy at the memorial in Macon. Aretha had already begun the sessions and I asked her if she wanted to join me. She said it would simply be too devastating. So we closed down the studio for a day when I flew off to Georgia. It was an amazing service. Joe Simon sang 'Jesus Keep Me Near the Cross.' Johnnie Taylor sang 'I'll Be Standing By.' Everyone was in tears—James Brown, Wilson Pickett, Isaac Hayes, Joe Tex, Arthur Conley, Solomon Burke, Don Covay—the complete soul royalty. I said, 'Otis's "Respect" had become an anthem of hope for people everywhere. Respect is something that Otis achieved. Otis sang, "Respect when I come home." And Otis has come home.' I only wished that Aretha had been there to sing that song.

"I was back in the studio the next day. Aretha wanted to hear all about the service and I spared her no detail. Tears fell from her eyes as I described the memorial. Aretha needed no extra motivation to sing her heart out. She did that no matter what. But if many of the vocals on *Lady Soul* seem to have an even greater depth, I believe it's because Otis was on Aretha's mind."

"I think *Lady Soul* contains Ree's best singing," said Carolyn. "I look at it as her greatest album—and not just because she sang my 'Ain't No Way.' I love it for the two tunes that Ree wrote, 'Since You've Been Gone' and 'Good to Me As I Am to You.' Erma and I sang on them both. Aretha liked to call me the writer in the family, but just as she had the big talent as a singer, she had that same big talent as a composer. The difference is that she pursued the singing with all she had but slacked off on the writing."

The two landmark songs from *Lady Soul* were not written by Aretha. "Chain of Fools" was composed by Don Covay, and "A Natural Woman" was the creation of Carole King and Gerry Goffin. (Wexler suggested the title and, in appreciation, King and Goffin credited him as a cowriter.)

Arif Mardin, the Turkish-American cohort of the Ertegun brothers who became a staff arranger and eventually a major producer at Atlantic, worked with Wexler and Tom Dowd on Aretha's early albums.

"I was listed as the arranger of 'Chain of Fools,' but I can't take credit," Arif told me. "Aretha walked into the studio with the chart fully formed inside her head. The arrangement is based around the harmony vocals provided by Carolyn and Erma. To add heft, the Sweet Inspirations joined in. The vision of the song is entirely Aretha's."

"We augmented Aretha's vision to some degree," said Wexler. "Joe South did a Pops Staples number on guitar by tuning his guitar down and boosting the tremolo. That created a signature intro that set off the fireworks. When we were through, I was so excited that I played the pre-mastered version for everyone I knew, including the great songwriter Ellie Greenwich. 'Aren't the backgrounds fabulous?' I asked. 'They are,' she said, 'but I hear another vocal part.' 'Impossible,' I said. 'Want to hear it, Jerry?' I did. Ellie sang it and, just like that, I whisked her into the studio, where she recorded it, making the super-thick harmonies that much thicker."

"Aretha didn't write 'Chain,'" said Carolyn, "but she might as well have. It was her story. When we were in the studio putting on the backgrounds with Ree doing lead, I knew she was singing about Ted. Listen to the lyrics talking about how for five long years she thought he was her man. Then she found out she was nothing but a link in the chain. Then she sings that her father told her to come on home. Well, he did. She sings about how her doctor said to take it easy. Well, he did too. She was drinking so much we thought she was on the verge of a breakdown. The line that slew me, though, was the one that said how one of these mornings the chain is gonna break but until then she'll take all she can take. That summed it up. Ree knew damn well that this man had been doggin' her since Jump Street. But somehow she held on and pushed it to the breaking point. I can't listen to that song without thinking about the tipping point in her long ugly thing with Ted."

If "Chain of Fools" defined Aretha's relationship to an abusive man, "Natural Woman" pointed to her inner strength, the elusive element in her character that Wexler recognized as essential to her emotional survival. King and Goffin placed the natural woman in a romantic context. It is a man who is "the key to her peace of mind." Aretha, however, took it to church. She told interviewers that she heard the song as a prayer. She was praising and singing to the Lord. When her soul was in the lost and found, it wasn't a man who claimed it, it was God.

"The song did have a hymn-like quality to it," Arif Mardin explained, "which was why we employed a more traditional written arrangement. Spooner Oldham played that very soulful introduction on acoustic piano. It was Aretha, though, who showed him exactly what she wanted him to play. She loved the song to the point where she said she wanted to concentrate on the vocal and vocal alone. I had written a string chart and horn chart to augment the chorus and hired Ralph Burns to conduct. After just a couple of takes, we had it. That's when Ralph turned to me with wonder in his eyes. Ralph was one of the most celebrated arrangers of the modern era. He had done 'Early Autumn' for Woody Herman and Stan Getz, and 'Georgia on My Mind' for Ray Charles. He'd worked with everyone. 'This woman comes from another planet' was all Ralph said. 'She's just here visiting.'"

Eric Clapton dropped by the session, brought to the studio by his mentor, Ahmet Ertegun. Clapton was at the Atlantic studios recording *Disraeli Gears,* the Cream album that included "Sunshine of Your Love." Coincidentally, on his record, Clapton was using Tom Dowd, Aretha's engineer.

"Eric came by when Aretha was laying down the vocal to 'Good to Me As I Am to You,'" said Wexler. "It was a blistering blues ballad, one of those songs with a strong autobiographical strain—Aretha sending a message to her man, or, for that matter, all men: Treat me right or get out. Later, when the copyright papers were turned in, I saw Ted White's name as a cowriter but Aretha said that was just for legal reasons. She assured me that she wrote the song all by her lonesome. Anyway, she was blowing the roof off the studio, singing the holy shit out of this song, when Ahmet heard a spot for some guitar licks. He encouraged Eric to take a stab. I was for it. But Eric, great as he was, was spooked at the idea of playing behind the mighty Aretha. He flubbed. Much to his credit, though, he came by the next day and, with Aretha no longer in the studio, played the part perfectly. His riffs were tasteful and right on time. Eric wasn't the first and wouldn't be the last musician to be intimidated by the Queen.

"Even though Felix Cavaliere and Eddie Brigati loved the way Aretha covered their 'Groovin',' I think they had some doubts later when her version got more praise than theirs. Earlier, Ahmet and I had signed the Rascals to Atlantic through their manager, Sid Bernstein, the man who brought the Beatles to America. I remember Sid asking me, 'Did she have to sing it so goddamn good? Now she's got fans thinking that the Rascals' hit — the fuckin' original — was a cover of her version.'"

"I love all of *Lady Soul,*" said Erma, "but the song that moved me most was 'People Get Ready.' Everyone in the Franklin family had nothing but respect for Curtis Mayfield, who wrote and had recorded the song. We called him the Gentle Giant and saw him as a modern-day Duke Ellington. He was touched with deep, divine genius. Ree felt the divinity in his music and if you listen to the fade of the song, you hear her break into prayer. Those are her words, not Curtis's, when she says, 'I thank you because I'm living,' before saying, 'I thank you today because I need a new beginning.' That's the perfect definition of where she was at. Our father taught us gratitude. She was grateful for all the wonderful things that were happening to her. But she was also in the midst of realizing that she couldn't go on this way for much longer. She needed a new beginning."

Despite that realization, Aretha saw the end of 1967 — the biggest year of her career — with Ted White still by her side.

"She was afraid to let him go," said Carolyn. "Fear had a hold on her."

"Her career was kicking into high gear," Wexler explained. "Contending and resolving both the professional and personal challenges were too much. She didn't think she could do both, and I didn't blame her. Few people could. So she let the personal slide and concentrated on the professional. Professionally, her career was rocketing into the stratosphere. With *Lady Soul,* she was easily the most beloved artist in the country.

"At the same time, she gave a large piece of her life over to the civil rights cause. She jumped into the political fray at this exact moment when everything was breaking loose. She could have easily excused herself from the political rallies and benefits that she headlined, but she didn't. When Dr. King called for her services, she was always there—in Chicago, in Atlanta, it didn't matter where. She was his staunch supporter."

"At the end of 1967," remembered Ruth Bowen, "I fully expected Aretha to have a breakdown. I don't say this disparagingly. Given her position, most people would break down. She was locked into a nasty marriage that she wasn't ready to end because she was afraid that if she left her husband/manager, he'd ruin her career. Also Aretha hates bad publicity and she thought negative press would also ruin her career. Her father and Dr. King were putting pressure on her to sing everywhere, and she felt obligated. The record company was also screaming for more product. And I had a mountain of offers on my desk that kept getting higher with every passing hour. They wanted her in Europe. They wanted her in Latin America. They wanted her in every major venue in the U.S. TV was calling. She was being asked to do guest appearances on every show from Carol Burnett to Andy Williams to the *Hollywood Palace*. She wanted to do them all and she wanted to do none of them. She wanted to do them all because she's an entertainer who burns with ambition. She wanted to do none of them because she was emotionally drained. She needed to go away and renew her strength. I told her that at least a dozen times. She said she would, but she didn't listen to me. I don't blame her. Entertainers are looking for glory, and at the end of 1967, Aretha was being offered more glory than at any time in her life. In 1968 that glory was magnified tenfold. But then again, so was the heartbreak that has haunted her ever since she was a child."

Heartbreak or not, she appeared on prime-time network TV when the *Kraft Music Hall* aired on December 27. Other performers included twenty-one-year-old Liza Minnelli and thirty-two-year-old Woody Allen.

In this same period, she appeared on Mike Douglas's TV show and, seated at the piano, sang a duet with Frankie Valli—a cover of Frank Sinatra's "That's Life." Valli, the superb lead singer of the Four Seasons and acolyte of the great Little Jimmy Scott, was practically blown off his stool. Aretha's power overwhelmed him.

In the December 28, 1967, year-end edition of *Jet,* this item ran in Charles Higgins's People Are Talking About column:

"Aretha Franklin tells chums she doesn't need a house because she recently purchased a four-bedroom beauty (estimated cost: $60,000) on Detroit's exclusive Northwest Side...her husband, Ted White, just bought her a lovely white mini-mink coat. So, she asks, 'How about Santa bringing me just a little more love?'"

"The world was showering love on my sister," said Erma, "but that at-home love—the kind of love we need to get by—wasn't coming her way. As a singer, she was enjoying more success than ever before, but that doesn't mean she wasn't suffering."

15. YEAR OF YEARS

In 1968—the year of the Tet offensive, the rising revolts in the streets of America, the assassination of Martin Luther King Jr., the race riots, and the brutal Democratic Convention in Chicago—Aretha Franklin, at twenty-six, became the most admired recording artist in the country. And yet, according to her siblings, manager, producer, and booking agent, she had never been more miserable.

"Ree was at the crossroads," said Carolyn, "and didn't know which way to go. She sang a song by Ronnie Shannon, the same guy who wrote 'I Never Loved a Man,' that said, 'I just can't see myself leaving you.' But then she sang another song, one that she wrote. She called it 'Think.' Ted put his name on it, but Ted had nothing to do with it. I was there when Aretha wrote it, all by herself. She tells him to think what he's trying to do to her. She cries out for her freedom. She sang 'Think' as powerfully as anything she'd ever sung in her life."

"I'm sure 'Think' had personal meaning for Aretha," said Jerry Wexler. "But it also resonated on a large cultural level. Young people were telling the war establishment to think what they were doing. Black America was telling white America to think what they were doing. The song spoke to everyone, and, like 'Respect,' became another way in which Aretha became a spokesperson for her generation."

"Think," part of *Aretha Now,* her fourth Atlantic album, didn't come out until the spring of 1968.

In January of 1968, backed by the miniskirted Sweet Inspirations, she had torn apart "Chain of Fools" on the *Jonathan Winters Show.*

Billboard reported that in Inglewood, California, on January 23, "Aretha Franklin launched the new $16 million Forum's entry as a concert facility." The article went on to say that, improbable as it might seem, she had opened the show with "No Business Like Show Business," a throwback to her mainstream Columbia material.

"We had nothing to do with her concert presentations," said Wexler. "That was strictly her domain. She had off nights, of course, but on her on nights, Aretha was the consummate performer. In my view she was challenged by what I consider lapses in taste. This has not only to do with some of her more outlandish stage outfits, but the songs she chose. I remember that I once gently asked Aretha whether she just possibly might think that her Judy Garland/Al Jolson–style numbers might not work in the turbulent sixties. She looked at me like I was crazy. She didn't say these words, but her expression told me, *You worry about the records and I'll worry about my show.*"

The accolades kept coming.

The mayor of Detroit, James Cavanagh, came to her concert at the city's Cobo Hall on February 16 to hand her a proclamation declaring Aretha Franklin Day. Dr. King himself flew in for the occasion, citing her extraordinary service to his Southern Christian Leadership Conference.

King's appearance was a complete surprise to Aretha. It was the last time she saw him alive.

That same night, three trade magazines—*Record World, Bill-*

board, and *Cash Box*—each presented her with a plaque calling her the female vocalist of the year.

"This was the point at which I believe she took the queen thing seriously," said Erma. "But who could blame her? Awards were coming from organizations all over the world. The honors were making her dizzy."

"The honors made her sing even harder," said Cecil, who was there that night. "The honors took her to a new place in her artistry. Never in my life—not in church, not at any show or any concert—have I heard folks scream like they screamed that night at Cobo. When she sang 'Respect,' the crowd woke up the dead and the dead danced a dance of joy.

"Daddy, of course, was beaming with pride. After the concert, he met with Dr. King. I heard Dr. King discuss the situation in Memphis where two sanitation workers had been crushed to death by a faulty truck. The conditions under which those workers operated were appalling, and the union struck. Dr. King told my father that he needed his help in what was shaping up as the next great battle in the civil rights struggle. Daddy assured him he would do what he could, and, in fact, in March my father did travel to Memphis and lend his support."

Reverend Franklin was back in Detroit when, on April 4, Dr. King was assassinated on the balcony of the Lorraine Motel.

"My father called me with the news," said Cecil. "I'm not sure how he heard but the first thing he said was that he'd been trying to call Aretha and had not been able to get through. Aretha was in the midst of her worst period with Ted. On top of that, the crazy demands of her career were growing each day. She was planning to go on this monster European tour and had the world on her mind. Daddy worried about what the news would do to her. His phone was ringing off the wall and he asked me to try to reach her. When I did, she had already heard and was very shook. Because Aretha was Dr. King's favorite singer, I knew that Mrs. King would want her to sing at the funeral. I said, 'Ree, you've got a lot going on. If you're not up to it, don't worry about it.' 'No, Cecil,' she said, 'if I'm asked, I'll go. I have to.' And of course she did."

Aretha chartered a plane to attend the funeral in Atlanta. When I asked her about her singing at the service, she had no distinct memory of it. Furthermore, she did not recollect what song Mahalia Jackson had sung. The only detail she recalled was the fact that Gladys Knight and the Pips, unable to find a commercial flight, had asked if they could fly on her plane. She accommodated them and distinctly remembered that they never thanked her. She insisted that this moment of what she considered ingratitude be recorded in her autobiography.

"We all have mechanisms for dealing with unspeakable pain," said Cecil. "Aretha's way is to focus on some little thing that happened to offend her. That's her way of coping with the enormous hurt inside. After the funeral—with so much craziness going on in her life—I wondered if she was going to cancel a big-band jazz recording session Wexler had set up in New York and the European tour to follow. I figured it'd be too much. But off she went— her, Ted, and a whole entourage of tour managers and musicians."

Before the start of the sessions and the tour, she signed a new contract with Atlantic. Wexler turned it into a media event. *Billboard* reported, "Aretha Franklin and Atlantic Records have negotiated a new contract even though her original contract with the label had several years to run. At a luncheon at the Hotel St. Regis to celebrate the new deal and her departure on her first European concert tour, Jerry Wexler, Atlantic's executive vice-president, said that Miss Franklin will receive one of the largest guarantees ever given to any recording star but to reveal the sum would be in 'gross taste.'" Wexler continued to hype the deal in the media. He told *Jet* that the contract was "the greatest that any single recording artist has signed in the history of the recording business." The magazine went on to say, "He refused, however, to divulge the amount of hard cash involved, but added, 'it was upwards of a million dollars.'"

On two days in April, Aretha showed up at the Atlantic studios in New York to start what Wexler was calling her first real jazz album. His idea was simple—to emulate the famous *Genius of Ray Charles* album that Atlantic had recorded in 1959 in which Charles performed with a Count Basie–style big band using actual members of Basie's band.

"It was time to get out of the rut," Wexler explained. "Aretha was as much a jazz singer as anything else—gospel, R-and-B, or blues—and I wanted the world to know it. We already had enough unreleased inventory in the can where I knew I could always release a single. This time I wasn't looking for a single. I wanted her wailing in front of a big band."

"I was given the honor of writing the arrangements," said Arif Mardin, "and used Ernie Wilkins—to me, the greatest of Basie orchestrators—as my inspiration. By then, Tommy Dowd was a coproducer along with Jerry."

"Jerry let me handle many of the logistics," Tommy Dowd told me, "and, with me behind the board, we had a good shorthand. He made several song suggestions to Aretha, and so did I, but in the end she picked the songs she wanted to sing. She came in with songs by Smokey Robinson, Percy Mayfield, and Sam Cooke. She had fabulous taste. I was surprised that the first thing she wanted to do was 'Today I Sing the Blues' because she had done it on her first Columbia album. 'I didn't do it right, though,' she told me. 'I didn't do it justice.' Well, when Arif got through with his chart, justice was done."

David "Fathead" Newman, the great saxophonist and charter member of the Ray Charles band, played on both the *Genius of Ray Charles* and these jazz sessions with Aretha.

"I thought that Ray album was a once-in-a-lifetime experience, but Aretha made it a twice-in-a-lifetime thing," David explained. "Like Ray, she came in and took over. I know Wexler and Tommy were called the producers, but it was Aretha who ran the show. She knew where she wanted every note. If the third trumpet was out of tune, she said so. If the rhythm section hadn't found the pocket, she found it for them. All energy came from her, whether she was seated at the piano or standing in front of the mic.

She didn't need more than one or two takes. She made us play above our heads. Joe Newman, Ernie Royal, and Snooky Young—all Basie cats who were also on the Ray album—had backed up everyone from Jimmy Rushing to Joe Williams to Arthur Prysock. But in Aretha's presence, they were humbled, just as I had heard that Miles and Dizzy had been humbled in the presence of Charlie Parker. I remember after we did 'Today I Sing the Blues,' Joc Newman shaking his head and whispering to me, 'Man, this bitch is so fuckin' good I may have a heart attack and drop dead right here, a happy man.'"

"Today I Sing the Blues" was recorded on April 17.

"We wanted to cut at least two or three songs a day," said Wexler. "That was the most economic way to do it. But after the first one, Aretha split. She didn't say why. She was simply gone."

The next day she showed up to record Smokey Robinson's majestic "Tracks of My Tears," a major hit for Smokey and his Miracles in 1965.

"It didn't seem like an obvious vehicle for a jazz big band," said Arif, "since it's essentially a rhythm-and-blues song. But Aretha was insistent that it would work. She gave me her ideas for harmonizing the horns and building up the chorus. Although she neither reads nor writes music, she was a co-arranger. She had the section sounds mapped out in her mind and I essentially adopted her plan."

The plan to complete the album before she left on her first European tour, though, had to be abandoned when, without explanation, Aretha canceled the rest of the April sessions.

"We weren't sure whether she'd make the European trip at all," said Carolyn, "but she did show up at the airport. I was happy to be invited to sing background vocals. When we got to Paris, it was early May, and Ree got happy in a hurry. Paris was beautiful. Paris was the highlight. The city has always played a big part in Ree's imagination. Aretha is a Francophile. At different points in her life, she's started to study French. She loves the French cooking and the French designers. So playing the Olympia was a major thrill. The Parisian audiences loved her. Atlantic recorded us for a live album.

The only problem was the band. Wexler didn't put it together. Ted did. The band lacked the fire that we'd been used to in the studio. And then the band became another point of contention between Aretha and Ted. She accused him of hiring the wrong musicians. He accused her of slacking on her singing. It got bad, even as the crowds kept getting bigger."

In London Aretha got to hang out with Ahmet Ertegun in his chauffeur-driven Rolls-Royce.

"Aretha loved Jerry Wexler because he was a passionate fan and a great producer and a salt-of-the-earth street guy who knew how to sell records," said Carolyn. "But I think she got even more of a kick out of Ahmet because he was so sophisticated. He was European royalty. He took us to exclusive private clubs and chic boutiques on Carnaby Street where you had to have appointments to shop. Ahmet was on the cutting edge. He dressed like he was on his way to visit the queen of England. The man was cleaner than the board of health. He took us by the store where a man custom-made his shoes. He told us he had over sixty pairs. I didn't even know a woman with that many shoes. The shoemaker's wife designed cashmere scarves, and Ahmet bought us each six scarves in different shades of soft pastels. It was a beautiful day. That night Ahmet came to our gig at the Finsbury Park Astoria, where Lou Rawls showed up and sang a duet with Ree."

The filmed Swedish concert, attended by Crown Prince Carl Gustav and Princess Christina, shows Aretha opening with "There's No Business Like Show Business" followed by "Come Back to Me." The audience seems somewhat in shock. They've come for a soul show, not a Broadway revue. But with her take on the Stones' "Satisfaction," she's off and running. In this, only her second year at Atlantic, she has enough Atlantic hits to round out the evening and give the crowd what they came to hear. She sits at the piano and invokes the spirit of "Dr. Feelgood" with supernatural force.

At what will later be tagged "The Legendary Concertgebouw" in Amsterdam, Ted has agreed to allow cameras backstage for a brief preshow interview. Aretha looks overwhelmed; she's painfully shy and awkwardly inarticulate. She answers questions with one or two words in a retiring little-girl voice. When the reporter asks her to explain the remarkable surge in her career, she simply says, "Atlantic Records." A nattily dressed Ted White lurks in the background. By the time Aretha gets to the stage, the promoter is struggling with crowd management. The fans reach for her, wave copies of her albums, scream hysterically. Some charge the stage. The security is woefully inadequate. Aretha appears frightened. Ted is onstage with her, ready to push back the crowd. Later, when she sits at the piano to do an astounding "Good to Me As I Am to You," fans are surrounding her, seated at her elbow. The scene is unsettling, and yet the moment she opens her mouth to sing, she's in full creative control.

Wexler didn't see it that way. "She's not at the top of her game," he said about her *Live in Paris* album, the set taken from her show at the Olympia Theater. "She and the band aren't on the same page. They're out of tune, they miss their cues, and they're struggling to find the right groove. Naturally she was excited to be performing in Europe for the first time, and naturally it had to be thrilling for her to see the international scope of her success, but when the music's not right Aretha's not right. Like Ray Charles, she hears every note being played by every band member. And when a note is wrong—and, believe me, there were scores of bad notes—for Aretha, it's like squeaky chalk on a blackboard. It hurts. When she came home, she was hurting. Here you had the premier singer of our time touring the Continent with a ragtag band suitable for backing up a third-rate blues singer in some bucket of blood in Loserville, Louisiana. It was outrageous."

Aretha didn't see it that way. Out-of-tune band or not, she had taken London, Frankfurt, Stockholm, Rotterdam, Amsterdam, and Paris by storm.

When she returned home at the end of May, her latest release, "Think," was flying up the charts. Her most recent album, *Lady Soul,* was hailed as her best yet.

She found time to accompany her father to the first Southern Christian Leadership Conference convention since the death of Dr. King, where she sang in honor of the great man's passing.

That spring she also sat down with jazz critic Leonard Feather for the blindfold test, in which *Down Beat* magazine played records that the interviewee tried to identify. Aretha was able to name Sam and Dave, Peggy Lee, Nancy Wilson, and Esther Phillips. But she didn't recognize Marlena Shaw and, amazingly, confused Barbra Streisand with Diahann Carroll.

Her next press appearance was the biggest of her career.

"When we learned that *Time* magazine was putting Ree on the cover," said Cecil, "we all saw it as the greatest honor yet. Presidents were on the cover of *Time*. Prime ministers. Nobel Prize winners. Aretha remembered that Barbra Streisand had been on the cover of *Time*—the same Barbra who had started at Columbia around the same time as Ree. So, as far as public relations go, this was going to be the brightest jewel in her crown. Then, of course, it turned out to be a tremendous embarrassment that took her years to get over. On second thought, I'm not sure she ever got over it."

The story that came out on June 28 contained comments that Aretha claimed were either inaccurate or taken out of context. For example, according to *Time,* she said, "I might be just 26, but I'm an old woman in disguise—26 goin' on 65."

Aretha was appalled by the treatment of her father, which she considered disrespectful. The article talked about how "his Cadillac, diamond stickpins and $60 alligator shoes testify to an eminently successful pastorate." It also mentioned his failure to file federal tax returns. The fifty-one-year-old minister was described as a "strapping, stentorious charmer who has never let his spiritual calling inhibit his fun-loving ways."

She was further infuriated by the implication that her mother had abandoned her and her siblings and by the description of Ted White as "a street corner wheeler-dealer" who had "roughed her up in public at Atlanta's Regency Hyatt House."

But it was the overall picture of herself that she found most disturbing. *Time* characterized her as a woman who "sleeps till afternoon, then mopes in front of the television set, chain-smoking Kools and snacking compulsively."

Cecil is quoted: "For the last few years Aretha is simply not Aretha. You see flashes of her, and then she's back in her shell."

Before *Time* ran the story, Aretha was eager for any coverage she could get. The more stories, the more sales. But suddenly she saw that in-depth profiles could be far more revealing—and unflattering—than she had ever imagined. She had been used to puff pieces in *Billboard, Down Beat, Ebony*, and *Jet*. She had assumed *Time* would offer her nothing but praise. Why else put her on the cover?

"The shock was severe," said Ruth Bowen. "It was definitely a turning point for Aretha. She'd never trust the press again. It took her a long time to agree to any more interviews. It became another one of her many fears—this fear of having secrets revealed. She and I argued about that. I said everyone has problems. Most women go through troubled relationships. Millions of women struggle with alcohol. There's no shame in that game—it's merely life. But Aretha, bless her heart, doesn't want to be seen like most women. She has an image she wants to maintain. And when *Time* blew that image, she went crazy. She even talked about suing them. 'For what?' I asked. 'It wasn't libel or slander. It was just a profile of how the reporter viewed you. Mainly, it was a valentine about your genius as an artist. Besides, a lawsuit will get even more people to read an article that you hate.' I convinced her, but I couldn't convince Ted. He did sue *Time,* though the suit never got anywhere. The irony, of course, was that Ted was furious to be described as a wife beater, while those of us with firsthand knowledge knew that to be the undisputed truth."

"Ree was pretty inconsolable over that *Time* piece," said Erma. "She was convinced it would ruin her career. In truth, though, nothing could ruin her career—not with her turning out hit after hit. The cover story came in the spring around the same time 'Think' was tearing up the charts. That summer she was offered all sorts of TV shows. She appeared on Johnny Carson, proof that the *Time* profile didn't hurt her at all. The opposite was true—it increased the public's appetite to hear her records and see her in person. Her fees went up, but her pride was hurt and she wouldn't stop talking about the lies that *Time* had spread. She wanted the world to believe that she had a happy marriage."

Ed Ochs's *Billboard* article from July 13 proves Erma's point. She told the reporter that, in addition to re-signing with Atlantic, she had also re-signed with her husband for personal management, adding, "We haven't had any real trouble so far."

After Carson, she played the new Madison Square Garden on Eighth Avenue to an audience of some twenty-one thousand fans. Wexler was there.

"I'd just come back from a music-industry convention in Miami, where I was to accept an award on Aretha's behalf," Wexler remembered. "In Florida, what I thought would be a pleasure turned into a nightmare. Gangster elements had taken over the industry's black-power movement. During the banquet, King Curtis came up to me and said, 'We're getting you outta here. You've been marked.' King escorted me out to safety. Later I was hung in effigy. Phil Walden, Otis's white manager, received death threats. Marshall Sehorn, a white promo man, was pistol-whipped. It was some scary shit.

"When I got back to the relative safety of New York City, I could not have been more grateful to King Curtis. I swore that I would convince Aretha to hire him as her musical director for live dates—not only because he had proved such an invaluable ally of mine but because he was the best man for the job. King was the consummate musician—a lean and mean tenor man who could go both ways in terms of jazz and R-and-B. The obstacle was Ted White, who had his own man. I did an end run around Ted and cornered Aretha. 'King Curtis is the right call,' I said. 'You know it as well as I do. King can groove you up in a way that no one else can.'

"Although she never acknowledged the fact that I had been

right about the third-rate unit she had been touring with, she finally agreed to turn the baton over to King. As a result, her live gigs, starting with the Madison Square Garden show, were starting to sound as sharp as the recordings. The switch also indicated to me that Ted was losing influence. In terms of their marriage, the handwriting had been on the wall for a long time. I just knew she was close to giving him his walking papers."

"Aretha was not one to discuss her intimate relationships," said Erma, "not even with her sisters—or especially not with her sisters, since we had fought over men. But after the *Time* article, she began calling me more and desiring my company. I had signed a new deal with Brunswick Records. Aretha certainly helped me. It wasn't only her own success that convinced another label to take a chance on me, it was her own involvement. She was the one who suggested the Carole King/Gerry Goffin song 'You Don't Have the Right to Cry.' She figured if she could hit with their 'Natural Woman,' I might hit with their 'Cry.' She even helped me place and voice the background parts. Of course I was disappointed when I didn't get major airplay, but I was so glad to have my sister back in my camp. The more she moved away from Ted, the closer she moved to the family. We all knew that she was under great pressure. It was evident because she started gaining weight. Aretha is an emotional eater. When she's not happy, she overdoes food. She was also drinking more than ever."

In its August 22 issue, *Jet* reported that friends were worried about Aretha's weight problem. "At a recent public concert in the Windy City, some were startled to see how much she had gained since her last time around."

A separate story in the same issue reported a disaster at Denver's Red Rock Amphitheater. When a few local opening acts were finally through performing, Aretha took the stage, and, according to the spokesman for the Denver police, "suggested the people get their money back because a contract between her and the producer had not been fulfilled and she would not perform." The fans' reaction was riotous—property was destroyed and three people arrested.

"That was the summer from hell," said Ruth. "I was booking her gigs with Ted's approval, but then Ted was no longer on the scene, and Aretha tried to manage herself. That proved to be a catastrophe. She's not good with details. Why should she be? She's an artist, and artists are not good at logistics. But she has a trust problem, and at some point there was no one around her she could trust. She'd call in Cecil, but Cecil wasn't properly informed of the plans that had been made long before he arrived. In short, it was a mess. She fired me several times that summer, claiming—falsely—that certain promoters had agreed to pay her certain fees. The truth, though, was that she had inflated those fees in her mind. On more than one occasion she flat-out refused to sing."

When she sang in the studio, though, the results continued to be positive. At the end of August, she had two hits climbing the charts, both recorded back in April. In a nursery rhyme turned soulful lament, "The House That Jack Built" reads like a metaphor for Aretha's crumbling marriage. The house that Ted built is collapsing. The second song, even more powerful and equally improbable, is a cover of the Burt Bacharach/Hal David "I Say a Little Prayer," a huge pop hit that had reached number four the previous December.

"I advised Aretha not to record it," said Wexler. "I opposed it for two reasons. First, to cover a song only twelve weeks after the original reached the top of the charts was not smart business. You revisit such a hit eight months to a year later. That's standard practice. But more than that, Bacharach's melody, though lovely, was peculiarly suited to a lithe instrument like Dionne Warwick's—a light voice without the dark corners or emotional depths that define Aretha. Also, Hal David's lyric was also somewhat girlish and lacked the gravitas that Aretha required.

"Aretha usually listened to me in the studio, but not this time. She had written a vocal arrangement for the Sweet Inspirations that was undoubtedly strong. Cissy Houston, Dionne's cousin, told me that Aretha was on the right track—she was seeing this song in a new way and had come up with a new groove. Cissy was on

Aretha's side. Tommy Dowd and Arif were on Aretha's side. So I had no choice but to cave. The Muscle Shoals rhythm section—Spooner Oldham, Jimmy Johnson, Roger Hawkins, plus funk master Jerry Jemmott on bass—followed Aretha's lead. I sat back and listened. I have to say that I loved it. She blew the fuckin' doors off the song, but I knew it wasn't going to be a hit. And, man, was I ever wrong! It stayed on the charts for three months. Just like she had found a way to appropriate Otis's 'Respect,' she did the same goddamn thing with Dionne's 'I Say a Little Prayer.' She redefined it, restructuring the sound and turning what had been delightful fluff into something serious, obsessive, and haunting."

"As much as I like the original recording by Dionne," Burt Bacharach told me, "there's no doubt that Aretha's is a better record. She imbued the song with heavy soul and took it to a far deeper place. Hers is the definitive version."

Outside the music world, Aretha continued to raise her profile. On August 26, Aretha opened the troubled Democratic National Convention in Chicago with a rendition of the national anthem.

"I cringed when I watched it," said Wexler. "The orchestra was woefully out of tune. Aretha did the best she could, but it was not her greatest moment."

"By then she had kicked Ted to the curb," said Cecil, "and asked me to go to the convention with her. We're lifelong Democrats, so it made sense for Aretha to do her thing there. Aretha follows politics, but not as closely as my father and me. Like Dr. King, we did not like the Vietnam War policies that Johnson had perpetuated and that Humphrey had embraced. We liked Bobby Kennedy, and had he not been killed earlier that summer, we would have supported him at the convention.

"The convention was chaos. The protesters were everywhere and it felt like an armed camp. The atmosphere did not help Ree's state of mind that was also under siege. Ted did not leave without serious protestations. Aretha had been his meal ticket for seven or

eight years and he wasn't going to give it up easily. The family—
Daddy, Erma, Carolyn, my wife, Earline, and me—had to be a
protective fence around our sister. We wouldn't allow Ted anywhere near her. Lawyers had been called. Restraining orders had
been issued. She was determined to live her life without this man
and we did everything in our power to support that decision.
Could she do it? Would she do it? We'd have to see. At least at that
moment, though, he was gone. That didn't help her drinking problem, but, hey, one problem at a time. We were off to Latin America
for a short tour, and, just like that, I was her manager."

"I was greatly relieved when Ted was out and Cecil was in,"
said Ruth Bowen. "I'd been campaigning for that switch for a long
time. Beyond the abuse, Aretha never really trusted Ted's business
activities. Aretha never really trusted anyone outside of family. I
came as close as anyone to gaining her trust, but I was often accused
of hiding or holding back money from her. On the other hand,
Cecil was a brilliant guy who quickly learned the ins and outs of
business and trusted me completely. We were allies in getting
Aretha back on track—to keep her in the studio, onstage, and off
the bottle. That took a while."

Billboard reported, "Aretha Franklin's brother, the Rev. Cecil
Franklin, has taken over management chores from Aretha's husband-
manager, Ted White. A reported split between the soul singer and
her husband-manager, who has managed her affairs for much of
their five-year marriage, has all but killed their 'business marriage,'
though White claims he still has Miss Franklin under contract.
Rev. Franklin, who accompanied the singer on her successful concert tour of South America, is assistant pastor of his father's New
Bethel Baptist Church in Detroit."

"The incident that I kept out of the press happened on our way
to Caracas, Venezuela," said Ruth. "When we got on the plane,
Aretha started throwing back the booze. Well, at that point I had
to give her a two-drink maximum, a restriction she resented.
'Mother Goose,' she said, using her nickname for me, 'you're not
my mother. I'll drink all I want.' By the end of the trip she gets so

loaded that she goes to the bathroom to hide out. She's gone so long that the stewardess goes to get her and winds up banging at the door, telling her that we can't land unless she gets back in her seat. Still no Aretha. The pilot decides to land anyway. Even seated with the belt on, it's a rough landing. Aretha must have gotten knocked around something silly. When we're pulling up to the gate she finally emerges. Her eyes tell me two things—that the landing has traumatized her, and that she's still drunk as a skunk. I look out the window and see a mob of reporters waiting on the tarmac. I just can't let them interview Aretha in this condition. So, with the pilot's help, I arrange for a limo to meet us at the bottom of the stairs by the plane's rear exit. I get her in the car and we're off. A minute later, she's out cold. The South American press is insulted. They write all sorts of nasty things. But given her condition, that's a helluva lot better than reporting about the arrival of the Queen in fall-down drunk condition."

Back from Latin America, Aretha returned to Atlantic's Manhattan studios to complete the big-band jazz album. On four days in late September, she recorded ten songs.

"I have many favorite Aretha sessions," said Wexler, "but that week ranks high. First of all, Ted was gone. Thank you, Jesus. His absence gave her a freedom to take more charge. Back in April, when she cut the first two tunes, she had loved the big band. For months she had been thinking about getting back to that band—especially after the lousy band Ted saddled her with in Europe—and when she hit the studio, she took off like a rocket."

The album, which came out in January of 1969, was called *Soul '69*, a title Wexler considered a mistake.

"I wanted to call it *Aretha's Jazz*," Wexler explained, "but jazz was the territory ruled over by my partner Nesuhi Ertegun. Nesuhi and brother Ahmet thought the jazz label would limit the market since, at that time, Aretha's market was pop. I liked the jazz handle because that's what it was. Say it loud and proud. The Erteguns outvoted me, though, and I've been unhappy about that decision ever since. *Soul '69* is, ironically, Aretha's greatest jazz album."

"*Soul '69* is one of my favorite Aretha albums," Carmen McRae told me. "It was when that small sorority of jazz singers knew that Aretha was a member in good standing. I remember listening to it at Sarah Vaughan's house. Like me, Sarah is a tough critic when it comes to other chicks that think they can blow. But not this time. She kept talking about how Aretha sang 'Crazy He Calls Me.' That was her favorite track. It became mine as well. It starts out slow, just Aretha and a trio. She takes her time. She sings it straight, but then she alters the lyrics when she sings, 'I say I'll go through fire, yes, and *I* will *kill* fire.' The *kill* is her invention and takes you to another place. You got Joe Zawinul playing organ behind her, Kenny Burrell giving her that soft gentle touch on guitar, and Fathead whispering in her ear. You gotta compare it to Ella or Billie or Sarah to understand its greatness. She doesn't sing. She flies."

"When she brought in 'Gentle on My Mind,'" said Wexler, "I was sure it wouldn't work. It had been a quasi-country hit for Glen Campbell and I didn't see how it would translate into big-band jazz. But she and Arif worked it out. That's because she put it in a seductive groove. That's Aretha doing the piano intro, that's Aretha voicing the background singers, Aretha creating that bongo break, Aretha leading the troops to victory. It was so good we released it as a single."

Aretha's national television appearances became more frequent. In early November she guest-starred on *The Hollywood Palace* TV variety show.

Sammy Davis Jr., replete with Afro and gold medallion, is the host. Still sporting a built-up beehive wig, Aretha appears chunky in a sleeveless yellow gown. Their musical exchange is uncomfortable—old-school, showbiz, desperate-to-be-hip Sammy asking Aretha the meaning of soul as they sing a mismatched duet on "Think," "Respect," and "What'd I Say."

That same week, Richard Nixon was elected president.

The year did not end well. After a bad fall in Hawaii, Aretha returned to Detroit, where she was hospitalized for a serious leg injury. According to *Jet,* the following week she was arraigned in Detroit traffic court for "reckless driving and operating her Eldorado with an expired driver's license. She is denying the charges, including one that the cops found a bottle of liquor under the front seat of the car she was driving."

"Aretha was big on denial," said Ruth Bowen. "She didn't want to hear that she had a drinking problem. It didn't matter how many falls she suffered, how many tickets she got, how many subpar performances she gave due to inebriation. Her talent protected her. Even drunk, she could sing better than ninety-nine out of a hundred singers. Most people couldn't tell anything was wrong. For example, back in October, she played two dates in New York at Philharmonic Hall that had fans standing on their seats and screaming. One of those nights her dad came onstage to present her with a gold album for *Lady Soul* and a gold forty-five for 'Say a Little Prayer.' It was all rosy and sweet. The world was at her feet, and you couldn't tell her she had a problem. But if you're truly an alcoholic—and I do believe Aretha was—the pattern gets worse, and even Aretha Franklin, as great as she was, could not contain the damage drinking was doing to her."

By the end of 1968, Aretha was exhausted. She had enjoyed extreme triumph and had suffered extreme setbacks. Her drinking was out of control. With her popularity at new heights, her career was more demanding than ever.

"I didn't see how she could go on," said Ruth Bowen. "But on the other hand, I didn't see how she couldn't. She was an entertainer, and, no matter what, entertainers entertain."

16. HIGH MAINTENANCE

Dennis Edwards, the powerful gospel-trained tenor and lead vocalist for the Temptations, told me about meeting Aretha in the late sixties. Our discussion took place in 1985 after a show he did in Los Angeles. He had left the Temptations for a solo career and his "Don't Look Any Further," a duet with Siedah Garrett, was a huge hit on the R&B charts.

"I met Ree in Detroit when she had her house on Sorrento Drive," he said. "Ted White wasn't around. I don't know if they were officially divorced, but everyone understood that their thing was over. I came to the house with the Tempts to show her some music and get her to sing with us. We were smokin' hot then. David Ruffin had quit to go on his own and Norman Whitfield had written these psychedelic-sounding tracks where I sang lead—'Cloud Nine,' 'Runaway Child,' 'I Can't Get Next to You.'

"Understand that the Franklins and Temptations had known each other forever. I knew Cecil, I knew Carolyn, and I'd gone out with Erma. I knew and respected their father and had been to church to hear him preach. We were family. I really saw Aretha as part of the extended Motown family, and I'd always been part of the extended gospel family. That day, though, it became clear that Aretha was interested in more than my music. To be honest, I wasn't that much of a one-woman man, but the word on Aretha was that she wasn't much of a one-man woman. She seemed ready to play, and so was I. The problem, though, was that I was still seeing Erma every once in a while. Erma was a great woman — funny and smart and a dynamite singer herself. I couldn't see myself playing off two sisters — that could get a man killed — and given that Aretha was far more aggressive, I took her lead."

"Aretha was very proprietary about men," Erma said. "I had no illusions about Dennis carrying me to a beautiful cottage surrounded by a white picket fence. I knew he was not famous for his loyalty to women. But he and I were going out, and we were having fun, and I didn't appreciate Aretha's refusal to respect that. She just up and snatched him away."

Aretha didn't see it that way. She told me that she didn't consider Erma's relationship with Dennis at all serious. Tensions built, and, one night over dinner at their dad's house, accusations started to fly. So did a glass. Aretha remembered Erma throwing a glass at her head.

"I was furious," said Erma, "but I threw a glass at the wall, not at Aretha. It didn't land anywhere near Aretha."

"I watched it happen," said Carolyn. "Daddy stopped them and told them to leave the table. They went upstairs and probably slapped each other around and did some hair pulling before it was all over. That wasn't unusual for my sisters. Their fights could get physical, but then the next day they'd be cool. When it came to Dennis Edwards, though, a man who had notably doggish ways, Aretha won the day. But if you ask me, she hardly walked off with a prize. She thought she had Dennis where she wanted him, but Dennis put her through some changes."

Aretha detailed those changes in *From These Roots*. She spoke of Dennis's high-rise apartment at 1300 Lafayette in downtown Detroit, where, on a whim, she would often visit. If Dennis wasn't there — and even if another of Dennis's girlfriends opened the door — Aretha would go on in and wait till he arrived. In one instance, bored with waiting, Aretha decided to give a party in the apartment and invited a group of her friends. When Dennis showed up, he was less than thrilled.

"Ree was high maintenance," Dennis told me. "She wasn't the easiest girlfriend. She had her demands and she had her ways. She was a much bigger star than me—hell, she was the Queen of Soul—and I think at times she saw her boyfriends like her servants. I love and respect her. But as far as being at a woman's beck and call, that's not my nature. When I told her that straight up, she had a strange reaction. She got up and went straight to the little piano that I kept in my crib. She sat down and started fooling with some chords. She didn't complete the song that day, but a year or so later when I heard 'Day Dreaming,' one of her bigger hits, I recognized that song. That hit song was about me."

When Aretha returned to the Atlantic studios, in January of 1969, "See Saw" was her current hit song and close to gold status. At these winter sessions, "Day Dreaming" was not one of the songs she recorded. That wouldn't happen for two more years.

"She said she had been writing," Wexler remembered, "and of course that was good news. I always encouraged her to come to the sessions with original material. But she said her new songs weren't ready. I knew not to push her. When it came to her own stuff, she took her own sweet time. There was also a little tension in that January session because I was coming off a hit album I'd done with Dusty Springfield, *Dusty in Memphis*. It was being called a soul classic and compared to Aretha. Aretha didn't like me producing other chick singers. I told her that she was Dusty's idol and Dusty was making no claims to her throne. Aretha smiled that little passive smile she's famous for—the smile that told me she wasn't happy. Making matters worse, 'Son of a Preacher Man' was the big hit off Dusty's record. That song had been written for Aretha, and, in fact, I had urged her to cut it the year before. Aretha had refused because she considered it disrespectful to her father and his church. I thought her reasoning was off but my argument got me nowhere. She was adamant. Now that it was a hit for Dusty, she wasn't at all pleased.

"No matter, we got four songs out of her in a week. The best was 'The Weight,' that had been a big hit for the Band on their *Music from Big Pink* that came out the year before. Aretha heard it and said she had no idea what the lyrics meant. I said I didn't know either but that the song had a vicious groove and she could kill it. I also thought the hippie flower-child market was there for the taking. They loved the Jefferson Airplane, but they also loved soul music, so why not throw them a bone?"

Wexler's reasoning won out. In the first quarter of 1969, Aretha's reading of "The Weight" went top-twenty pop and as high as number three on the R&B charts. Even in the aftermath of Sly and the Family Stone's refashioned funk, Aretha held her own.

It was also in early 1969 that Aretha met Ken Cunningham, a dashing gentleman with whom she would soon cohabitate.

"Jerry Wexler had moved to Miami and was urging Ree to record down there," Cecil said. "He put us up in a suite at the Fontainebleau Hotel. He had us out on his boat and was showing us a big time. Sister was still distracted from her breakup with Ted. She and her lawyers were in the middle of the divorce negotiations that got a little rough. It would take many more months to finally get settled. Ree was in no mood to record. She didn't even want to go out on Wexler's boat. Well, I did. Wexler was a great host. When I got back, Aretha was all excited about a guy she met who was looking for investors. His company was called the New Breeders, and they were making Afro-style clothes and shoes. She described him as a handsome guy in a dashiki and big freedom 'fro. It was a time when we were all converting to Afros. Would I meet him? Would I hear his sales proposal? Sure, why not?"

It's unclear whether Aretha financially invested in the New Breeders, but there's no doubt that she invested emotionally in Cunningham. When she left Miami for New York, he was part of the entourage.

"She never showed up for the recording sessions I had planned in Miami," said Wexler. "That was disappointing. Criteria Studios was a hot spot. It was where James Brown had recorded 'I Got You

(I Feel Good).' I had assembled the best players in the South to back up Aretha on some new tracks, but where the hell was she? Later I learned through Cecil that love had blocked her path from the hotel to the studio. There was no arguing with love. After what she had been through, Aretha deserved some righteous love. That same winter when I met Ken Cunningham in New York, he seemed like a good guy. At the moment when black America was going through a period of Afro-centricity, he was a proud proponent of the movement."

When Cunningham met Aretha, he was married and had a young daughter. Aretha told her siblings that the marriage was already over and that Ken, whom she called Wolf, had previously decided on a divorce.

"Ken's a good man," said Brenda Corbett, who began to sing backup for her first cousin both in concerts and in studios. "He helped Aretha get it together. He helped her stop drinking. By the early seventies, Aretha had stopped drinking and it never became a problem again. That was a huge blessing. Ken was also serious-minded about art and books and he loved all kinds of music. He came along at just the right time. Aretha needed a man who could point her in a positive direction."

"When I visited Aretha in New York," said Earline, Cecil's wife, "she and Ken were living in a high-rise in midtown off Seventh Avenue. First thing she said was that Ed McMahon, Johnny Carson's sidekick, was her neighbor. It was a big spread with a beautiful view. Her sons Clarence and Eddie were back in Detroit being cared for by Big Mama. Teddy was being raised by his father's folks. So Ken and Aretha had it all to themselves."

"It was something she deserved," said Carolyn. "She hadn't known domestic happiness for a long while. Wolf was all about healthy lifestyle—healthy eating, healthy thinking. He addressed her drinking problem in a way that the rest of us could not. If she wanted him around, she'd have to cut down and stop playing the fool. His approach worked. He became a wonderful addition to her life."

"Everyone liked Ken Cunningham," said Ruth Bowen, "and I was no different. He helped soften some of Aretha's rough edges. Everyone was saying that he was turning her into a new woman. While I believe that Ken helped Aretha considerably, I also know that geniuses like Aretha have personalities not easily altered or, in most cases, not altered at all. People show up and no doubt have a large influence, but—especially in the case of women like Dinah Washington and Aretha Franklin—those people tend to come and go."

"When Ken showed up," said Erma, "he was universally liked. And Aretha became much easier to deal with. The problem I foresaw, though, was Cecil. By then, Cecil had solidified his position as Aretha's manager. I'm not sure Ken didn't have his own managerial ideas concerning Aretha's career. In that sense, a clash was inevitable."

Political clashes were also threatening the Franklin family.

On March 29, 1969, there was a deadly battle at Reverend Franklin's New Bethel Baptist Church between members of the Republic of New Africa, a militant black-power group, and the Detroit police force.

"My father rented out the church to many organizations," said Cecil, "as long as their ideology reflected his pro-black-power stance. They did not have to agree with my dad's nonviolent position to use our facilities for their meeting. The Republic of New Africa was one such group. When the RNA met on that particular evening, they showed up heavily armed with loaded rifles. Daddy, who was not present, had no idea that would be the case. A cop car patrolling the area spotted some of the RNA members outside the church with guns. One of the policemen was shot to death and the other called for backup. Within fifteen or twenty minutes, fifty cops stormed the church—they actually vandalized the church— and arrested nearly a hundred and fifty people and apprehended a considerable cache of rifles and guns. The sensational news took

Detroit by storm. Daddy was criticized for harboring radicals, but Daddy would not apologize for his support of black power. Next day he even convened a press conference. He spoke of the fallen policeman and offered his deepest sympathies to the man's family. But he also did not back down in his sympathy with the RNA goals while restating his disapproval of their methodology. Ralph Abernathy came out to our church the next day and backed up Daddy. In fact, Daddy said he would continue to rent to the RNA as long as they pledged not to bring arms into our church."

"The New Bethel Shootout," as the incident was tagged, did serious damage to Reverend Franklin's reputation as a civic leader. His church had been turned into a battleground. A month later, he traveled to Dallas, where he was planning an African musical and cultural event, the Soul Bowl, starring Aretha. On his return flight, American Airlines misplaced his bags. When they were located, police officials searched them and found a small amount of marijuana. Charges were pressed. Franklin claimed the drugs had been planted in order to further embarrass him. The charges were dropped a month later, but by then, because of the negative publicity, the Soul Bowl had been canceled. Franklin sued the airlines, only to learn that the State of Michigan was pursuing him for back taxes.

"My father was sought out and victimized by government officials, both national and local, who resented his political positions and were determined to humiliate him," said Cecil. "He fought back, he answered every charge, he eventually paid his tax bill, and, as far as his congregation was concerned, he cleared his name. But I have to say that after what happened to him in that particular season of 1969, he was never quite the same."

On another front, Aretha had a tough time tolerating the career ambitions of her sister Carolyn. When a *Jet* article from April 3, 1969, reported that Carolyn had received $10,000 to sign with RCA, Aretha was not happy.

"She was miffed because she assumed I'd just continue to travel with her and sing backup," Carolyn told me. "She said she was counting on me. I said I had to count on myself. I figured it was about time to go back out there and give it a try. I was about to turn twenty-five and felt like I'd lived at least five or six lives. There was the life with our mother. There was the life with our father. There was the life when Daddy said I couldn't live with him anymore and turned me over to neighbors who became foster parents. There was my life as a responsible adult when I'd worked at the post office. And then there was my musical life that had actually started when I was nineteen and, through Erma, met Lloyd Price, who signed me to his Double L label. Back then—to make sure I had my own identity—I called myself Candy Carroll. I cut a few singles but nothing happened. That didn't discourage me because I knew I could sing and I knew I could write. When 'Ain't No Way' broke out of *Lady Soul* and became big for Aretha, she encouraged me to concentrate on my writing over my singing. My attitude, though, was *Why not do both?* Who says one has to preclude the other?

"Aretha's success no doubt helped Erma get her deal at Shout. Her 'Piece of My Heart' was an R-and-B hit, but when Janis Joplin covered it and made it into a million-seller pop hit, Erma kept on keeping on. She got another deal at Brunswick Records. Aretha isn't the only driven and determined Franklin sister. If Aretha's heat could help Erma, it could also help me. And no doubt it did. I'm not sure I would have gotten the RCA deal if I had continued to be Candy Carroll. But once I was in the door, I was going to give it all I had."

And she did. *Baby Dynamite,* Carolyn's debut album, is rock-solid soul. Her vocals measure up to the strongest singers of the day. The charts are tight and the songs—especially her own haunting "I Don't Want to Lose You" and ingenious "Boxer"—are infectious. The sound is the end-of-the-sixties Sly Stone–Stax/Volt-Muscle Shoals horn-punched groove-and-grind R&B.

"I sang on those sessions," said cousin Brenda Corbett. "It had the same kind of feeling as Aretha's sessions. Very free, very loose, very spontaneous. We all knew that Carolyn, like Erma, was a sensational singer, and she proved us right. We were thrilled with the results."

"My idea was to play it for Ree and have her give me an endorsement by writing the liner notes," said Carolyn. "I gave her an early version and waited weeks for her reaction. When she never responded I finally called and put her on the spot. 'I've heard it,' she said, 'and I love it, but I don't know what to write.' 'Write that you love it,' I said. 'Write whatever you want, Ree, but just write something. My label is counting on your endorsement.'

"Finally, I turned to my dad. He said he'd get Aretha to write something. But even he couldn't move her. Instead, he wrote the notes himself and did a beautiful job."

"Musically," wrote Reverend Franklin, "in terms of formal training in music, Carolyn possibly excels both her sisters (Erma and Aretha). She has a rich background in music training as she majored in music theory and harmony at the University of Southern California. She also possesses a genius for composing which is well known to entertainers and most people in the industry."

Attempting to make peace among his daughters, Reverend concluded his remarks on a diplomatic note: "As Carolyn embarks on her own career as an artist, I think I will use the words of her sister Aretha, whom she asked to write the liner notes for this album. Aretha wrote, 'This is my sister Carolyn, and she is ready!' When Aretha was told that this was not sufficient for the liner notes, she said, 'That's all there is to say.'"

The record earned some critical praise but yielded no hits. Within weeks, Erma's "Gotta Find Me a Lover (Twenty-Four Hours a Day)" was also released but did not catch on. Meanwhile, Aretha's "I Can't See Myself Leaving You" rose to number three on the R&B charts, where it remained for nine weeks.

On April 14, Frank Sinatra introduced Aretha Franklin at the forty-first Academy Awards. She sang "Funny Girl" as her former Columbia label mate Barbra Streisand watched from her front-row seat. Nominated for best actress for her work in the film *Funny*

Girl, Streisand shared the prize with Katharine Hepburn for *The Lion in Winter.*

"If I must say so myself, I pulled off that coup," Ruth Bowen told me. "The producer wasn't sure Aretha could handle a song like 'Funny Girl.' 'Pah-leeeze,' I told the man, 'Aretha could sing the French national anthem better than Edith Piaf. When she's through with "Funny Girl," Ms. Streisand will never want to touch the goddamn song again.' He listened to me and the day after the ceremony apologized for ever doubting my word. The appearance put Aretha in the center of mainstream American entertainment—a place she'd never lose."

Aretha's memories of the event were the Frank Sinatra introduction, the Arnold Scaasi gown Diahann Carroll wore to the Governor's Ball, and her own outfit with an extravagant gold antler headdress. (She chose a color photograph of that Academy Awards appearance to grace the back of her autobiography.)

The higher her public profile, the greater her entrepreneurial ambitions. In May, for example, *Jet* reported that Aretha was planning her own magazine, *Respect,* and her own label, Respect Records.

"Both these ventures went nowhere," said Ruth Bowen. "The plain truth is that Aretha lacks fundamental business sense. She's not organized. She's not disciplined. Every one of her nonmusic schemes has failed. I kept telling her—leave the business to us and just stick with your music."

On May 26, Aretha returned to the music. She was back in the Atlantic studios in New York with the Muscle Shoals rhythm section—Barry Beckett on keys, Jimmy Johnson on guitar, David Hood on bass, and Roger Hawkins on drums. Eddie Hinton, whom Wexler called "the white Otis Redding," and Duane Allman doubled on guitar on Aretha's searing version of Jessie Hill and Dr. John's "When the Battle Is Over." She also sang Jimmy Reed's "Honest I Do" and Carole King and Gerry Goffin's "Oh No Not My Baby."

By then Arif Mardin and Tommy Dowd had become full-fledged coproducers with Wexler.

"They were mainly in New York," Wexler explained, "and I was mainly in Miami. Of course I came to every vocal session, but I was less hands-on. I was feeling less controlling and more willing to turn over many of the in-studio decisions to Tommy and Arif. To get the right sound, my presence really wasn't required."

"Aretha should have been listed as the fourth producer," said Cecil. "She should have been listed as the main producer. She was the one who was really in charge at those sessions. I spoke to Wexler about it, but he wasn't willing to budge. His point was that she got credit as the artist. She got all the glory she needed. Besides, he said, no one really cares about the producer anyway. Maybe so, but fair is fair and I felt strongly that her role was being hidden from the public. Aretha felt this way as well, but, given her lucrative history with Atlantic, she was unwilling to make waves. Her position was that Wexler's promotional skills were as great as his producer skills. He had such high enthusiasm for everything Aretha did, he became her greatest cheerleader. She thought if she insisted on getting producer credit, he might be miffed and back off on that enthusiasm. I didn't agree. Wexler and the Erteguns were making a fortune on my sister. They weren't about to back off no matter what. Give her the credit she was due. Give her extra points for producing. Just be fair."

That wouldn't happen for several more years. Aretha went along with the program but not without resentment.

"There are passive-aggressive parts to my sister's personality," said Erma. "She lets her anger stew for weeks, months, or even years. Then something inconsequential will set her off and suddenly all the anger comes spilling out."

Around the time of the "Honest I Do" session, Aretha learned that she was pregnant by Ken Cunningham.

"She was happy to know she was having a child with Ken," said Ruth, "but she was also determined not to marry. She said one marriage had been enough. She was glad to be living with the man without any legal commitments. One commitment, though, that was damaged by her pregnancy was a weeklong engagement I had booked her in Vegas. This was a breakthrough for Aretha, both in terms of venue and fee. Vegas was the obvious next step up in her career. But then, Aretha being Aretha, she canceled at the last minute. When she told me it was because of morning sickness, I reminded her that she didn't have to sing in the morning, only at night. The result was a legal mess."

Jet reported, in its People Are Talking About column: "Soul singer Aretha Franklin and her whereabouts since she fell ill in Las Vegas and was unable to complete her engagement at the prestigious Caesar's Palace. It was announced at the time that Miss Franklin was being rushed to Detroit to be put under the care of her physician, but a check with her home days later brought the information that Miss Franklin was not there and, in fact, had not been home in several weeks."

"Aretha was always getting caught in her little fibs," said Ruth, "and it was my job to clean up after her."

On July 24, 1969, Jet referred to its previous story:

"The mystery was cleared up when her friend and booking manager Ruth Bowen revealed that Aretha had been in Detroit's Ford Hospital being treated for a throat infection and Mrs. Bowen declares, Aretha is 'sicker over the fact I had to cancel two engagements, one in Tampa, Fla., and the other in New Orleans that would have enriched her bank account by $100,000.' The two dates have been rescheduled as has the cancelled Caesar's Palace engagement."

That same summer, Carolyn remembered her sister's reaction to the Stonewall riots in Greenwich Village, the spark that ignited the gay rights movement.

"My friends and I were talking about it as a great thing," said Carolyn. "Civil rights had been a topic. Women's rights were being discussed. Now for the first time there might be a conversation about gay rights. When I mentioned this to Aretha, though, she said that she found the topic distasteful."

On July 26, the New York Times reported, "Aretha Franklin, the soul singer, pleaded guilty to a charge of disorderly conduct yesterday and was fined $50 in the Highland Park Municipal Court. The charges resulted from a traffic accident Tuesday night when, the authorities said, Miss Franklin became belligerent toward the police who investigated."

"Her pregnancy was not easy," said Ruth Bowen. "She was moodier than usual. One day she could be funny as hell—doing her Jimmy Durante or Judy Garland imitation. Aretha had a wonderful sense of humor and was also a great mimic. But the next day, forget it. When items about her 'disorderly conduct' appeared in the paper, her first instinct was to fire whatever publicist she had hired. Then she'd call one of her friends at *Jet* to clean up the story and give it another spin. Sometimes *Jet* cooperated, but sometimes they didn't."

On August 7, *Jet* reported, "High-strung soul queen Aretha Franklin, claiming to be too distraught over the death of the Rev. A. D. Williams King and the earlier death of singer Judy Garland, missed a court date in Highland Park (Detroit), Mich. and forfeited a $50 bond. In court the next day, however, a subdued Miss Franklin made an appearance and paid a $50 fine on disorderly conduct charges. Police said the 27-year-old singer, driving a Cadillac, hit a parked car in a parking lot, became 'belligerent' and refused to cooperate with police. They said she also threw a $100 bill on the desk and left when her bond was set at $50 and she didn't have any change."

Meanwhile, her music kept selling. In August Aretha's blistering version of Al "TNT" Braggs's "Share Your Love with Me," a hit for Bobby Bland, was an even bigger hit for the Queen. It crossed over to the pop charts, where it climbed to number thirteen.

A week later, Carolyn's "It's True I'm Gonna Miss You" found its way to the R&B charts—renamed the soul charts—but never rose above twenty-three.

Then in September, Aretha canceled all personal appearances and concerts for the rest of the year.

"The wrangling with Ted over the divorce settlement was

driving her crazy," said Cecil. "Ted felt entitled to a lot since, in his mind, he was responsible for her success. Naturally, Ree didn't feel that way at all."

"Aretha never personally told me about the cancellations," Ruth Bowen said. "I learned about it in the trades like everyone else. Naturally, I was furious. Since I had booked those gigs, wasn't I entitled to an advance notice about cancellations? I couldn't get through to Aretha, but I gave Cecil hell. I felt bad about that because I knew that Cecil, like all of us, was merely serving a whimsical queen."

In *From These Roots,* Aretha wrote that, even though she was with Ken Cunningham, she occasionally saw Dennis Edwards as well. She admitted that her fascination with the Temptation had not entirely quieted, and, despite her domestic arrangement with Cunningham, she also found time for Edwards. When pressed, she said that Cunningham was not threatened by her friendships with other men.

"When she showed up in Miami in October, she was in a pissy mood," said Wexler. "She decided to record 'Son of a Preacher Man,' now claiming that she had always wanted to sing it but I had given it to Dusty Springfield before she had a chance. She refused to remember that I had offered it to her first. No matter, she sang the shit out of it. She sang the shit out of everything during those Criteria sessions. It was a great studio, and the Muscle Shoals boys had come down to back her along with the Sweet Inspirations. It was the first time she did Beatles songs—'Eleanor Rigby' and 'Let It Be.'

"McCartney and Lennon had written 'Let It Be' specifically for Aretha, but when I played her the demo, back many months before, she wasn't sure whether the religious implications were compatible with her Baptist background. She thought the Mother Mary reference might be a bit Catholic. So she put off recording it. Paul and John knew they had a hit, got tired of waiting for her, and put out their version first. Aretha's version is magnificent, but by then the

Beatles had made the first and most lasting impression. It could have been another one of her signature songs but, as with 'Preacher Man,' her equivocation proved costly."

"When it came to the lyrics of songs and what they meant," said Ruth Bowen, "Aretha was hard to read. For example, she called me one day and said that she just walked out of an interview because some reporter had wanted to know how her father felt about her singing such sexy songs. 'I don't sing sexy songs,' she told the writer. 'I sing soul songs.' He pointed to 'Dr. Feelgood' as an example of an explicitly sexy song. ' "Dr. Feelgood," ' she told him, 'is about romance, not sex.' When the reporter gave her other examples, like the 'sock-it-to-me' line in 'Respect,' she got up and left. She told me that she wasn't going to tolerate questions from someone who reads sex into every line. Naturally I didn't say a word because it really wasn't my business. But for someone like Aretha, who wasn't exactly reticent about voicing her sexual needs, her prudish attitude seemed somewhat ridiculous."

"She was also a little hesitant about doing 'Dark End of the Street,' that haunting song by Dan Penn and Chips Moman," said Wexler, "because the story was about adultery. James Carr had the R-and-B hit in 1967, but I was convinced that Aretha could take the blues-based lament to another level. We went over the lyrics many times before Aretha finally rationalized that the couple were merely *discussing* what they might do at the dark end of the street. They really hadn't done anything yet. Thank God she saw her way to singing it because her version, though never released as a single, is definitive.

"She had no ambivalence about singing the Bacharach/David 'This Girl's in Love with You,' a number-one song for Herb Alpert. The idea, of course, was to revisit the procedure she had applied to 'I Say a Little Prayer'—funkify the fluff. She was so certain that it would work twice that she insisted that we give the album the title of the tune. Turned out, though, the real breakout hit from that session was something Aretha had written herself—'Call Me,' a song reminiscent of Carolyn's work. It was sweet and heartfelt and filled with longing. She brought in another wonderful Carolyn song, 'Pullin',' with an especially alluring hook. At that same session Aretha also sang another one of her originals, 'Try Matty's,' a spirited blues about her favorite rib joint. When the session was over, we all ran out for barbecue.

"When she was in the right mood, Aretha was also famous for arriving at the session with buckets of barbecue. She liked to feed the boys in the band. She also sought out great food joints. I remember she was staying at the Presidential Suite of the Fontaine-bleau when, through my DJ friend Fat Daddy, she learned of a pig's-feet emporium on the other side of town. She ran over there, copped a big grocery bag filled with the delicacy, and headed back to the hotel. Walking through the lobby, though, the wet pig's feet broke through the bag and spilled all over the fancy carpet. Didn't faze Aretha at all. She reacted by snapping into queen mode. She didn't look alarmed, didn't bend down, didn't bother to try and pick them up. With back erect, she walked straight to the elevator and rode up to her room.

"At the end of that week in Miami, we had more material than we needed. 'Pullin'' and 'Try Matty's' were put on the shelf and not included in *This Girl's in Love with You,* which came out in January of 1970. We put them on *Spirit in the Dark,* released in the summer of 1970. Anyway you looked at it, 1970 was shaping up to be Aretha's biggest year yet."

At the same time Aretha was recording at Criteria in Miami, Motown released the Jackson 5's first single, "I Want You Back." The Sly Stone–influenced quintet would soon become the hottest crossover sensation in soul music since Aretha.

Musically, the rest of 1969 was about the Archies' "Sugar, Sugar," Neil Diamond's "Sweet Caroline," Johnny Cash's "A Boy Named Sue," and the Rolling Stones' "Honky Tonk Women."

A few months earlier, men had walked on the moon. That same summer, the Manson murders shook Hollywood to its core. In

August the hippie nation peacefully rallied at Woodstock. In December, the peace was broken at Altamont. In Washington, President Richard Nixon, who cited reconciliation as his first priority, presided over a nation painfully—and often violently—divided.

Come January 1970, Aretha Franklin, seven months pregnant, found herself embroiled in heavy domestic drama that, despite her best efforts, could not be kept out of the press.

17. SPIRIT

From *Jet*, January 15, 1970:
   "Sam Cooke's Brother, Charles, Is Shot in Detroit: Detroit police were investigating the early morning shooting of Charles Cooke, 42, brother of slain singer Sam Cooke. Police said Cooke, a guest at the house of Soul Queen Aretha Franklin, was shot in the groin following an altercation with Miss Franklin's estranged husband, Theodore (Ted) White, 38."

White told *Jet*, "I have a right to go to my home," explaining that he had bought the house, which he had visited only twice in the past two years since separating from Aretha. When Ted asked Cooke to leave the room so he could speak privately to Aretha, Cooke refused to go. "Cooke felt he had to protect Aretha like I was some kind of gorilla or something," said White, who admitted he pushed Cooke out of the room. "When Cooke returned," *Jet* reported, "White shot him." Cooke was rushed to New Grace Hospital, where he survived an emergency operation. Officers at Detroit's Twelfth Precinct brought Aretha in and questioned her; she gave a statement and returned home.

"Aretha was infuriated that *Jet* would publish something like that," said Ruth Bowen. "She said she felt disrespected. Well, *Jet* is the neighborhood newspaper for black America. Black folks have always been curious about Aretha. She's our queen. *Jet* was merely getting out the news on our queen. They were reporting facts. Aretha couldn't handle that. She said, 'They make it sound like ghetto stuff.' I said, 'Well, it *is* ghetto stuff. You were the one who married this man.' She didn't want to hear it. 'I'm pregnant,' she said, 'pregnant women shouldn't be treated this way.' 'Pregnancy has nothing to do with it, Aretha. You're still at war with Ted and until the war stops, the newspapers are going to report the battles.'"

"My second album for RCA, *Chain Reaction,* was dropping just about the time of all that hullabaloo about Ted shooting up the house," said Carolyn. "I thought it was the best thing I'd done and was looking for some play in the press. When I let Aretha hear it, she was generous with her praise. She saw how this record could be my breakthrough. One reporter said he'd do a story on me if Aretha would also agree to be interviewed about her feelings for me and Erma, who also had some great songs out there. Aretha refused, saying that she couldn't trust the press. She said that they'd wind up asking her questions about Ted shooting up the house. 'Don't answer those questions,' I told her. 'Just talk about music.' She said it doesn't work that way. She pointed to the title of my album. 'It's a chain reaction,' she said. 'They got my professional life chained up with my personal life. Well, I'm not going near any of it. I've had it with the press.'"

The next news item appearing on Aretha was a happy one: In March she gave birth to her fourth son, Kecalf (pronounced "Kalf"), his name an acronym formed from the initials of his father, Ken E. Cunningham, and his mom, Aretha Louise Franklin.

"Aretha always went home to Detroit to have her children," said Erma. "She left her New York penthouse and all that glamour for the comfort of her father and grandmother and all her family. I believe she only stayed a few weeks, though. She dearly loves her children—as I love mine—but we were part of that generation of young female singers who definitely sacrificed time with our kids to attend to our careers. We did so knowingly. We did so with the support of Daddy and Big Mama and so many other caring relatives. But we also did so with heavy guilt. We were mothers who had made the decision to put our profession as entertainers first. I'm not sure Aretha will ever admit to that, but that's the truth. As a result, we did a great deal of silent suffering."

Five weeks after giving birth, Aretha was in Miami to complete what would be the album *Spirit in the Dark*, to be released in late summer.

"She was radiant," said Wexler. "She was off the sauce and on the one. She came to the studio with an armful of songs she said she'd written during her pregnancy. I was elated. They were all good, but the killer was 'Spirit in the Dark.' It was one of those perfect R-and-B blends of the sacred and the secular whose lyrical ambiguity appealed to fans of every stripe. What is it, the spirit? Is it God? Or is it the god of the good orgasm? It's Aretha conducting church right in the middle of the smoky nightclub. It's everything to everyone. It helped that when she recorded it, I had the Dixie Flyers in place. That was my house band in Miami that included Jim Dickinson on keys, Charlie Freeman on guitar, Tommy McClure on bass, and Sammy Creason on drums.

"She also came in with B.B. King on her mind. She was set on covering his 'The Thrill Is Gone,' King's first real pop hit, and his evergreen 'Why I Sing the Blues.' Listen to her deep-fried deep-funk piano solo on 'Thrill' and you'll understand why I begged her to do an instrumental album, just as I begged her to do an all-gospel album. In between takes, she spoke of her father's relationship with B.B. 'My daddy is B.'s preacher and B. is my daddy's bluesman,' she said. 'It's a beautiful thing.' "

"If you go through the vaults," said Cecil, "you'll also see that Ree cut a version of 'My Way,' the song that Paul Anka wrote for Sinatra. If Anka would ever hear it, he'd be convinced that he subconsciously wrote it for Aretha, because she turned it sunny-side-up soul style. After she sang it, we were ecstatic. We thought it was going to be the new 'Respect.' It had that anthem feel. When

Wexler decided not to release it as a single or even put it on the album, we were amazed. But there were so many hits coming out of Aretha, we couldn't really complain."

When I mentioned Aretha's "My Way" to Wexler in 1992, he couldn't remember her doing it. But in 2007, when we listened to it together for a reissue we were coproducing, *Aretha Franklin: Rare and Unreleased Recordings from the Golden Reign of the Queen of Soul,* his memory was jogged. He called it "a discovery of enormous value. Listening to it now, I forget about Paul and Frank and think only of Aretha, Aretha, Aretha. She builds her case and claims the victory. The song becomes a royal pronouncement of incontestable truth. It's a masterpiece."

"Spirit in the Dark" was the first single off the album. In May it entered the R&B charts, rose to number three, and stayed for nine weeks. The flip side, "The Thrill Is Gone," was the second single and remained on the list for eight weeks. The third single, Aretha's remake of Ahmet Ertegun's "Don't Play That Song," a cover of Ben E. King's 1962 hit, went number one R&B and number eleven pop.

On the home front, things were peaceful.

"We went to New York to visit Aretha practically every weekend," said sister-in-law Earline. "She had furnished her high-rise apartment to where everything was sparkling. Ken also had her on a good personal program. She was slimming down and not drinking at all. She was wearing an Afro and spending less time fussing with makeup and such. Ken took this 'natural woman' thing seriously, and the change suited Aretha. She seemed more relaxed."

"All her songs were hitting big," said Carolyn, "and I was still having trouble getting on the charts. To be honest, I think that gave her some relief. Now that she saw that I was no competition, she began calling me. I think she felt a little guilty about not having written my liner notes. Anyway, I had begun working with Jimmy Radcliffe, the writer and producer, on a Broadway show based on gospel music. This was before the advent of hit musicals like Micki Grant's *Don't Bother Me, I Can't Cope* or Professor Alex Bradford's *Your Arms Too Short to Box with God.* Jimmy and I were ahead of the curve. Ree liked the idea. Barbra Streisand had been a star on Broadway and there wasn't any reason my sister couldn't be as well. Jimmy and I wrote the central role with her in mind. She even put some seed money into the project. But somehow she lost interest along the way. Aretha is easily distracted, and, though she means well, follow-through is a big challenge for her."

"People were always coming to Aretha with investment ideas," Cecil confirmed. "Because she's an openhearted person, she's an easy sell. And if you're a relative, she's doubly easy. She's always wanted to help her family. But to tell you the truth, I didn't even hear about the project that Carolyn and Jimmy Radcliffe were putting together until I read an item in *Billboard.* By then Ree had moved on to something else entirely. By then she had met Donny Hathaway."

Hathaway, the most influential soul singer since Sam Cooke, had been a producer for Curtis Mayfield's Curtom Records in Chicago. After hearing Hathaway at a music convention, King Curtis urged Jerry Wexler to sign him. Wexler needed little convincing. He described Hathaway's voice as "plush-velvet, broad-stroked and big-bottomed. It's a misty-blue pop-jazz church voice of tremendous power and conviction. He's the third component to Atlantic's Holy Trinity of Soul. First there was Ray Charles, then Aretha, now Donny."

Hathaway's first album, the self-produced *Everything Is Everything,* included "The Ghetto," a critical sensation and an R&B hit.

"When I played Aretha 'The Ghetto,'" said Wexler, "she was excited. The first thing she said was 'I want to work with this guy. We come from the same place.'"

"Aretha had the opposite reaction," said Joel Dorn, another high-ranking Atlantic producer, "when she heard the first Roberta Flack things we did at the label. Although they are vastly different artists, Aretha saw Roberta as a threat. She actually got up and walked out while I was playing her that first Roberta album. She later complained to Ahmet that it wasn't appropriate for Atlantic to be trying to break another female soul singer. Ahmet smoothed her feathers, as only Ahmet can, but she was never happy with Roberta as a label mate. On the other hand, she loved Donny—until Donny started having those duet hits with Roberta."

King Curtis, Aretha's musical director for the previous thirteen months, asked her to play along with Donny Hathaway on Sam Moore's first solo album, a sensational record that sat in the vaults for over thirty years before it was released in 2002. Curtis was the main producer as well as the tenor sax player; the Sweet Inspirations did the background vocals, and Aretha and Donny played keyboards on several tracks.

"I never thought it would happen," said Cecil. "Never thought Aretha would ever make a date strictly as a 'sideman,' without singing. But these were special circumstances. Sam was always fighting with his partner Dave Prater. They were harmony dynamite onstage but offstage couldn't stand each other. Curtis wanted to make Sam a star on his own and he put together a great recording group to back him up. When he needed the icing on the cake, he looked to Donny and Aretha. Aretha loved Curtis and had great respect for Sam. Wexler had been telling her about Donny and she was curious to go in the studio with him. She wasn't disappointed."

"Don't know why they held the album back except that Sam was having serious drug problems back then," said Wexler. "Drug problems or not, the album was a monster."

"Aretha hadn't performed live in nearly a year," said Ruth. "She had given birth to Kecalf, she had gone in the studio and cut *Spirit in the Dark,* and I thought she was ready to finally do the big Vegas gig. I couldn't get her back at Caesar's, where she had canceled, but I did convince the International Hotel to book her. The engagement came in June. She was not in great shape. I don't know whether she had started drinking again, but I suspected as much. Her voice was not in top shape. Emotionally, she was extremely fragile. When I asked Cecil if there was anything I could do to help, he said, 'We just need to leave her alone. She'll get through this.' She did, but just barely. When I learned what happened a few weeks later in St. Louis, I was not surprised."

"Aretha Falls Ill in St. Louis; Treated in New York" read the *Jet* headline from July 16, 1970. In the article, WVON DJ and promoter Pervis Spann said, "I had to refund about $50,000 to fans. I'm the big money loser. And I want to say I was with Aretha, went to Detroit and got her for the show we were staging at St. Louis's Kiel Auditorium. We had a 6,000-person audience and after she sang one song ('Respect') she couldn't sing another. She broke down. She's now in New York under special care. I want everyone to know there was no stimulants involved whatsoever. The woman just took sick. She had a nervous breakdown from extreme personal problems."

"The sudden disappearance of Aretha was a frequent occurrence," said Wexler. "Ruth Bowen or brother Cecil would call and simply say, 'She needs to get away. It may take a while.' No one used the word *nervous breakdown,* but we knew."

"Sometimes she'd call me," said Erma, "or sometimes she'd call Carolyn. She'd talk about getting away from it all. She'd say she was going too fast, that the demands were too great, that too many people were pulling her in too many different directions. There were times when Carolyn and I would go and simply sit with her. Cecil of course would do the same. 'Please don't tell Daddy what I'm going through,' she'd tell me. 'He doesn't need to know.' But of course he knew. He knew better than anyone. He knew that, for all her drive to keep making recordings and doing shows and increasing her status as a star, she was a mess inside. She had huge fears she was not willing to look at or even name. But when those fears got too big, she'd break down. Cecil would put her in a hospital somewhere in remote Connecticut so the press wouldn't find out. Cecil called it 'nervous exhaustion.' She'd get her rest, she'd renew her strength, and she'd be back out there again. This is the pattern that continued for years."

When I asked Carolyn what Aretha's exact fears were, she said, "I think she was basically afraid that she wasn't enough. Crazy as it sounds, she was afraid that she wasn't good enough as a singer, pretty enough as a woman, or devoted enough as a mother. I don't know what to call it except deep, deep insecurity. Psychoanalysts might have determined the source of the insecurity had she gone into therapy, but that's not her style. Her style was to either drink away the anxiety or, when that stopped working, disappear for a while, find her bearings, and go right back onstage and wear the crown of the impervious diva."

She was, in fact, back onstage that summer when she played the Antibes Jazz Festival on the French Riviera. Also on the bill were Archie Shepp, Grant Green, Erroll Garner, Lionel Hampton, the Clara Ward Singers, and Stan Getz.

"I had been told that she looked at Clara Ward the way I looked at Lester Young," Getz told me. "Clara was the original. Clara was the template. And Clara was terrific, an inspired gospel singer who knew how to entertain. But Aretha went so much deeper. She cried with pain that was almost too intense to consider. I was deeply moved and artistically inspired. But I felt afraid for her. She was channeling more emotion than one human being could bear. I remember approaching her, just to say a few words of appreciation. Her brother was a jazz fan and knew who I was. Aretha knew my work as well. She said something like 'Oh, yes, Mr. Getz, I enjoy your recordings,' and then looked away. She couldn't look me in the eye. She wouldn't allow any discussion whatsoever. She was too troubled to deal with me, a stranger eager to offer words of comfort and encouragement."

She returned to the United States in mid-August and showed up at the Atlantic studios in New York, ready to record.

"They were all covers," said Wexler, "but what's fascinating is which covers emerged as hits and which didn't. She sang Elton John and Bernie Taupin's 'Border Song (Holy Moses)' with great passion, and it did all right, but it languished on the R-and-B charts and never got anywhere on the pop charts. That's significant because our sales strategy with Aretha never changed. It was the same sales strategy that had been in place with black artists for decades. They hit on the R-and-B charts and then you hope the success crosses over to the white charts, the pop charts. The R-and-B audience, though, didn't relate to the opaque lyrics of the 'Border Song.' The flower children were into ambiguous stories with disconnected imagery, but not Aretha's core fans. Those fans did relate, though, to Paul Simon's 'Bridge Over Troubled Water,' which can be read as straight-up gospel. It's a magnificent hymn, a song of hope and redemption, the kind of message Aretha and her audience love. It shot to number one on the R-and-B charts before going top-ten pop."

After the sessions, Aretha traveled to California to fulfill several professional obligations. There were indications of her fear of flying, a phobia that would build over the next decade.

In September 1970, *Jet* reported on the cross-country train trip Aretha would be making with "warm friend Ken Cunningham." The article spoke about her European tour, where "the demand for her appearance had been building to a deafening crescendo," as well as her upcoming TV appearance. It also noted that she was taking the train from New York to Hollywood because of her trepidation about flying. "The slow trip will be kinda romantic," said Aretha.

In October she recorded the *This Is Tom Jones* television variety show in Los Angeles and was brilliant. She appears healthy, vibrant, and happy. In the first sequence, she wears a glittery silver turban and, with ferocious confidence and subtle aplomb, tears up "Say a Little Prayer." From then on, she shares duties with Tom, who is obviously inspired and at his blue-eyed soul-singing best. The second sequence has Aretha in a black-and-gold African headdress giving a delicious reading of Tom's "It's Not Unusual," a further demonstration of her rare ability to turn the superficial into the profound. Together she, Tom, and a gang of go-go dancers rock through "See Saw" and find the beating heart of "Spirit in the Dark." In the third sequence, seated at the piano—no headgear this time, just a perfectly coiffed Afro—Aretha sings "The Party's Over" with exquisite restraint and unerring taste. Tom has some trouble making the switch from soul to straight-up jazz, but Aretha shows him the way.

"The show was wonderful," said Ruth Bowen, "and I congratulated her on her success, but I couldn't allow her to stay in California. She wanted to hang around and just bask in the sun. Aretha has a strong lazy streak. But I wasn't about to cancel the New York date I had booked. Philharmonic Hall was sold out. I can't tell you how many previous New York gigs she had canceled. I just couldn't go through it again. But she kept putting off the return trip until there was no time to take the train. So I had Cecil, Erma, and Carolyn fly to LA and fly back with her to New York. That's how Erma and Carolyn wound up singing with her that night."

"Erma opened the show," remembered Carolyn, "and broke it up with 'Little Piece of My Heart.' I followed and sang 'Chain Reaction.' We each had fifteen or twenty minutes, and we were grateful for the chance. We had helped Ree get through a couple of very difficult months and now she was helping us get the exposure we had both been seeking. She also had dancers and percussionists from Olatunji's school. When she came out after intermission, there was a symphony orchestra, an eighteen-piece jazz band, and the Sweet Inspirations behind her. It was among her greatest performances. Not that many weeks earlier she'd been in the throes of a breakdown, yet here she was, commanding the stage and thrilling the audience. I realized that, in fact, the truest healing Aretha receives happens when she sings. That's when she's able to purge her demons, find her center, and connect with the creative power of a loving God."

In November, Aretha and Wexler were back in the Atlantic studios in New York where she recorded two songs. The first, "Oh Me Oh My (I'm a Fool for You, Baby)," would be released on the flip side of the single "Rock Steady" a year later. The second, "Young, Gifted, and Black," would wind up on her 1972 album of the same name.

"Wexler had me come in and play organ that day," Billy Preston told me. "Naturally, I was honored. I'd known Aretha forever. We'd come up in church together. We were both students of James Cleveland and made in the same musical mold. I love this lady. I remember feeling the way I felt when I first got to play behind Ray Charles. The electrical charge was almost too strong to be contained. I also remember that she and Jerry Wexler were discussing whether she should sing 'Young, Gifted, and Black.' Wexler was trying to be diplomatic. He said that Nina Simone had not only written it but nailed it so strong that maybe Aretha should leave it alone. Wexler told Aretha the story of how Ray Charles had told him that he'd never sing 'The Christmas Song (Chestnuts Roasting on an Open Fire)' 'cause Nat Cole had nailed it so strong. While this discussion was going on, I kept quiet. I was just there as a sideman. But when Aretha turned to me and said, 'What do you think, Billy?' I had to say, 'I think you'll crush it, Ree. I think you'll make them forget about Nina.' And that's just what she did."

After the session, Aretha flew to Las Vegas, where, *Jet* reported, Sammy Davis Jr. had promised the International Hotel that if she did not show, he would perform in her place.

"Sammy was a client and a dear friend," Ruth Bowen said. "He made this guarantee for Aretha as a favor to me. Sammy has had his share of emotional breakdowns so he's especially sensitive to fragile artists. Besides, given the dozens of cancellations that had marred her history, this was the only way I got the International to book her for two weeks."

In addressing rumors of a nervous breakdown, Aretha told *Jet*, "I was all fouled up." The article goes on to say, "Today, apparently at ease with the world, she credits her triumph over her 'hangups' to a Detroit doctor and 'mindreader' who, she says, 'straightened me out.' When the subject gets around to her these days, she confides: 'I'm together now. Everything's groovy.' And she adds, 'I want to get into acting. And I'm not talking about acting in musicals. I'm talking about dramatic acting.'"

A month later, in its December 3 issue, *Jet* caught her in an unusually political mood.

"There was a period when, like many of us, she expressed a degree of militancy," said Cecil. "We'd come from this highly charged political background and were raised by a father unafraid to speak his mind. And though it might not have been anything the mainstream wanted to hear, Aretha wasn't about to hold back. Why should she?"

The *Jet* headline read: "Aretha Says She'll Go Angela's Bond If Permitted." The article stated that Angela Davis, the twenty-six-year-old former UCLA philosophy instructor, was being held in New York without bond pending extradition to San Rafael, California, where she faced kidnapping and conspiracy indictments in connection with a courtroom escape attempt that took four lives. "My daddy says I don't know what I'm doing," Aretha told *Jet.* "Well, I respect him, of course, but I'm going to stick to my beliefs. Angela Davis must go free. Black people will be free...I know you got to disturb the peace when you can't get no peace. Jail is hell to be in. I'm going to see her free if there is any justice in our courts, not because I believe in communism, but because she's a Black woman and she wants freedom for Black people. I have the money; I got it from Black people—they've made me financially able to have it—and I want to use it in ways that will help our people."

Two weeks later, *Jet* reported that Franklin and her family were forming a charitable foundation into which funds from "at least five concerts a year" would be funneled. Aretha said she wanted the money to be used primarily to help welfare mothers.

"I encouraged my sister's political stances," said Cecil. "I think they helped her. When she was politically engaged, she regained a stronger sense of herself. Political involvement took the concentration off herself and her personal problems. It got her out of herself. When her emotional fragility was at its greatest, I'd often give her an article about what was happening in politics—just to bring her back to earth. Some say that her 'Spirit in the Dark' was about sex. Some say it was about God. But there was also a powerful political spirit that was sweeping through the country in the early seventies. Aretha was part of that spirit. She contributed to it and, in many ways, gave it a voice."

18. RIGHT REVEREND

In late January, Aretha was in New York, where, at the Atlantic studios, she recorded "First Snow in Kokomo," certainly her most abstract composition. It is the only Aretha song written out of rhythm. There's no groove whatsoever. Aretha explained to me that Kokomo, Indiana, was the home of Ken Cunningham's mother, a woman she adored. She had gone there with Ken on a family visit, and she fell into a reflective mood as she described how Cunningham and his New Breeder artist friends were hanging out and playing music. A couple expecting a child dropped by. The atmosphere was calm. For a few blissful days, Aretha found a way to get off the grid. No touring, no recording, no career demands.

"There were moments in her relationship with Ken when she could finally relax," said Carolyn. "In many ways, that relationship was healing. You listen to 'Kokomo' and you begin to understand the kind of life that, from time to time, Aretha fantasized for herself—a life of domestic bliss. When she played the song for me in the studio, I felt sad, knowing that, given her talent and ambition, that kind of calm and easy life would probably never be realized. At the same time, it was a beautiful moment that she let you see the completely chilled-out Aretha. It's Aretha as the observer of life rather than Aretha in the center of the action. Erma and I both sang background on the song and were extremely moved. It showed us that Aretha had the quiet heart of a poet. It was a very simple but also a very poignant statement. In the end, though, it was something of a fairy tale."

"The song really resonated with me because it came at a time when I was at the end of my own fairy tale," said Erma. "Mine was about having a big career and becoming a major star. In truth, I had forged a small career and was a minor star. In 1971, I felt it was time to wake up to reality. I loved singing. I loved show business. I loved the records I had made. But I could not maintain myself as an entertainer. I was no longer able to make a living. I decided to leave New York, move back to Detroit, and raise my children. I needed a regular job with a steady paycheck and benefits. I found that job at Boysville, a wonderful child-care agency and the largest in Michigan, where I worked my way up as a program developer and fund-raiser. I bought a house in northwest Detroit and was blessed when my daughter, Sabrina, then a teenager, moved in with me. I found a great deal of domestic happiness that eluded me for years. To me, that's the theme of 'First Snow in Kokomo'—the dream of domestic happiness."

"Being a single woman without children," said Carolyn, "I was in a much different position than Erma. My intention was to continue to pursue my career, both as a performing artist and writer. I still had my deal with RCA in place, and I was planning on not only composing the majority of the songs for my next album but producing it as well. I hated to see how Aretha never got the credit for being her own full-fledged producer at Atlantic. I was determined that would not happen to me."

"Aretha came out of the sixties, when producers dominated," said Ruth Bowen. "The artists were beholden to the producer. Wexler ran his operation with an iron fist. He wasn't about to give up producing money to an artist. Look at Motown. The producers were in control. The artists were interchangeable parts. It wasn't until Marvin Gaye rebelled against the system and produced his own *What's Going On* that things began to change. But that wasn't until 1971."

"I started pushing for Aretha to get producer credit around the time of *Spirit in the Dark,*" said Cecil. "Everyone knew that she was the key element in putting those records together. But if you look at the albums, you keep seeing the names of Jerry Wexler, Tommy Dowd, and Arif Mardin as producers. It's true that Jerry was the man in charge. It's true that Tommy was a great engineer and Arif a great arranger. But Aretha had the big vision for how the songs should sound. Aretha had the arrangements—both instrumental and vocal—in her head. She provided the harmonies, she provided the grooves, she had the musical vibe that made her records distinct. But Aretha didn't want to rock the boat. She was making big money with this team. She was turning out hit after hit, and she was afraid of making too many waves. She figured that she had enough problems of her own without creating problems with her record company. She was not a happy person."

"The fast-paced thrills that are an essential part of show business do not promote personal happiness," said Ruth Bowen. "Most entertainers are too overstimulated, by adulation or wealth, to keep their feet planted firmly on the ground. Aretha is no exception. Even though she was deeply in love with Ken Cunningham, she also had not cut off her relationship with Dennis Edwards. That complicated things enormously. But even more demanding than her romantic desires was her career. Her career wanted her attention and got it. And, believe me, she wanted her career as much as her career wanted her. If you ask me, that was her essential relationship."

On the musical front, Wexler was able to coax Aretha down to Florida. On February 16, Aretha showed up at Criteria studios in Miami together with her sisters and her cousin Brenda. She was also armed with three original compositions.

"Aretha had written the basics of 'Day Dreaming' some time

earlier," said Carolyn, "and when I first heard it, I knew it was a monster. It was about Dennis Edwards and a famous limo trip the two of them had taken together from Saratoga Springs to New York City with the champagne flowing and the curtains drawn. It's a head-over-heels-in-love song with a silky-smooth feel-good groove. Ree had Erma, Brenda, and myself come to Miami to sing it with her. We were all stoked. It had *hit* written all over it."

"That was a marvelous day," said Erma. "At that same session Aretha cut her 'Rock Steady.' Jerry Wexler had the good sense to fly in Donny Hathaway. He was an almost painfully shy guy, but, brother, when he played that opening line on organ, we were off and running. That line defined the song. Aretha absolutely tore up the vocal. We knew it was an instant classic."

"The third original Aretha wrote for that session was 'All the King's Horses,'" said Cecil. "If 'Day Dreaming' was the upside of Aretha's friendship with Dennis Edwards, 'King's Horses' was the downside. As she said, all the king's horses and all the king's men couldn't put their two hearts together again. I'd been trying to tell her that Dennis was hardly a staunch supporter of monogamy, but she had to learn that for herself. No matter, she got a couple of good songs out of that relationship. And on 'King's Men,' she switched over to celeste, an instrument that gave the song a sad and lonely feeling."

When released in 1972, "Rock Steady" and "Day Dreaming" were top-ten hits on both the R&B and pop charts. "All the King's Horses" reached number seven on the R&B charts.

A month later, Aretha was in California. Wexler had convinced her to record a live album over three nights at Bill Graham's Fillmore West in San Francisco, one of the principal palaces of late sixties/early seventies hippie culture. Making that happen wasn't easy. The first obstacle was money.

"Aretha was getting from forty thousand to fifty thousand a show," said Ruth Bowen, "and Graham wouldn't pay anywhere near that. His club didn't have that kind of capacity. Neither Aretha nor I was willing to compromise."

"I stepped in and said that Atlantic would make up the difference," said Wexler. "We'd underwrite the funding. That's how much importance I ascribed to the project."

The next problem was Aretha herself, who was not enamored of the alternative-culture crowd.

"She was afraid she didn't belong there," said Wexler. "She saw the flower children as devotees of bands like the Jefferson Airplane and the Grateful Dead. She was afraid they wouldn't understand or relate to her. She had, after all, come out of gospel and R-and-B. She saw hippies as somewhat alien. But I liked the venue—Bill Graham was a friend—and I saw it as a chance to broaden her market. The hippies loved the blues. Graham had booked B.B. King and Buddy Guy, and I saw no reason why Aretha wouldn't be absolutely sensational in that setting."

"I've played a million gigs," said Billy Preston, her organist during those nights. "I've played a million churches, a million buckets of blood, a million nightclubs, and a million concert halls. But never, ever have I experienced anything like playing for Aretha at the Fillmore. It wasn't that the hippies just liked her. They went out of their minds. They lost it completely. The hippies flipped the fuck out. Fans say that *B.B. King Live at the Regal* or *Ray Charles Live* in Atlanta or James Brown *Live at the Apollo* are the greatest live albums of all time. And, no doubt, they are great. But, brother, I was there with Aretha at the Fillmore. I saw what she did. And I'm proud to say that I helped her do it. What she did was make history."

"Give King Curtis major props," said Wexler. "By the time she got to the Fillmore, his Kingpins were tighter than tight. What Basie was to jazz, King was to R-and-B. His band was locked and loaded, a unit that included the Memphis Horns, a rhythm section of Billy on organ, Cornell Dupree on guitar, Jerry Jemmott on bass, Bernard 'Pretty' Purdie on drums, and Pancho Morales on congas. I suggested that, in addition to her repertoire of hits, she add 'Love the One You're With,' a hit for Stephen Stills, and 'Make It with You,' a Bread hit. She smashed them both."

"The highlight, of course," said Billy Preston, "was when she left the stage to get Ray Charles, who was sitting somewhere in the back of the club. I know Ray well. I know how he hates to sit in. That's not his style. But even Ray couldn't refuse the Queen. That happened on our last night. It was a Sunday."

"I rarely go out to hear anyone," Ray told me. "But I happened to be in San Francisco that night when my friend Ruth Bowen called to say that Aretha was performing in the city and I should go see her. There are many female singers I like—I love me some Gladys Knight, I love me some Mavis Staples—but Aretha is my heart. It also doesn't hurt that Aretha is the name of my mother. Anyway, I love Ruth and I love Aretha and I figured that I'd have my man find a table way in the back where I'd slip in, hear a set, and slip out. When I got there, who do I run into but my old friend Jerry Wexler. He tells me that they're recording an album that night. 'Ray,' he says, 'will you sing a song with her?' 'Don't think so, Jer. Not tonight. Besides, I really don't know her material.' 'Her material is your material, Ray.' 'Just came to listen,' I say, 'not to sing.' So Jerry leaves me alone and I'm just digging the show. Excuse my French, but I have to say that this bitch is burning down the barn—I mean, she's on fire. She does a version of 'Dr. Feelgood' that's a hundred times better than the record. She's turned the thing into church. I'm happy all over when suddenly she turns up at my table shouting to everyone, 'Look who I've discovered! I discovered Ray Charles!' That was a line that Flip Wilson was using on his TV show, when Columbus comes to America where he tells everyone he's discovered Ray Charles. Next thing I know, she's taking me by the hand leading me to the stage. What could I do? This is Aretha Franklin, baby. She sits me at her electric piano and has me doing her 'Spirit in the Dark.' Never played the thing before. Didn't know the words. But Aretha's spirit was moving me and I got through it. She had me play a long solo on electric piano. Couple of months later, Wexler called and said he wanted my duet with her on the record. I messed up the words so bad, I said no. But then Aretha called and begged me and finally I said, 'What the hell.' Looking back, I see it was history in the making. Aretha and I did some Coca-Cola commercials together that turned out great, but in terms of real records, this is the only one. At the end she calls me 'The Right Reverend Ray,' a label I'm proud to say has stuck."

"I remember there was discussion about how she should end the concert," said Cecil. "Aretha wanted to do 'Reach Out and Touch (Somebody's Hand),' the Ashford and Simpson song that Diana Ross had turned into a megahit. Wexler thought it might be corny for the flower children. But Aretha argued that it was perfect because the hippies were all about handholding and love."

"We were all crying," said Brenda Corbett, Aretha's cousin, who was a member of the Sweethearts of Soul vocal trio. "It was one of those times when you thought, despite what was happening in the world, that peace and love might really prevail. Of the hundreds of concerts I did with Aretha, this was probably the most exciting."

"I saw it as a breakthrough," said Wexler. "The crowd at the Fillmore was not only emotionally connected to Aretha but proved to be musically sophisticated. They were deep into every riff played by King Curtis and Billy Preston and Ray Charles. They followed Aretha's every vocal nuance. If she had let them, they would have carried her from the stage and held her on their shoulders like a conquering monarch."

Before he left, Wexler encountered a reporter who questioned him about Aretha's drinking problem. "That pissed me off," said Wexler. "Here she had just sung the concert of her life. She was at the absolute height of her artistic powers. And all this schmuck of a scribe wanted to know is was she smashed on booze. Well, who gives a fuck? Everyone at the Fillmore was high that night, me included. You had to be an idiot not to be high. If Aretha was a little tipsy, it didn't make a shit. She sang her ass off and that's all that mattered."

Wexler described himself as Aretha's greatest defender, but a *Jet* article implied that he was seeking to control her nonmusical activities. The magazine reported that "Atlantic Records' bigwigs moved relentlessly behind the scenes to quietly, but quickly put the kibosh on Soul Queen Aretha Franklin's publicly announced plans to stage a benefit concert in Los Angeles for imprisoned Black activist Angela Davis. As a result, there'll be no such benefit by Miss Franklin in Miss Davis' behalf."

"That was absolutely bullshit," said Wexler. "Aretha and I share a common politics. We are both fire-breathing liberal Democrats. We might have had different lefty causes, but not in a million years would Ahmet or I even hint that she suppress her point of view."

Aretha backed up Wexler, as indicated by a follow-up report in *Jet* on May 27: "Aretha Denies Being Told Not to Perform to Aid Angela Davis: Soul Queen Aretha Franklin told *Jet* that she is angry over reports that officials at Atlantic Records (her label) had stymied her plans to stage a concert for Angela Davis." Aretha insisted that neither "Atlantic nor anyone else" dictated what she could or could not do. She explained that the cancellation was due to confusion over dates for the proposed concert at UCLA.

"Aretha was always going off and scheduling benefits without checking with me," said Ruth Bowen. "She drove both Cecil and myself absolutely crazy by willy-nilly arranging charity events. Her intentions were good. She has a big heart and a passion for genuine altruism, but when it comes to logistics, she's not home. Supposedly she was committed to leaving the organizational piece of her professional life to her brother and me, but at least once a month I'd get a call from the head of some political or charitable organization telling me that Aretha had agreed to perform for free. Inevitably Aretha chose a date when I already booked her elsewhere. Massive confusion would result. I'd be left to clean up the mess. I usually did—but not always. There are some promoters as well as heads of nonprofit charities who will go to their graves furious at me."

That summer she joined Stevie Wonder, who had just turned twenty-one and released his first self-produced album, *Where I'm Coming From,* at a benefit charity at Fisk University in Nashville. Aretha had told Stevie how much she liked the hit song he had written for the Spinners, "It's a Shame," and she wondered when he'd write a song for her. He told her that he already had. Aretha wouldn't record the song—"Until You Come Back to Me (That's What I'm Gonna Do)"—for another two years.

In May she played the Apollo, where, according to *Billboard,* she gave a stirring performance despite her tendency to cheapen her concerts with cheesy effects. Reviewer Ian Dove wrote, " 'She's home' ran the marquee billing. Aretha at the Apollo—the natural woman in a natural setting. There it was, the cohesion and knitting together of singer and audience and song... Aretha had King Curtis' big band, her own chorus and it was more than enough without some attempt to dress up the evening with sets, curtains that dropped and rose throughout, and dancers."

"Aretha thought she had the capacity to arrange her shows in terms of dancers and props," said Ruth Bowen. "I'd argue with her that she needed help. But she had little patience with my arguments. So I turned the matter over to Cecil."

"I stopped arguing with Ree about her shows," said Cecil. "It wasn't worth it. People came to hear her sing. If she overdid the stage settings, well, no one really cared. Same thing is true of the elaborate gowns she began wearing in the early seventies. Some fans complained they were over the top and didn't reflect a sense of refined taste. Well, Aretha had her own taste in clothes, refined or not. Far as I was concerned, it was her taste in music that brought out the crowds. Wasn't the stage lighting, wasn't her hats or her plumage, it was her voice that gave the thrills and had 'em shouting for more—her voice and nothing else."

Her voice was still in great demand in Europe when she returned in June. Her performance in Montreux, Switzerland, was a triumph.

"This was Aretha in her absolute glory," Montreux Jazz Festival founder and director Claude Nobs told me. "It was hell trying to arrange the date. She must have canceled four times. But I was determined. I'd come back to her and beg. Then she'd make another demand—a bigger dressing room, an extra hotel suite—and I'd cave every time. I sent her flowers, candies, and chocolates. She said it was the chocolates that won over her heart. She agreed to come! I was afraid she'd arrive with that terrible orchestra she had used before in Europe. When I learned that she'd be using King Curtis and the Kingpins, I wept with joy. Cornell Dupree was on guitar. We treated her like royalty and she was so grateful she asked did I have any favors she might grant me? Yes, I did. 'Play piano, Aretha. Please play piano as much and as often as you like. I'll have the world's finest Steinway grand onstage just for you. Play it. Stay on it. Do me the favor of playing piano all night long! You see, Queen Aretha, I think you're the funkiest piano player out there. I adore your singing, but I adore your piano playing just as much!' She laughed and said that yes, she would play. And she did. If you look at the set, which I videotaped, it's unusually keyboard heavy. It's splendid. Her 'Dr. Feelgood' and 'Spirit in the Dark' are masterful. This happened when the festival was celebrating its sixth year. We had imported everyone from Bill Evans to Duke Ellington to Carlos Santana. But Aretha was the highlight."

In Italy, though, she ran into trouble. *Jet* told the story in its July 15 issue: "Soul Queen Fumes Over Treatment by Italian Cops." Angry about an incident at the airport in Rome, Aretha vowed to call a conference of black men who would start, in her words, "to deal with how the Black woman specifically and Black people in general are treated around the world."

"I'm going to get Muhammad Ali, the Reverend Jesse Jackson, Huey Newton, Cong. Charles Diggs and we are going to have ourselves a conference and come up with a plan," said Aretha after she described being "manhandled" by Roman law enforcement officers for no apparent reason. After a scuffle with the police,

Aretha and two of her sons—Clarence and Eddie—were interrogated for four hours before being released. "The only reason I can think of why they did this," she added, "was because I had to cancel my last concert in Rome but I played a series of nine one nighters and I was tired."

The next brouhaha erupted over South Africa. Ruth Bowen was in the middle of the controversy, doing her best to protect her client. In its July 29 issue, *Jet* reported that Aretha had canceled her upcoming trip to South Africa. Ruth Bowen told the magazine that the singer would reschedule the tour, despite criticisms from the American Committee on Africa, Chicago chapter. The ACA had rebuked Aretha for agreeing to play in Soweto. Bowen claimed, though, that the postponement of the tour had nothing to do with those criticisms. "We have other dates in the USA to fulfill first," she said. "We are not politicians. That committee, which is headed by a white man, called me. I told them that I am black and explain to me why a black entertainer can't entertain black people. We are going to entertain blacks only. They want it and that's what we are going over there to do. I am opposed to black artists going over there to entertain black audiences, then white audiences. I would shoot any of my acts that did it. But we are not going to deny our black brothers over there from seeing our acts."

"The trip never happened," said Cecil. "It got mired down in politics and confusion. We were hammered by both sides—left and right—and for no reason whatsoever. The left could have no beef with Aretha. The Franklins have always been a freedom-loving family with absolutely no tolerance for racial bigotry of any kind. Aretha would never have anything to do with a racist regime in any country. Our mission in South Africa was to point out the moral bankruptcy of apartheid, not endorse it. The right could not possibly claim that we had agreed to entertain all-white audiences, because nothing could be further from the truth. In the end, extremists on both sides polluted the waters, and South Africa was deprived of the chance to see one of their queens."

★   ★   ★

A tragedy befell the R&B world on August 13, 1971. Aretha's musical director King Curtis was murdered on the streets of New York City.

"When I got the call, I was dumbfounded," said Wexler. "Couldn't speak. Couldn't move. Didn't know what to do. Didn't know how to process it because it came from out of nowhere. King was going home to the apartment building where he lived, on West Sixty-Eighth Street. King was at the top of his game—a healthy man, a vibrant man, a fabulous artist, a great guy. A couple of junkies were hanging out on the steps, shooting up and acting crazy. King told them to move on. They told King to get fucked. King made a move, but one of the junkies got to him first, stabbing him with a blade. The knife went through his heart. His life was over."

"It was a devastating loss," said Cecil. "King Curtis had proven to be the best conductor Ree had ever known. He was fast to pick up her cues and keys. He was a dynamite musician himself, both in the studio and onstage. He gave her that snap that every great rhythm singer needs.

"I'll never forget the funeral. My father flew in from Detroit to officiate. Jesse Jackson spoke. Everyone was there—from Brook Benton to the Isley Brothers to Stevie Wonder to Dizzy Gillespie. Curtis's band, the Kingpins, played 'Soul Serenade.' When Aretha sang 'Never Grow Old,' everyone lost it.

"The fact that King was killed in cold blood made it that more shocking and tragic. Like so many people, Aretha had a fear of sudden violence, and Curtis's death added to that fear a hundredfold."

Bernard Purdie, the great drummer who had been recording and touring with Aretha for years, took over King's job.

"He was our leader," Purdie told me, "and it was a sad, sad time. And the strange part is that Aretha didn't even want his name mentioned. It was like she couldn't take the sadness. If someone happened to say something about King, she went into her shell. I understood. She couldn't handle it. When Aretha was around, it was better to act like it had never happened."

In the summer of 1971, Aretha's take on "Spanish Harlem," written by Jerry Leiber and Phil Spector, shot up the charts and proved to be one of her biggest smashes, outselling Ben E. King's original version recorded ten years earlier. At the same time, Atlantic scored another hit, the Donny Hathaway/Roberta Flack cover of Carole King's "You've Got a Friend," a song Aretha would sing five months later in a radically different context.

One of Aretha's most vivid memories of this summer was Freda Payne's "Bring the Boys Home," a Vietnam protest song that Aretha told Wexler she would have gladly recorded had it been brought to her first. (The songwriting/production team, Motown's Holland-Dozier-Holland, had sued Berry Gordy, left Motown, and signed Payne to its own label, Invictus.)

The warm months in the city were not without diversion. *Jet* reported that Aretha dropped by the Roman Pub in the Hilton Hotel to hear jazz/gospel/cabaret singer–pianist Emme Kemp, an artist she had long admired. Aretha stayed for only a tune or two, then left a bottle of champagne for Emme with a note that said, "After a day's shopping, my feet hurt, stopped in for a delightful rest, thanks so much for the lift. Your sister in soul, Aretha."

Returning to concerts, she played Madison Square Garden in October. In the *New York Times,* Don Heckman wrote, "The feeling Miss Franklin radiates to her listeners, the feeling that makes virtually every muscle in one's body vibrate with an independent life of its own, was omnipresent."

The arrival of winter saw another Franklin song soar to the top—"Rock Steady." In November, she returned to Madison Square Garden to headline a tribute concert for her father. The audience included Coretta Scott King, Jesse Jackson, Ralph Abernathy, and Stevie Wonder.

Ever since the *Time* cover story in 1968 exposed her troubled relationship with Ted White and detailed her dark side, Aretha had scrupulously avoided in-depth interviews. But in the winter of 1970, she began to soften. She agreed, for example, to do *The David Frost Show*. At the end of the awkward interview, she was briefly joined by her dad before going to the piano and singing "Precious Lord."

"That show was my coup," said Ruth Bowen, "and it almost blew up in my face. Frost wanted it but Aretha was reluctant. So I arranged for the show to do a pre-interview with Aretha in my office. If she didn't like the way it went, she could pull the plug. I'm glad to say that it went beautifully. Aretha was charming and had lots to say about everything. The questions were respectful, and her answers were right on point. The topics weren't too personal, but personal enough for Aretha to display her confidence. At the same time, she and Ken were doing great, and she was happy to report on her romantic bliss. She agreed to do the show. At the actual taping, though, another Aretha showed up. This was timid-little-girl Aretha, the shyer-than-shy Aretha, the Aretha who would rather hide in the corner than be interviewed on TV. She sat there frozen. When Frost asked his questions, she gave one-word answers. She wouldn't elaborate on anything. In the middle of the taping, she said, 'Excuse me,' got up, walked to her dressing room to get a cigarette, and came back on set smoking. Frost was stunned. He finally got her to open up a little, but not much. When Aretha decides to close down, the door stays shut."

"As my career in child care developed," Erma told me, "I worked with many psychologists and learned a great deal about mental health. I finally had a way of understanding Aretha's volatile personality. I knew she was often depressed, and I knew that she had used drinking as an antidepressant. When she was drinking much less—and later in the seventies, when she stopped drinking altogether—her depression emerged unexpectedly. In between there were moods of hyperactivity when, in a manic state, she'd switch into overdrive. This is when she'd start planning to take over the world. She was going to buy her own restaurant. She and

Ken were going to open their own clothing store in Harlem and call it Do It to Me. She was going to fire Ruth Bowen and open her own booking agency. But none of these grandiose plans ever happened."

In *Ebony*'s cover story on her that December—"Aretha: A Close-Up Look at Sister Superstar"—she mentions the record label and booking agency and claims to have already signed her protégé, sixteen-year-old gospel singer Billy Always, the godson of Mahalia Jackson and the son of one of her dad's former girlfriends. These business ventures, however, never made it off the ground.

The profile by Charles L. Sanders is a seven-page feature that follows the singer from her New York apartment to concerts on the road. We learn of her interest in all things African. She's depicted as kindly, sympathetic, even-tempered, and abstemious. She says she no longer drinks. Despite having a cold in Greensboro, North Carolina, she visits seventeen-year-old fan Luther Williams. Still, she's reticent because, according to the reporter, "she considers interviews in about the same light as she does, say, splinters under the fingernails: painful indeed. She has always been a very private, extraordinarily shy person." The article goes on to say that her problems with Ted White "actually weren't any more special than the problems that a whole flock of women wrestle with and try to solve. Aretha says that she's feeling more confident in herself, how she used to want to appear more glamorous, but the Black Revolution, as she calls it, helped her attitude. 'I suppose the Revolution influenced me a great deal, but I must say that mine was a very personal evolution—an evolution of the me in myself.' "

During the course of the interview, Aretha mentioned one plan that she would soon realize—returning to church to record, a homecoming that would become the artistic triumph of her career.

19. AMAZING

W hen you look back and see what are now considered the great Aretha Franklin albums of the late sixties and early seventies," said Jerry Wexler, "they really aren't albums at all. They're compilations of singles. There was never any organizational principle. We just threw 'em together. *Soul '69*, the mislabeled big-band album, was as close as we came. But some years after Isaac Hayes's breakthrough *Hot Buttered Soul*—where his entire LP consisted of extended versions of four songs—at a time when Marvin Gaye was telling a complete story with his *What's Going On*, neither Aretha nor I had any narrative in mind. For example, you could interchange the tunes on *Spirit in the Dark* with those on *Young, Gifted, and Black*. Mix and match as you please. The formula remained the same—Aretha did superlative covers and came in with originals, notably songs by her or her sister Carolyn. Well, all that was well and good, but I felt we needed to stir up the pot.

"I've always loved gospel and, at one of the early seventies sessions, got Aretha to sing 'Heavenly Father,' by Edna McGriff, who had a hit on Jubilee back in the early fifties with a song called 'Note Droppin' Papa.' Like Aretha, Edna was equally skilled at sacred and secular. Aretha absolutely devastated 'Heavenly Father' but she felt it didn't belong on a pop album so it was never released until 2007, when I put out the *Rare and Unreleased Recordings*. I didn't argue with her when she refused to put it out back in the seventies, but I did suggest she do an entire gospel album. She was a little reluctant. She thought it might hurt her fan base. I said the opposite was true. It would expand her base. She said she'd think about it. She did and started suggesting songs. I liked all her suggestions but not the one that had us recording in our New York studio. I wanted it to be live in church. Again, she hesitated. She would have less control that way. But the more she thought about it, the more she liked my idea."

Aretha had a completely different view of the project's genesis. On more than one occasion she told interviewers that the idea of recording a gospel album—and doing it live in church—was hers, not Wexler's. She added that if she had not remained adamant, it would not have happened. She grew angry when people said she had abandoned the church. She insisted that she never could leave the church, since church was her essential inner core. This album would be her reaffirmation of that belief. Other people said that pressure had come from her father, but Aretha denied that. She denied that she felt pressure of any kind. She had sung blues. She had sung rhythm and blues. She had sung Broadway songs and folk songs. She had sung jazz. Now she wanted to revisit the music that had captivated her as a small child, the music that had birthed her artistry. She said that you could sing for man for only so long. At some point, you must sing for God.

Aretha was also careful to underline the notion that, to do justice to her tradition, merely recording a gospel album in a church was not enough. The music had to be the centerpiece of a larger concept—an actual church service. She reminded me that when she and her dad had traveled the country in the fifties, they didn't put on concerts. Reverend C. L. Franklin conducted services in which music played a vital role. That's the kind of record Aretha wanted. And, to a large degree, that's the record that she eventually got with *Amazing Grace*.

Aretha's version of the story in *From These Roots* has her taking charge of the project. It was, in fact, the first time that she was listed as a coproducer, along with Wexler and Arif Mardin. It was her choice to record in the New Temple Baptist Missionary Church in Los Angeles and have the choir directed by Reverend James Cleveland, the former minister of music for her dad's New Bethel Baptist Church in Detroit and the duly proclaimed King of Gospel.

"I was thrilled when Aretha called," Cleveland told me, "and I saw it as a chance to bring gospel music and message to a wider audience. I believe she called not only because of my friendship with her family but because my reputation was built on harmonizing choirs in new and dynamic ways. My Southern California Community Choir was known far and wide for its precise voicings. They were like a crack military unit. When it came to singing, they were sharpshooters. Alexander Hamilton, my first lieutenant and assistant choir director, was impeccable. No one was out of tune — ever. From the sopranos to the basses, the parts were enunciated with feeling and flair. Aretha knew that she'd be among her peers — blood-washed believers ready to sing the glory of God in every note."

Wexler knew just how to balance Cleveland's contribution. "I was determined to sneak the devil's rhythm section into church," said Wexler. "It was fine for Aretha to pick the choir. She loved James Cleveland, and James was a great choice. But I needed my guys — Bernard Purdie on drums, Chuck Rainey on bass, Cornell Dupree on guitar, and Pancho Morales on congas — to keep the rhythm right. My original choice for keyboards was Richard Tee. Then James made a strong case for his protégé Ken Lupper. Minute I heard Ken on the Hammond B-3, I was sold. Ken had crazy chops."

Aretha said the decision to fly in her New York–based Atlantic recording-session rhythm section was hers. By then Purdie had become her musical director and Rainey her favorite bassist. She had high regard for Cornell Dupree's funky guitar and thought that Pancho Morales would add just the right spice. She saw no

SOMETHING DIFFERENT • PREACHING AND SINGING

REV. C. L.
FRANKLIN

Rev. C. L. FRANKLIN

AND HIS DAUGHTER

ARETHA FRANKLIN
OF DETROIT

STAPLE
SINGERS
OF CHICAGO

STAPLE SINGERS

MISS BRYANT

MISS SAMMIE BRYANT
THE LITTLE LADY WITH THE BIG VOICE (3 FEET TALL) OF DETROIT

HOWARD HI-SCHOOL
CHATTANOOGA • 8:00 P.M.
MON. APR. 4

ADMISSION: $1.00 ADVANCE • $1.25 AT DOOR

H. NASH PRESENTATION   SOUTHERN POSTER PRINTING CO., ATLANTA, GA.

Gospel poster from the 1950s (Rock and Roll Hall of Fame and Museum, Cleveland, Ohio)

With John Hammond (Don Hunstein. Sony Music Entertainment)

With Bob Mersey (Don Hunstein. Sony Music Entertainment)

Clyde Otis and Aretha (Don Hunstein. Sony Music Entertainment)

With Ted White (Sony Music Entertainment)

Young Aretha (Sony Music Entertainment)

Jerry Wexler and Aretha, 1969 (GAB Archive/Redferns/Getty Images)

Duane Allman (standing), from right end of board to left: Tom Dowd, Arif Mardin, and Jerry Wexler, 1969 (Stephen Paley/Michael Ochs Archives/Getty Images)

Donny Hathaway and Aretha, 1973 (Estate of David Gahr/Premium Archive/ Getty Images)

With Glynn Turman, 1978 (Michael Ochs Archives/Getty Images)

With blood, sweat and tears, Ruth Bowen, founder and president of Queen Booking Corp., transformed her once fledgling New York talent/booking agency into a multi-million dollar empire. The agency—named for its first client, the late Dinah Washington, known as the "Queen"—has many of the nation's top black entertainers as clients.

FIRST LADY OF TALENT BOOKING

Ruth Bowen beats odds to gain success in competitive world of show biz careers and contracts

SHE describes herself as "a tough broad, taught by necessity to wheel-and-deal with the best of them" in a business she terms "dirty." Her competitors in the talent agency game think she flatters herself. "Tough? She's more like nails," says one, while another adds, "merciless . . . she's paying back with interest and relish the crap she took getting started in this industry."

She is also described as "my friend as well as my agent and," continues Aretha Franklin, "she is unique in that she cares as much about you, the person, as the you that earns her 10 percent. She tells you straight when she thinks

you've gone crooked—on or off stage."

She is Ruth Bowen and there is no precedent for her success. No woman has held as exalted a position in the entertainment industry as she does as founder and now president of Queen Booking Corp., one of America's major talent/booking agencies. Prior to Ruth Bowen, the only black women seen in the halls of such competitors as the William Morris Agency and Creative Management Associates dealt in mops and pails rather than careers and contracts. When Mrs. Bowen began QBC 12 years ago, few gave her an inch and even fewer a chance of becoming a multi-

Continued on Next Page 73

Ruth Bowen in *Ebony*, 1974 (David Ritz Collection)

Erma Franklin, 1960s
(Michael Ochs Archives/
Getty Images)

Carolyn Franklin,
1970s (Gilles
Petard/Redferns/
Getty Images)

With Cecil Franklin in *Jet*, 1976 (David Ritz Collection)

Aretha in the pulpit (Alan Elliott)

Reverend C. L. Franklin, with James Cleveland looking on (Alan Elliott)

Reverend James Cleveland (Alan Elliott)

Clara Ward, seated next to C. L. Franklin (Alan Elliott)

Father wiping his daughter's brow (Alan Elliott)

With Luther Vandross, 1980 (Afro Newspaper/Gado/Archive Photos/Getty Images)

Narada Michael Walden, Aretha, and Whitney Houston, 1989 (Michael Ochs Archives/Getty Images)

With Clive Davis, 1990 (Ron Galella, Ltd./Ron Galella Collection/Getty Images)

With Luciano Pavarotti, 1998 (HENNY RAY ABRAMS/AFP/Getty Images)

contradiction in using secular musicians in a sacred service and said that Wexler's notion of sneaking in the devil's rhythm section was absurd. She wanted the best players, the best choir, and the best songs.

To rest up for the grand event—two services over two nights (Thursday, January 13, and Friday, January 14, 1972)—Aretha and Ken Cunningham traveled to Barbados with an entourage that included brother Cecil as well as Bernard Purdie and Chuck Rainey. Cunningham shot the album cover photo at Sam Lord's Castle, which had been converted into a luxury hotel, with Aretha adorned in African garb.

In *Amazing Grace,* Aaron Cohen's insightful book on the making of the album, Rainey reflected back on this period: "I was with Aretha for three years and if I were to count the words I heard her say, other than singing, it couldn't have been more than 200 words. She very seldom said anything. When she did, she said it hard and quick. Mahalia Jackson was the same way. Sat in the chair with her knees close together, with her arms folded in front of her. Honoring whatever. That was the way she was. I've never been around Aretha where I was, 'Wow, Aretha!' I never saw that at all. She would speak to the wives more than to the band."

"I understand that Aretha's not a talker," said James Cleveland. "She's a musician who talks through music. She and I had our own shorthand. We communicated with nods. We were always on the same page. We rehearsed at the church that I pastored—the Cornerstone Institutional Baptist—where I would have preferred to hold the services. But Wexler had bigger plans. He not only had a recording crew, he had a film crew. That's why we moved the whole operation to the larger church down in Watts."

"Through Warner Brothers, who owned Atlantic, I had arranged for Sydney Pollack to film both nights," said Jerry. "This was after he directed *They Shoot Horses, Don't They?* and just before he did *The Way We Were.* Sydney loved the idea and showed up with a multicamera crew."

"While Wexler was running around and worrying about the

movie director and big stars he had invited, Aretha and I were tending to the music and the arrangements," said Cleveland. "Don't get me wrong. I knew King Curtis and I loved his rhythm section. Purdie and Rainey and the boys were great. Arif Mardin helped out with the arrangements. Wexler was a good traffic cop. But the truth of the matter is that Sister Aretha and I put the whole thing together.

"She came in with the new songs. Marvin Gaye had *What's Going On* out and she asked me if I thought 'Wholy Holy' from that album would be inappropriate for church. Well, sir, I'm made from the same musical mold as Aretha's daddy. I'm a musical liberal. It's all God's music and it's all good. Marvin was essentially a minister and I welcome his songs in my church. The other big album back then was Carole King's *Tapestry.* Carole had written 'Natural Woman' for Aretha, and Carole had deep soul. What did I think of incorporating her 'You've Got a Friend' into the service? I loved the idea, especially since we both wanted to change the words a little to say that the friend is Jesus. I suggested a little Rodgers and Hammerstein. I remember seeing *Carousel* and weeping when they sang 'You'll Never Walk Alone.' That might be Broadway but, hey, Broadway and gospel are not incompatible. Broadway can preach. So could the Beatles. That's why we put George Harrison's 'My Sweet Lord' in there.

"Of course, the core of the service would have to be straight-up gospel, what they had begun to call old-school gospel, the kind of gospel with lots of meat on the bones, the same gospel Aretha and I grew up on. Can't remember whether it was me or Aretha, but we agreed that we needed traditional material like 'What a Friend We Have in Jesus' and 'Climbing Higher Mountains.'

"Because Aretha idolized the Caravans and because I was their piano-playing disciple, we needed the Caravans' spirit in this service. Albertina Walker, the queen Caravan, hired Inez Andrews, who put together her own version of 'Mary, Don't You Weep.' 'Precious Lord, Take My Hand,' the famous Thomas A. Dorsey hymn, was something that Dr. King always requested and we wanted to include it. It was the idea of my trusty and worthy assistant Alexander Hamilton to combine it with 'You've Got a Friend.' It was my idea to get Aretha to sing a song she had sung as a child— a song I heard her sing when I was working at her daddy's church in Detroit—'Never Grow Old.' If you compare the version she recorded as a teenager with the one she does with New Temple, you will have the best demonstration of the flowering of genius that anyone could ask for. As a kid, she was a prodigy. As a twenty-nine-year-old woman, she has fulfilled the promise of her gift.

"Clara Ward holds a special place in Aretha's heart," Cleveland continued. "Every artist needs a role model, and Clara is Aretha's. Clara has style and class and rare musical character. I believe that Aretha has surpassed Clara because her range is greater and her material more varied. Aretha has gone farther afield. Aretha has conquered every musical ground there is to be conquered. But that doesn't take away the importance of Clara in Aretha's maturity. It was Aretha's idea to do 'Old Landmark,' a song associated with Clara, as well as 'How I Got Over,' one of Clara's biggest hits. It was a sure bet that Clara, along with her mother, Gertrude, was coming to one of the services. When I mentioned that, Aretha got all flustered and said, 'Of course Clara is coming, but I can't believe I completely forgot to invite my father.' 'Well, you better get on the phone right now and tell Reverend to catch the first plane out.' She did, and her dad, in the company of Clara Ward, sat right there on the front row.

"Aretha insisted that I sing 'Precious Memories' with her. I knew Sister Rosetta Tharpe's version, but Aretha had another notion of how to do it. She had this slow-walk-through-the-muddy-water-to-Sunday-morning-church-service groove that fit it just right. She gave it a fresh coat of paint and made it sound new without losing its ancient wisdom. Even at twenty-nine, Aretha was an old soul. She'd been here before. And have no doubt about it, she was also a preacher. That didn't happen during the services themselves, but at rehearsals she let loose. My most precious memories of the entire event were the rehearsals."

"The rehearsals were the joint," Bernard Purdie told Aaron Cohen. "While we were in church, Aretha preached. The actual recording of the date was nowhere near like the rehearsals...She was actually being a minister. The choir and everyone was totally in shock because the lady was preaching. She went someplace else."

For the services themselves, there was some concern that the presence of the recording technicians and equipment would over-whelm the church's physical facilities. Alexander Hamilton was especially worried that the film crew would be intrusive.

"The one thing that you don't want is for the things with the light and the director to distract you from doing what you're able to do," Hamilton told Aaron Cohen. "He [Sydney Pollack] had a camera in the Baptismal pool, behind the choir, shooting. Was it OK to do that? Noooo. The good sisters and brothers would have had a cow! Normally, somebody going up there with a camera, they'd be Baptized for real!"

"I had to keep reminding everyone that this was church," said Cleveland, "and not some rock-and-roll show. There's a notion out there that the black Baptist church is all about hysterical peo-ple waving their hands and jumping up and down in the aisles. There surely is joy in the way we celebrate God's grace, but the service itself is, above all else, sacred. It is no joke, no show, no sham. We worship Christ in complete and absolute sincerity—and the music, born out of our genuine love of a caring God, carries that same sincerity."

Before the music began, Cleveland took the time to explain to the congregation that this was a serious church service. They had assembled, first and foremost, to praise the living God.

Aretha's first solo on the first night of services was Marvin Gaye's "Wholy Holy." A dozen years after the night she sang it in the church in Watts, Marvin and I listened to it together on a rainy night in Ostend, Belgium. Marvin was deep into one of his long periods of exile from his Los Angeles home.

After it played, Marvin sat in silence. I was reluctant to break the spell, but there were so many questions I wanted to ask.

"When did you learn she was going to record it?"

"Not until the record came out," he said.

"So you were surprised."

"Stunned. As stunned then as I am now. Not only was I stunned with the knowledge that Aretha had decided that I had written something worthy of her voice, I was stunned by the beauty of her interpretation. *What's Going On* hadn't been out all that long. Because it came out of controversy—that whole business of Motown not thinking it was commercial—I was still a little battle-weary. I told my label that I'd never record again if they didn't release it. I won the fight, and the public seemed to be validating my stance—the record was selling—but I was still in a state of uncertainty. I knew it was good, but when Aretha sang 'Wholy Holy,' I saw just how good. She and I have similar musical backgrounds—watching and listening to our dads preach and sing—so I knew she had especially discriminating taste when it came to this kind of material. To me, gospel is the ultimate truth and ultimate test. I once heard a story about Duke Ellington, who had devoted a good piece of his later life to composing sacred music. He was in the middle of writing one of his great suites when a woman friend invited him out to a club. Duke demurred. The woman kept insisting, saying, 'You'll have time to finish the music later.' 'Darling,' said Duke, 'you can jive a lot of people a lot of the time, but you can never jive God.' That's the essence of gospel music—its connection to the divine makes it incorruptible. Aretha is incorruptible. Her God spirit is incorruptible. When I sang the song, I overdubbed my voice and devised a kind of self-harmony. I shadowed myself. I had strings and saxophones and a host of sound effects. Aretha had only her voice and that beautiful full-bodied choir. She built it up. She beefed it up. I believed she immortalized it."

"What about the rest of *Amazing Grace*?" I asked Marvin.

"If you ask true lovers of soul what's my best record, the answer is usually *What's Going On*. And if you ask true lovers of gospel what's the best record, the answer is *Amazing Grace*. Ask true

Aretha fans to name her best album, and the answer is the same—
Amazing Grace. No one loves 'Respect' and 'Natural Woman' and
'Chain of Fools' more than me. *Sparkle* turned me green with envy.
Curtis Mayfield got to write and produce an entire album on
Aretha! I'd die for that chance. But no matter how marvelous that
material, none of it reaches the level of *Amazing Grace*. I don't think
I'm alone in saying that *Amazing Grace* is Aretha's singular master-
piece. The musicians I respect the most say the same thing. It's her
greatest work. It's the Aretha album I cherish most."

"I look at *Amazing Grace* as an interlude in her life," said brother
Cecil. "It's a beautiful and healing interlude that I wish had been
longer. It came at just the right time. When Aretha had signed with
Atlantic, she hit the ground running. The first record was a hit—
and so was the second and third and so on. She took off like a
rocket. At the same time, she was all messed up in a negative marriage. She and Ted were like oil and water. That relationship was
hellish. But she thought she needed him and wouldn't let him go.
He knew he needed her and he wouldn't let her go. They'd break
up to make up and make up to break up. It was nuts. The drinking
got out of control, the press got ugly, and yet the hits kept coming.
So did the bookings. After she got rid of Ted and had me and Ruth
running things, the bookings got bigger, the travel got crazier, and
her moods got shakier. Ken came along, and Ken helped. Ken's a
good cat, but there was still a void in her life. The void was church.
By church, I don't mean her missing regular Sunday services at
New Bethel, but the *spirit* of the church. Her soul was craving that
spirit. Her heart was crying for it. Church wasn't only the appreciation of the saints who had encouraged her every note since she was
a little girl. Church was the presence of God's all-accepting love.
Church was home, mommy and daddy, a place where she could
completely be herself. Just as God is the source of every good thing,
church is the source of every good musical thing in Aretha's life.

"Don't get me wrong. I'm not saying that singing jazz or pop or
R-and-B hurt her in any appreciable way. And of course neither

my father nor myself ever did or would discourage her from singing other forms. But at the beginning of 1972, given the whirlwind nature of her life, it was, like the Beatles song says, time to get back to where she once belonged.

"After all is said and done, *Amazing Grace* was a homecoming—a joyous and heartfelt homecoming. You hear it in the excitement of the choir. You hear it in the reaction of the congregation. But mostly you hear it in my sister's voice. Of course, it helped tremendously that she was reuniting with James Cleveland, one of her main mentors. James was about the most reassuring presence you could have. The only thing possibly more reassuring was the presence of our father, who attended in the company of Clara Ward. When they arrived for the second service on Friday night, the scene was set in complete perfection. The person who mattered most to Aretha was seated in the front pew. And the female singer who had served as her musical mother was seated right next to him. It was a moment when Ree returned to those formative years, those days and nights when she was singing for both her Heavenly Father and earthly father at the same time. The difference, though, was this: Sister was no longer a prodigal child but a full-grown woman who, having captured the heart of the world, had come home to acknowledge and thank Jesus for the gift of her genius."

"She actually got some criticism from old-school church people," said Carolyn, "who accused her of putting on some Hollywood event. They said it was exploitation. They didn't like her including pop tunes like 'You'll Never Walk Alone.' They didn't like her singing stuff by Carole King and Marvin Gaye. When the showbiz columns reported that Mick Jagger had showed up for one of the services, the traditionalists saw it as proof that the whole thing was a staged event. But I was there and I'm telling you that it was real. It was righteous. We had no idea that Mick Jagger was in the church, and we couldn't have cared less. It was all about Aretha and James and that smokin' choir. It was all about digging deep into the roots and renewing the tradition that got her over."

*   *   *

To watch the raw footage of the *Amazing Grace* film shot by Sydney Pollack is an illumination. Alan Elliot, a former Atlantic producer, showed me a copy in 2010. For years, he had painstakingly labored to save, restore, edit, produce, and release the film. Long before I saw the images, I had memorized the record. To see it, though—to actually witness the performance—was not only thrilling, on every aesthetic and emotional level, but shocking. I hadn't thought I could ever appreciate the music more. But watching the film caused me to do just that.

First there is the image of Aretha herself. She glows with soft confidence. There is no swagger in her gracious self-assurance, but rather a sweet humility. In the presence of her dad and Clara Ward, that humility is easy to understand. She is there not to outdo them, but to honor them. She is completely comfortable, totally in control of her surroundings and her material. James Cleveland's strong presence is reassuring.

When her father is asked to speak, the emotions behind his words match the emotions of his daughter's music.

"This music took me all the way back to the living room at home when she was six and seven years of age," he says. "I saw you crying and I saw you responding, but I was just about to bust wide open. You talk about being moved—not only because Aretha is my daughter, Aretha is just a *stone* singer."

When Aretha hears her father's praise, a sweet and bashful smile breaks over her face.

"Reverend James Cleveland knows about those days. When James came to prepare our choir . . . he and Aretha used to go in the living room and spend hours in there singing different songs. She's influenced greatly by James. If you want to know the truth, she has never left the church!"

After her father speaks, Aretha replaces James at the piano, where she plays and sings "God Will Take Care of You." At one point, seeing his daughter's brow wet with perspiration, C.L. gets up, walks over, takes his handkerchief, and gently dries her forehead. It is an exquisite gesture, a touching moment—a father caring for a child.

The high points are many: During the "Precious Memories" duet with Cleveland, teacher and student both cry out *sacred secrets* in voices that chill the blood. Just as riveting is her reading of "Mary, Don't You Weep." The quirky 12/8 time signature creates a ferocious groove that sharpens the edge of Aretha's biblical storytelling. When Mary chastises Jesus for allowing her brother Lazarus to die, Aretha voices her grief in terms of a stammer. She addresses Christ as "my master" followed by "my my my my my my my my my my my sweet Lord." As Billy Preston once told me, that stutter might be the greatest riff of Aretha's career. The church explodes. But that's only the pre-climax. The full weight of the story comes when Christ summons Lazarus from the dead and gives him new life. Jazz singer Dianne Reeves, in describing her experience of first hearing Aretha's "Mary," told Aaron Cohen, "It makes you feel like you're standing there watching Jesus calling Lazarus. The thing that really gets me is that in the background, how the choir is very far in the back, like when Lazarus gets up he may be kind of dizzy. You hear these choir members in the background going 'woooo, woooo'... The way that she sings it, the way that she tells the story, you're right there seeing the whole thing go down."

"The whole record is punctuated by little miracles," said Carmen McRae. "And that's coming from me—a person who's always thought Baptist church singing can be overwrought. In this instance, though, the art approaches perfection. She's turning traditional gospel to pop and turning pop songs into gospel."

"It's an important moment in the history of black gospel," added Billy Preston, "because it lights up the crossroads. She gives a nod to old time by including those Clara Ward and Caravan songs. But she also anticipates modern gospel. She actually helps invent modern gospel by including Marvin Gaye and allowing a funky R-and-B rhythm section and razor-sharp choir to dress up the sounds. It's more than Aretha's greatest performance. It's really a radical record."

The record—which was heavily edited and resequenced back in Atlantic's New York studio—turned out to be a success on every imaginable level. Not only did critics call it her crowning achievement, but the public came out in droves to buy it. Since its release in June of 1972, it has sold well over two million copies. It remains the biggest-selling album in Aretha's career as well as the biggest-selling album in the history of black gospel.

"I see it as more than a hit record," said brother Cecil. "I see it as the sacred moment in the life of black people. Think back. We had lost Martin; we had lost Malcolm; we had lost Bobby Kennedy. We were still fighting an immoral war. We had Tricky Dick in the White House. Turmoil, anger, corruption, confusion. We needed reassurance and recommitment. We needed redirection. So when Aretha helped lead us back to God—the only force for good that stays steady in this loveless world—I'd call it historical."

"I'm a hard-core, card-carrying atheist," said Wexler. "I don't believe in God, but I do believe in art. And though it might sound like hyperbole, my assessment of *Amazing Grace* is that it relates to religious music in much the same way Michelangelo's Sistine Chapel relates to religious art. In terms of scope and depth, little else compares to its greatness."

20. HEY

While Aretha was praising God in James Cleveland's church, she was also singing his glory on national television. On the same Friday night of the *Amazing Grace* recording, an episode of the network drama *Room 222,* shot a few weeks earlier, was aired in prime time. Although her speaking part was small, Aretha sang a stirring full-length version of "Guide Me, O Thou Great Jehovah" to people in need of rehabilitation.

In the dialogue within the show, a man watching her sing asked, "Is she a minister?"

"No," answered a woman. "She's not a minister, but she ministers."

That same month, *Time* reported Jesse Jackson's break from Operation Breadbasket to start Operation PUSH in Chicago. The article described Jackson's split from other leaders of the Southern Christian Leadership Conference following Dr. Martin Luther King's death. Aretha Franklin was mentioned among the "prominent blacks" helping Jackson raise $250,000 for his new organization. Others included Ossie Davis, Jim Brown, and Manhattan borough president Percy Sutton.

Aretha played the Apollo Theater in January, where she received a standing ovation for her one-hour performance, a benefit concert for families of the victims of the Attica prison riots.

On January 27, Mahalia Jackson died in Chicago. Over fifty thousand admirers passed by her casket at the Greater Salem Baptist Church. Her funeral, held at the Arie Crown Theater at McCormick Place, was attended by six thousand people. Aretha was there to pay tribute. She sang "Precious Lord," the same hymn Mahalia had sung at the funeral of Dr. King.

"Mahalia represented the end of a glorious era that brought traditional gospel to the white masses," said Billy Preston. "She was the reigning matriarch of that genre. Mahalia was also a purist. Aside from 'Come Sunday,' a religious song she sang with Duke Ellington as part of his *Black, Brown and Beige* suite, she avoided jazz at all costs. Clara Ward sang in Vegas, but not Mahalia. She wouldn't carry gospel into a nightclub. She was the last of her kind. Some say that with her passing, Aretha assumed her throne, but that's wrong. Aretha had already been crowned Queen of Soul, a category that included gospel—but much more. Mahalia wouldn't have accepted the Queen of Soul title because *soul* sounds too street. That doesn't mean that Mahalia didn't sing with a blues cry in her voice. God knows there were jazz notes all over her style, but the story had to be religious. Even after *Amazing Grace* went through the roof, Aretha would never go the way of Mahalia. Aretha would never restrict herself to gospel. What's really interesting about that, though, is that the black gospel community— both singers and fans—are insistent that you are either in one camp or the other. They don't like their artists switching back and forth. Good examples are Little Richard or Al Green. They both tried to be as popular as gospel stars as they were in the R-and-B field but failed. Aretha's the one exception. She's accepted in whatever field she chooses to work. The doors of the church are always open to her. The saints welcome her whenever she chooses to honor them with her presence."

In February, Aretha expanded her repertoire even further. On a network TV comedy show, she ventured into vocal impressions.

"From the earliest days, she had this knack for throwing her voice and sounding like just about any female singer out there," said Cecil. "When we were kids, she could do everyone from Ruth Brown to Kay Starr. She was a phenomenal mimic. She always wanted to put it in her act, but I always thought it might be a little cheesy. But Aretha's gonna do what Aretha's gonna do. When Ruth booked her on the *Flip Wilson Show,* Aretha brought it up again. We mentioned it to Flip's producers, who liked the idea. So she did Diana Ross, Sarah Vaughan, Dionne Warwick, and Della Reese. She nailed every single impression, and from then on, it became a regular part of her act. She thought it added to the entertainment value of her show. Many of her fans didn't like it. They came to hear Aretha, not Aretha imitating Diana Ross. But other fans got a kick out of the accuracy of her impressions. I'd say the reaction was equally divided. But, as in all matters, Ree got the final vote, and the impressions stayed."

A *Jet* magazine article underlined Ken Cunningham's influence. He told the reporter, "The one most important change in Aretha's life is that she is happy and she's now being related to as a Black woman and a sister."

On March 24, she celebrated her thirtieth birthday by giving herself a party at New York's Americana Hotel. Guests included Richard Roundtree, Cannonball Adderley, Miriam Makeba, Nikki Giovanni, Betty Shabazz, and Quincy Jones, whom she had named the producer of her next album.

"Aretha asked me if I had any objections," said Jerry Wexler. "And I assured her that I had none. I had produced ten albums on Aretha in five years and there was no reason why she shouldn't venture out in a new direction. I thought Quincy was a good choice. He had done work for Atlantic in the past. He was one of the arrangers of the *Genius of Ray Charles* album. He had a reputation for missing deadlines, but I figured that, working with an artist of Aretha's caliber, he'd have to be on time. The quality of his musicality was beyond reproach. I also liked the idea of an Aretha/Quincy jazz album. *Soul '69* had been a successful Aretha jazz record and it was high time for another. The locale was another plus. Quincy was based in LA. Aretha had cut studio records in Muscle Shoals and New York but hadn't worked in a West Coast studio. I thought the change would be good."

"This was the Quincy Jones that was getting his feet wet with soul and R-and-B," said Cecil. "Ree and I saw Q as a jazz cat. We wanted a jazz album. He said he wanted to use some of the best jazz musicians, like Phil Woods and Joe Farrell."

"That's when the delays started," said Wexler. "The delays drove me crazy. We were used to doing an Aretha Franklin album in a couple of weeks. Get the songs together, get the musicians, the backup girls, book the studio, and bang out ten songs in a few sessions. That's how Aretha works best. She's a very assertive recording artist. She likes to jump on the material. Deliberation isn't her style. Procrastination on the part of the producer does not help."

"Q had lots on his plate," Cecil explained. "He was juggling lots of projects—writing for the movies and TV as well as producing the studio. I love the man but never felt that we got his full attention. I'm not saying that Aretha didn't contribute to the delays. There were more than a couple of times when she canceled West Coast trips. Her fear of flying was building up. When we did arrive in LA for the meetings, Q was always the most hospitable and loving man you can imagine. But his concept was changing. He was talking less about a straight-ahead jazz album and more about a mixed bag—a jazz tune, an R-and-B tune, maybe a show tune. Aretha said she had several originals that she wanted to include. Q liked the idea. Wasn't long before we were all over the place. Wexler was concerned. He was calling me every day, asking, 'What the fuck is taking so long?' 'Take it easy, Jerry,' I'd say. 'The record is developing.' 'I don't want it developing,' he'd say, 'I want it *delivered.*'"

What was delivered from the sessions that started in the spring and didn't conclude till late summer was disappointing. That Quincy/Aretha project, *Hey Now Hey (The Other Side of the Sky)*, was Aretha's first Atlantic album that did not land in the top twenty-five on the pop chart. In Quincy's autobiography, *Q,* he failed to give an account of his time in the studio with Aretha. The record got only a passing mention.

Neither fish nor fowl, it's an unfocused hodgepodge of unrelated songs. The cover art, conceived by Ken Cunningham, is amateurish and bizarre—a strange sketch of an angelic Aretha, a dope needle, a black matador, and Quincy sleeping in the clouds. Aretha told interviewers that she was baffled by the drawings.

Two of Aretha's originals—the title track and "So Swell When You're Well"—are subpar. Her rendition of Leonard Bernstein and Stephen Sondheim's "Somewhere" from *West Side Story* is overwrought and strained. When she sings James Moody's bebop classic "Moody's Mood," her vocalese feels rushed and uncertain. And yet for all its faults, *Hey Now Hey* cannot be ignored. Four of its tracks are fine. And one of those four—"Angel," written by sister Carolyn—is among the powerful and poignant singles in Aretha's career. It was the album's only hit.

Aretha's simple and sincere spoken introduction to "Angel" has become as much a part of the song as the melody or lyric. It's the one song she has sung—and continues to sing—at her every concert. She never fails to start with her prologue:

"I got a call the other day," she says. "It was my sister Carolyn saying, 'Aretha, come by when you can. I've got something that I want to say.' And when I got there, she said, 'You know, rather than go through a long-drawn-out thing, I think the melody on the box will help me explain.'"

The opening line—"Gotta find me an angel, to fly away with me"—is, in the words of sister Erma, "a prayer with wings. It's Carolyn's most beautiful song—and that's saying a lot because my sister wrote dozens of beautiful songs. But 'Angel' took it to a higher level—to the Curtis Mayfield/Marvin Gaye level, where there's really something divine about her composition. I can't tell you how proud we were of Carolyn. Daddy, Cecil, myself, and especially Aretha realized that she had finally realized the potential of her God-given gift."

Aretha's one successful original is "Sister from Texas."

"She wrote it for Esther Phillips," Cecil told me. "When Ree won her Grammy for *Young, Gifted, and Black,* she gave it to Esther, who that same year was nominated in the same category—Best R-and-B Album—for *From a Whisper to a Cry,* a great record that Aretha loved. Esther had fought off a lot of demons at that point in her life and the struggle wasn't over. Like Aretha, Esther had been a child star. Aretha had deep respect for her and wanted to help the sister in every way she could. It was one of those times when Aretha showed the love and generosity that I knew to be at the core of her character."

Her exposition of Bobby Womack's "That's the Way I Feel About Cha" is a study in overdubbing. A year earlier, Marvin Gaye had layered and harmonized his many voices in *What's Going On,* and the impact was immediate. In covering Womack's big hit from his *Communication* album, Aretha surely has Marvin in mind. She shadows herself to chilling effect. The intensity of three or four Arethas coming at you at once—especially out of that fat, kicked-back Bobby Womack pocket—is thrilling.

The final thrill on *Hey Now Hey* is Quincy's reconstructed and newly expanded treatment of Avery Parrish's "After Hours," a classic 1940 instrumental hit for Erskine Hawkins that Aretha had learned as a little girl. When Reverend Franklin woke his prodigal daughter to play for his party guests back in Detroit, "After Hours" was one of his requests.

"It's essentially a jam," said Billy Preston, who played the original Avery Parrish part on the track. "I start off just duplicating the record. But then Q wrote this killer big-band chart that kicks in. I mean, it's like a Basie chart. All Q did was tell Ree, 'Sing the blues, baby.' That's all he needed to say 'cause Sista turns it out. She's making up the words as she goes along. She's moaning low. And before long, she's screaming, she's soaring, she turns in the best straight-up blues singing I've heard since Ray Charles. Funny thing is that at the end of what was supposed to be a pure jazz album, Aretha turns in about the best blues performance anyone's ever done since the blues were invented somewhere in the middle of a muddy cotton field in Mississippi."

In mid-June, before completing *Hey Now Hey,* Aretha gave a triumphant performance at Chicago's Arie Theater.

"I've never seen her better," said Ruth Bowen. "I was a little worried because she wasn't exactly happy with the record she was making with Quincy. It was taking forever and the lack of progress put her in a bad mood. You wouldn't know that, though, by her demeanor onstage."

In the *Chicago Tribune,* Lynn Van Matre wrote about the concert:

"Even done up in a white satin dress with rhinestones for the first of two concerts Saturday, she wasn't exactly pretty. But more important, she was beautiful, and even with her 12-piece recording orchestra and three backup singers in saris on stage with her, there was never any doubt who was the center of attention... and why."

In the same edition of the *Tribune,* there was mention of her scheduled performance at the outdoor "Jail Show of 1972 for more than 3,200 inmates of Cook County Jail."

"Ken Cunningham has a heart for the downtrodden and less fortunate," said Cecil. "He was always arranging for Aretha to sing benefits and concerts for those who were ordinarily not privileged to see her. In that respect, Ken was a great influence. His political conscience went along perfectly with Aretha's and mine. I remember that was the summer that Nixon was running for reelection. My good friend Marvin Gaye put out a highly political single called 'You're the Man.' Like everything Marvin did, it was shot through with biting irony—a jab at the establishment. Aretha and I must have listened to that two dozen times in a row. That's when she told me that she really wanted to collaborate with Marvin. Wasn't long after that when I ran into Marvin in Detroit. 'Any time, bro,' he said. 'I'm ready.' For years we went back and forth, trying to make the arrangements. We were always running in different directions and it never happened. That still bothers me. I can only imagine what kind of music my sister and Marvin would have made together."

Ruth Bowen also remembered that year's hit parade, but for a different reason. "Sammy Davis Jr., one of my favorite people in all the world—I was very close to him and his mother—pulled a big surprise. Given the fact that we were in the soul era, everyone said that Sammy—essentially a Broadway belter—would never have another hit. Trying to be current, Sammy had actually signed with Motown, but they didn't know what to do with him. Then this movie came out— *Willy Wonka and the Chocolate Factory*—that had a song called 'Candy Man.' Turned out to be Sammy's only number-one hit in his career. 'I'm happy,' Sammy told me, 'but I want a hit with the kind of soul song Aretha sings.' 'Count your blessings,' I said, 'and eat your candy.'"

Jet reported that in August, back in New York after her recording sessions with Quincy Jones, Aretha was into a vigorous cycling routine in Central Park. She told the magazine that she had embraced a new diet and exercise regimen that required her to drink lots of water mixed with vinegar and honey.

A watershed moment arrived in September with the release of Aretha's version of "Wholy Holy," the first single from *Amazing Grace*. When the record failed to climb the charts, doubts began to set in. Would the project prove to be a commercial failure?

"After Aretha's huge success in the R-and-B and pop market," said Wexler, "[Atlantic] thought promoting a gospel album would disappoint her secular fans. There was also a feeling that once you leave the field of gospel music—as Sam Cooke had—there's no going back. So when 'Wholy Holy' failed to chart in any meaningful way, the naysayers had a field day. But not for long. Fans didn't look to *Amazing Grace* for singles. As it turned out, they embraced it in its entirety, as an organic and whole listening experience. In less than six weeks, it sold more than a million copies. That's unheard-of for a gospel or R-and-B album—especially one without a hit single. This record was on its way to making history. The reason had to do with nothing but quality. When quality is this fantastic, a record sells, no matter what genre. Take Miles Davis's *Kind of Blue*. No one would ever believe a jazz album would sell in the multimillions. But that particular jazz album is simply so good—the compositions, the playing of Miles, Coltrane, and Cannonball, the new modal sound—that it outstripped anything before or since. What *Kind of Blue* is to jazz, *Amazing Grace* is to gospel. It set a new standard."

This was the same moment—the summer of 1972—when Wexler was hearing the final masters from *Hey Now Hey*.

"Naturally, I loved 'Angel,'" Wexler said. "Everyone loved 'Angel,' and everyone knew 'Angel' was a hit. Carolyn saved Aretha's ass on that record. If it weren't for 'Angel,' the album would have been a total wash. Even with 'Angel,' the album was still seen as a flop. It slowed down Aretha's momentum. Careers have trajectories, and, ever since joining Atlantic, Aretha's was up, up, up. Quincy Jones has won his fabled place in the history of the music. His big band was wonderful. His small band arrangements for Dinah Washington were great. As a pop guy, he did Lesley Gore's 'It's My Party,' and you don't need for me to tell you about the incredible work he did with Michael Jackson. When it came to Aretha, though, he didn't serve her well. Maybe it was her fault. Maybe she was back on booze. Maybe she knocked him off his jazz course. I don't know. All I do know, though, is that the issuance of that album represents the end of her golden age on Atlantic."

Wexler was right. Aretha never recaptured the mojo or momentum of her first remarkable series of albums at Atlantic. Hammond and his colleagues had eventually run out of fertile ideas for the artist, and Wexler and his colleagues were on the verge of doing the same.

21. SHOP AROUND

A retha and Ken Cunningham were always hatching grand plans," said Ruth Bowen. "He convinced her that he could direct a film that she could star in. If Barbra Streisand could do it, so could Aretha. Aretha had a thing about Barbra Streisand. Because they'd started out together on Columbia, she always saw her as competition. Ree saw all female singers as competition. Because Barbra had a big soaring voice, she was seen as super-competition. Then, when Barbra busted out with *Funny Girl* and won an Academy Award, Aretha saw herself doing the same. Next comes Diana Ross. When Berry Gordy had Diana play Billie Holiday in *Lady Sings the Blues,* Aretha had the same reaction—why not me? 'Well, honey,' I said, 'because you don't have Berry Gordy. Diana does.' Aretha saw herself as being outdone by women who didn't have any more talent than her. If they could get a movie, she could too. Nothing wrong with that attitude. In show business, a competitive spirit is good. It makes for motivation, and—for someone who didn't always relish working—Aretha could use all the motivation she could get. But Ken wasn't always realistic about what it meant to get a movie made. He just didn't have the financial muscle. He was her man, though, and even though I believe in talking straight with my clients, early on I learned that straight talk never beats pillow talk. Pillow talk wins every time."

The October 12, 1972, issue of *Jet* mentioned that Cunningham and Franklin were scouting locations in Spain "for a film that he will direct and which she will star in." The movie never happened. The magazine later reported that Aretha was "taking the first half of the year off from concert dates to help friend and confidant Ken Cunningham put together a movie on Black women."

While the film projects were never realized, Aretha kept up her public appearances and joined Isaac Hayes, Gladys Knight, the Jackson Five, and Donny Hathaway in Chicago at the PUSH Expo '72 headed by Reverend Jesse Jackson.

Her personal appearance was the subject of a *Jet* article addressing her "mini meals" diet plan. She said she had lost twenty-five pounds and was close to meeting her goal—135 pounds. She also said, "Well, I'm not going to get that small. I'm going to leave enough there for somebody to grab hold to." Accompanying the article was a photo of Franklin in a bikini in Nassau.

The magazine also noted that Cecil was shopping for a new Aretha Franklin record deal. With her Atlantic contract up on March 31, he was reportedly talking to ABC-Dunhill, Columbia, and Warner Brothers. Her price tag was $5 million.

"I had some doubts about our bargaining position," Cecil told me. "Of course, Ree had this incredible run of hits. But the truth is that her only platinum-plus album was *Amazing Grace*. She had a great string of singles that somehow hadn't turned into blockbuster LP sales. And then, on the heels of *Hey Now Hey*, which wasn't looking all that good, I felt we were a little vulnerable. On the other hand, Ruth and Aretha felt we were in a strong position."

"Atlantic said they'd give her three million," said Ruth. "I said that was nothing. She needed twice that. Aretha was behind me but Cecil was a little cautious. I told Cecil to start talking to other labels. That would get Ahmet and Wexler good and nervous. In the early sixties, they had lost Ray Charles to ABC Paramount. That's when

Ray went on to his big country hits. His leaving cost Atlantic a fortune. I didn't see those boys making the same mistake twice."

"I didn't like how Cecil began making the rounds," said Wexler. "I didn't appreciate that. Of course Aretha was a free agent and entitled to see what was out there. But after all was said and done, Atlantic was where she had rediscovered herself. Her tremendous talent notwithstanding, our input was critical to her fabulous success. She didn't reinvent herself in a vacuum. That reinvention happened in the specific culture of Atlantic Records. Surely we deserved special consideration."

"Aretha's first choice was to stay at Atlantic," said Cecil. "She felt that she owed them both gratitude and loyalty. But business is business. In this case, I followed Ruth's lead. I worked hard to make Wexler worry."

"The guy who worried me most was Clive Davis," said Wexler. "He was running Columbia. Now, Clive is shrewd. He's the guy who took Columbia from a classical-and-Broadway-musical-cast-recording-driven label—they'd made a fortune on *My Fair Lady*—to the era of rock and roll. Clive had gone to the Monterey Pop Festival and heard the future in Janis Joplin. He saw the money in rock and roll. In the early seventies, he also saw the money in rhythm and blues. That's when he went after a bigger share of the black music market. He signed Earth, Wind, and Fire and also cut a distribution deal with Kenny Gamble and Leon Huff at Philly International, who were terrific writers and producers. Clive saw that Philly International—red hot with the O'Jays and Harold Melvin and the Blue Notes—was positioned to be the new Motown. I have no doubt that Gamble and Huff had the chops to produce Aretha, but there was no way I was going to be outbid."

"When Wexler put four million on the table," said Cecil, "my inclination was to take it. After all, Aretha had originally signed with the label for twenty-five thousand. Sure, she was a big earner, and sure, she had decades of more hits in her, but Atlantic had sweetened their original offer by a million. As usual, I asked Ruth Bowen's advice."

"I told Cecil and Aretha both, 'Stick to your guns,'" said Ruth. "'Atlantic is no longer an independent label. Atlantic is owned by Warner, a major corporation with deep pockets. You're into a new era. Demand the six million.'"

Aretha got the six million.

"Ahmet and I felt like we had no choice," said Wexler. "We were haunted by the memory of losing Ray Charles and weren't about to let that happen again. We convinced the brass at Warner to do the deal. Champagne all around. Aretha took the money, bought a glamorous town house on the Upper East Side on Eighty-Eighth Street between Fifth and Madison and hired a decorator and went to town."

"The place was beautiful," said sister-in-law Earline. "Aretha was proud of her home and entertained often—mainly her family. She was generous in having me and Cecil and her sisters stay over whenever we wanted. It was a good period. She seemed stable, but stability with Aretha is an illusion. Her emotions—her big highs and her deep lows—don't let her stay stable. If the stability lasts for a few months, she's lucky. After that—watch out!"

On January 16, 1973, her stability was shaken by the death of Clara Ward. C. L. Franklin was by Clara's side. Both he and Aretha performed at her funeral in Philadelphia.

"It was a great loss for our family," said Cecil. "My father lost perhaps his closest friend. And Aretha lost another mother figure—the singer whose style, in music and fashion, influenced her the most."

After her sister's death, Willa Ward found a notebook in which Clara had recorded her impressions of key figures in her life. "My baby Aretha," wrote Clara. "She doesn't know how good she is. Doubts self."

In February, Aretha was in California to perform on the Quincy Jones network television special *We Love You Madly,* a tribute to Duke Ellington. Aretha was especially thrilled to be appearing along with Duke, Count Basie, Ray Charles, Sammy Davis Jr., Tony Bennett, Joe Williams, Billy Eckstine, Sarah Vaughan, and Peggy Lee. Among her seniors, she more than held her own. She was part of the show's youth contingent, which also included Roberta Flack and the band Chicago.

"She had no objection to Sarah and Peggy," said Ruth Bowen, "but she didn't like Roberta Flack being on the show. She felt that one so-called soul singer was enough. Ever since Roberta had joined Atlantic, Aretha didn't like the attention they were giving her. I had to reassure her that Roberta was a much different kind of artist and that she in no way stole Aretha's thunder. The issue came up over and over again and finally I gave up trying to calm her down. I let Atlantic deal with it."

"Aretha knew that I was Roberta's producer," said Joel Dorn. "Because of that, every time I ran into her at the studio, she looked at me with daggers in her eyes. I was always extra polite, but I never got past her cold-blooded stare. I've dealt with chilly women before, but she was absolute ice. You'd think I killed her dog."

In March 1973, she returned to the studio to cut *Let Me in Your Life*. The hope was that, back with the Wexler crew, she could reverse the downward sales slide that had started with *Hey Now Hey*. The hope was not realized.

Bill Withers's title song is a routine cover. Other covers are more convincing: Ashford and Simpson's "Ain't Nothing Like the Real Thing," Bobby Womack's "I'm in Love," Leon Russell's "A Song for You" (with Richard Tee on keys), plus a well-wrought dramatization of "The Masquerade Is Over." But there is also tedious filler—"Oh Baby" and "If You Don't Think So," two inferior Aretha originals. The feeling is of uninspired obligation. The only showstopper chart topper is "Until You Come Back to Me (That's What I Got to Do)," by Stevie Wonder, Clarence Paul, and Morris Broadnax—the single that went number one on the R&B charts, crossed over to number three on pop, and became a permanent part of Aretha's repertoire.

In his liner notes to the album's reissue, soul scholar David

Nathan pointed out that for the first time during a recording session Aretha had let a journalist watch the proceedings. Loraine Alterman from London's *Melody Maker* quoted Wexler about why these sessions were so different from her earlier work on Atlantic.

"These are the first arranged sessions we've done with her," he tells the reporter. "Everything we've done with her has always been woodshedded in the studio with just the rhythm section there."

In retrospect, the decision appears to be a mistake. Spontaneity is missing.

The album cover reveals a slimmed-down mink-covered Aretha, her Afro a bit softened and highlighted with a hue of red.

"After the six mill we paid for her new contract," said Wexler, "the album didn't perform. Stevie's song wasn't enough to save it. On the heels of *Hey Now Hey,* another underperformer, I knew that the Franklin franchise was in trouble. We needed something new. I don't say this to disparage Aretha because, in all ways, she was a great contributor to her own productions. And when we agreed to list her as a coproducer, her attitude changed. She was less accepting of our ideas and far more emboldened to initiate her own. I had to fight with her to let Donny Hathaway play on these sides. She thought it would be over-soul. She also wasn't thrilled about having Deodato play on 'Let Me in Your Life.' She thought it would be under-soul. We were starting to have our issues. Earlier, she'd basically go along with my program. Now she had a program of her own. Well, in the case of Quincy, that program didn't work. This was another instance where I felt her concept was scattered and emotionally disconnected."

An emotional disconnection was also evident in Aretha's personal life.

"It wasn't long after she moved into the town house that she started having what she described as nightmares," said Erma. "She started calling me back in Detroit nearly every day with stories of these terrible dreams. She said they were foreboding. Her voice sounded shaky—which is not at all typical of my sister. She asked whether I could come stay with her in New York, but my job wouldn't allow it. Carolyn was able to get away, though, and Carolyn wound up staying with her for a while."

"She was really off-kilter," said Carolyn. "I'm not sure what was causing the distress—maybe all the travel with Ken, maybe the pressure of the gigs, maybe the tension over her negotiations with Atlantic; I'm not sure. But it became increasingly difficult for her to get out of bed. She did an enormous amount of crying and ultimately we had no choice but to get her to a hospital."

From *Jet*, April 12, 1973: "Aretha Buries Rumors About 'Going Crazy': It was no small wonder that many of [Franklin's] followers registered dismay over erroneous reports coming out of New York that Miss Franklin was 'hospitalized for a nervous breakdown.' So moved was the soul queen by the concern exhibited by her admirers that she called the first press conference of her career to explain that her three-day hospitalization at Mount Sinai Hospital in New York was caused by acute physical exhaustion, a medical fact attested to by her personal physician, Dr. Aaron O. Wells." In the same issue of *Jet*, there was an additional item: A "hot rumor that Aretha Franklin has a semi-nude scene in a soon to be released movie. The movie, still untitled, was filmed last fall while the Soul Queen was vacationing in the Bahamas."

"Aretha used *Jet* for decades to clean up and clear up her image," said Ruth Bowen. "The truth is that she had suffered something of a breakdown but was adamant that the public see her as healthy. I tried to tell her that there is no shame in having mental-health challenges. Most of us have mental-health challenges in one form or another. But she couldn't tolerate letting me know that. 'Who *doesn't* know that you have the blues, Aretha?' I'd ask. 'For God's sakes, you're a blues singer. You're supposed to have the blues.' Didn't matter what I said. My job was to keep what she considered 'dirt' out of the press and to drop in items—like the one about her appearing semi-nude in a film—into the magazines. I invented half of those, but if it made her happy, so be it. In turn, she made me happy by helping me put together a testimonial dinner. By then she had completed her hospital stay and was regaining her emotional balance."

That same winter, Aretha—together with Sammy Davis Jr. and Ray Charles—sponsored a testimonial dinner for Ruth Bowen at the New York Hilton, the proceeds going to the foundation for research and education in sickle cell disease and to the Miss Black America scholarship fund.

"It was a beautiful evening," Ruth remembered. "Aretha was fully recovered and at her best. She could not have been more gracious. Before singing like an angel, she praised me to the sky, like a grateful daughter acknowledging the love of a mother. The ballroom was packed with every star in the galaxy of show business. I told them that I've been blessed to have served two queens in my life—first Dinah and now Aretha. Tears were flowing so strong until I made a mess of my makeup."

"The evening for Ruth turned out good," Cecil remembered, "but afterwards Aretha fell back into depression. These were rough times. I couldn't figure out how to break her out of the blues. These blues were deep. Ken certainly wanted to help, but you can only help Aretha so much. At a certain point she resists help. She says, 'You're making me feel helpless. Leave me alone. Back off.' I know when to back off. I'm not sure Ken did."

"The other thing is that Ken was encroaching into Cecil's territory," said Ruth. "Aretha's first serious man—Ted White—had managed her and I could understand why Ken saw himself falling into that role. But after Ted, that role had been given to Cecil by none other than Reverend C. L. Franklin, the man Aretha respected more than anyone in the world. When it came to management, Cecil was a lock. I was able to mentor Cecil, but I knew better than to invade his territory. When it comes to advising talent, boundaries are critical. You don't want to step on the toes of people who have known the artist a lot longer than you. I'm not sure Ken was wise to get Aretha in so many different business situations—from movies to clothing lines. Looking back, those plans faded. I'm not blaming Ken. Aretha's always been big on branding. From the first years we worked together she talked about opening an Aretha soul-food restaurant in every major city. Not even one ever appeared. Cecil and I couldn't tell her outright that she lacked the business skills to pull it off, but we knew how to distract her. Ken kept pushing."

In speaking about Ken, Aretha was always complimentary. In her long litany of male friends, he received her highest marks. However, the relationship didn't last because she felt that Ken didn't grant Cecil the respect that her brother deserved.

"The cracks in Ree's relationship to Ken certainly contributed to her nervous condition," said Carolyn. "This was her second or third so-called full breakdown. I mean that literally—where she just couldn't write, rehearse, record, or perform."

"But here's the thing about my sister," said Erma. "You think these breakdowns are a pervasive pattern. And in a sense, they are. Ultimately, though, she doesn't stay down. Ultimately, she gets back up. It may take her a while, but her commitment to her career is strong as steel."

By springtime, Aretha felt renewed.

"Rev. Wyatt T. Walker's Canaan Baptist Church in Harlem got a surprise visit Easter Sunday morning from soul sister No. 1 Aretha Franklin," wrote *Jet*. "In response to a request from Rev. Walker, Aretha got up and sang 'Amazing Grace' for surprised church-goers. According to one observer, it was almost 30 minutes after she finished singing before the church calmed down so the service could continue."

That same month she sang "Rock Steady" on *Soul Train*.

In July, she played the Newport Jazz Festival concert at the Nassau Coliseum along with Donny Hathaway, Duke Ellington, and Ray Charles.

"Angel" started making its climb up the charts.

"'Angel' definitely revived her spirits," said Carolyn. "She was really afraid that *Hey Now* would be a total sales failure. I think she sent me a dozen roses two or three different times to thank me for the song. The hit put her back on track, and she and Ken were getting along again. When you're in the music business, a hit is something that makes everyone happy and seems to solve all your problems — at least for a while."

By the holidays, Aretha was upbeat. She hired a yacht and went on a cruise to the Bahamas, resting up before her upcoming 1974 tour. In addition to Ken Cunningham, she brought Cecil, his wife, Earline, and Norman Dugger, her personal assistant and longtime road manager.

"After being in and out of all those hospitals, the cruise did her a world of good," said Dugger, who would serve as Aretha's fiercely loyal lieutenant for the next thirty-eight years. "She was just about as relaxed as she could ever be. Aretha's never ever completely at ease, but for the most part the cruise did a lot to cool her out. She kept talking about all these dishes she wanted to cook up and put into a book."

Jet reported that "Aretha Franklin returned from a yacht cruise around the Bahamas with ideas for a cookbook that would include recipes like Ken's paella (for Ken Cunningham), Norman's potato salad (for Norman Dugger), and a collection of other jaw teasers like pecan pie, fried ribs, home made ice cream and cracklin' bread. The Soul Queen still insists that despite all the tasting and testing she'll maintain her size nine to 10 figure after dealing with all the good recipes. She's still on the vinegar cider and honey and water conditioner. A mixture of the three ingredients three times a day will keep those calories away."

On January 14, 1974, she went into the studio to start recording what would be *With Everything I Feel in Me*, an album that would mark a further decline in quality and sales.

The revealing cover has her in a mink coat that's slipped down her shoulders to show major cleavage. She has a come-hither, check-me-out smile on her ultra-slender face. There are two Carolyn originals, an original Aretha song, and a bunch of covers, all in the heavy-gospel-pop-R&B recipe cooked up by the singer and her coproducers.

"There's only so long you can continue the formula," said Wexler. "We were aware of this. We thought that by including a couple of Bacharach/David songs—'Don't Go Breaking My Heart' and 'You'll Never Get to Heaven'—we might strike lightning in the bottle, but we didn't. Because she had successfully thinned down, she was in an ebullient mood. She wasn't high on drugs but definitely on an emotional high. She was certain this would be the greatest album of her career. I remember questioning her about her inclusion of a love song by James Cleveland. James is King of Gospel but hardly king of love songs. I thought it was filler. Aretha thought it was great. It stayed. And the entire album laid a giant egg. It's the first time an Aretha Franklin Atlantic album failed to have a single in the top forty."

Before the record was completed, Aretha went on tour. In early March, she played Chicago, where, according to *Jet*, "She electrified the capacity audience at the Auditorium Theater with her new size-8 figure. Garbed in a painfully-tight white satin, silver-trimmed backless pant suit, her majesty leaped to the piano and revealed to her subjects: 'I looked at myself in the mirror and said to myself, Go on child, you done really got yourself together.'"

A week later, she played the Apollo. John Rockwell's review for the *New York Times* indicated what the Aretha Franklin show would be like for decades to come:

"Miss Franklin seems intent these days on approximating a kind of Liza Minnelli cabaret glamour, complete with glittering cutaway costumes, a top hat and supper-club bumps and grinds."

On March 25, 1974, Aretha celebrated her thirty-second birthday.

"Ken gave her a surprise party at their East Side town house," said Ruth. "Ken is almost as dangerous in the kitchen as Aretha. The boy can burn. He assembled us in the living room, and when

Ree came downstairs, wearing her dressing gown, we jumped up and sent her into shock. She loved it."

Three days later *Jet* hit the newsstands with this item:

"Ken Cunningham, Aretha Franklin's consort and manager, is also a screenwriter and has a dynamite movie script...and is looking for investors to match his bread and turn it into a movie."

"I planted that item," said Ruth Bowen. "I planted most of the press items that Aretha felt would help the cause. The black press was always more than willing to accommodate her. I didn't always like doing it because many of the items were nothing more than ads for investors in the projects that she and Ken were cooking up. I knew those projects weren't going anywhere, but rather than argue with the Queen, I did her bidding. After all was said and done, that was my job."

In May, *Jet* published still another cover story of Aretha, and this one didn't make brother Cecil happy. The reporter wrote, "It is to Ken that she looks for direction in most of what she does professionally. He produced the show that she recently put on at the Apollo and which she will be taking to Japan for a concert tour this summer and to Europe in the fall. Ken also influences greatly when and where she'll appear."

"More and more the world was getting the idea that Ken was her manager," said Cecil, "not me."

"'No one is going to drive a wedge between you and your sister,' I told Cecil when he called to complain," said Ruth. "'Just be patient. Things will come around. Meanwhile, if she wants to give Ken a little of the spotlight, let her. Now is not the time to make waves. She's happy, and that's all that counts.' Cecil listened to me. He always did."

In the June issue of *Ebony*, Ruth turned the spotlight on herself. She arranged for a feature article with a headline that read: "First Lady of Talent Booking." The piece described Bowen's toughness in the white-male-dominated business. At the time, Queen Booking was twelve years old. Her star client remained Aretha, who told the reporter that "Ruth is my friend as well as my agent and she is unique in that she cares as much about you, the person, as the you that earns her 10 percent. She tells you straight when she thinks you've gone crooked—on or off stage."

A photo showed Ruth consulting with Aretha on her wardrobe for an upcoming performance. Bowen was also quoted as saying how she "represented most of the Motown acts, from the Supremes to Stevie Wonder." As the acts grew, though, they were raided by big-time bookers and often "placed with a white agency." According to Ruth, her biggest star resisted the raiders. "Those cats just didn't know Aretha," said Ruth. "Nothing can shake her from her loyalties and her love."

During the summer when the Watergate scandal resulted in Nixon's resignation, Cecil remembered a certain joy in the Franklin camp.

"All of us—Daddy, Ken, Aretha—couldn't wait to see Nixon bite the dust," said Cecil. "We had a Good-Bye, Tricky Dick party the weekend after his resignation."

In October, the relentless public relations campaign in the black press continued. Once again, it was Ruth Bowen who convinced *Ebony* to put Aretha on the cover.

"I promised them total access and exclusive photos," she said. "I said I wanted the emphasis to be on the New Aretha—slim, trim, and sexy. That's the story I got. Aretha was thrilled."

The article talked about her favorite designers—Stephen Burrows of New York and Boyd Clopton of LA. The thrust of the story was her weight loss. Photos showed her playing pool in her town house, practicing a golf shot on a New York course, and modeling a revealing new outfit. There was also discussion of a diet book (which was never written). She revealed that her weight-loss method was moderation. She liked to take a spoon and dip it in the corner of a pot filled with fattening food.

"When I read the article," said Ruth, "I thought, *Girlfriend is talking way too much about food. If she ever puts on that weight again, she's gonna have some backtracking to do.* But Aretha has an obsession with food. There are times she can leave it alone. This was one of those times. But ultimately the obsession bites her back. The way some folk get comfort of drugs, that's how Ree is with food. I forget the exact year, but it was sometime in the seventies that she finally gave up booze and never really drank again. But food's different. You can never give up food. So if you're addicted to sugar or bread or fried chicken, well, it's almost too easy to fall off the wagon and get your fix."

At the end of January 1975, Franklin appeared on *The Midnight Special* television show. With her red-hued blown-out Afro and her turquoise feather wrap, she sat down on the piano bench next to Ray Charles and belted out "Takes Two to Tango," a revisiting of the song Ray had recorded with Betty Carter fourteen years earlier.

She continued her tradition of throwing herself splashy birthday parties. Her thirty-third took place at the Hotel Pierre in New York, and the Spinners performed.

"The Spinners owed Aretha big-time," said Ruth Bowen. "When their Motown contract was up in the early seventies, it was Aretha who pulled their coat to Atlantic. She got them on the label. That's around the time when Philippe Wynne became their lead singer. Aretha, like all of us, recognized Philippe as one of the most original soul styles to come along since Sam Cooke. And of course it was on Atlantic that the Spinners had those monster hits like 'One of a Kind (Love Affair)' and 'Mighty Love.' That night, they sang for free. Hell, they would have paid Aretha for the honor of singing at her party."

A week later she flew out to LA for the Oscars. *The Godfather Part II* dominated the show. For the second time, Frank Sinatra introduced Aretha to the worldwide Academy Awards audience. She sang a forgettable song from a forgettable movie: "Wherever Love Takes Me" from *Gold*.

In June, *Jet* reported this Ruth Bowen plant:

"The soul queen is and should be especially proud of her two eldest children, Clarence and Edward, who are 'A' students. She took them out of private school a year ago and put them into a public school in New York so they could stay close to 'real people.' "

"I love each of Aretha's children," said Ruth, "and diligently reported exactly what Aretha had instructed me to report. But I also knew that, like all children, they had their challenges. Those challenges would continue throughout the years. But whenever there was a problem, Aretha worked fast and furiously to make sure it stayed out of the press. She was adamant on telling the world that her kids were normal. Well, I don't believe anyone is really 'normal,' especially children of stars. At the same time, I didn't blame her for protecting their privacy. And to this day, no one can get any information about them out of me. That's how it should be."

A *Billboard* review of her May 27 concert at the Westchester Premier Theater in Greenburgh, New York, gave a composite picture of her mid-1970s show:

"Besides looking like an angel in a white, slightly sequined outfit, Aretha Franklin managed to sing like one."

In addition to her hits, she covered the pop standard "With a Song in My Heart," Barry White's "Can't Get Enough of Your Love" and the Staples' "Respect Yourself," with her pitch-perfect imitation of Mavis. Accompanying herself on piano, she sang "Bridge Over Troubled Water."

"She always seems to soar on arrangements with a call-and-response structure," wrote the reviewer, "where she can weave her voice up, around and through a simple but strong rhythmic line."

In early September, she returned to Manhattan. There, according to one press report, "the soulful singer" was "redecorating her home and putting together some material for a television special that will feature the high points of her career." That special never happened.

For all the enthusiastic reviews of her live performances, her recorded performances were not selling.

"When *You* came out in October," said Wexler, "we were deeply concerned. Aretha was certain that the song she'd written—'Mr. D.J.'—would be a smash. I had my doubts but we released it as a single anyway. Today no one can remember the song. No one can remember any of the material from *You*."

"I was called in to do the arrangements," Gene Page told me, "because Aretha thought well of the charts I had done for Barry White. Those are the kinds of orchestrations she was looking for. Of course Aretha sang heavenly. And of course I loved being in the studio with her. But I'm not sure the songs she chose were up to her usual level. I remember a tune by Van McCoy that we cut, 'Walk Softly,' and a beautiful one by her sister Carolyn, 'As Long As You Are There,' but that was about it. Nothing hit, and, though I cherish my time with the Queen, the sessions were tense. She and Jerry Wexler seemed at odds. They both knew they needed a hit, but the hits just weren't there."

The album's cover shot showed Aretha in a summery two-piece outfit of sunshine yellow—lots of leg and a slim midriff.

"The look was fine," said Wexler. "But the music wasn't. We knew that her franchise was in trouble. People were saying that she had had a fabulous run, and the run was over. There was reason to believe that. For a pop star to have a run that lasts nearly a decade is nothing to sneeze at. But I knew Aretha was more than just a pop star. Neither she nor I was about to call it quits. We were not going to stop trying to find new musical combinations.

"The problem was that the cultural climate was changing. The first rumblings of disco were being felt. That's why we called in Gene Page. His Barry White arrangements contained the seeds of the disco era. Aretha always dismissed disco, but I think her song 'Mr. D.J.' definitely had a pre-disco consciousness. Aretha is always conscious of the marketplace. Aretha always wants to adapt. But after *Hey Now Hey*, *Let Me in Your Life*, *With Everything I Feel in Me*, and *You*, the string of lousy-selling albums was getting long. We needed help, and, quite frankly, we didn't know where that help would come from."

"We loved Jerry Wexler," said Cecil. "For a long time he and Tommy Dowd and Arif Mardin were the right team for Aretha. Their work together will probably live forever. But all good things come to an end, and more and more it looked like Wexler's day as her producer was over. Wasn't anything personal, but purely practical. The hits had stopped. We had to look around and say, 'Who has the hits?'"

After *You*, Aretha decided that the answer was definitely not Wexler. He never produced her again.

During the winter of 1975, she made another major move—she moved to Southern California. Both she and Ken Cunningham had been courting the film community for years. She was certain that living in the Los Angeles area would help their cause.

"She had been planning the move for some time," said Cecil, "and urged me to move as well. But I never did. I didn't want to leave Detroit. Earline and I flew out every few weeks. That went on for years."

"I also lived in her house in Encino on Louise Avenue to help with Kecalf," said cousin Brenda. "It was a beautiful suburban home just around the corner from the Jacksons."

One of the reasons she chose the neighborhood was her hope that her boys and the Jackson brothers could become friends. That never quite happened.

"She thought the transition from heavily urban New York City to the suburbs of the peaceful San Fernando Valley would do her a world of good," said Erma. "I didn't discourage her. I knew that New York was wearing my sister out. After all, she'd fallen apart in New York a couple of times. She'd become an expert at putting herself back together, so why not try kicked-back California? Why not live an easier life?"

By year's end, Aretha seemed to be in a more comfortable setting.

Her last performance of 1975 had her singing "Auld Lang Syne" with the Guy Lombardo Orchestra, long thought to be the squarest of all pop musical aggregations. Her rendition brings to mind something James Cleveland said about Aretha: "The girl could sing the Yellow Pages and make you weep."

Her singing, of course, was never in question. The big question in her professional life was whether she could climb back onto the charts. On the personal front, the issue was whether she could preserve her emotional equilibrium, sustain a romantic relationship with a man, and maintain a household where her four sons all lived under one roof.

In short, could she hold it all together?

22. THE SPARK

My job," said Ruth Bowen, "was to let the world know that Aretha had found domestic bliss in California and was ready to get into the movies."

Ruth did her job well. On February 26, 1976, *Jet* quoted Aretha explaining that she had moved to Southern California because she considered it the center of show business. She spoke about her plans to star in both an upcoming TV special and a major motion picture. She also mentioned one of her sons: "Clarence is ready to record on his own. He writes as well as sings and plays, and we're looking for a record company that will sign him." There was a brief discussion of her fondness for golf, deep-sea fishing, and tennis. The article included a picture of Ken and Aretha on the tennis court.

The problem of finding a hit record remained. The hit did come, but its origins go back to before Aretha's move to California. According to Carolyn Franklin, the hit was originally designated for her. The hit's creator, Curtis Mayfield, had known the Franklin family for years.

"We loved Curtis when he was with the Impressions, and we loved him when he went solo," Carolyn told me. "Not only was he a fabulous singer, he possessed genius as a songwriter. 'People Get

Ready,' 'Keep On Pushing,' 'Gypsy Woman'—the list goes on forever. So much positive energy. Then came *Superfly,* one of the greatest movie scores ever. So when Curtis and I ran into each other in Chicago and he mentioned another score he was working on for a film about three sisters who start out in church and wind up singing R-and-B, naturally I thought of Aretha, Erma, and myself. I was intrigued. When Curtis played me some of the songs, I was completely knocked out. He also said that, in addition to writing the soundtrack, he was producing an album in his own studio. He thought two of the actresses, Irene Cara and Lonette McKee, were excellent singers for the movie but wanted a more experienced R-and-B vocalist to cut the album. Was I interested?

"Was I! It had been a couple of years since *I'd Rather Be Lonely,* my last album for RCA, and I was eager to start another project. With some help, I'd pretty much been writing and arranging my own material. By then I considered myself a full-fledged producer. But I was more than willing to give up that role for the chance of being produced by Curtis. The songs were not only sensational but, taken together, told a story I could relate to—the hopes, aspirations and heartaches of sisters who saw singing as a way to make it in the world. It was just perfect. I remember thinking that it was too good to be true. And on that score, I was right."

"Things got very complicated," said Ruth Bowen. "Cecil and I had a meeting with Ahmet Ertegun. Wexler was an Atlantic owner, but Ahmet was the big boss. We wanted to let him know that, although Wexler had been great, Aretha wanted to cast around for another producer. Could he give us some names? On the list was Curtis Mayfield. Well, I had booked Curtis for years, knew him well, and loved him like a brother. I knew he'd be thrilled to work with Aretha and vice versa. What I didn't know, though, was that he'd been talking to Carolyn."

"We also didn't know about the movie project," added Cecil. "When Curtis's name came up, we all broke into smiles—especially Ree. I called him and mentioned the possibility. I figured he'd be overjoyed. 'Oh, wow, Cecil, I've got a great project but I've promised it to Carolyn.' When I asked about the project, he mentioned *Sparkle*. That's the first I heard of it. I knew we had trouble."

"There shouldn't have been any problems," said Erma. "Aretha should have left it alone. She should have let Carolyn sing those *Sparkle* songs and then, afterwards, do her own record with Curtis. But somehow Aretha got a copy of the songs. They were so good that she felt she had to sing them."

"I was watching all this from the sidelines," said Wexler. "I had been benched, and, to tell you the truth, I wasn't all that surprised. At that point there were many more producers hotter than me. An artist has the right to pick any producer he or she wants. I admired Mayfield's work. And Mayfield, like everyone in the civilized world, admired Aretha. That's why he sent her the songs. He wanted hits, and no matter what he might have said to Carolyn, once he knew that Aretha was in the mix, she was his first choice. He'd be crazy if she weren't."

"It got a little nasty between the sisters," said Cecil. "The verbal catfights were intense. Carolyn didn't want to let go, but Aretha wanted those songs. When Ree wants something, watch out! She asked me to settle the matter—which meant telling Carolyn she was off the project. I couldn't do that. I loved all my sisters equally. So I turned the matter over to the only man with the authority to resolve the conflict—our father."

"Daddy didn't want any part of it," said Erma, "but had no choice. It was an extremely difficult situation because they both had their arguments. Carolyn's argument was that she was there first. And that she needed hits a lot more than Aretha. Aretha's argument was that Curtis preferred her, and, given her long dry spell, she also needed hits. None of us were surprised that Daddy came down on Aretha's side. He loved all his children—he lavished all of us with attention and care—but Aretha always had her special place. It took Carolyn a long time to get over this. She kept saying that she was being denied her big break. And then when the record broke open for Aretha—the critics loved it, the public loved it, the world loved it—that made things even more difficult for Carolyn."

"I was at the Franklin family home when this mess over *Sparkle* came to a head," said Ruth Bowen. "They were down in the basement, where they were doing a lot of drinking. The Franklins, from C.L. on down, has always been a family of hard drinkers. The drinking emboldened Carolyn, who had already been told by her daddy to drop the subject of Aretha singing these Mayfield songs. She called Aretha a name and Aretha retaliated with an even worse name. That's when Carolyn grabbed a fireplace poker and threatened Aretha. 'If you can't fight me like a sister,' said Aretha, 'don't fight me at all.' For some reason that sounded funny and broke up the tension. We all laughed, Carolyn regained her reason, and no one got hurt. But for a minute there, I wasn't sure what was going to happen."

"It's hard for me to talk about it now," Carolyn told me. "It's hard for me to say that Aretha sang those songs better than anyone could have. But I do have to say it because it's the truth. It's not that I couldn't have sung *Sparkle*. It's not that I might not have had a couple of hits off the album. But even if I had—and God knows I wish I had—I still couldn't have given what Aretha gave: Aretha gave it her genius."

Sparkle sparkles like nothing Aretha has done before or since. There was the tender young jazz-soul prodigy singing the soaring "Skylark" during her Columbia days. There was the feverish perfection of her sensational early records on Atlantic. There was the holy fire of *Amazing Grace*. And then comes *Sparkle,* arguably her most impassioned secular singing. From start to finish, her collaboration with Curtis Mayfield is a triumph of kindred spirits.

The stars are perfectly aligned. The songs are perfectly suited to Aretha's sure sense of storytelling. For the first time in her Atlantic career, she turns out a cohesive work. When she worked with Quincy Jones and the latter-day Wexler, her albums were a grab bag of originals and covers. *Sparkle* is a tightly woven tapestry, a long-form concept album tied to a cinematic narrative that lends it a flow and feeling all its own.

Aretha absorbs Mayfield's aesthetic with joyful ease. "'I sparkle,'" she sings in the first line of the first song. "'Loving the way I do...I feel so good.'" The story is all about good feeling. The mood is irresistibly upbeat, informed by what Aretha called Curtis's "sweet funk." Like Marvin Gaye, Mayfield possessed an extraordinary ability to mix sugar and spice in just the right measures. Also like Marvin, Mayfield was a subtle groove-meister. In the suite of songs that make up *Sparkle,* the rhythms are sequenced seamlessly.

Lush orchestrations—replete with strings, flutes, and harps—had been the hallmark of Isaac Hayes. His *Shaft* was a masterpiece. Working in a similar style, Marvin and Mayfield created masterpieces of their own—Gaye's *What's Going On* and *Trouble Man,* and Curtis's *Superfly. Sparkle* carries on the tradition. Here, though, the central character is neither a gangster nor a damsel threatened by a menacing world but instead a young woman in love with life. She floats on a cloud of aspirational energy. The mood is one of hope and promise.

"People said that Aretha was singing about being in love with Ken Cunningham," said Ruth Bowen, "but I don't agree. She wasn't singing about being in love with a man. She was singing about being in love with these songs. She knew that Curtis had written some of his greatest work, and she was riding those melodies all the way to the moon. When I showed up in Chicago at Curtom Studios, where the record was being cut, I couldn't believe my ears. I never thought Aretha could outdo 'Respect' or 'Natural Woman.' But, believe me, this singing was on a whole different level. Girlfriend was shouting. She was going for broke. After being lost in the woods for a couple of years, she found her way out. And Curtis Mayfield, one of the smoothest gentlemen in the funk business, was leading the way."

"It was perfectly harmonious in the studio," said Cecil. "Curtis may be mild-mannered but he's strong. These were his songs and arrangements and he knew how he wanted them sung. At Columbia and early at Atlantic, Aretha responded well to direction. But at this point, with so many hits under her belt, she was more assertive. When it came to 'Something He Can Feel'—the first single—they argued over how she riffed over the vamp at the end of the song. He wanted even more emotion than Ree was giving. She thought she had it nailed in a couple of takes. But somehow, in his gentle way, he got at least a half dozen more takes out of her. When the song shot to number one, he proved his case."

"Humility isn't my strong suit," said Jerry Wexler. "But when Mayfield sent us the masters, I had nothing to say but 'Bravo!' I realized that Aretha was back. Their rapport was evident. 'Hooked on Your Love' and 'Look into Your Heart' contain some of Aretha's most subtle singing. She's inspired. I couldn't have provided that inspiration. Only a peer like Curtis could have done that."

"I was happy and heartbroken at the same time," said Carolyn. "The same year that *Sparkle* came out, I released my last RCA album, *If You Want Me*. It had several good songs and I thought my performances were fine. But nothing hit. At that moment—the same moment that *Sparkle* had revived Aretha's career—I knew that my own recording career was over. Confirmation came when RCA dropped me."

"Carolyn was disappointed and had every right to be," said Cecil. "A deep freeze set in between her and Aretha. But I knew that, given enough time, the wounds would heal. My sisters fought tooth and nail, but the bad blood never lasted."

"Some singing groups begin together as sisters but end up as adversaries," said Erma. "Take the Supremes. No one could have been closer than Diana Ross, Mary Wilson, and Florence Ballard. But their circumstances and conflicting personalities ultimately broke them apart—never to reconcile. When Florence passed away, in 1976, my dad officiated at the funeral at New Bethel. It was one of the saddest days I can remember. So much talent, so much heartbreak. In the case of us Franklin sisters, though, it's important to remember that, for all our fighting, we always got back together. *Always.*"

In April, the same month *Sparkle* was recorded, *Jet* had this news for its readers: "Aretha Franklin's soul mate, Ken Cunningham, is trying to establish himself in a filmmaking career. He recently spent some time in San Francisco scouting locations for a movie, *Asili-Genesis,* for which he wrote the script." The magazine reported that Aretha had spent a month preparing for the role but that plans had been postponed due to a strike by West Coast film technicians.

That summer of America's bicentennial saw *Sparkle*'s release. The critics applauded it, the fans loved it, and the first single, "Something He Can Feel," held down the number-one spot on the R&B charts for nineteen weeks. The question that had been looming—could she still sell records?—had been answered in the affirmative. The other question, of whether she could find harmony at home, was not as easily answered.

"When she asked me to place a puff piece on Cecil," said Ruth, "I had to wonder why. Cecil was always a behind-the-scenes man. He wasn't looking for glory. When it came to the press, Aretha's sole purpose, like most artists', was to make herself look good. So why all of a sudden an emphasis on Cecil?"

"Maybe Ken had pushed her too far," said Cecil. "Maybe she wanted to let the world know that she had one manager and one manager only. I didn't need that confirmation. I always knew I had my sister's trust, but for some reason she needed the world to know."

In July, *Jet* called the article "Aretha Franklin's Hidden Asset: Her Brother Cecil" and said, "Not only does he manage her, but he is also vice president of the four small companies she owns."

By August, Ken Cunningham was gone.

"I asked Aretha if she was sure that she wanted it in the press," said Ruth Bowen. "Maybe it was better to keep these matters pri-

vate. 'No,' she said, 'my fans need to know. Plus I want the world
to know that I'm eligible.'"

Jet, August 12, 1976: "Aretha Franklin, Her Soul Mate End
Their Love Match: Aretha Franklin and her soul mate, Ken Cunningham, have separated after one of the more durable 'soul mat-
ings' in show business."

The magazine reported that Ken was no longer living in her
Encino home. It was also noted that at a recent TV-show taping,
when Aretha gave her father an Ebony Music Hall of Fame award
for his contribution to gospel music, her entire family was onstage —
with Cunningham conspicuously absent.

Ironically, the cover of this same issue of *Jet* featured Glynn
Turman, the soon-to-be-next man in Aretha's life. The story promoted Turman's new movie, *J.D.'s Revenge.* Interviewed on his
ten-acre ranch in Malibu, the actor discussed his upbringing on the
streets of Harlem and Greenwich Village, his tenure at the Tyrone
Guthrie Theater in Minneapolis, his ongoing role on the TV soap
opera *Peyton Place*, his volunteer teaching job at the Los Angeles
Inner City Cultural Center, and his passion for raising Arabian
horses.

Aretha didn't recall seeing the splashy profile in the same *Jet*
that announced her breakup with Cunningham. It would be another
five months before she and Turman met.

Press reports of Aretha's upcoming film appearances continued:
She was slated for the starring role in a remake of *Morning Glory,*
the 1933 classic in which Katharine Hepburn played an aspiring
actress; she would play Bessie Smith in a biopic directed by Gordon
Parks. But *Morning Glory* was dropped, and the Smith project
abandoned.

"Our first discussions were promising," said Gordon Parks, the
photographer and director of *Shaft*. "Aretha was talking to several
acting coaches and seemed serious about learning the craft. By
nature, singers are actresses. The lyrics of their songs demand a

certain kind of dramatic reading. But then came her crazy demands about the script. She wanted a sanitized version of Bessie's life that would avoid any comparisons to her own. She was insistent that Bessie not be seen as an excessive drinker. Bessie's biographers had all detailed her bisexuality, but that was also a no-no for Aretha. Musically, Aretha would have been perfect—that's what got me interested in her to begin with—but I couldn't go along with her restrictions. Her point was that a less-than-heroic Bessie Smith would besmirch her own image. I pointed out that a less-than-heroic Billie Holiday did not besmirch the image of Diana Ross. In fact, it got her nominated for an Oscar. But Aretha wasn't persuaded, and our discussions broke down. I can't remember who walked out first—me or her—but neither of us was about to budge."

While *Sparkle* continued selling, Aretha returned to the studio, this time with Lamont Dozier, a member of the Holland-Dozier-Holland writing-producing team responsible for a slew of the great Motown hits with the Supremes, the Four Tops, the Isley Brothers, Junior Walker, and Marvin Gaye. Given Dozier's enormous talents, the new album, *Sweet Passion*, was strangely uninspired.

A year earlier, Donna Summer's erotic "Love to Love You, Baby" pushed disco into the center of pop culture. In 1976, Diana Ross entered the disco fray with her "Love Hangover," a decided hit. Other sixties soul artists, like Johnnie Taylor, jumped on the bandwagon. Taylor's smoldering "Disco Lady," for example, is one of the great tracks in all rhythm and blues.

"I understood Aretha's attitude about disco," said Wexler. "She didn't like it. And I didn't either. She saw it as a passing fad and a superficial form. She thought it lacked soul. She was certain that the giants in her field—like Curtis Mayfield and Marvin Gaye—wouldn't pander to popular tastes in such a vulgar manner. Lamont Dozier was certainly one of those giants, and I was glad to see her team up with him. The problem was that she insisted that he include no less than four of her original songs, none of which were really record-worthy. But [people] couldn't tell that to Aretha—especially not a producer like Lamont, who's a lovely man and an especially gentle soul."

"I had a different attitude about disco," claimed Cecil. "I saw it as R-and-B with a busy bass line and heavy four-on-the-floor beat. The best of disco was as good as anything. If Aretha had been given 'I Will Survive' instead of Gloria Gaynor, it would be one of her hallmark anthems. If Aretha had hooked up with Giorgio Moroder and Pete Bellotte, the guys who produced Donna Summer, I guarantee that she'd have a hit. I always thought Ree should do a duet with Barbra Streisand. To me, that always made sense—marry two markets. But Aretha wasn't interested. So here comes Donna Summer singing 'No More Tears (Enough Is Enough)' with Barbra. Number-one hit. I can name a dozen number-one disco hits that Aretha passed on. She thought classic soul and disco didn't mix. Given the right artist like an Aretha Franklin, disco could be turned into classic soul. Look at what Nile Rodgers and Bernard Edwards did with Chic."

"Jump," the one dance song from *Sparkle,* was as close as Aretha came to a disco hit. It was released as a single in September 1976 with "Hooked on Your Love" as the B side, but it never rose above number seventeen.

"I wouldn't call 'Jump' true disco," said Carolyn. "When I heard the original version—the first draft of the song that Curtis showed me—it was a more traditional R-and-B dance groove, more related to 'Chain of Fools' than 'YMCA.' When he started recording with Aretha, Curtis modified the groove to sound a bit more current, but the song never made it into the clubs where disco fever was really happening."

In November, Aretha, forever a loyal Democrat, sang at Jimmy Carter's victory celebration at the Sheraton Park Hotel in Washington, DC.

Earline Franklin, Aretha's sister-in-law, remembered that the first month of the new year—1977—was marked by two events.

"Cecil and I were staying at the Beverly Comstock," she said, "when we learned that, at this very same hotel during the same time we were there, the actor Freddie Prinze had shot himself. That shook us all up. The next night we were at Aretha's house in Encino when she was all excited about having met Glynn Turman at a benefit for Rosey Grier's youth foundation, called Giant Step. Aretha's always been man-crazy—she falls in and out of love easier than anyone I've ever known—so I didn't pay all that much attention. But the next day she was still talking about him. And the next day as well."

In March, though, *Jet* reported that "the fizzled breakup of Aretha Franklin and her longtime mate Ken Cunningham was now sizzling again." When the magazine called Aretha to ask about their relationship, she said, "Well, Ken is on the patio reading *Roots.*"

That same month, *Billboard* carried a photo, taken at the benefit concert for Giant Step, of Aretha Franklin, Jacqueline Onassis, and Rosey Grier above a caption that read "Impressive Trio."

She threw herself a thirty-fifth birthday party at the Beverly Hills Hotel, hiring a caterer to provide the soul food. She was miffed when she learned that the hotel prohibited outside food. So she rented a private bungalow at the hotel, and, after entertaining her guests in the lavish Crystal Room, Aretha invited her guests— some 150 of them—back to her rooms, where the soul food was brought in the side door.

Sweet Passion, the Lamont Dozier–produced album, came out in May to tepid reviews and weak sales.

"Jerry Wexler was no longer with us," Ahmet Ertegun told me, "and I tried to get more involved. My hope was that the momentum from her Curtis Mayfield album, so spectacularly good and such a strong seller, would favorably impact *Sweet Passion*. It didn't. Unfortunately, after *Sparkle,* Aretha never had a successful album on Atlantic again. I saw her several times during my trips to Los Angeles, but she was mainly concerned with breaking into the movies. Her focus on music had lessened. I recall casually mentioning Natalie Cole and how I thought that Natalie's producers, Chuck Jackson and Marvin Yancy, might be ideal for Aretha. The idea incensed Aretha. I had no idea of the history between Aretha and Chuck and Marvin. I had stepped into a land mine. It must have been two years before Aretha talked to me again."

Back in 1974, two Chicago producers, lyricist Chuck Jackson—Jesse's brother—and music man Marvin Yancy, had brought Aretha a group of songs. At the time, Aretha was recording *You*.

"She turned them down cold," Yancy told me in the early 1980s. "She had absolutely no interest in cutting them. She said that they weren't up to her standards."

A few months later, the Jackson/Yancy team recorded those songs with twenty-five-year-old Natalie Cole, a superb vocalist with a phenomenal stylistic range who was then at the beginning of her career. Natalie's interpretations were strikingly Aretha-like.

"There's no soul singer who isn't markedly influenced by Aretha," Natalie told me when we collaborated on her memoir, *Love Brought Me Back*. "In the beginning, I thought of myself as a straight-up soul singer. All those comparisons to Aretha, my idol, were incredibly flattering. Personally, I didn't think I was in her league."

The result of the Cole/Jackson/Yancy hookup was a string of blockbuster hits, including "This Will Be (an Everlasting Love)," "Inseparable," "I've Got Love on My Mind," and "Our Love." Natalie was suddenly a star, and Aretha was infuriated, especially when, in 1975, Natalie ended Aretha's eight-year Grammy streak by winning best female rhythm-and-blues vocal performance.

"The first time I saw Aretha was at an industry banquet," Natalie remembered. "She gave me an icy stare and then turned her back on me. It took me weeks to recover. I mean, this is the woman whom I revere! She began this make-believe feud that I still don't understand. I give her the highest respect—then, now, and always."

"Natalie's rise corresponded with Aretha's decline—at least in terms of sales," said Carolyn. "To many, Natalie looked like the future and Aretha represented the past. That idea enraged Aretha. Unfortunately, she took out her frustration on Natalie."

"It took many years to accept Natalie," said Cecil. "It really wasn't until the nineties when Natalie started singing her father's pop material that Aretha felt less threatened."

"Berry Gordy used to say that competition breeds champions," said Ruth Bowen. "So maybe Aretha's competitive spirit helped maintain an edge. Personally, I thought that attitude didn't come from a will to win but just old-fashioned insecurity and fear. It didn't matter who the female vocalist happened to be—Mavis Staples, Gladys Knight, Diana Ross—Aretha was convinced they were after her throne. I'd say, 'Look, Ree, these ladies have thrones of their own. They don't need yours.' But she didn't like hearing that. But it was more than just female singers. It was females *period*. Other than the women closest to her—her sisters, her sister-in-law Earline, her cousin Brenda, and me—she couldn't maintain a relationship with another woman. In nothing flat, she'd find fault with them and cut off the friendship before it started. Even in those relationships that did last—like mine—there were endless fall-outs when I was on her shit list for months at a time.

"I kept saying, 'Aretha, Natalie's a wonderful girl. Just wish her well and move on.' But it got to be a thing with Aretha. I'd call it an obsession. Then she told me to call *Jet* and get them involved."

Jet, on June 23, 1977, ran an article entitled "Still on a Throne, Aretha Loses Weight, Looks Ahead."

The weight gain she attributed to not being able to exercise due to a pulled muscle. A photo of her and Ken Cunningham underlined their reconciliation. She discussed film roles under consideration. Concerning Natalie, Aretha claimed that she wanted to avoid a rift: "It's easy for a singer to sometimes pick up on another singer's sound," she said, "but that's just copying. It's really a compliment that she sounds like me on some songs. In fact, when I listen to her I hear little things that remind me of myself at the beginning of my career. I think Natalie's doing a fine job but in my estimation she's just a beginner."

A month later, the magazine said that Aretha was out on the town with Glynn Turman. In response, Ken Cunningham told *Jet*, "If I have to pick up a newspaper to find out what's happening between us, that is just kind of cold. Every time I pick up a paper, I'm finding out something about Aretha." He was referring to a column appearing in the *New York Daily News* indicating that the Franklin/Cunningham relationship was over. "I love Aretha," Ken added, "and I know that we are going to be together. She is the mother of my son, so she is a part of me. We've been through so much together and I want her to know that I still love her."

"No doubt Aretha kicked Ken to the curb," said Erma. "Later she said it was due to the conflict between Ken and Cecil, but I don't think so. I think she fell for a handsome and charming movie star—Glynn Turman. End of story."

Delighted to feed the flames of the Aretha/Natalie feud, *Jet* put both their pictures on the cover—along with Diana Ross's. The headline: "Is There Room at the Top for Big Three of Song?" When asked about Natalie, Aretha said, "I don't think she has the ability or the equipment to take anything from me and I'd say that to Natalie herself."

In October, *Billboard* mentioned that Aretha would play England for the first time since 1968. Jeffrey Kruger was named as the promoter.

"The deal was set," Kruger told me. "I had spoken to both Cecil Franklin and Ruth Bowen. It was to be a tremendous event. There were to be six concerts in London alone—plus other dates in Ireland and Scotland. This was to be Aretha's grand tour of Great Britain."

Six weeks later, the deal was off. On December 3, 1977, under an article headlined "U.K. Pact Flap Axes Aretha Gig," *Billboard* noted that a "controversial contract flap, promising still-to-come legal repercussions, resulted in Aretha Franklin canceling three SRO dates at the London Palladium" less than twenty-four hours before the scheduled opening.

"I was incensed," said Kruger, "because I had no warning and was given no real reasons for the cancellations. There were some last-minute demands about stretch limos and extravagant hotel suites that I was only too happy to agree to. But then I was told that she wanted a bigger fee to match what a promoter had promised her to play Paris. She also wanted to eliminate a date and demanded a chartered jet to fly her and her entourage over the pond. This was *after* contracts were signed. Outrageous! These new costs were prohibitive. Then came word that she didn't fancy working in England during the winter. Could we move the dates to the spring? No, the dates were set in stone. By this time, I understood that she acted out of pure whimsy. She simply didn't feel like playing London. Well, I'd had it. I turned the matter over to my solicitors."

"The lawsuits came, as I knew they would," said Ruth Bowen. "The lawsuits cost Aretha a pretty penny, and she blamed me. She claimed that I had booked her for more dates than she had agreed to. But the number of dates never changed. What changed was her mind. At this point she was far more interested in pursuing her romance with Glynn Turman than playing London."

At the end of December, *Jet* ran a photo of Aretha and Glynn on a plane to France. Cecil was shown seated behind them.

During her concert in Paris, she sang "La Vie en Rose."

"Josephine Baker had sung it there," said Cecil, "and so had Louis Armstrong. But when even the sternest critic heard Aretha do it, they forgot about the earlier version. I'll never forget this one cat running up to me and saying, 'Tell your sister to move to France. She'll be loved here more than anywhere in the world.' I did tell that to Aretha and I know she believed it to be true."

Billboard's review was far less kind: "Aretha Franklin disappointed here at a show at the Palais des Sports, after an absence of 10 years. Though the hall is not ideal for this kind of soul concert, critics and audiences felt she paid more attention to the television cameras than to the paying audience."

Although in coming years she pined for France — the cuisine, the fashion, the adoring audience — she never made it back.

23. FAIRY-TALE PRINCESS

"I was living alone in LA when my apartment got robbed," said Carolyn. "That shook me up. Aretha was kind enough to invite me to live there. By then time had healed much of the hurt from the *Sparkle* fiasco. Our sisterhood had recovered.

"I moved in when Ree's romance with Glynn Turman was blossoming to full flower. Glynn was great—smart, artistic, socially conscious, an altogether wonderful man. But I wasn't optimistic about their relationship. Aretha had her four boys and Glynn had two boys and a girl of his own. That comprised a very large and complicated family dynamic. Plus Glynn's career drive is as powerful as Ree's. They're both extremely driven people. The question was, Could they drive in the same lane or would they drive over each other? Glynn's insider role in the movie industry interested Aretha, and so did his reputation as an acting teacher. She was ready to be taught—or at least she said she was. But I don't think she lasted for more than one or two of his classes. Glynn's method was to mine the depths of your emotions and bring them to the surface. He has his actors go all out. That was Aretha's singing style but in the context of a class, she's way too self-conscious to express any kind of vulnerability. If anything, she guards her feelings. She's got that tall protective wall around her. She might have been feeding the magazine stories about how she and Glynn were going to be the new Hollywood power couple, but I just didn't see them living happily ever after."

"There's something very sweet about my sister's vision of herself as a princess in a fairy tale," said Erma. "She meets a successful and handsome man and, in her mind, turns him into a brave knight on a black stallion. He's going to carry her off, slay all her dragons, and solve all her problems. It's the way a little girl thinks, not a grown woman. In that way, Aretha never grew up."

In March of 1978, Aretha announced plans to marry Turman.

"Because she and Ted White had basically run off to marry," said her cousin Brenda, "Aretha felt that she had missed out on a storybook wedding. She was going to make up for that with Glynn. No one loves to throw herself a party more than Aretha—she's been doing that her whole life—but she told me that this would be the party to end all parties. In fact, there'd be two huge parties. First they'd get married by her dad at New Bethel in Detroit and then come back to California and have another blowout for their Hollywood friends."

The wedding took place on April 11.

"Aretha produced her own wedding," said Erma, "but it almost didn't come off. She'd given Glynn a prenup to sign. He agreed to sign but then said he'd misplaced it. Apparently another copy was sent.

"An hour before the ceremony, though, the agreement has not been delivered. Ree and I are waiting with Daddy in the pastor's study. Ree is incensed. Reporters and photographers have come from all over the world. Spectators are lined up and down the block. The church is packed. But my sister is unmoved. 'No prenup,' she says, 'no wedding.' 'Will she really call it off?' I ask my father. 'You know your sister,' says Daddy. 'She's likely to call off anything.' We're holding our breath. A few minutes before she's due to walk down the aisle, the signed prenup arrives.

"It was a glorious event. Lou Gossett was Glynn's best man. I was the maid of honor. The Four Tops sang Stevie's 'Isn't She

Lovely.' There were at least eight bridesmaids and eight grooms-men. Ree wore a fabulous off-white silk-and-mink gown with a seven-foot-long train. She walked down the aisle to a Carolyn composition, 'I Take This Walk with Thee.' She had the choir singing all her favorite gospel songs. She had cousin Brenda singing 'Amazing Grace.' She had Big Mama crying her eyes out. The wedding cake was a work of art — eight feet tall, four tiers."

A week later, the party continued in Los Angeles. Aretha rented out the ballroom at the Beverly Hilton. A thirty-five-piece orchestra played arrangements on personal loan from Barry White. The Four Tops flew out to LA to entertain the thousand-plus guests, as did Lon Fontaine's dance troupe. *Jet* reported that "hun-dreds and hundreds of pounds of the choicest filet mignon, giant silver tubs of shrimp, and an array of Indian foods and French des-serts" were served and that "the evening's only sour note was that somebody stole four cages of live doves that were intended to sym-bolize the newlyweds' happiness."

A few weeks later, Aretha was telling the press that she and Glynn had written a song together — "If You Feel the Need, I'm Your Speed" — and a theme song to a movie in which they would star.

In May, Aretha was in New York, where she appeared at Car-negie Hall. She did three extremely brief sets — the first was dedi-cated to her hits and to covers like "You Light Up My Life"; for the second, she appeared in a Josephine Baker costume singing Jose-phine Baker–related songs, like "Brazil" and "La Vie en Rose"; and the third she devoted to gospel.

Aretha told the press that she had invited some movie produc-ers who were interested in having her play Baker in a biopic. The gospel numbers were in tribute to Miss Clara Ward, who, accord-ing to Aretha, had the courage to sing church songs in jazz clubs and even Las Vegas casinos.

In June, Aretha took out an ad in *Variety*. ARETHA in big block letters was plastered across a full page. Below were the words *Car-negie Hall — Gross $126,000*. Reverend C. Franklin was listed as her manager and Howard Brandy as her press agent. No mention of Ruth Bowen.

"I was out of her good graces for several years," said Ruth. "This was because of her refusal to admit that she had agreed to those dates with Jeffrey Kruger in England. The lawsuit cost her a small fortune and she blamed it on me. I kept my cool and realized all I needed to do was bide my time. Aretha is the kind of artist who will always spend more than she makes. That means she'll always need to work to live. And because I have a unique ability to book extremely lucrative dates, I knew it was only a matter of time before she and I would be doing business again."

In July, *Ebony* ran another Aretha/Glynn puff piece: "They look like a pair of happy kids, but they have seven of their own. Aretha denied that, despite her weight gain, she was pregnant." There was more talk of her taking Glynn's acting classes and of their plans to produce a movie in which they both would star.

When *Essence* published its own puff piece about the wonders of the two-career Franklin/Turman marriage, Glynn gave a hint of the trouble that would come from her star shining brighter than his.

"It's a thing of being a prideful man raised in this society with the idea of being a breadwinner with the head-of-the-household thing," he said. "I'm not used to being referred to as anyone's husband. I'm used to a woman being referred to as my woman…After I had worked 17 years in the business at the time we got married, suddenly being recognized as Aretha's husband was a heavy burden to carry."

Aretha disagreed, saying, "I don't think it's so hard."

Glynn responded: "But you're not in my shoes, baby."

Aretha's summer appearance in Vegas included her impressions— Gladys Knight's "Midnight Train to Georgia," Mavis Staples's "Respect Yourself," and Diana Ross's "Ain't No Mountain High Enough."

Back in Los Angeles, she agreed to attend a charity event arranged by her brother at LA's Good Shepherd Baptist Church.

"Daddy flew in for the occasion," said Cecil. "We were set for a special evening, but unfortunately Aretha had forgotten about the commitment. She wanted out but it was too late. The result was not particularly pleasant."

Billboard's Jean Williams reported on July 22 that "Aretha Franklin was the special guest of honor, but Aretha did the least to make the occasion special…She sang with no enthusiasm as the audience whispered, 'What's wrong with her?' while others were overheard to say, 'She acts as if she's angry with the world.'"

"It was a period when she was angry a good deal of the time," said Cecil, "because record sales were off so drastically. *Sweet Passion* was pretty much a flop, so we decided to go back to Curtis Mayfield. *Sparkle* was such a hit, we figured that a second helping of an Aretha/Curtis dish was sure to work. Besides, Curtis took the same hard line against disco that Aretha did. They were both set on turning the tide. But in the end, the tide was too strong and the sessions weren't all that happy. Aretha was convinced that Curtis was giving her his B-list songs, and Curtis didn't like the one original that Aretha demanded go on the record, the 'I'm Your Speed' song she wrote with Glynn."

A rare Curtis miscue, the second Mayfield-produced Aretha album, *Almighty Fire,* lacks fire. The songs are missing the sturdy soul underpinnings that mark Curtis's best efforts. Aretha realized some of her most impassioned vocals on *Sparkle,* but this time around, she sounds detached and uninterested. Without a single hit, the album sank like a stone.

With the exception of *Sparkle,* Aretha's previous seven albums had been commercial failures. In marketing terms, she was clearly in danger of becoming an irrelevant artist.

This was 1978, the year of the Bee Gees and *Saturday Night Fever.*

"I tried to tell Aretha the Bee Gees' 'Stayin' Alive' and 'How Deep Is Your Love' owed as much to Marvin Gaye as they did to disco," said Cecil. "I heard it as a modern take on dance-crazy R-and-B. I kept telling her that, whether she liked it or not, the groove changes and we have to change with it."

★   ★   ★

The rhythm-and-blues groove is one of pop music's most elusive motifs. The groove emanates from the street. As the street changes, so does the groove. Those changes come fast. R&B has always been a streetwise fashion-first music. Few R&B artists or producers have been able to keep a current groove for more than a few years. In the forties, Louis Jordan had it for a while. In the fifties Chuck Berry, Little Richard, Ike Turner, and Ray Charles each came up with original grooves. The happy-go-lucky Motown producers of the sixties, along with Stax men Dave Porter and Isaac Hayes, were superb groove masters, as was James Brown. Curtis hit the right groove for Aretha in *Sparkle,* but as the seventies were winding down, disco was still winding up—and Mayfield, at least in his second collaboration with Aretha, missed the mark.

"It had been some time since I had been at Atlantic," said Wexler. "I was working as a freelance producer and talent scout for Mo Ostin at Warner Records. But of course I never stopped tracking Aretha's career and listening to her records. I'd never call her to give advice—not because I didn't have any but because I knew she really wasn't interested. That's why I was surprised when she called me during the depths of her dry period to ask me what kind of record I thought she should make. I spoke to her about the relationship between Ella Fitzgerald and her manager/producer Norman Granz. Granz was the one who masterminded Ella's masterful albums in which she sang the songbooks of Gershwin, Cole Porter, Jerome Kern, Duke Ellington, and all the others. I suggested a similar strategy for Aretha. There's no reason why she couldn't sing a Duke Ellington songbook as well—not to mention Percy Mayfield, Bobby Womack, or Isaac Hayes. She could avoid chasing fashion and concentrate on time-capsule material. The idea of her and Ray Charles collaborating on a duets album was something I would have killed to produce. He did it with Betty Carter and there was no reason he couldn't do it with Aretha. She said she'd think about it, but I don't think she ever did. Ray hadn't had a hit in years, and, as far as Aretha was concerned, that was reason enough to disqualify him."

"If you look back at the early Atlantic stuff," said Cecil, "it's both classic and commercial. That's always been Aretha's aim. She always wants a hit but never wants to compromise quality. With disco, she didn't see the quality. She spent a couple of years bad-mouthing the fad. I remember one evening when we met up with Marvin Gaye in LA. Marvin had the same complaints about disco as Ree. It was ruining R-and-B. It had no soul. But then Marvin did 'Got to Give It Up,' a disco hit. Typical Marvin, it was a song about how he hated to dance. That was his way of bending to current fashion. Aretha said she wouldn't but in the end she did. She went out there and made a disco record."

24. THE HUSTLE

Aretha never admitted that she had, in fact, decided to do disco. During our discussions, she clung to the position that during that dance-craze era, she remained one of the few artists to buck the trend. When shown a copy of *La Diva,* the album in which she presented herself as a disco queen singing disco music directed by one of the most celebrated disco producers, she said the record was not disco at all, merely modern rhythm and blues.

Her search for a disco hit had begun with Nile Rodgers and Bernard Edwards, architects of Chic, one of disco's more elegant aggregations.

"They came in with completed tracks that were smokin'," said Cecil. "I thought it was a slam dunk, but Ree had reservations. She thought the songs needed retooling and she also had some tunes of her own that she wanted included. Nile and Bernard were very respectful of Aretha, but at that point they were riding high. They had those huge Chic hits like 'Good Times.' Aretha needed them far more than they needed her. They were happy to produce her—everyone wants to produce Aretha Franklin—but on their terms, not hers. Those discussions didn't get very far.

"The crazy thing is that the Rodgers/Edwards songs that Aretha rejected—'I'm Coming Out' and 'Upside Down'—were the same songs they gave to Diana Ross. Both were big hits. When that happened, Aretha acted like she didn't care. She thought the songs didn't measure up to her standards. She'll never admit to a mistake, but, boy, passing on the Chic producers was a huge mistake."

Enter Van McCoy, whose training as a producer began under the tutelage of Leiber and Stoller, one of the greatest writer/producer teams in the history of R&B. Erma had recorded McCoy's "Abraca-dabra" and Aretha sang his "Sweet Bitter Love" during her years on Columbia. In 1975, McCoy's own album—*Disco Nights*—included "The Hustle," an international hit and one of the most enduring of all disco anthems. He had also produced a smash on David Ruffin, "Walk Away from Love," a masterpiece of seventies soul.

"Van was a humble cat," said Cecil, "and was easy to work with. Maybe too easy. Aretha was still convinced that she had songs of her own—and one written by her son Clarence—that were smashes. She loaded up the record with that stuff. Van was able to get her to do a couple of his tunes, but, far as I'm concerned, it should have been *all* McCoy songs, since he was on a hot streak. That would have increased our chances. I don't blame Van for going along with Aretha's program—you always want to please the Queen—but I think we paid a price."

"I realized that if this record had no hits," said Ahmet Ertegun, "it would probably be Aretha's last on Atlantic. Her contract was coming due and of course I wanted to keep her. I was more than happy to accommodate her ideas for the cover. She felt as though other singers—like Gloria Gaynor and Donna Summer—had become grand divas during this disco period. She wanted to rees-tablish herself as the grandest of the divas. Thus the title, *La Diva,* and the cover art in which she was in a Cleopatra recline. I saw some humor and irony in the imaging, though I'm not sure Aretha did. In any event, we gave the record a concerted promotional push. Van McCoy was a bankable producer and I thought a few of his tracks had hit potential. What I thought, though, made no dif-ference. When the record came out in 1979, it made no impact on the marketplace. From then on, I had a hard time getting Aretha on the phone."

"When it became clear that *La Diva* was not selling," said Cecil, "Aretha blamed Atlantic."

"In my very long career," added Ertegun, "I've yet to have worked with an artist who took responsibility for a commercial failure. The fault is always with the label."

"One of the times that Aretha renewed our relationship was when she was thinking about leaving Atlantic," said Ruth Bowen. "When it came to the most serious matters, she always got in touch. She'd forget whatever she was mad at me about and we'd chat like the old friends that we are. She was convinced that her long dry spell had to do with Atlantic's lack of promotion. She didn't think they were pushing her product the way they used to. I couldn't say that Aretha wasn't delivering the kind of product worthy of her artistry. To say that would cause another rift in our relationship. In all honesty, I could say that I didn't think Atlantic was the same kind of R-and-B-centric company as when she'd signed with them in the sixties. They'd gotten so heavy in white rock and roll that maybe they had forgotten how to sell soul. Of course that's what Aretha wanted to hear. She wanted to hear me say that it never hurts to look around and see what's out there. Maybe there was someone who could do a better job promoting Aretha Franklin. In the meantime, she asked me to put out some press items about how happy she was with Glynn Turman. I had no problem doing that."

In the winter of 1979, *Jet* ran a cover story celebrating Aretha's happy marriage: "Aretha Adopts New Lifestyle with New Family." She called Turman her "sweet gorgeous man" and described her domestic situation as nothing less than perfect—no tension, no arguments, harmony all around. While Glynn was in New York doing off Broadway, Aretha said she was delighted to play the part of the happy homemaker in LA. She vowed never to do another taxing national tour of one-nighters again. Always eager to preview future plans, she revealed that she was "working out the final details of opening a very elegant boutique in Detroit—either downtown in the new Renaissance Center or in the suburb of Birmingham, Michigan. It'll be called Aretha's Champs-Elysees de Paris of Detroit and it'll have all the beautiful and unusual things you can't find in other stores." The article pointed out that a year earlier she had weighed 108 pounds and she was now up to 145. But that didn't seem to bother her. She would trim off the weight for her upcoming gig at Harrah's in Lake Tahoe. Besides, she said, "I can take off the pounds whenever I really want to, or when Glynn tells me, and he ain't doing no complaining—yet."

"If you read the version of her life that Aretha gives to the magazines," said Carolyn, "you'd never think she had a care in the world. Everyone was always beautiful—her family, her man, her career. She loved to give that impression. I know that was her heart's desire. She longed for simple happiness. But I was living there and I know that things were anything but simple. Sure, there were times when Ree would stay at home and cook and enjoy the simple pleasures. But if you think she stopped thinking about how to get her career back on track, you're wrong. And if you also think there weren't career clashes between her and Glynn, you're doubly wrong. Aretha liked to think of herself as the kind of woman who put her man first. But that was fantasy, not reality. In reality, she always came first."

On January 10, 1979, Donny Hathaway, suffering from severe mental illness, committed suicide by leaping from the fifteenth-floor balcony of his room at the Essex House in New York City. He was working on a second album of duets with Roberta Flack.

"I was the one designated to call Aretha with the news," said Jerry Wexler. "After all, I had brought Donny to Aretha in the first place. She had seen his talent and called him one of the most marvelous players, writers, and singers she had ever encountered. Because Aretha had suffered with depression of her own, she was sympathetic to Donny's disease, but she had no idea of just how sick he was. None of us did. When I told her the tragic news, she let out this small cry of absolute anguish. He was thirty-three years old."

"Donny's suicide devastated Aretha," said Cecil. "He was one of the few artists whose musical soul was comparable to hers. She related to him on a very deep level and put him in the same class as Marvin Gaye and Stevie Wonder. She was in shock for weeks. A month later, when we went to play Harrah's in Vegas, she dedicated her performance of 'You Light Up My Life' to Donny."

According to *Billboard,* at that same show she did a Judy Garland/Al Jolson takeoff on "Swanee."

In March, *Jet* ran a picture of Aretha and Glynn together with President Jimmy Carter and his wife, Rosalynn, at a Lincoln Center tribute to Marian Anderson.

In the spring, Cecil began speaking to other labels.

"He and I had several candid talks," said Ertegun. "I knew that Jerry Wexler had discussed the idea of doing classic Norman Granz/Ella Fitzgerald songbook albums with Aretha. I made it clear that I disagreed with the concept. I knew that Aretha wanted hits and so did I. I saw no reason in the world why she couldn't have hits. After all, Atlantic was still in the forefront. We had Chic on our label. That's when Cecil told me that Aretha and the Chic producers had not proven compatible. 'No problem,' I said. 'I'll call my friend Robert Stigwood and get Barry Gibb to produce her.' Stigwood's label, RSO, had put out *Saturday Night Fever.* Cecil liked the idea and said he'd take it to Aretha. I was convinced I had come up with the perfect solution."

"Aretha called me one day and said, 'What do you think of Clive Davis?'" Cecil remembered. "'I think he's one of the sharpest shooters in the music biz,' I said, 'but no one's sharper than Ahmet.' That's when I mentioned Ahmet's idea of working with Barry Gibb. She seemed intrigued."

"I was absolutely adamant on keeping Aretha at Atlantic," said Ahmet. "I flew out to California and was pleased to be invited to her home for dinner. Aretha's a marvelous cook. She could not have been lovelier. It was old-home week. We reminisced about the past and I expressed my faith in her future at our label. The Barry Gibb idea came up briefly. When I left, I felt good about having done damage control. A few weeks passed before word came back from Cecil that Aretha found the Bee Gees–style production 'unsuitable.' Gibb went on to write and produce an album on Barbra Streisand that yielded 'Guilty,' an enormous dance hit."

"Aretha kept talking about Clive," said Cecil. "How Clive had started his own label—Arista—and had big hits with Barry Manilow. How Clive had big hits on Melissa Manchester. And, more to the point, how Clive had revived the career of Dionne Warwick with 'I'll Never Love This Way Again,' produced by Barry Manilow. Aretha thought Manilow might also be the right producer for her. I didn't see that. To me, Manilow was far too pop for Aretha. No matter, I had my marching orders. Put out feelers and see if Clive Davis was interested in signing her. 'Of course he's interested in signing you,' I said. 'There's no label out there who's not interested in signing you.' That wasn't entirely true. Columbia and RCA had told me that we were asking too much money for an artist who hadn't had a hit in years. But that wasn't the kind of thing that Aretha wanted to hear, so I never mentioned it. On the other hand, I proved to be absolutely right about Clive. He was dying to have Aretha on Arista."

In May, Aretha played for Jesse Jackson's Operation PUSH Excel-A-Thon at LA's Dodger Stadium to raise money for deprived students.

And then, on June 10, after having ended her show at the Aladdin Hotel in Las Vegas with a rendition of Earth, Wind, and Fire and the Emotions' "Boogie Wonderland," Aretha was given news that would permanently change her life.

During a robbery at his home on LaSalle Boulevard in Detroit, her father had been shot.

Part Four

ARISTA

25. DADDY'S LITTLE GIRL

The panic was immediate.

Minutes after hearing the news from Detroit, Aretha received a call from Pops Staples, an old family friend, saying that he had just heard that Reverend C. L. Franklin had passed.

"Mavis Staples called me with condolences," said Carolyn. "She spoke as if she were certain that Daddy had been killed."

"Because Aretha, Carolyn, Brenda, and I were in Vegas when it happened," said Cecil, "it took a long time to figure out the truth. Great relief came when Erma called us from the hospital. She was the one who assured us that he was alive."

"The story didn't come together for quite a while," said Erma, "but the bottom line was that six burglars had been casing the neighborhood looking for a house to rob. They hadn't pinpointed Daddy. They didn't know who he was. The fancy stained-glass windows of Daddy's house on LaSalle gave them the idea that the owner had to be rich. One of the guys somehow got up to the second floor, took off a screen, and slipped through a window. Daddy was down the hall in his bedroom, also on the second floor, watching TV. Daddy had the ears of a wolf. He also believed in self-defense. That's why he kept a loaded pistol by his bedside. Daddy got the gun and was waiting when the thug burst into his bedroom.

The burglar was armed with a semiautomatic handgun. Four shots were fired. Daddy got off two but they missed. The thug didn't miss. Daddy got shot twice, in his right knee and right groin. I don't know how much time passed before the neighbors, hearing the gunshots, found a way into the house. Maybe a half hour, maybe more. Maybe if they'd acted quicker, he wouldn't have lost so much blood. But of course, if they hadn't acted at all, he might not have survived.

"Neighbors found him unconscious on the floor. They called 911. The ambulance came, but all that blood loss caused a series of cardiac arrests. At Ford Hospital, one of the doctors said it was too late to do anything, but then another doctor recognized him as Reverend C. L. Franklin. So they resuscitated him again."

"We flew home and raced over to the hospital," said Cecil. "First thing the doctor said was that his brain had been deprived of oxygen for up to a half hour. That's what threw our father into a coma."

"It was a sickening feeling to see him," said Erma. "The most vibrant man in the world. The most energetic man, the most articulate man, a man whose brain never stopped working, not for a second. Now this man, who was only sixty-four, was without speech or motion. He was comatose. That wouldn't change for the next five years—the most difficult time our family has ever known. These were our toughest years."

"Of course our concern was for our father," said Carolyn, "but we were just as worried about Aretha. He was close to all of us, but Aretha was always Daddy's little girl. Their bond was super-special."

Years later, Carolyn expressed this concern about Aretha during a filmed interview. When Aretha heard what her sister had said, she stopped talking to Carolyn for months. Aretha told interviewers that Carolyn had no right to portray her as an emotionally weak person.

"The truth is that Aretha got through this crisis when many people thought she never would," said Cecil. "In her own way, she managed. Instead of worrying about her, we should have been worrying about those nasty rumors concerning our father. Nasty rumors were running wild."

Because Reverend Franklin had been charged with marijuana possession in the past, some speculated that the shooting had something to do with a drug deal gone bad. Others claimed it was related to C.L.'s overactive love life. But none of those theories were based on fact. The truth of the matter was that he was shot during a random burglary.

"Aretha called me a few days after she had returned to Detroit," said Ruth Bowen. "She wanted me to put out the word that her career was on hold and that she was devoting all her efforts to her dad's recovery. She made it plain that he required all her attention. 'That's beautiful,' I said. 'That's a noble and wonderful thing that you're doing, but—' 'No buts about it, Ruthie,' Aretha said. 'My mind's made up. I don't even want to think about business.'"

"Aretha's heart was in the right place," said Cecil. "Her first priority was for Daddy. And when it became evident that the coma was going to be long lasting, she was the only one of us in a position to pay for his home care. That would require money. Because Aretha has never been one to accrue savings, that would mean ongoing work. She'd have to tour and record."

"The doctors described his condition as a light coma," said Erma. "That meant that he did not require machines. He could sustain life on his own. Yet he remained unconscious. He was with us and not with us at the same time. It was a bewildering and frightening situation that took a long time to adjust to. I'm not sure any of us really did adjust. All we knew is that we wanted him home, in his bedroom, and not in a hospital or long-term-care facility. That meant round-the-clock nurses. The cost was astronomical."

"My first thought was to move home," said Carolyn, "and I did. I moved back into the house on LaSalle to be by his side. I wasn't a nurse by any means, but I was certainly capable of making sure that the nurses we hired were doing their job. I knew Aretha wanted to move back as well, but she had her husband, Glynn, in

Los Angeles, her children, and a life she had worked hard to sustain."

Less than a month after her father was shot, Van McCoy, the man who produced *La Diva,* died of a heart attack at age thirty-nine.

"Our sadness was profound," said Cecil. "No matter what her detractors said, Aretha loved *La Diva* and thought the world of Van. She counts his 'Sweet Bitter Love' as one of the best songs she's ever cut. She was looking forward to doing more work with Van. In this same period, Glynn's uncle was shot and killed. These were tremendously heavy blows that made the summer of 1979 the most difficult of Aretha's life."

"Her moratorium on her career didn't last long," said Ruth Bowen. "She called back to say that she thought it was best for her mental health to go back to work. I agreed with her. I also knew that she needed money. Aretha always needs money. And then came this piece of irony: for all the work that she had done with both Ken Cunningham and Glynn Turman in trying to produce a movie, a movie finally came to her from out of nowhere. It wasn't anything for her to produce or star in. It was basically a cameo— an appearance that gave her a small talking part but a chance to sing an entire song on film. She had hoped for a drama, but this was a comedy. It was *Blues Brothers.*"

Aretha plays a waitress whose husband is leaving her to go on the road with the John Belushi/Dan Aykroyd band. It's a far cry from the glamour role she had envisioned for herself. Nonetheless, she lights up the screen. In her waitress costume, she gives her man holy hell before breaking into a hair-raising version of "Think," her hit from the late sixties. She tears up her man, tears up the song, and delivers a knockout punch, a highlight of the hugely successful film.

"At first she wasn't all that sure about the role," said Cecil. "She wasn't sure about playing a servant in her first movie role. But when it comes to confronting a no-good man, Aretha has no equal. She realized that this part gave her a chance to tap into that attitude. The combination of her being real and then topping it off with a song was too great to resist. Ray Charles had a cameo in that film, and so did James Brown and Cab Calloway. But the one musician everyone remembers is Aretha telling you to 'Think.'"

In August she was back on the road, playing the Kool Jazz Festival at Giants Stadium in Hackensack, New Jersey. *Billboard* loved her:

"Franklin gave her strongest performance in this market in almost five years. She performed 'Ain't No Way,' 'Seesaw' and 'Chain of Fools.' While her physical appearance is not what it has been, Franklin's voice is as strong as ever. The inconsistent live and recorded performances in recent years have obscured her unequaled vocal skills and it was good to see that one of the best voices around can still do it."

In September, the same month that *La Diva* was released to harsh reviews and poor sales, Aretha received a star on the Hollywood Walk of Fame.

"Right after that honor, she came to Detroit to see about Daddy," said Cecil. "She always stayed with me and Earline. She was obviously distressed about our father and wanted to be with him more. She carried some guilt about still living on the other side of the country. I told her what I believed—that she had to live her own life. She needed to move forward. It was a critical time in her career. She didn't like hearing that *La Diva* was perceived as a failure, but that was the stark truth. By then, Clive Davis had already flown to LA to meet with her. He was very clear in his desire to sign her. She still had some doubts. She'd been at Atlantic for twelve years. Atlantic was where she'd broken through. Atlantic was also Ahmet Ertegun, one of the slickest salesmen in the business. He hadn't given up on Aretha. By then Ahmet was a rock-and-roll kingpin. He promised to book her on huge stadium shows with the Rolling Stones and Led Zeppelin. All this weighed on Aretha's mind. She had to decide between two super-powerful music moguls. As expert promoters of their own labels, both of them were promising her the moon. When she asked my opinion, I told her it was a close call but that I felt like she needed a fresh start with a fresh label. I gave Clive the edge. She was leaning in that direction anyway."

In December she appeared on *Soul Train*. Playing the piano accompaniment herself, she offers an impromptu version of "Ooo Baby Baby" as an ultra-sensitive duet with the song's composer, her childhood friend Smokey Robinson. The short musical encounter is breathtaking.

As 1980 kicked off, Aretha signed with Arista and began discussing her new album with Clive Davis as well as her siblings.

"I had written a group of songs that I thought were perfect," said Carolyn. "Some were dance-oriented but others had a strong message. They dealt with the courage of the heart. The lyrics weren't religious, but they were inspirational. Aretha had been singing 'You Light Up My Life' for years and I thought that kind of song, especially in the light of our father's condition, would help her cope. But she didn't want to go spiritual. She said that Clive wanted her to go pop. Clive would be picking out the songs, and Clive would be picking out the producers. They wanted only upbeat tunes. They didn't want to fool with anything deep. They wanted hits. Well, 'Angel' and 'Ain't No Way' were deep. 'Angel' and 'Ain't No Way' were hits. But Ree said that 'Angel' and 'Ain't No Way' were about pain, and she had enough pain. She was all about ignoring pain. She kept talking about how she needed a new team with new ideas. That team, no matter how good it was, did not include me. When she started recording in LA, I thought I'd get a call to come out there and at least help, but I didn't. I stayed in Detroit, where Daddy showed no signs of progress. They had called it a 'light coma,' but to me it was the heaviest thing imaginable."

"I think Aretha knew that her emotional survival depended on her keeping her distance from Detroit," said Erma. "The situation was simply too heavy for her to take. In the first year or two that Daddy was in the coma, she was right to visit only occasionally. Anything else would have been too much. The emotional toll was enormous on all of us, but Aretha was the one who was in the midst of trying to keep her career alive. That took all her effort."

"Carolyn, Erma, and I discussed Aretha all the time," said Cecil, "and what we could do to keep her on an even keel. Since I was both her brother and manager, I had a special responsibility. No one wanted her to suffer another breakdown. And something like this could do it. She needed to keep on keeping on. That meant a new label and a new record. Carolyn was convinced the new record should deal with the real emotions she was facing. Carolyn argued that Ree's biggest hits—like 'Respect' or 'Chain of Fools' or 'Think'—came from real-life situations. She was singing about what was really happening. But I told Carolyn that Aretha didn't want to sing what was really happening. During those moments when she was recording, she needed to forget about what was really happening and concentrate on the positive. She and Clive talked about a lighthearted pop record. Well, far as I was concerned, that's just what the doctor ordered. A pop record would mean money—and at this point, money was just what Aretha needed."

In April, the Franklins organized a benefit concert in Detroit to help pay C.L.'s medical bills. James Cleveland, Jesse Jackson, the Staple Singers, and Aretha herself appeared at Cobo Hall, where, according to *Jet*, $50,000 was raised.

That same spring, work began on her debut Arista album. In conjunction with Clive Davis, Aretha selected two producers. Ironically, both were from her past. Arif Mardin, a celebrated musician and arranger, was one of the trio that had produced the lion's share of her Atlantic albums. Chuck Jackson was a member of the production team that had brought Natalie Cole to stardom. He was also the composer of that group of hit songs that were rejected by Aretha and later sung by Natalie.

"Aretha and Clive were very clear in that they wanted this record to have a certain sheen," Arif told me. "They did not want the old Atlantic sound. They came to me with four songs. The one they liked most was 'Come to Me,' a big ballad that had the resonance of a movie theme. Aretha was very specific about the musicians. She read *Billboard* carefully and knew exactly who was hot and who wasn't. Toto was extremely hot back then, and, at Aretha's urging, I used three of their members—David Paich on piano, Jeff Porcaro on drums, and Steve Lukather on guitar. I employed a young David Foster to play synths. I borrowed bassist Louis Johnson from the Brothers Johnson, another hot group, and was only too happy to follow Aretha's suggestions and hire the Sweet Inspirations plus her cousin Brenda Corbett. In addition to the ballad, I was asked to produce two covers—Otis Redding's 'Can't Turn You Loose' and the Doobie Brothers' 'What a Fool Believes'—and the slightly funky 'Love Me Forever.'

"It was a great honor for me to participate. This was, after all, something of a new debut for Aretha. Knowing the extremely difficult circumstances surrounding her father, I tried to be especially sensitive to Aretha's needs in the studio. In that regard, I must say that she was not in the least demanding. She was open to my ideas and the ideas of others. We were all on the same page. This was not to be a heavy-handed Aretha Franklin album. This was to be her introduction to the pop market that Clive had cultivated with such finesse. The songs needed to soar. The record needed to shine."

"Aretha loved Arif's light touch," said Cecil, "and the fact that he's the ultimate gentleman. Arif put her at ease. Chuck Jackson was also cool. He came in with a group of his songs. One of those—'Together Again'—he cowrote with Aretha and Phil Perry. But it was 'School Days,' the song that Ree cowrote and coproduced with Chuck, that gave my sister the biggest kick. She's nostalgic by nature, and this song—her answer to Stevie Wonder's 'I Wish'—took her back to the fifties, where, in her memory, life was all about simple fun."

Aretha's psychological pattern remained firmly in place: She avoided present trauma by idealizing her past. Her "School Days" is a walk in the park, an ode to an era that exists only in her imagination. The song celebrates the innocent fifties of "hoop skirts... petticoats...and fringe suede jackets." The heartbreaks are edited out. There is no motherless childhood. There is no promiscuous father. There are no teen pregnancies.

The result of the record is similarly superficial. The soul does not cut deep. Mardin and Jackson are efficient producers, but the material is thin.

"The hope," said Arif, "was that her cover of 'Can't Turn You Loose' would do for her career at Arista what 'Respect,' her earlier Otis Redding cover, did for her career at Atlantic—kick it off in high gear. Ultimately, her vocal won a Grammy, but the single never approached the kind of success she experienced with 'Respect.' Today it is largely forgotten."

Robert Palmer reviewed the Arista album, called simply *Aretha,* for the October 24 issue of the *New York Times:* "There should be a way for her to make contemporary music without having to keep her wonderful voice under wraps, but she hasn't found it yet. One wonders if she's looking."

The issue of Aretha's outrageous costuming always popped up in the press. *Billboard's* Jean Williams wrote, "Does Aretha Franklin need a new costumer? Appearing on 'The Tonight Show' recently, Franklin was outfitted in a tight, clinging costume designed for a lithe singer like Diana Ross rather than a lady of ample proportions like Franklin."

During her slender days, Aretha was understandably eager to show off skin. Interestingly, though, this penchant didn't change when she gained weight. Defiantly, she continued to wear outfits that did nothing to hide her curves, no matter how extravagant the curves became. She would adorn herself with bodice-busting fashion items of questionable taste for decades to come.

Whenever her taste was questioned, Aretha was quick to tell the press that she studied fashion as closely as she did the music charts. She followed the latest trends and knew exactly what was appropriate for her body type and what was not. Any criticism came from people who were merely jealous.

"When it comes to her outfits," said Carolyn, "Ree is no one you want to criticize. She's super-sensitive. Yes, I think she can be over the top, and yes, I think some of her stuff is tacky. But I also think there's a method to her madness. Her wild stage outfits bring her even more attention. They get her press. They keep her in the magazines. Crazy-ass clothes are part of her strategy for staying in the public eye. You may not like what she's wearing, but you'll notice what she has on. The first rule of a long-lasting diva like Aretha is always *You will not ignore me.*"

"At the start of the eighties," said Cecil, "there was an upsurge in her career. The move to Arista worked. The critics might not have loved the album, but the public knew that she was back. The Arista team was hell-bent on making the record a hit. Clive was in the Aretha business for the long haul. The first single, Chuck Jackson's 'United Together,' got to number three on the R-and-B charts and stayed for months. When *Blues Brothers* came out, Ree got raves. Everyone was talking about how she threw down. Then came the trip to London and the Netherlands."

"In the early Arista days, I thought I'd get back with Aretha," said Ruth Bowen. "She called several times to ask about whether I could find her lucrative dates. I knew she needed money for her father's medical bills. The new label was pushing the record hard and I had several hotels in Vegas ready to book her. Next thing I learn is that she's signed with ICM. Cecil called and said they were booking her. Why?"

"ICM came to her with dates for concerts in London," said Cecil. "The London dates had Ree remembering the fight she had with Ruth over British promoter Jeffrey Kruger. That's when she made up her mind to cut off Ruth again and go with ICM. She liked the idea of being repped by an international talent agency."

"The thing with Aretha is that you're in on Monday and out on Tuesday," said Ruth. "I understood that. So when I heard I'd been fired before I was rehired, I just kinda chuckled. I knew she'd be back."

In November, the month that Ronald Reagan was elected president, Aretha played a command performance for Queen Elizabeth and the royal family at the London Palladium, with Sammy Davis Jr. introducing her. Two days later, she moved to the Royal Victoria Hall for three more concerts.

"Glynn was on that trip where we also played for Queen Beatrice of the Netherlands," said Cecil. "Aretha was in a great mood 'cause, before we got there, she'd finally taken off weight."

Jet reported that she had been losing fifteen pounds a month: "Aretha said she plans to write a book about her weight loss. She has dropped several dress sizes to slip into a Jean Louis creation made from three layers of black and white chiffon with silver and white beads and rhinestones."

In January 1981, *Ebony* reported that her Arista contract was worth nine million dollars.

"An exaggeration," said Ruth Bowen. "If Aretha got a contract for four million, she'd tell the press it was worth eight million. Back in the day, if I got her twenty-five thousand for a date, she'd have me tell *Jet* she was getting fifty thousand."

"Aretha wasn't wrong to worry about going out of style," said Cecil. "The music business is all about current style—who's got it and who's lost it. I remember how upset Ree got over the Steely Dan hit 'Hey, Nineteen.' It was all over the radio. I liked it. I thought Steely Dan had a great jazz/soul groove going, but I didn't pay that much attention to the lyrics. Aretha did. She pointed out that it was a story about the singer's hookup with a younger chick who's nineteen. The cat sings, 'Hey, Nineteen, that's 'Retha Franklin…she don't remember the Queen of Soul.' Then he says something about how the soul singers are having a hard time. Ree didn't like hearing that. She wanted to sue the writer. 'Sue for what?' I asked. 'Sue for libel. He's defaming me. He's saying I'm old hat.' I had to calm her down and convince her that no lawyer was gonna take a case like that. Plus it would bring even more attention to the lyrics. But that's how sensitive she was. She didn't want to be reminded of the fact that she hadn't enjoyed a big pop hit since the early seventies."

That winter, Aretha revved up her live show, the usual combination of unintentional camp and brilliant singing.

Robert Palmer, in his *New York Times* February 27 review of her City Center concert, described her "unerring instinct for picking the most inappropriate material and for sabotaging the pacing of her sets with gimmicky, utterly banal stage routines." Still, he noted, "during 'Amazing Grace,' her closing number, she sang so movingly that she began to cry."

The same week Aretha sang at City Center, the Grammy Awards ceremony was televised from Radio City Music Hall. She had been nominated in the best R&B female vocal category for "Can't Turn You Loose," and she was asked to sing the number at the telecast. A win would end a six-year dry spell. From 1967 until 1975, the year her streak was broken by Natalie Cole, Aretha had won eight straight Grammys in the category.

"It was a crazy night," Cecil remembered. "We started out at Radio City, where she crushed 'Can't Turn You Loose.' Her live performance was better than the record. Aretha was a little worried because Diana Ross was nominated in the same category for her 'Upside Down.' She wanted to beat Diana in the worst way. She wanted back in the Grammy game. So she wasn't happy when, to everyone's surprise, Stephanie Mills won for 'Never Knew Love Like This Before.' Losing to Stephanie, though, was a lot better than losing to Diana."

Predictions were for Barbra Streisand and Barry Gibb's "Guilty" to rule the Grammys, but the night's big winner was Christopher Cross and his "Sailing."

"From Radio City we jumped into the limo to head over for her gig at City Center," Cecil remembered. "There wasn't a second to spare, so when the limo driver kept turning down the wrong streets and got us caught up in a traffic jam, Aretha lost it. She screamed so loud I thought there'd be nothing left for the stage. I calmed her down but she was really frazzled. She made it in time, the concert was great, and then it was time for this huge party Clive Davis was giving to honor Aretha's comeback. You know how much Clive likes throwing parties—well, this was the party of the year with every music and movie star in the city waiting on Ree's arrival. The press coverage was going to be tremendous.

"I know damn well that I'd told her that the party was in a swanky private club on the top floor of a skyscraper. But when we got there, she claimed I hadn't warned her. This was when Aretha's fear of heights was building. 'I'm right next to you, sis,' I said. 'I've got you.' Well, we made it up to the tenth floor. But then we had to walk over to another elevator bank that would take us to the fiftieth floor, where the party was happening.

"'Oh, no, we're not,' Ree said when she learned we had forty more stories to go. My pleas did no good. She turned right around and went back down. Yes, sir, that was the night the honored guest decided to skip the honor. Next day she apologized to Clive, but not before she told him that if he wanted to give her another party to make sure it was low down—like in a basement. Turned out, though, that Clive's next party was in his penthouse apartment up on Park Avenue, and, as you can imagine, Aretha wasn't about to get on the elevator and go up that high."

Three days after the Grammys, Aretha appeared on *Saturday Night Live* singing the same Arif Mardin chart of "Can't Turn You Loose."

"Then it was back to California for rest and relaxation," said Cecil. "That New York situation wore her out. She needed the comfort of family life."

"I'm not sure how much comfort life with Glynn was giving her at that point," said Erma, who visited her sister in Encino. "Ree loves to cook, but she was spending so much time in the kitchen that weight had become a problem again. She said she wanted time off from her career but she's never been able to leave her career. She was deep into her new record, picking songs and producers. Her first Arista album hadn't been the blockbuster she had hoped for, so, in her mind, this second one had to do it.

"And then she was torn up because of Daddy. Daddy had made no progress. He was still in a coma. Aretha felt that if she were with him in Detroit, maybe it would make a difference. Maybe he'd respond to her. So she flew back with me for a few weeks. Her presence didn't make any difference—at least, none that we or his doctors could detect. Through all this I sensed that her first priority was not her marriage. I saw Glynn moving deeper into his acting and his family, and Aretha moving deeper into her career and our family."

In the May issue of *Ebony,* though, when Aretha, along with a group of black women that included Lena Horne and Roberta Flack, was asked to rank the top ten most exciting black men, she "emphatically insisted that to her there is only one exciting man: her husband, actor Glynn Turman. No prodding or pleading or threats could get the 'queen of soul' to expand her list. 'Put him down 10 times!!' she demanded. 'He is my boyfriend, my husband, my big brother, my protector and sometimes even my little boy. I look at him from time to time and I can't believe he's really mine. Now that's exciting.'"

"What did Shakespeare say?" asked Ruth Bowen. "'Methinks the lady doth protest too much.' That's Sister Aretha. She always wants the world to think that not only is everything hunky-dory but everything is absolutely totally glorious. She couldn't be richer, she couldn't be happier, she couldn't be living a more satisfying life. Aretha gets up every day and starts creating her own reality. Because she is who she is—a queen—she can call in that reality to the press. And they'll usually buy it. At the same time, she's trying to sell herself that reality. But, believe me, honey, her reality ain't real. Far as a relationship goes, the real of the matter is that any man with a serious career of his own is gonna have a hard time with Sister Ree. Because she's career fixated, he's gonna have to take a backseat. And a strong man and seriously gifted actor like Glynn Turman is not about to take a backseat. I didn't care what she was telling *Ebony* about her happy home life, I knew it was just a matter of time—especially during those early Arista days when she was desperate for a hit. Nothing was going to interfere with her getting back on track."

26. BACK ON TRACK

W hen Aretha called to say she wanted me to coproduce her second Arista album, of course I was pleased," said Arif Mardin, "but my first question was, 'Who's the other producer?' Her answer came quickly. 'Me,' she said. When she was in the studio, she was focused. But there were several trips to Detroit to see about her dad that understandably had her distracted. As it turned out, she actually only coproduced two of the songs that she had written—neither of which was especially strong—'Kind of Man' and 'Whole Lot of Me.' She also coproduced and wrote the rhythm arrangement for 'Truth and Honesty,' a snappy little ditty by Burt Bacharach, Carole Bayer Sager, and Peter Allen.

"Like many artists who have written hits, Aretha was convinced that she could write another 'Dr. Feelgood,' 'Think,' or 'Spirit in the Dark,'" Arif told me. "She was proud of her compositions, and, even if I had tried, I could have never dissuaded her from including them on her record. Clive Davis is a true diplomat, though, and rather than discourage her songwriting, he urged her to collaborate. That's how she got together with Sam Dees and George Benson, a hot artist at the time. George had just won a Grammy for 'Give Me the Night,' written by Rod Temperton, who had enjoyed great success with Michael Jackson on *Off the*

Wall. Sam, George, and Aretha wrote 'Love All the Hurt Away,' which became the title of the record and an R-and-B hit. She was certain it'd cross over and become a pop hit, but it never got higher than number thirty-six.

"Overall, *Love All the Hurt Away* was a very ambitious album that did not quite realize its ambitions. It was Aretha's idea to cover 'It's My Turn,' the pop smash Michael Masser and Carole Bayer Sager had on Diana Ross. It was one thing to cover a sixties soul chestnut like Sam and Dave's 'Hold On, I'm Comin'' or a rock anthem like Keith and Mick's 'You Can't Always Get What You Want.' But 'It's My Turn' was only a year old, and it was far too early to forge a cover version. Aretha disagreed. She felt strongly that the song was more suited to her style than Diana's. Yes, but Diana already had the hit. 'I don't care,' Aretha said, 'it's *my* turn.' She sang the song with undeniable conviction. She did feel it was her turn for a pop hit, but, alas, the marketing people agreed with me. They saw no hope for its success as a single.

"I had more hope for a song like 'Living in the Streets,' a Rod Temperton song that bore traces of his work with Heatwave, his own band, and his productions for Michael's *Off the Wall* and, later in the eighties, *Thriller.* I'm not sure, though, that Aretha's voice was quite suitable for the kind of slick dance grooves that were Rod's specialty. 'Living in the Streets' became a decent album cut and nothing more.

"We used many of the same sidemen—pop stars like the guys from Toto, and pop-oriented musicians like David Foster, Greg Phillinganes, and Louis Johnson, who'd worked with Quincy and Michael Jackson, and bass player Marcus Miller, who'd started recording with Luther Vandross. We definitely pulled out all the stops. Other than the title track, though, there were no hits. On the other hand, the reviews were strong, and I think the overall quality of the album gave steam to Aretha's slow-building resurgence."

"Aretha loves all her albums," said Cecil, "but the thing she loved most about *Hurt* was the cover. She got George Hurrell to do the photography. He's the guy who shot those old stars like Bette Davis and Joan Crawford. She wanted the film noir black-and-white look of old Hollywood. The image of her, turned out in her white fur shawl, sitting on a stack of suitcases, made her feel she had finally arrived. In the movie capital of the world, she was sitting pretty. Yes, Mr. DeMille, she's ready for her close-up."

The record has its charms. The title song is an infectious ballad, and it's fun to hear her riffing with the Stevie Wonder/Donny Hathaway–influenced George Benson. I like her assault on "It's My Turn." It's thrilling to hear her go full throttle on Masser's already over-the-top anthem to the glories of self-assertion. For the rest, though, the album feels like an out-of-breath attempt to catch up to current musical fashion.

The *New York Times*' Stephen Holden felt otherwise. When he reviewed the album on October 11, he wrote, "It has been nine years since Aretha Franklin, the greatest soul singer of her generation, made an album as strong and as emotionally compelling as 'Love All the Hurt Away.'"

During this same period, Aretha addressed her image in a cover story in *Jet*. The headline read: "Aretha Franklin Tells Why Weight Doesn't Worry Her Anymore." She argued that when she was a size eight or nine, she looked too small. "I feel better at a thirteen," she said. "It looks better to me, more healthy…I would certainly prefer to be healthy and well-fed than svelte and hungry." She added that Glynn liked her with extra padding.

"If you read her press from any period of her life," said Ruth Bowen, "it's always the same. It always comes down to four words— *I have no problems*. Aretha's philosophy is, if you say it enough, maybe it'll come true. Sweep the problems under the rug. Don't worry about anyone looking under those rugs 'cause no one's allowed in your house."

That fall Aretha played the Claridge Hotel in Atlantic City. Included in the show was a medley of old-fashioned showbiz songs, among them "Up a Lazy River," "Me and My Shadow," "Yankee Doodle Dandy," and "Over the Rainbow."

Two decades after she had sung this material on her early Columbia records and at her nightclub performances, they remained part of her act.

"She got criticism that singing something like 'Swanee' might be corny," said her longtime musical director H. P. Barnum. "But Aretha was never too moved by criticism. She's not prone to change. She sees herself as an old-fashioned entertainer who wants to put on a splashy show to please all the different kinds of fans in the audience. She comes from that school that says you better cross over or you'll wind up crossing back. Crossing over means going for the most mainstream material. Besides, she likes Judy Garland and knows that if she sings a Judy Garland song, she's gonna sing it better than Judy ever could. That gives Aretha great satisfaction. At the same time, she's concerned with her core audience—the R-and-B audience. She realizes in that arena she's got to be current. That's why in her live show she'll have me, an old-school conductor, taking charge. But in the studio, you best believe she's running after the hottest producer around. Like Ray Charles, you can get by at these big venues in Atlantic City and Vegas by performing your old hits. But if you want to stay on the radio, you need new hits. Aretha never stopped chasing after new hits."

"Because *Love All the Hurt Away* had only one semi-hit," said Arif Mardin, "I wasn't surprised that I was not asked to produce her third Arista album. I suspected she'd go off after one of the more up-to-date guys, like Rod Temperton. Rod wasn't available, but Luther Vandross was. Luther proved to be the best choice she could have made. Yet for all their artistic compatibility, I heard that it wasn't a match made in heaven."

Luther laughed when I asked him about Arif's comment.

"Well," he said, "it's a long story. Are you ready for the epic tale?"

"I am."

"Understand where I was in 1981. My first record, *Never Too*

Much, had come out—and it was a hit. Turned gold and made me a bunch of money. Even though I'd grown up in the projects of New York, I was already used to money, since I'd made a small fortune doing backgrounds and jingles. Patti Austin and I were probably the most successful studio singers of our time. I was also in Chic. In fact, that's me saying 'Yowsah, yowsah, yowsah' on 'Le Freak.' I paid my disco dues and then some. It was one thing to sing behind David Bowie or Bette Midler but another to break out on my own. That happened when I entered my thirties. I saw myself as an artist who had been raised on the glorious voices of the great divas. I also adored the girls' groups, especially the Shirelles. But it was the female solo stars that captured my heart. To me, the holy trinity of divas consisted of Aretha, Diana, and Dionne. It never dawned on me, though, that it would be my fate to produce all three of those stars. I knew I could produce. I wrote, arranged, and produced *Never Too Much,* but my concentration was on my own career, not helping revive someone else's.

"For the first time in my life, I started doing interviews with major publications. Naturally I talked about my influences, and naturally I kept mentioning Aretha. I told *Rolling Stone* that the idea of producing Aretha one day would be a dream come true. Turned out that day would be tomorrow. The afternoon the interview ran, Clive Davis called me. 'Are you serious about producing Aretha?' 'Well, yes,' I said, 'you caught me by surprise—but of course. No one in his right mind could pass up the chance to produce the Queen.' 'I'll make it happen,' Clive said. 'When?' 'Soon.'

"A week later I was at home when they said Aretha Franklin was on the phone. I started whooping it up like a little boy on Christmas morning. Ran to the phone. 'Aretha?' 'Yes, this is Miss Franklin. Is this Mr. Vandross?' That's when I first saw that it wasn't gonna be all hugs and kisses. Miss Franklin was formal. Miss Franklin wanted to know if Mr. Vandross had any songs that were suitable for her. 'Not now, Miss Franklin, but I can sure write some.' 'Do that, Mr. Vandross, and I'll give you my evaluation soon thereafter.'

"Clearly I had to audition. Well, why not? The Queen has certain prerogatives. One of them is that her subjects must submit their credentials before being awarded an audience. I asked her to give me a little time. She said that she didn't have a lot of time. If I wanted to be considered as a producer, I'd have to turn out product quickly. She also added that she enjoyed that rendition of 'House Is Not a Home' that I did on *Never Too Much*. 'I've been planning to sing that song myself,' she said. 'What would you think of including it on my album?' 'I'd think you'd be better served by originals, songs fresh and new.' 'I dare to say that I'm also known for doing covers.' 'You're known for singing anything and everything beautifully, Miss Franklin.' 'Why, thank you, Mr. Vandross.'

"It was a strange and somewhat strained conversation. The Aretha that I had heard throughout my entire childhood on the radio—warm and down-home—wasn't the Aretha I heard on the phone. I'd get to know down-home Aretha, but the planet would have to take a couple of spins before that happened.

"Working with Marcus Miller and Nat Adderley Jr. on my first album, we had already formed a production team. Along with Doc Powell's guitar, Marcus's bass, and Nat's keyboards, I had the rhythm section of life, silky-smooth with just a taste of the dance-disco-dazzle that delights the club-goers. In quick order, Marcus came up with the track. The track was on fire. I knew it was a smash. I wrote the words to the rhythm. Wasn't looking for anything deep. The thing just jumped off the tape, so I called it 'Jump to It.' I was all about, hey, respond to the rhythm, respond to love, jump to love.

"Aretha heard it and loved it. She was ready to roll, but the challenge was my schedule. I was touring heavily behind my own album, gigs practically every weekend. I had to fly in to LA from wherever I was—Chicago or Atlanta or Miami. At the same time, I had agreed to produce an album on my label mate Cheryl Lynn, also in LA, so I was doing three things at once. I was a little frazzled.

"The sessions with Aretha began with the same formality. But instead of calling me Mr. Vandross, she changed it to Vandross. From then on I'd always be Vandross to her, never Luther. When I told her it was okay to address me by my first name, she said, 'If I call Curtis Mayfield [by the name] Mayfield, I know you have no objections if you're Vandross.' 'If I do anything half as good as *Sparkle*,' I said, 'you can call me [late] for dinner.' 'Dinner is already here,' she said, indicating that her assistant had brought us enough fried chicken to feed an army.

"After dinner, Aretha finally indicated that I should call her Aretha. We bonded over food. We loved the same stuff—everything greasy and sweet. We struggled with the same overeating addiction. I'm certain we enabled each other because when Aretha and I were in the studio, good food was as much a part of our collaboration as the harmonies. Good food always brought Aretha down to earth.

"There were a few sharp disagreements. Aretha doesn't like her vocals critiqued—and understandably. Hey, she's Aretha Franklin. On the other hand, the heart of the album was comprised of the four songs that I wrote either alone or with Marcus. We also knew damn well that 'Jump to It' was a stone hit, and, because we had composed it, we knew how it should sound. It was a production thing, a vision thing. I could have well kept the song for myself, sung it on my second album and had a surefire smash. But we had it earmarked for Aretha, and as long as Aretha was willing to bend a little to her producers, we were game.

"The bending was a problem. For example, I wanted to establish the groove with a long instrumental intro. Aretha didn't think the listener would wait that long to hear her voice. I assured her that the listener would be hooked on the groove and would be delighted to wait. She wanted to come in sooner. I said no. 'Who's the one with the most hits here?' she asked. Of course the answer was her. I just had one; she had dozens. 'But who's the one with the *latest* hit?' I asked. She didn't answer. She stormed out.

"But she came back. And she sang it the way I wanted it. Not only that, she came up with that whole spoken business of her chit-chatting with her girlfriend Kitty about dishing the dirt on who's drop-kicked who. She fell into the story with a coyness that suited the song perfectly. I also have to say that Aretha rode the groove like a surfer riding a wave. She rode it better than anyone could have, throwing in just the right scats and side licks that punctuated the lyrics in all the right places.

"Aretha's not only a great soaring singer, a great gospel singer, soul singer, and jazz singer, but she's a percussive singer. By that I mean she has the sensibility of a drummer. So if a groove is slick, she'll find a way to kick back and push it in the most subtle ways. 'Jump to It' is basically a rhythm thing. For it to work, enormous vocal variations are required to keep it interesting. Aretha has variations to spare. The track was already hot, but she completely burned it up and set the studio on fire."

When "Jump to It" was released in the summer of 1982, it shot to the top of the R&B charts, her first number-one hit since her work with Curtis Mayfield five years earlier. At age forty, Aretha had emerged from her sales slump to reconfirm her commercial status.

When I first heard "Jump to It," I reacted as most Aretha fans did. I loved it. I couldn't stop listening to it. I found the groove irresistible. Luther had relit the fire. Over three decades later, I still rank it among her greatest confections. It's hardly profound, but it's sweet and funky as the devil.

"I didn't think Aretha wanted profound," said Luther. "Aretha was looking for airplay and single sales. Those days of 'Respect' and 'Think' were behind her. She didn't want to be political. She wanted to be current. She wanted to sound fresh. I was fascinated to see that her focus was more on the container that the content. On a personal level, she played it very close to the vest. She'd sit down and rap with me but she kept the talk light. Before I met her, I had the wrong idea of what she might be like. Having grown up on

Ebony and *Jet,* I remember reading all these articles about her. Seems like there was one every week. In every one, you got the idea that she lived the perfect life. Happy at home. Happy with her man. Her career going full blast. She had it all. But in person, I encountered this rather lonely woman who wasn't happy at all. Naturally, a lot of that had to do with her daddy. Our work together all took place while he was still in a coma. But beyond that, I sensed that her marriage was also a source of anguish. Reading in between the lines, it seemed clear that her relationship to Glynn Turman was on the verge of collapse. She was also fighting with her sisters."

"Long ago I lost track of all the times Aretha wasn't talking to me," said Erma, "but I do recall things being especially tense in the early eighties. She had accused me of not getting the right care for our father. We had words, and for a while we had no communication. But when she started recording with Luther, things took a turn for the better. I think she realized that she finally had found the right producer. She used Cissy Houston and Darlene Love on some tracks but invited our cousin Brenda and me to sing on others. I took note that the song she asked me to do backgrounds on was called 'I Wanna Make It Up to You,' the thing she'd written for her and Levi Stubbs of the Four Tops. To us, Levi has always been one of the strongest soul singers, and their duet is about the best Aretha had ever and would ever do. I also sang on her cover of the Isley Brothers' 'It's Your Thing,' and we reminisced about the time she and I had once partied with the Isleys at their home in New Jersey. It was a good reunion. I wish Carolyn had been there as well. Ironically, though, just as Aretha and I made up, she and Carolyn fell out. Can't remember why."

"Luther brought a lot of light back in Aretha's career," said Cecil, "and there's no doubt he gave her a contemporary sound. Can't stress enough the importance of this. We'd seen that the move from Atlantic to Arista was a good one. It was Clive who identified Luther, and it was Luther who had what the kids wanted to hear. I'd call it a born-again moment."

Billboard's review from July 31 summed up the industry's attitude about *Jump to It.*

"Arista's efforts to return the Queen of Soul to the top of the
pop charts may pay off with this frisky, eight-song collection,
while the title cut is already causing excitement on black radio."

Nelson George, in *Billboard* on September 25, wrote that the
highlights of her appearance at the Budweiser Superfest in Madison
Square Garden were her duets with Smokey Robinson and Luther:
"The contrast between her gospel shouts and Robinson's crooning
delivery on 'I Want to Make It Up to You' was thrilling...Van-
dross came out to sing a chorus of 'Jump to It' with Franklin and
show that he too could have had a hit with this bubbly dance tune."

After completing the *Jump to It* project, Aretha told the press that
she'd never felt better. When reporters mentioned the issues she
was facing—her dad's ongoing coma and her marital difficulties—
she dismissed them. She kept saying that positive people see life
positively—and that's all there was to it.

A perfect example was in the August 9 issue of *Jet*, in which she
said that her dad, although he had been unable to speak for the past
thirty-six months, was "a picture of health and communicates with
his eyes and smiles."

"Aretha was convinced that one day he'd come out of that
coma," said Carolyn, "and everything would be rosy. The doctors
said that would never happen. Aretha saw expressions on his face—
happiness in his eyes and smiles on his face—that no one else saw.
She was imagining."

That wasn't all that was going on. On August 23, *Jet* reported
that "Queen of Soul Aretha Franklin and her leading man, actor
Glynn Turman, won't talk about the threatened dissolution of their
two-career marriage because they're too proud and feel their problem is personal and private."

"When it comes to admitting failure, no one expresses more
pride than Aretha," said Ruth Bowen. "There is no failure in her

universe—or if there is, it can never be her fault. I remember talking to her just before the breakup with Glynn became public. 'Ruthie,' she told me, 'don't believe those lies. I'm happier than any time in my life.'"

"Poor baby was miserable," said Erma. "And understandably. Her marriage to Glynn was billed as the perfect Hollywood relationship. A handsome, dashing, and successful actor marries a beautiful, glamorous, and successful singer. After her fairy-tale wedding and her enormous effort to paint a perfect picture in all the magazines, the end of this relationship was especially painful."

"If you go to any Twelve Step meetings," said Carolyn, "they tell you not to pull a geographic. A geographic is when people pull up stakes and move rather than face their problems and pains. Move to another house, another city, or another state. Aretha did all three. I was happy to have her move back to Detroit and stay with me and Daddy on LaSalle. It was her home as much as anyone's. She was paying the mortgage and the utility bills. I liked having my sister help me supervise Daddy's nurses. But I knew that her move was predicated on her running from her problems in California."

"I was surprised that Aretha decided to go home to live—and then I wasn't surprised at all," said Cecil. "She had been so set on living the Hollywood life. She had high hopes that California was the answer to all her domestic trouble. Like any woman, she just wanted simple happiness. Problem is, Ree is not a simple woman. She's a genius, and geniuses are plagued by their talent. Their talent takes over their lives and overwhelms everything else. It's almost as if their talent is too strong to be controlled. I'm not making excuses for my sister, I'm just saying that her genius gave her a sensitivity and vulnerability ordinary people can't understand. She feels too much. She feels too deeply. She can be hurt too easily. I don't know if she made too many demands on Glynn or whether Glynn made too many demands on her. I know that they're both wonderful people with a creative spirit. They both live in the world of competitive backbiting show business. That world is not conducive to long-term romance. And to be frank, I don't think Ree was built for long-term romantic commitment. Her main commitment is to her music. That's the one commitment that will never die. Her other unshakable commitment has to do with our dad. She felt like if she could be home by his side, a lot of her anxieties and fears would disappear. After all, of all the people in the world, it was Daddy who had the most calming effect on my sister. She wanted calmness. Aretha has always yearned for calmness. So she came home to find it."

27. HOME

In late 1982, Aretha retreated to Detroit, and as of this writing, Detroit remains her home.

I say *retreated* because, according to her siblings, first cousin, and sister-in-law, she began to close in and build a wall around herself. Her world became far more circumscribed. Rather than dissipate, her fears increased.

"As soon as she moved into LaSalle," said Carolyn, "she insisted on more security. Bigger bars on the windows. New locks on the door. More guards. She was definitely more uptight. I understood because I had been living there with Daddy for four years. Being in the same house with someone in a coma can make anyone uptight. Aretha thought that the proximity to Daddy would help her. She'd feel more useful. But there wasn't really anything to do. The frustration was mind-boggling, and the frustration certainly messed with Aretha's emotions."

"When she flew out to Los Angeles from Detroit to start our second album together," said Luther Vandross, "I could see she was under great strain. I knew being back in her dad's house wasn't easy for her, so I tried to be as sensitive as I could, but it was impossible. She bristled at any suggestion I made. Once again, these were my songs and my arrangements. These were my guys—Marcus Miller and Nat Adderley Jr.—the same guys who worked on *Jump to It*. She had to know that we knew what we were doing since the first album had been a runaway hit. But no. Anytime I gave the slightest comment, she screamed, 'If you think you can do it better, then you sing the damn thing.' 'Fine,' I finally said. 'I'll see you later, Miss Franklin.' My second album—*Forever, for Always, for Love*—had gone gold. I was doing just fine. So if Miss Franklin wanted to have her diva fits and torture another producer, that would be his problem, not mine. I washed my hands of the matter. But then she went running to Clive, complaining about my mental cruelty. I hadn't been cruel at all. I'd been a gentleman and a complete professional. 'Just apologize,' said Clive. 'That's all she wants.' If anyone deserved an apology, it was me. 'You need to be bigger than that,' said Clive. I listened to the man and apologized. Aretha came back to the sessions, but with the demand that she record a song written by her son Clarence. She also insisted that another one of her sons, Teddy, play guitar on it. Both sons were talented, so I accepted both demands. I did so knowing that, no matter how much she needed to put her two cents into the production, we already had one smash in the can. That was 'Get It Right,' something whipped up by me and Marcus Miller. It went straight to number one, her second top-charting R-and-B [song] in twelve months. After she saw we had another hit together, she was sweet as sugar."

Aretha's version of the story in *From These Roots* was the opposite: She had been both reasonable and cooperative; Luther had been a bully. After the final session in LA, she felt so disrespected that she couldn't wait to get away. She booked herself on the first flight to Detroit. The plane encountered extreme turbulence. She had always been a nervous flier, but, for better or worse, had dealt with the anxiety. Suddenly the anxiety increased exponentially. Nonetheless, she flew back to LA that summer to be the honoree at a gala concert sponsored by the Brotherhood Crusade, a charitable organization active in the black community.

A few weeks later she flew to Atlanta, where she was to headline two shows and be honored by her friend Mayor Andrew

Young. According to Aretha, the mayor was out of town and his tribute plans went awry. The two performances went well but she missed her scheduled flight home. Eager to get back to Detroit, she decided to take a twin-engine prop plane. The weather was stormy and the ride extremely rough. Aretha was terrified and, the minute she landed safely in Detroit, swore never to fly again. She never has.

"We were all scared," said Cecil, who was with her on the flight. "Any normal human being would have to be. Falling into those steep air pockets, it felt like we were falling out of the sky. But after a bad flight, the best thing you can do is fly again—and as soon as possible. I urged Ree to do just that. If not, I was scared that her fear would just keep growing. She'd keep remembering what happened and how it could happen again—as opposed to picking a sunny day and experiencing a smooth flight. 'You gotta work through this fear, Ree,' I kept saying, 'or it'll wind up costing you millions. Your livelihood depends on your getting to your fans, and you have fans all over the world.' She heard me. She knew I was right. But she was just too scared to act. That's when everything in her life started to change. She became a prisoner of her fears."

"Money became a central fear," said Ruth Bowen. "She claimed that Arista was extremely slow in paying royalties on her recent hits. Her cash flow had stopped. Her decision to stop flying meant the cancellation of several dates that she had asked me to book for her. That cost her a fortune. And that's when she decided to host what she called her Artist's Ball.

"When Aretha decides to throw a ball or a party for charitable purposes, she has the best intention. But her party planning is the same as her financial planning. It's always a mess."

Jet reported the story in its November 7 issue with an item headlined "Aretha Franklin Sponsors 2nd Annual Artist's Ball to Benefit Comatose Dad." Family members were "optimistic" that Reverend Franklin would come out of his coma, the article noted, although the twenty-four-hour-a-day nursing care was costing the Franklin family some $2,500 a week. According to the magazine,

Aretha had been paying 98 percent of her father's medical bills, with the remainder coming from church donations and a 1979 fund-raiser.

"The only family member optimistic about Reverend Franklin coming out of the coma was Aretha," said Ruth. "She clung to that delusion when everyone else knew the reality. The other delusion was that the event would make money. Even if it had proven profitable, I was against it. I thought it looked tacky for an artist of Aretha's caliber—still in demand and still commanding top dollar—to plead poverty. In fact, the event was not successful and wound up costing Aretha. That's why she sued Arista, which, I told her, was like biting the hand that was feeding her."

In November 1983, the same month Jesse Jackson announced his bid for the presidency of the United States, an article in *Jet* reported: "R-E-S-P-E-C-T! That's what Queen of Soul Aretha Franklin says she wants from Arista Records. She has hired a lawyer to help her get it."

"It didn't turn out to be Arista's fault at all," said Cecil, "but a misunderstanding on Aretha's part. She thought she hadn't received a certain check that, in fact, had been deposited in her account months before. Being the gentleman that he is, Clive Davis understood and forgot about the accusation."

Finance was always a great challenge, but no more so than romance.

Aretha spoke often about a man that she called one of the great loves of her life. She would not name him. In her autobiography, he is called Mr. Mystique. She said that their affair started in the sixties and went on through the eighties, overlapping her relationships with Dennis Edwards, Ken Cunningham, and Glynn Turman. She insisted that no one knew his identity, not even members of her family. She claimed their affair was rekindled shortly after her return to Detroit.

It sounded a bit like a soap opera.

"Aretha has been hooked on soap operas ever since I've known her," said Ruth Bowen. "Her days revolve around *The Young and the Restless*. At some point she started seeing her love life like a soap opera. She began writing a soap-opera script—just making up shit, fantasizing about men and relationships that never existed. I don't care what she said in her book about some damn Mr. Mystique. I don't think the man existed. I think she fabricated the whole thing. That became a new pattern for her—making up stories about these beautiful love affairs that happened only in her mind."

When I asked Cecil and Erma if they knew about Mr. Mystique, they diplomatically said no.

"Anything's possible," said Cecil. "I didn't tell Aretha about all the side trips in my life and she didn't tell me about all the secrets in her life. But if there had been this one guy who kept coming round year after year, I think I would have known about him."

"Ree has a vivid imagination," said Erma. "Her genius as a musical storyteller has to do with her ability to imagine romantic situations. When she sings, she becomes a great actress. She places herself in those situations. That's part of her creativity."

"She needed to get her mind off Daddy," added Cecil. "It wasn't easy living in that house. And because of her unfortunate fight with Arista, there were long months when she wasn't recording. Time weighed heavy. She was looking for some kind of relief. She was looking for romance. What woman isn't?"

In February 1984, Aretha's divorce from Glynn Turman was finalized.

"Another fairy tale without a happy ending," said Erma. "Even though I never thought Ree was realistic about the chances of this relationship working out, it pained me to see her hurting. Given my sister's tremendous need for security, this was a big blow. You also can't imagine the terrible stress of being in the same house with Daddy. I wish Aretha hadn't moved back in, but that was her choice. She had to follow her conscience."

"Me and Ree in the same bedroom—our childhood bedroom—was no picnic," said Carolyn. "We fought the same way we fought when we were kids. She accused me of snoring. I accused her of snoring. She set up a tape recorder to prove that I was the one doing the snoring. But when she played it back, the noise I heard was her snoring, not mine! Anyway, we went from fighting to writing together to singing together and then back to fighting. Daddy was still in his coma, but I know he had to be laughing inside. His daughters were still going at it."

That winter Jackie Wilson, the great Detroit soul singer, died at age forty-nine.

"It happened during that same time that my dad was still so deep in his coma," said Cecil. "Our father was close to Jackie. In fact, we all were. We were shocked when he had his heart attack. I was told that it happened when he was singing that line in 'Lonely Teardrops' that says, 'My heart is crying.' After that, like Dad, he fell into a coma. I know he suffered a lonely death, and I know that Aretha wanted to visit him at the hospital where they were keeping him, in New Jersey, but she never went. With our father incapacitated, that would have been too much. The other part of the tragedy was that Jackie Wilson, one of the greatest all-around entertainers of his time, died stone broke. That news shook us up and made us even more fearful of how, in this business, you can lose everything at the drop of a hat."

The financial challenges mounted when, in 1984, Aretha was sued for $102,000 in back taxes by the State of New York. The state claimed that she had not paid taxes on the recording work she had done in Manhattan from 1973 to 1977. Aretha claimed that because the master tapes were the property of Atlantic, not her, she should not be liable.

"This added to the tension and the money woes," said Cecil. "We worked it out, but it cost a pretty penny."

Then, on April Fools' Day, the day before his forty-fifth birthday, Marvin Gaye was shot and killed by his father in Los Angeles.

"After Smokey," said Cecil, "Marvin was my main man. Maybe there were more powerful singers in terms of volume or projection, but no one more sensitive or artistically advanced. That's why Ree loved his work so deeply. Like her, he had all the big three elements mixed inside his music—gospel, jazz, and R-and-B. We talked for years about an Aretha/Marvin collaboration. I hate that it didn't happen. I also hate that Marvin's problems with drugs did him in. I should have read it as a cautionary tale, but I didn't. I still had some years to go before I dealt with my own drug issues."

In May, while Michael Jackson was being honored by Ronald Reagan at the White House, Aretha was in Detroit signing a contract to star in a musical, something she had been discussing for years. She finally agreed to play Mahalia Jackson in *Sing Mahalia!* The plan was to perform it in Cleveland, Chicago, and Detroit before bringing it to Broadway. According to *Jet,* Aretha Franklin was "thrilled and honored" to appear onstage as Mahalia Jackson, whom she described as "an absolutely great lady, a devout Christian, who was warm with a great sense of humor."

"Humor was the key," said Cecil. "Aretha, like Mahalia, can be funny as hell. She can crack jokes with the best of them. That humor was in the script. Musically, we never had doubts. Musically, it was a match made in heaven. No one except Aretha could approach Mahalia's majesty. But it wasn't until we saw the writing that we knew for sure. Mahalia was portrayed as a down-home sister from New Orleans who could cook as well as she could sing. There were some great moments in the play. The thing had *hit* written all over it."

"Because Aretha had experienced frustration with the movie industry in Hollywood," said Erma, "she felt this Broadway offer was a godsend. It wasn't a pie-in-the-sky project. It was real. It didn't require a screen test or an audition. The producers wanted Aretha and only Aretha. It was just the pick-me-up that she needed. Her attitude was, *The world knows I can sing; well, now the world will see that I can act!*"

Before she had a chance to take on the role of Mahalia, though, her father's five-year coma came to a tragic end. Reverend C. L. Franklin died on July 27, 1984.

"I knew it was coming soon," said Cecil. "So did Erma and Carolyn. But I really believe Aretha had convinced herself that ultimately Dad would come out of this coma and be fully restored."

"After the death of her dad," said Ruth Bowen, "Aretha was never the same."

28. OUR FATHER

The day of the funeral, I felt deeply for Aretha," said her sister-in-law Earline. "I felt for my husband, for Carolyn and Erma and Brenda. I felt for everyone. Reverend was the anchor of their lives. He was the strongest force they had ever known. He had shaped them in the most fundamental ways imaginable. He'd been their father and mother, been there for every decision. He'd been their chief adviser. Any crisis and they came running to their daddy. Say what you want about Reverend and his worldly ways, but the man was a wonderful father. In a culture that isn't exactly famous for devoted single fathers, he was all that—and more.

"Reverend adored Cecil. He had encouraged my husband to go to college and to become a minister. He had encouraged him to learn management and protect his sister. Reverend also adored Carolyn and Erma. He had encouraged their higher education as well. He never stopped telling them how talented they were. He listened to their records with pride. But when it came to Aretha, that was a whole 'nother thing. Aretha was his favorite. You had to be blind not to see that. And if Reverend had genius—and I do believe that, as a preacher, he did possess genius—he couldn't help but be extraordinarily close to his genius daughter. That's why on the day of his funeral, I wanted to be especially sensitive to Aretha. I knew how bad she was hurting.

"But here's the thing about Aretha. She takes her suffering—and God knows she was suffering that day—and turns it into anger. That's just her way. So when we were assembled outside the church doors and prepared to walk down the aisle towards the casket where Reverend had been laid to rest, she somehow got the idea that I wanted to walk in first. Well, I didn't. I was happy to follow behind the siblings. But Ree went off on me, claiming that I was somehow looking to boost my status as a family member by leading the way into the church. Nothing was further from my mind.

"Just like that, she threw a fit. There was shoving and shouting until it took Reverend Jesse Jackson to come in and settle her down. I have no idea why she chose that moment to start this ridiculous family feud, but I'm afraid that's Aretha. I'm not a psychologist, but if I had to describe my sister-in-law's psychology, I'd say that it's all about diva drama. That's her default position. It's hard for her, just like it's hard for all of us, to deal with extreme sadness and loss. Rather than deal, she acts out. She goes to rage. Rage without reason. It's crazy."

"I can't even remember what happened that day," said Cecil. "I know that Ree and Earline had words, and I know that Ree was angry that the arrangements weren't to her liking. But I was so lost in the memories of my dad, the greatest man I have ever known, that I wasn't paying attention to anything else."

"It was silly," said Erma, "but it was also appropriate. Daddy was always there to break up family's fights. But now that he was gone, who could stop the fights?"

"It was all about control," said Carolyn. "Aretha had made the calls to those preachers that she wanted to eulogize Daddy. She had sent for Jesse and Jasper Williams. She had picked out the gospel songs she wanted sung. She had gone as far as to select the pews and seats where she wanted the family and honored guests to sit. She also wanted to control the procession. But when something seemed to go out of order, she lost it. I understood that. She was really losing it over the death of our dad. None of us can control death, so if we can control other stuff—a seating arrangement or a processional—that makes us feel less vulnerable and maybe less afraid. I know that with Daddy gone, Aretha felt more afraid than at any time in her life."

"I remember talking to Aretha after the funeral," said Ruth Bowen, "and thinking that this poor child would never be the same. I thought that his death would do one of two things—either make her more confident because she had to stand on her own, or make her more anxious because she had to live in a world without that magnificent man. She kept saying that she would be fine, that she just wanted to be certain that the press covered his death with the dignity that he deserved. I assured her that, with all my various contacts, I would do all I could to help.

"It wasn't more than two weeks later that she called and said that she wanted me to ask one of my reporter friends to set up an interview. She wanted to explain that, now with her father gone, she was prepared to return to her career. I wasn't quite sure what she meant. 'For the past five years, since Daddy got sick, I've had to put my career on hold. I've had to sacrifice many things.' I agreed that she had, in fact, sacrificed a great deal. At the same time, I pointed out that after his coma, she had hardly retired or put her career on hold. She'd done the *Blues Brothers* movie; she'd jumped from Atlantic to Arista, where she'd cut four albums and was about to cut a fifth. Rather than slow down, she had sped up. With the help of Clive and Luther and many others, she had revived her career. The story was just the opposite of the one she wanted to tell—rather than get down and depressed over what had happened to her daddy, she got up and got moving. Why not tell *that* story?

"'Because it's disrespectful and not true,' said Aretha. 'These things happened only after I made sure Daddy was cared for. I cared for him full-time while I worked on everything else part-time.' There was no use arguing. As usual, Aretha was rewriting history the way it suited her. She wanted the history to show how the long-suffering devoted daughter gave up everything for her father. Well, it was one thing for Aretha to sell herself that story, but I sure as hell couldn't sell it to a reporter. I didn't even try. The facts just wouldn't bear it out. Aretha finally dropped the idea. But not more than a year or two passed before I heard her tell some writer that same fable, only this time there was a twist. She said that only after her dad had passed could she really concentrate on turning out hits. She explained that the first time she really got back into her career wasn't until after his funeral. That's when Clive hooked her up with Narada Michael Walden and they had those hits—'Who's Zoomin' Who?' and the big one, 'Freeway of Love.'"

In the mideighties, Narada Michael Walden was in the center of Clive Davis's phenomenal pop-music mix. He had started off in the early seventies as a drummer. Replacing Billy Cobham in the Mahavishnu Orchestra, John McLaughlin's celebrated jazz-fusion group, he made a name for himself as a percussion prodigy. By the late seventies, he had a deal with Atlantic, making soul-jazz-pop records under his own name. His first success came as a pop producer for teen soul singer Stacy Lattisaw.

"Clive was the one who hipped us to Narada," said Cecil. "Clive has those ears for who's hot and who's not. He also had a feeling—and he was right—that Narada's upbeat personality would be the right medicine for what had been ailing Aretha. Because of her legal dispute with Arista, she hadn't recorded for a long while. And because of her fights with Luther, she was down on big-name producers. She thought they had too much ego. Clive said that she'd love Narada—and she did. Everyone does. He's a new-age cat who believes in nothing but love, love, love. He does everything he can to make you happy. He understood that Ree needed to be treated like a queen. And more than anything, he came with the goods. He and his boys Preston Glass and Jeffrey Cohen had the smoking-est tracks."

Narada, so named by his guru Sri Chinmoy, realized that the Aretha Franklin paradigm had shifted. There was a time when she had been willing to venture outside Detroit to record. But that time had passed. Now the world would have to come to her. She had set up permanent camp in Detroit. After her dad died, she lived with Cecil and Earline for a year before moving to a sprawling home in Bloomfield Hills, a woodsy, affluent suburb twenty miles north of the city. Over time, she would buy and sell several houses in Greater Detroit, but Bloomfield Hills would remain her command post. She could sing over tracks made elsewhere. Narada could work up the music in his Northern California studio and then fly out to Detroit for the vocal sessions at her preferred recording studios, like United Sound.

"Aretha dug in," said Erma. "She moved way out there, bought a big house, and angered the neighbors by putting big ugly bars over all the windows. I said that, given the upscale neighborhood, she didn't have to worry about crime. But after Daddy's death, Aretha worried about everything a lot more. She said those bars made her feel secure — so the bars stayed."

"Narada's vibe helped her tremendously," said Carolyn. "He had a carefree spirit that was the perfect counterbalance to what we'd just gone through with our father. He had good cheer and positive energy. His songs were all about bouncing along through life with a song in your heart — nothing dire or deep. Of course, Luther's songs — like 'Jump to It' and 'Get It Right' — also had a happy spirit, but Luther had emotional baggage, whereas Narada was a free spirit. I know that Narada was seen as a gift from Clive, but I saw him as a gift from God. He lightened the mood and led Ree, then in her early forties, into green pastures."

"My relationship with Aretha," Narada told me, "actually began when Dionne Warwick, who was recording for Clive, rejected a bunch of my songs. I adore Dionne but for whatever reason, we weren't on the same page. Clive suggested that I work with Aretha. I jumped at the chance. I considered her hookup with Luther — 'Jump to It' — the height of new funk. I was inspired to take that funk even further. Our first call went well. I tried to be as delicate as I could because I knew her dad had just died. I said, 'Aretha, I know you've gone through a lot recently, but when you want to relax, what do you do?' She talked about going out to a club and seeing a cute guy at a nearby table. 'I might look his way, he might look mine, and just when he thinks the fish is about to take the bait, the fish jumps off the line and he's wondering, "Baby, who's zooming who."' She cracked me up and I took careful notes of her storytelling nuances. It was really her story, so she and my close partner Preston Glass and I became co-composers of 'Who's Zoomin' Who?' Because she wasn't leaving home, I flew to Detroit to produce that and another I wrote, 'Until You Say You Love Me.'

"The minute she walked into Studio B of United Sound, where she did all her recording, I could feel the strain she'd been under. Nothing is tougher than losing a parent. I'd never met anyone so vulnerable. I could do little more than gently touch her hand. I knew it was my responsibility to treat her with ultimate sensitivity and respect. She appreciated that and slowly warmed to me and my approach. I wanted her to give 'Zoomin'' the full 'Retha treatment— and she did just that. Before starting, she warmed up with these incredible octave runs and then sang the hell outta the song. Did all the parts. Nailed the sucker in no time. Same with the ballad 'Until You Say You Love Me.' I was thrilled when she said she wanted more.

"Went back to my studio by the San Francisco Bay and, at the suggestion of Preston Glass, took a song I'd written with Jeffrey Cohen for my album and decided to give it to Aretha. This was 'Freeway of Love.' I sent her the track and heard back immediately. 'Let's go,' she said, and the next day I was flying back to Detroit. First day the weather was bad. Got a call from Aretha saying, 'See that snow outside?' 'Yes, Queen, I do.' 'Well, I don't drive in the snow.' 'No problem.' Second day it was still snowing. Another call from the Queen. 'Sorry,' she said, 'but if you look out the window you'll understand why I'm still not coming down to the studio.' 'I understand.' Third day was the same. On the fourth day the weather broke and she showed up in her mink splendor. I poured on the honey. With the Queen, you can't pour on too much honey and you can't display too much patience. She has that Aries streak. Confrontation will not work with Aretha. Sweetness will."

That recording—"Freeway of Love"—would become Aretha's biggest record since "Respect."

"It was a monster hit with all the right elements," said Cecil. "Narada had the smarts not only to plug into the mythology of motor-crazy Detroit, but he tapped into the Springsteen vibe by using Clarence Clemons on tenor sax. Clarence tore up the track. In the MTV age, the song was also video-friendly. Fact is, it was Aretha's first real video hit. She got her hair shorn in a super-hip extra-edgy mod cut and was ready to roll. It crossed over, became a pop hit, became Ree's first number-one dance hit, and got her another Grammy. It did everything we could ask for—and she never had to leave Detroit."

The success came at just the right time. Aretha's money problems had returned due to her last-minute cancellation of the Mahalia Jackson project. She not only refused to fly to any of the venues where the play was scheduled but also decided that the drives were too long.

"Naturally we got sued," said Cecil. "The entire enterprise rested on Aretha playing Mahalia. The contracts had been signed and the excuses didn't wash. Aretha's attitude was *Well, our legal expenses will be good tax write-offs.* When our accountant told us those expenses couldn't be written off, Aretha fired the accountant."

Responding to the success of *Who's Zoomin' Who?*, Aretha told the *Chicago Tribune,* "This is by no means a comeback. I am a contemporary artist. Artists like myself and Smokey and Tina and Diana are firmly established artists and kind of roll right along. I used to tell Jerry Wexler that everything is not about a hit; some things are purely artistic."

Wexler laughed when he read the quote. "She turned that scenario around," he said. "I was the one who told her that not everything is about hits. I told her to go for the art. Look, 'Freeway' was a clever pop confection—a bit of radio-friendly airplay—but it was nothing more than a product of the Clive Davis hit machine. It was ear candy. You can't put her vocal on 'Freeway' in the same category as 'Dr. Feelgood' or 'Think.' Credit Aretha and Narada for being clever and slick. Getting a hit is never easy and not to be taken for granted. I applaud them for staying current. Not everyone can stay current. But whatever you do, don't call it art."

"A great dance groove," said Luther, "is undoubtedly artful. I gave Aretha several of those grooves, and so did Narada. The creation of those grooves, like the creation of a fine silk suit or a piece of jade jewelry, is considerable work. For my part, I call it art."

"Doesn't matter what you call it—soul, R-and-B, or rock and roll," said Cecil, "the song sold and sold big. If you wanna be a big-time player in the music biz, sales is all that matters. And no matter what Ree says or does, whether she's living the high life in California or kicking back in the burbs of Detroit, Aretha is a player. And nothing is ever gonna change that."

In order to increase her presence as a major player, Aretha realized that she had to be more mobile. She called *Jet* to publicly announce the end of her flying phobia. The magazine reported, "After ending her period of mourning the death of her father Rev. C. L. Franklin Sr., singer Aretha Franklin returned to the concert circuit with four shows in her Detroit hometown. The Queen of Soul not only conquered the enthusiastic show crowds, but she has also harnessed her fear of flying and is ready to start jetting across the nation on a concert tour."

That proved not to be the case.

"I booked a couple of tours," said Ruth Bowen, "only to cancel them. Aretha never made it further than the airport. This is when my patience started running out. I got on her case. I said, 'Girl, these last-minute cancellations are costing you a fortune. You can't afford to keep messing up like this.' She accused me of being insensitive. She said I lacked understanding, and the next thing I knew, I was fired. A few weeks later Dick Alen, a big-time agent at William Morris in LA, began booking her."

"The first time I heard 'Freeway of Love' on the radio, I knew it was going to be huge," Alen told me. "I contacted her lawyer and asked whether she might consider new representation. My timing was good. She was no longer with Ruth Bowen and was open to the idea of working with a prestigious international agency. We had briefly met earlier in her career. In the sixties, I had managed King Curtis, her musical director. I knew Jerry Wexler as well as Clive Davis. We had many mutual friends. In the light of what would soon become a major hit, I thought she had a huge earning potential. To land her as a client was a major coup."

For the next twenty-seven years, Dick Alen booked the majority of Aretha's engagements. On several occasions he was fired—as Aretha would fire practically all those who worked for her—but he exhibited more staying power than even the remarkably tenacious Ruth Bowen.

"That's because Dick never had a really personal relationship with Aretha like I did," explained Ruth. "With Dick it was always business. And that's good. That makes it easy. But because I was something of a mother or older sister to Aretha, I got tangled up in her emotional life. Even in the years after Dick was booking her, she'd call me. The call might have to do with her make-believe fairy-tale love life. Or it might have to do with her financial woes. She might be crying the blues about Mr. Wonderful having two-timed her. Or she might want to know if I had a high-paying gig that would let her pay off some debt. 'I thought Dick Alen was getting you your gigs,' I'd say. 'He is, but that doesn't mean you can't earn a fat commission if you come up with something quick.' I got pissed at her and she got pissed at me. But we knew each other very, very well and we loved each other. I knew that deep down, she has a good heart. Aretha's a loyal daughter and a good sister. She has her problems and I understand all of them.

"Dick Alen didn't know her on this level. And to his credit, he didn't need to. He just needed to keep making her money. And he also needed patience. He had patience—that's one of his strongest traits. Look at his other major clients—Little Richard and Chuck

Berry. He worked for those guys as long as he worked for Aretha. For an agent to rep Aretha, Richard, and Chuck and not suffer a nervous breakdown requires fortitude. Hand it to Dick—the man put up with as much shit as any manager or agent in showbiz history."

The year after C.L.'s death, 1985, proved positive for Aretha. She had new management in place, her dispute with Arista was resolved, and she recorded a new album with a new producer.

"Above all, Aretha is resilient," Erma explained. "She goes through losses, she goes through moods, she has her falling-outs with family members or friends or management, but she bounces back. I admire that. She takes her reign seriously. She once told me that if Queen Elizabeth gets to be queen for the duration of her life, why not Queen Aretha? Ree loves and protects her throne. She's not about to let anyone come and grab it. I see that as a good thing. That's the thing that gets her through."

The record that helped sustain her upward climb—*Who's Zoomin' Who?*—is a product of its time. Overall, it has a cold and mechanical feel, typical of the eighties obsession with hard-driving studio-created sonics. Its influences range from Michael Jackson's "Beat It" to Michael Sembello's "Maniac." In comparison to disco—the prominent dance music of the previous decade—this material has a far more frantic feel. There's little emotional softness, little vulnerability.

"I see the eighties as a time when music went for the jugular and artists went for the money," said Luther Vandross. "You can hear the influence of the Reagan years where the idea is every man for himself. Sixties music had a high political awareness. Seventies music was about liberation in many areas. But the eighties are when blatant materialism comes to the forefront. I'm not saying great artists didn't emerge in the eighties. Prince came on strong, and Michael Jackson did his greatest work. *Thriller* was the ultimate eighties album. The eighties was when I found my own voice.

What we all had in common, though, was a burning desire to sell, sell, sell."

"Aretha likes being on the cutting edge," said Cecil, "and that's exactly where she was with Narada. It was Clive's idea to pair Ree with Annie Lennox. Clive is the king of duets. He likes to say that the heat from one artist can benefit another. The Eurythmics were coming off their big hit 'Sweet Dreams (Are Made of This),' and Annie supposedly idolized Aretha. Dave Stewart, the other half of the Eurythmics, was called in to produce it. He and Annie wrote 'Sisters Are Doing It for Themselves.' A few people said it was too feminist for Aretha, that Aretha has always been a man's woman. But, man, Ree is the original feminist. If she ain't the one in charge, who is?"

Interviewed about the duet some years later in *Billboard,* Annie Lennox said, "Well, I'll tell you the honest truth about that. In my mind, that song was written for Tina Turner. Aretha didn't know who we were; she didn't have a clue. I was quite intimidated, because how can you sing with Aretha? It's just, 'Try to stay on the bicycle.' I just wanted her to feel comfortable."

"Next, Clive put Aretha with Peter Wolf," said Cecil, "the voice of the J. Geils Band. The idea was to capture some of that white rock-and-roll market. Aretha didn't mind. She agreed, as long as Clive let her sing and produce two tracks of her own choice. She wrote 'Integrity' and then decided to sing 'Sweet Bitter Love,' the same Van McCoy she sang in the early sixties on Columbia."

It's fascinating to compare the two versions. The earlier "Sweet Bitter Love" has a purity that's heartbreaking; the eighties interpretation is bolder. Aretha's riffs are far more daring; she's determined to drain the song dry—and she does.

"I followed Aretha's career," said Carmen McRae. "All serious singers did. We knew she had the deepest chops and the deepest soul. You had to wonder about what she was going to sing next. When I heard 'Freeway of Love,' I wasn't happy. Because it was a hit, I knew she'd probably go on making similar-type records. They weren't bad but they didn't match her genius. They sure as hell didn't bring out her genius. A good comparison is Sarah

Vaughan. She had only one big hit, 'Broken Hearted Melody,' back in the fifties. It was cowritten by Hal David, the guy who wrote all those hits with Burt Bacharach. It was probably the weakest song Sarah ever sung—and she knew it. She told me that Hal David gave her other songs, but none of them sold. If they had, they might have ruined her career artistically. Without any more hits, Sarah went back to singing jazz. She spent the rest of her life singing old standards and new ones like 'Send in the Clowns.' She recorded the greatest music of her career—all because she wasn't a hit maker and had to rely on quality and quality alone. That's what I was hoping Aretha would do. I was hoping that she'd pick a piano player like Ella had picked Tommy Flanagan and just go out there with a trio. I was hoping she'd take her place as one of the greatest jazz singers of the century. That wouldn't mean she couldn't sing her hits. With a super-tasteful trio, she could do her R-and-B material. The emphasis, though, would be on the beauty of her voice. We'd get to hear her interpret and improvise and make every song her own. Look, I understand the temptations of the marketplace. But some artists are made to transcend the marketplace. Some artists are made to record the absolute best material without consideration to commerce or any other goddamn thing. When I heard 'Freeway,' I knew that Aretha was moving in a whole 'nother direction. She was moving to the money."

On August 3, *Billboard* reported, "Aretha Franklin's 'Freeway of Love' this week leaps to No. 1 on the black and dance club charts, and to number 12 on the pop chart. It's Lady Soul's 20th No. 1 black hit, which is more than any other artist has had in the chart's 36-year history."

By winter *Who's Zoomin' Who?* had sold a million copies. In December, Nelson George in *Billboard* wrote, "The platinum success of Aretha Franklin's *Who's Zoomin' Who* is a textbook example of the fact that, in the age of mass communications, touring is becoming increasingly anachronistic...Franklin has delivered the most commercial album of her post-soul career."

Nelson went on to explain that three of her videos—"Freeway

of Love," "Who's Zoomin' Who?," and "Sisters Are Doing It for Themselves"—gained heavy airplay, while interviews with *Entertainment Tonight,* the *CBS Morning News,* and *People* magazine kept her profile high. He also mentioned a McDonald's commercial that Aretha taped with the great Chicago soul singer Jerry Butler.

"No doubt, Aretha's comeback was in full swing," said Erma. "Once again, it was my sister's time. It was also a time when two other important black women came on the scene, who gave Aretha credit in very different ways. I'm talking about Whitney Houston and Oprah Winfrey."

Winfrey, whose morning talk show had overtaken Phil Donahue's and was on the brink of national syndication, told *Ebony* that when she ran away from home at thirteen, she found herself walking the streets of Milwaukee, where she happened to see Aretha sitting in a limo. Oprah invented a sob story that the singer bought, to the tune of two hundred dollars. That act of kindness endeared Aretha to Oprah forever.

Through his A&R staff, Clive Davis had heard about Whitney Houston, the daughter of Cissy Houston. He saw her potential, signed her to Arista, closely supervised her debut album, *Whitney Houston,* and promoted it unceasingly. The record's three number-one singles—"Saving All My Love for You," "The Greatest Love of All," and the Narada Michael Walden–produced "How Will I Know"—would eventually help the album sell some twenty-five million copies.

Whitney told *Jet* that she cherished the memory of going to the studio to watch her mom work with Aretha, whom she called Aunt Ree.

"Whitney's star was rising at the exact same time Aretha had clawed her way back," said Ruth Bowen. "There was real affection between the two women, but there was also resentment on Aretha's part. This was a replay of Aretha's reaction to Natalie Cole. It was Whitney's 'Saving All My Love for You' that knocked Ree's 'Freeway' from first position. And, in the months to come, it was Whitney who was getting the lion's share of publicity. Whitney was being called the great new diva. Some were even calling her the new Aretha. Whitney was a gorgeous reed-thin model, while, with each passing year, Aretha was putting on the pounds to the point where she was no longer pleasantly plump. Girlfriend was fat."

"Doesn't take much to bring out my sister's competitive side," said Cecil, "and Whitney did just that. In the same way [Aretha] never liked how Atlantic had Roberta Flack on the label at the same time as her, she wasn't thrilled that Clive seemed to be spending more ad sales on Whitney than her. Ree was naturally thrilled that she won a Grammy for 'Freeway'—best R-and-B female vocal—but was dismayed that Whitney won the best pop performance for 'Saving All My Love for You.' Aretha thought—and I agree—that 'Freeway' was basically pop and 'Saving' basically R-and-B. Of course, all R-and-B singers want pop awards and pop sales because pop is bigger. Aretha saw *Who's Zoomin' Who?* as her big pop album and she was convinced that it would have been far bigger if Clive hadn't been preoccupied with turning Whitney into a crossover act."

29. DIVA-FICATION

The repacking of Aretha Franklin was no easy task," said Jerry Wexler. "I never could have done it. I lacked the vision of a Clive Davis. Only someone like Clive, with his uncanny understanding of the marketing behind music, could have realized how to sell her on a grander scale. Clive knew that he had to more than pick her producers, writers, and duet partners. He had to turn her into a diva."

"I call it the diva-fication of Aretha," said Erma. "And it all came about because of Clive. He saw that the public loved divas. Fans loved to see women who appear larger than life—women who wear fabulous gowns and date dashing men. These are women with tempers even bigger than their talents. Through sheer will, they can overcome anything. We like them because, even though they may make unreasonable demands and throw all kinds of fits, they entertain us. They make us feel good because nothing can defeat them. That's Aretha.

"She had called her last album on Atlantic *La Diva,* but at the time, the label didn't stick. It was too early. And, sales-wise, she was too cold. But by the middle of the eighties, she had more than earned that title. It also helped that Clive commissioned artists like

Andy Warhol and Peter Max to do the covers of her albums. That was the final touch on the diva-fication."

"I thought she should have called the album with the Andy Warhol portrait *Look to the Rainbow* because she sang that old standard—the one we knew from Dinah Washington's version—so beautifully," said Carolyn. "She agreed. But when Ree saw the Warhol portrait, she said the album had to be called *Aretha*. 'But that was the name of your first Arista record,' I said. 'This is your sixth.' 'Makes no difference,' she said. 'It's my name and I'll use it for as many titles as I want.'"

The album, produced by Narada Michael Walden and released in 1986, contained one huge hit—"I Knew You Were Waiting (for Me)," a duet with George Michael, that went to number one on the pop charts in 1987. Clive Davis viewed Michael, who had recently left Wham! and had scored solo hits on his own, as another crossover key for Aretha.

"I thought the song was boring," said Carolyn, "and rather routine. The lyrics were lame. But my opinion didn't matter. It was a marketing decision made by Clive and embraced by Aretha. And it worked."

"George Michael was incredibly stoked to get to sing with the Queen," said Narada. "He flew to Detroit the day after Aretha had done her vocal. He did his on day two, and on day three they got together for the ad libs. She destroyed everyone. I noticed that when it came to women, Aretha had this sharp competitive edge, but with men she was perfectly cool."

Pleased that her forays into rock were working, Aretha decided to up the ante.

"It was her idea to sing 'Jumpin' Jack Flash' and get Keith Richards to produce it," said Cecil.

In Richards's autobiography *Life,* he confirms Cecil's statement: "Aretha Franklin called up because she was making a movie called *Jumpin' Jack Flash,* with Whoopi Goldberg, and she wanted me to produce the title track for it."

Actually, Penny Marshall was making the movie, and the song, sung by Aretha with Whoopi in the background, would be included as a musical highlight. Aretha was adamant, though, that it was Keith who called and recruited her to redo his song.

Either way, she growled her way through the rock anthem with both Keith and Ron Wood on guitar, future *American Idol* judge Randy Jackson on bass, and Steve Jordan on drums.

"Give Keith credit," said Jerry Wexler, "because when he produced his song, he made sure Aretha not only sang but played piano. Keith understood what I had learned years before—when Aretha is anchored at the keyboard, it's a stronger and more organic overall performance. She becomes her own rhythm section and all power flows from her."

Whoopi, Keith, and Ron then flew to Detroit to shoot the video, in which Aretha styled her hair in a purple punk ponytail.

"Aretha was loving these collaborations," said Cecil. "It was her idea to do the next one with Larry Graham."

A brilliant bassist and contributing architect to the newfangled funk developed in the sixties as a member of Sly and the Family Stone, Graham led his own band, Graham Central Station, in the seventies and had enjoyed solo hits as a singer in the eighties, notably "One in a Million." Aretha liked the quality of his bass-baritone voice and thought he'd make a good duet partner.

"It's another so-so ballad," said Carolyn. "I'm not saying it's terrible, but Aretha knew damn well that I had at least a half dozen ballads that were four times as good. When I asked her why she wasn't singing any of my songs, all she said was that Clive had to approve everything—and he thought my stuff sounded like the seventies. I did notice, though, that she was able to get one of her songs on the album, 'He'll Come Along.' That song went nowhere. The truth is that it had been fifteen years since Aretha had written a hit. 'Rock Steady' was way back in 1971. But that didn't stop her on insisting that nearly every album she cut include at least one or two of her own songs. I understand that she did that to get the publishing income. But in doing that, she also hurt herself by ignoring the work of other songwriters—namely, me."

A mediocre melody, "He'll Come Along" was, according to Erma, a song about Willie Wilkerson, the fireman who would become Aretha's only public boyfriend for the next twenty-five years. The song is about Aretha waiting for Mr. Right.

"In many ways, Willie was Mr. Right," said Erma. "He's warm and affable, a wonderful guy who has the even temperament to deal with Aretha. He became one of the steadiest influences in her life. He put up with a lot but always remained loyal. I give him major credit."

"Willie stayed around while Aretha started talking to the press about her fantasy lovers—that Mr. Mystique business," said Ruth Bowen. "He knew that they were fairy tales. But Willie was real. Nothing Hollywood or phony about him. I admire him for staying by her side—especially later in the eighties, when things got really rough for Aretha. Willie became her anchor."

One other track on *Aretha*—"Jimmy Lee," a Motownish-sounding throwback—went to number two on the R&B charts.

"Any way you look at it, this album was a success. The Aretha–George Michael duet was huge. The video with Keith and Whoopi was in heavy rotation on MTV, and they were playing 'Jimmy Lee' in all the dance clubs. Far as I was concerned, Narada proved that *Who's Zoomin' Who?* was no fluke," said Cecil. "What Luther had started, Narada continued and took to a higher level."

"In the eighties, Narada was Clive's golden boy," said Jerry Wexler. "He was a superb producer. I remember Whitney's mom, Cissy, telling me how excited she was about the work he was doing with Whitney, infectious songs like 'I Wanna Dance with Somebody' and 'So Emotional.' It's catchy, upbeat material and I don't argue that he helped Aretha move into what became the most profitable chapter of her career—at least in terms of pure pop hits. But when I listen to their work together, I don't hear her voice soaring. I hear her screaming. I hear her over-riffing and what I call over-souling. Aretha is a baroque singer by nature. That's the nature of her gospel background. Extravagant flourishes are part of her essential vocal grammar. But then comes a time when you're no

longer twenty-five or thirty-five but forty-five. This is when you
have to start singing smart. Because you can no longer reach the
high notes that were once your second nature, you have to learn to
avoid them. You have to learn restraint. Yesterday your voice could
do anything, but today it can't. So you kick back, modify your
style, and trim your sails. Vocally, you tend to be a little less assertive, less aggressive. Rather than paint enormous landscapes, you
paint miniatures. What you lack in strength, you make up in subtlety. You work your way around the edges of a song, discovering
those nooks and crannies that allow you to display the depths of
your musical intelligence. In short, as a vocalist, you age gracefully.
Did Aretha do this? I'm afraid not."

"This goddamn business is about survival," said Ray Charles,
who in the eighties unsuccessfully sought the kind of pop hits
Aretha was enjoying. "And I admired how 'Retha kept on surviving. Survival comes before anything. I don't really give a shit if
they play my records in a hundred years from now 'cause I won't be
around to hear 'em. But I do care if they play me on the radio
today, or tomorrow, or next week, 'cause I've got a payroll to make
and bills to pay. So when folks say, 'Brother Ray, you're too old to
keep trying to cut hit records,' or, 'Brother Ray, you already done
made your mark. Why are you still trying to get over?' I say,
''Cause I ain't interested in being an exhibit in some fuckin'
museum. I ain't about to be put out to pasture. I'm gonna keep
grinding and humping 'cause that's all us entertainers know how to
do. That's what we're born to do.'"

Reviewing for the *New York Times,* Jon Pareles was less understanding than Ray. "'Aretha' may yield some hit singles," he wrote,
"but it comes across as an impersonal piece of pop product."

On April 21, 1986, Luther Vandross brought his show to the
Joe Louis Arena. He was touring behind his fourth Epic album, the
highly successful *The Night I Fell in Love.*

"I got word that Aretha was coming, and of course I was glad,"
Luther told me. "There was some drama in the aftermath of *Get It
Right* and we were not on speaking terms, which, as the years went

on, was perfectly normal for us. She asked for a dozen front-row seats and I was happy to accommodate, but she also asked that we perform onstage together. She wanted to do a duet with me on 'If This World Were Mine,' but I didn't think that was wise. I had produced and sung the song on Cheryl Lynn's album as a tribute to Marvin and Tammi. It became a hit. Some were even calling it a classic comparable to the original. It was something special between me and Cheryl. Surely there was another number that Aretha and I could do. She was insistent and so was I—and so there we were, doing battle again. But it was my show and I held my ground. She finally capitulated and asked if we could do 'Jump to It.' Well, that's hardly a duet. It's a song where Aretha sings lead and I sing background. But since it was my song and my production, she figured I might agree. She was right. I did agree and she came onstage to perform her hit. The crowd loved her performance. I loved it as well—and so there was peace between us. At least for a while."

Aretha publicly announced that she had truly made peace with one of her most persistent anxieties. She told the press yet again that she was over her fear of flying and promised her fans a full summer concert schedule.

"Our money was getting funny again," said Cecil. "Aretha bought a third or a fourth house in Detroit—I can't remember which—and that squeezed her financially. She was insistent that the royalties from Arista for her recent hits were not flowing in fast enough. When I checked with Clive, though, I was assured that the checks were coming. But because Aretha is always changing accounting firms and bookkeepers it wasn't clear where the checks wound up. Things were getting chaotic and we had no choice but to turn to Dick Alen and Ruthie Bowen to find her big-money concert gigs. There were gigs, but touring on the bus made it impractical. It cut down on the number of gigs—not to mention eliminating the huge markets of Europe, Latin America, and Asia. To make the kind of money she needed, she had to fly."

"She signed up for a program [for people who are afraid of flying] that one of the airlines offers," said her cousin Brenda Corbett.

"We all supported her in that effort. You'd go out to the airport, sit in the plane, and they took you through the sounds of a flight. They did it step by step, carefully explaining just what was happening, so you got used to the experience. After doing this a few times, they'd pick a clear day and take you on a short flight. So far, so good. Aretha went through the program, but on the day of the short flight, she said, 'Oh, no. This is not happening. I am not ready.' And she was out of there."

In July, *Billboard* reported that Aretha had "canceled a series of concerts at New York's Radio City Music Hall with no explanation... The Queen of Soul has limited all concert dates to shows within driving distance."

"She didn't consider the six hundred and twenty miles from Detroit to New York a driving distance," said Cecil. "For Aretha, a driving distance meant getting to the gig in less than a day. She didn't like the limo or bus driver to go faster than fifty, and she liked to take a break every few hours. That meant a drive to Manhattan was a matter of two days, something she considered too taxing. Rather than go to the fans, we found a way for the fans to come to us. We taped an hour-long Showtime special in Detroit and arranged for Westwood One to broadcast a stereo simulcast."

"It was another summer from hell," said Ruth Bowen. "I can't remember the number of dates we booked and then canceled."

"I didn't keep count of cancellations," said Dick Alen of William Morris. "My attitude was to accommodate Aretha as best I could. Going in, I realized that she was someone likely to change her mind at the last minute. I couldn't change her and didn't try. I accepted that an essential part of my job was to clean up after her. I didn't try to understand her moods. I wasn't her psychologist; I was just the guy who negotiated her fees."

"Part of the reason she was in a bad mood that summer had to do with Anita Baker," said Ruth. "Like Aretha, Anita is a Detroit girl. And also like Aretha, Anita is an artist who applies a highly sophisticated jazz sensibility to rhythm and blues. Remember that *Rapture,* Anita's second album, came out in 1986 and was an international sensation. It far outperformed *Aretha* and wound up selling something like eight million copies. Then to add insult to injury, Anita beat out Aretha, who was nominated for 'Jumpin' Jack Flash,' for best R-and-B female vocal performance. Before Anita, Aretha had Detroit locked up. She was without a doubt the biggest star in the city. Now here comes Anita, produced by Michael Powell, another budding local Detroit talent. None of this made Miss Thing happy. She used to say, 'If I toured as much as Anita, I'd be selling in the millions myself.' 'Well, why don't you?' I asked. 'I will — just you watch.' But she didn't. She couldn't sustain a multicity, much less a multicountry, tour that involved a dozen or two dozen dates. Aretha went out and worked only when she had to — that is to say, when she was broke. Which was often."

In January 1987, the second annual induction ceremony of the Rock and Roll Hall of Fame took place in the grand ballroom of the Waldorf Astoria in New York City. Along with nonperformers Ahmet Ertegun and Jerry Wexler and artists B.B. King, Jackie Wilson, Marvin Gaye, and Smokey Robinson, Aretha was an inductee, the first woman to be selected.

"She saw it as a huge honor," said Cecil. "She thought that they would have chosen Ruth Brown or Etta James, women that came before her. Maybe it was because they were seen as rhythm and blues and not rock and roll. We'd always seen rock and roll as the white version of R-and-B — Georgia Gibbs singing LaVern Baker or Pat Boone singing Fats Domino. But an honor is an honor, and since Ree had been recently breaking into rock, this honor was right on time. We were also happy to hear that Keith Richards, who'd been working with us on 'Jumpin' Jack Flash,' was personally giving her the award. We were all set to go, but then the weather got bad and Aretha got nervous about the drive. She sent me instead. I had a ball hanging out with my main man Smokey.

When he got up to get his prize, the whole audience started singing his 'Ooo Baby Baby.' It was beautiful."

"Not showing up to be inducted as the first-ever female in the Rock and Roll Hall of Fame could not be seen as a good public relations move," said Ruth Bowen. "As a friend who continued to care about her, I mentioned this to Aretha. I also said that, because Jerry Wexler and Ahmet Ertegun were being inducted that same night, it would be beautiful to see her standing on the podium with two men so instrumental in her career. 'Ruth,' she said, 'that part of my career is in the distant past. I've moved on.'"

30. IN THE STORM TOO LONG

Aretha dedicated the first half of 1987 to a project for which she had great passion—a follow-up to *Amazing Grace,* the bestselling gospel album of all time and the record that many of her most ardent fans, myself included, consider her best.

"She wanted to honor her gospel heritage, of course," said Cecil, "but mainly she wanted to honor our father. That's why she made sure that the live concerts were religious services, just like *Amazing Grace.* Where *Amazing Grace* was based in Los Angeles because of James Cleveland, she wanted the follow-up to be done in Detroit, at New Bethel. And where Jerry Wexler was the organizing force and chief supervisor of *Amazing Grace,* Aretha wanted to run this operation entirely on her own. Clive had let her produce several cuts of her own, but never an entire album. 'It's time,' she told me. 'No co-supervisors, no co-producers, just me.'"

The Arista label head agreed. In Aretha's liner notes to the album that she titled *One Lord, One Faith, One Baptism,* she wrote, "With much appreciation to Clive Davis for giving me the opportunity and entrusting such a mammoth project to my sole creative judgment."

"The beautiful thing about the album," said cousin Brenda, who was Aretha's assistant production coordinator, "was that Aretha, her two sisters, and her brother Cecil were all together in their daddy's church. That would be the last time. Thank God it was all caught on record."

"Given the talent she assembled," said James Cleveland, a prime contributor to *Amazing Grace,* "it should have been a much better record. But I could tell from the outset that it was going to be rough riding. Aretha took it all on herself—every little detail. I tried to tell her that she needed a producer and nominated myself for the job. I tried to tell her that it was enough that she simply be the main vocalist. She didn't need to be an organizer. Organization is her greatest weakness. She took offense. In fact, she never called me back, and my invitation to come to Detroit was put on permanent hold. I never knew why."

The album was composed of three separate concert/services at New Bethel in the summer of 1987—July 27, 28, and 30. Aretha committed to a double LP, mirroring the format of *Amazing Grace.*

"Aretha was able to delegate a lot of the work to me," said Brenda, "and I loved doing it. As the production coordinator, I oversaw all the rehearsals. I managed the choir and made sure it all ran smoothly."

"Ree simply took on more than she could manage," said Cecil. "She was picking the talent, picking the musicians, picking the hymns, and picking the various ministers. Up until the last minute it wasn't clear who was going to sing what and when."

"Because of Aretha's position," said Erma, "she could command the presence of whomever she liked—and she did. She invited the crème de la crème of the gospel world—Mavis Staples, Thomas Whitfield, Joe Ligon of the Mighty Clouds of Joy, and Reverends Jesse Jackson, Donald Parsons, and Jaspar Williams. I was thrilled and grateful to participate."

From the start, the project was ambitious. In addition to producing a gospel record of lasting value, Aretha wanted to outperform and outsell *Amazing Grace.* If *Amazing Grace* lives as a luminous moment in the history of gospel, that is partially due to the extraordinary supporting cast surrounding its recording. Wexler was a strong and single-minded producer. He got the super-funky secular rhythm section he wanted. He made sure that, in choosing James Cleveland, Aretha got a choir director who could direct her when needed. In addition, the Aretha of 1972 was a far cry from the Aretha of 1987.

Twenty-nine years old at the time of *Amazing Grace,* Aretha conveyed both a genuine humility and a longing to thrill the two gospel greats seated in the first pew, whom she admired above all others—her father and her father's lover Clara Ward. Fifteen years later, that humility was lost. She was determined to prove to the world that she no longer needed a Hammond, a Wexler, a Clive Davis, a Luther Vandross, or a Narada Michael Walden. When it came to gospel, she felt that her taste was unerring. After all, she was a child of the gospel world. Gospel was her first passion. Gospel was her teacher. It was gospel that turned her into a child star.

"The album contains some moving moments, I'll grant you that," said Reverend Cleveland. "I found myself tearing up when Aretha sang those two Clara Ward songs with her sisters and cousin Brenda—'Jesus Hears Every Prayer' and 'Surely God Is Able.' That goes to the deepest part of their childhood. It was also stirring to hear Aretha sing 'I've Been in the Storm Too Long' with Joe Ligon. But overall, I have to say that it sounds scattered—a little bit of preaching, a little bit of singing, but nothing unified. *Amazing Grace* was a whole story with beginning, middle, and end. This time around, Aretha lost sight of the story."

"Aretha was very generous in allowing everyone to have his or her say," said Cecil. "She invited me up to do a little preaching, just as she invited Jesse Jackson to say whatever he liked. But it all went on for too long and needed to be cut when it came time to put the record together. There were also problems with the mix."

"After Aretha, the biggest star was Mavis Staples," said Erma. "The Stapleses and the Franklins have known each other since the very beginning, and it was appropriate that Aretha invited Mavis to do two duets with her. Ree even spoke of how, as children, traveling with our folks on the gospel circuit, we all met on a muddy Mississippi road. It was a beautiful memory. But when the record was mixed and Aretha listened to those duets, she was convinced that Mavis's voice overwhelmed hers. Singing with the one other gospel singer who could rightfully be called her equal, Aretha felt threatened. I told her she had nothing to worry about, that the two of them sounded great together. Their voices were completely complementary. But Aretha didn't hear it that way. She put Mavis's voice so low in the mix that you could barely hear it. It became an ordeal and caused a serious falling-out."

In the *New York Times*, John Rockwell called the record "one of the most eagerly awaited albums of the year. Which makes its failure all the more disappointing...One suspects that Miss Franklin, eager to appease all the various dignitaries who had assembled for the occasion, and perhaps constrained by the grandeur of the event, lost sight of the unbridled enthusiasm that has defined her own best gospel work." Rockwell went on to complain about what he termed the record's "speechifying." There was too much talking between songs, the songs themselves were too often truncated, and the production was disjointed.

In the liner notes, Aretha included her own review, writing, "It's truly a *pièce de résistance* of Gospel."

The public didn't see it that way. The record languished on the charts and, in comparison with *Amazing Grace,* a perpetual seller, made little impact on the marketplace.

"*Amazing Grace* is Aretha's gospel landmark," said Reverend Cleveland. "As a young lady she had recorded gospel before that and, with this Arista release, she recorded gospel after that. But in my opinion and the opinion of most gospel lovers, none of it comes close to those miraculous performances that happened back in 1972. For another great Aretha gospel production to succeed, she'd need the help of a producer to harmonize the elements. But Aretha remained blind to the fact that she's never her best producer."

A sad undercurrent of *One Lord, One Faith, One Baptism* was the declining health of Aretha's sister Carolyn and her brother Cecil.

"Carolyn had been diagnosed with breast cancer," said Erma. "Initially there was reason for optimism, but a second opinion indicated that the cancer was extremely virulent. She was advised to undergo radiation. Carolyn had spent a great deal of time in various colleges without having earned a degree and, at the time of this medical crisis, was enrolled at Marygrove College. She was close to fulfilling all her requirements, and, cancer or no cancer, she wasn't about to give up. She was gonna get that degree.

"We all interrupted our lives in order to help our sister, but Aretha above all. She was wonderful. She moved Carolyn into her home and hired a full-time nurse to care for her. There was a moment when it seemed as though the treatments were working and the cancer had moved into remission, but those hopes were quickly dashed. At the start of 1988, Carolyn was suffering mightily. And yet she somehow continued to do her course work, write her papers, and pass her exams.

"Infections set in and there were any number of hospital stays. The prognoses became more and more dire. A new surge of hope came over all of us when we learned that Carolyn would be given her degree. Aretha gave her a graduation party, a big, happy catered affair. At that point Carolyn could no longer walk, but that didn't stop her from wearing her cap and gown in bed, where she was handed her diploma. We were cheering and crying."

When Carolyn Ann Franklin died, on April 25, 1988, she was two weeks short of her forty-fourth birthday and had been a college graduate for only a few weeks. Services were held at her father's church.

"I consider her a great woman," said Erma, "a powerful artist with a tremendous writing and singing talent. She went her own way, lived her own life, and found freedom in her individuality. Like me, she experienced great frustration in her career. We were both challenged by the success of our extraordinary sister. In the end, though, Carolyn more than proved her own worth. She left behind a legacy of enduring music."

"When you think of how Carolyn and Aretha fought their entire lives—I mean, they were literally at each other's throat—it was amazing to see how Aretha rallied to Carolyn's side at the end," said sister-in-law Earline. "The Franklin sisterhood is something to behold. No sisters are more competitive. Every two weeks Aretha would have a nasty falling-out with either Carolyn or Erma. Yet when push came to shove, Aretha was their biggest protector.

"When it came to my husband, though, it was a different story. Cecil was Aretha's protector. And Aretha could never—and still can't—admit that Cecil fell into heavy drug addiction. In the eighties, when freebase cocaine swept through the neighborhood, my husband got hooked. He stayed hooked. Somehow he still managed to do his work with Aretha, but just barely. She wouldn't recognize this. She viewed Cecil the same way she viewed her father—a perfect man with no faults. But like his father, Cecil, despite his brilliant mind, was vulnerable to the world and all its temptations. Finally, I had enough. I told him that if he didn't go to rehab, I was gone."

I visited Cecil in Detroit just before his rehab. He spoke a great deal about his friends who had been crushed by crack. "I knew Marvin Gaye was on the pipe," he said, "because he told me to stay away from it. Marvin's whole history with drugs was a cautionary tale." He also mentioned David Ruffin, who was struggling with a crack cocaine addiction that, in a few years, would take his life. Cecil discussed how he, his father, and his siblings had all operated in a world of stimulants. "Whether it's wine, whiskey, or weed," said Cecil then, "the stuff has always been around us—and all of us have had to deal with this stuff in one way or another. Now it's time for me to finally come to terms with my addiction and win this long battle."

When I saw Cecil after his stay in rehab, he described himself as clearheaded for the first time in decades. He said he was facing the future with new determination and fresh energy.

"I was so proud of him," said Ruth Bowen. "Cecil was my pro-tégé, one of the smartest people I'd ever known. So you can imag-ine how much I hated seeing him get lost in all those drugs. When he got clean, I rejoiced. But then, when Earline called to say that they'd found a spot on his lungs, I fell apart. I was just devastated, and I could only imagine what this would do to Aretha. But Aretha did not fall apart. She rarely does. Her way of coping with adversity is to stay in the social swim. That helps her keep her head above water."

Bowen's point was made by a photo in *Jet* of Aretha at her "annual masquerade ball" in which she was dressed as an Egyptian queen, and her date, Willie Wilkerson, as an old-time convict.

In this same summer of 1988, her Chicago nightclub show was filmed for PBS's *Soundstage* and later released as *Live at Park West,* first in videocassette and then on DVD. At forty-six, she appears to be in good shape. She wears a twenties-style sleeveless flapper dress, cut low in the front. Her enormous cleavage is on full display. Her mood is carefree. She's feeling frisky and sexy and even jokes about doing a striptease. After an unsteady opening—her cover of Frankie Beverly's "Love Is the Key"—she renders a fabulous "Love All the Hurt Away," her hit duet with George Benson. She sings both her part *and* his, and her Benson imitation is a comic/musical master-piece; she opens up the song, a lovely ballad, and gives it wings. Her scat singing, a slick soul variation of the Ella Fitzgerald/Sarah Vaughan variety, is superb and wholly original. Her spoken vamp at the end, shadowed by the great guitarist David T. Walker, becomes a sermon on sexual anticipation. ("I'll meet you at the front door with one of those sweet kisses," she says-sings. "I'll put a big pot of greens and hot-water cornbread on for you, baby...and we'll slide under those silk sheets.") The medley of her Atlantic hits is less convincing, but both her reading of sister Carolyn's "Ain't No Way" and her return to the Columbia-era gem "Sweet Bitter Love" are startling, reminding us that, on any given night, she has the God-given ability to turn the secular sacred and, in the case of her interpretation of Mahalia Jackson's "Didn't It Rain," the sacred secular.

She had promised her old friends Ahmet Ertegun and Jerry Wexler that she would appear that May at Atlantic's big fortieth-anniversary concert at Madison Square Garden.

"Everyone was coming," said Ertegun, "from the Rascals to Ruth Brown to Wilson Pickett to Led Zeppelin. The idea was to celebrate the triumphs of the label. Since our most meaningful triumph was our work with Aretha, I couldn't imagine the evening without her. We arranged for a luxurious private bus to drive her from Detroit. We booked the penthouse suite at the Waldorf Towers for her. I was overjoyed when she accepted, and saddened when, for reasons that were never explained, she failed to show up."

During the summer, PBS featured her on its *American Masters* series, a routine piece of television docu-biography with sketchy facts and loads of old concert footage. As Mark Bego astutely pointed out in *The Queen of Soul,* his biography of Aretha published a year after the broadcast, the only telling moment is when Aretha, asked about her love life, replies, "I have always maintained that a real man is not going to be intimidated by me. Some can rise to the occasion, and others cannot."

"With its sexual innuendo, that statement is pure Aretha," said Ruth Bowen. "It's also an honest expression of her feeling about the opposite sex. Her challenge to her suitors is always, Are you man enough to handle me?"

In November, the family suffered a great loss with the passing of the formidable Rachel Franklin, mother of Reverend C. L. Franklin, at age ninety-one.

"Big Mama was the great link with our past," said Erma, "and a tremendous spirit in all of our lives. She really raised us all. She was a country woman who was quirky and funny and faithful in all ways. She had her little dance, she had her little laugh, and she had her big, big heart. She was the essence of old-time religion. I never met anyone with such a rock-solid belief in God. In the last years, she'd been living in a home but hadn't lost her love for life. Every Franklin child and grandchild, every niece and nephew, every cousin and every family friend simply adored this woman."

After Big Mama's funeral, Aretha had to decide whether to fulfill her contract with Trump's Castle in Atlantic City.

"I wasn't sure she'd go," said Ruth Bowen, "and would have taken bets that she wouldn't. It had been several years since she had left the state of Michigan for any reason whatsoever. Besides, Big Mama had just died, and Big Mama was, for all practical purposes, the main woman of Aretha's childhood. After wavering back and forth, she decided to go, much to the delight of everyone. I think one of the reasons was that she wanted to wear a gown she had designed that looked like something Josephine Baker wore in Paris."

Self-reflection was never Aretha's strong suit, and yet in the late eighties, she began discussing the idea of writing her memoirs. Before she hired an agent to shop a deal, though, she spoke about her life to reporter Ed Bradley for a *60 Minutes* segment. The resulting profile was little more than a puff piece. Yet Aretha was extremely unhappy with the interview because of one particular question. Bradley wanted to know about the sexual content in so many of her songs.

"I mean, it's in a lot of your songs," he said. "Lust. A feeling— good feeling."

"You got me mixed with somebody else, Ed," said Aretha indignantly.

A few months after the interview aired, I spoke with Bradley.

"I've done some tough celebrity interviews," he told me, "but Aretha ranks among the toughest. When it came to personal revelations, she was completely shut down. Given the openness in her music, that shocked me. There was no introspection whatsoever. So when I learned that she was planning to write her autobiography, I was surprised. I couldn't imagine her making any emotional disclosures."

Yet in early 1989, she decided it was time to work on her memoirs. Shaye Areheart, an editor at Doubleday in New York, was among those contacted by a local Detroit agent to be interviewed by Aretha at her home. Areheart had worked for five years with Michael Jackson on his recently published memoir, *Moonwalk*.

Areheart told me that she flew to Detroit and showed up at Aretha's home in Bloomfield Hills with two dozen white roses. The women spoke for over two hours. Areheart described Aretha as "gracious, lovely and funny." There was no written book proposal or any indication of a ghostwriter. Based on their meetings with Aretha, Areheart and her competitors were asked to submit bids in an auction for the publishing rights. Areheart was delighted to learn that her offer—she called it "a fortune"—had won. While on vacation, though, the editor learned that Aretha was now demanding $350,000 more. This isn't how auctions work. The top bid wins—period.

"Aretha doesn't care about the rules of auctions or proper negotiations," said Ruth Bowen. "She simply wants what she wants. It's the most common thing in the world for her to entrust a representative to do her negotiation and then, on a whim, undercut the process by demanding more."

Areheart assured me that she wrote Aretha a diplomatic letter explaining that, as she had won the auction, it was unreasonable for her to be asked to bid against herself. She never heard from Aretha again.

31. THE MIXTURE AS BEFORE

When the English novelist Somerset Maugham published a new collection of short stories in 1940, the London *Times* labeled it "the mixture as before," criticizing it as the same-old-same-old. A few years later, Maugham, a master of irony, released his next collection, called *The Mixture As Before,* and thanked the *Times* critic for the title.

Aretha's attitude was similar to Maugham's. When I mentioned to her that some critics and fans viewed her late eighties/early nineties Arista records as commercial packages with a certain redundancy, she spoke of her interest in staying current. She was not ready to be put out to pasture and join the oldies circuit. I asked whether at some point the marketplace ceases to be the main concern. She answered that it's never the main concern. She insisted that her motivation was always to find the best songs and that, in her mind, the best songs were usually hits.

Looking for a hit, Aretha returned to the studio in 1989 and, with the help of Arif Mardin and Narada Michael Walden, put together another something-for-everyone album. This time the hodgepodge would include no fewer than three duets.

"Clive Davis had this notion that when an older singer's sales start to sag," said Ruth Bowen, "the best way to market that singer is to do duets with other singers who bring a different audience to the party. So pairing Whitney with Aretha made sense because Whitney was red hot. Putting her with Elton John made sense because Elton was pure pop and could help her with crossover. Same idea applied to getting Kenny G to play on the album. Kenny G might have started in R-and-B, but he wound up with a huge white market. James Brown was another thing altogether. That was just a matter of bringing two legends together. However you looked at it, it was all about profiting from different combinations."

The major labels enjoyed enormous earnings in the eighties. The introduction of compact discs, with their huge profit margins, was the most lucrative innovation since the long-playing album. Reissues became a windfall. Because millions of consumers were eager to repurchase their old LPs and cassette tapes in CD form, the record companies could eliminate the costs of original productions. Meanwhile, a string of blockbuster new albums—by everyone from Bruce Springsteen to AC/DC to Prince to Michael Jackson to Bon Jovi to Whitney Houston to Guns N' Roses to Phil Collins to Madonna—fattened the coffers. In retrospect, the eighties were the last decade in which the music business prospered from the sales of factory-manufactured products bought in brick-and-mortar retail stores.

"Given these crazy profits," said Jerry Wexler, "you'd think that someone would say, 'Okay, now we got the money to go and do something for the ages. Now we can get Aretha out of the pop-confection business and back to doing what she does best—playing piano and singing live in the studio with a great rhythm section.'"

"There was no disagreement between Aretha and Clive about what the direction should be," said Ruth Bowen. "They wanted hits. And why not? It's all about hits."

Unfortunately, neither the silly duet with Whitney Houston ("It Isn't, It Wasn't, It Ain't Never Gonna Be") nor the bland duet with James Brown ("Gimme Your Love") had significant sales.

The album's title track, "Through the Storm," Aretha's perfunctory duet with Elton John, did make it into the pop top twenty, but that was hardly a landmark for either artist. None of the artists on the album sounded committed or even terribly interested in singing the songs.

Her duet with Whitney Houston was fraught with problems.

"There was all sorts of drama between Whitney and Ree," said Ruth, "until it nearly fell apart. Aretha kept calling it a mismatch. She said that Whitney lacked her wisdom and maturity as a recording artist, but I just think Aretha was nervous about being outsung by someone from the next generation. It hardly mattered because the song was forgettable. The year after it was out, even the most devoted fans of Aretha and Whitney had forgotten that shit had ever happened."

"What happened was this," said Narada. "Whitney flew to Detroit, all excited about singing with her Auntie Ree. But when Auntie Ree walked in the studio, she didn't enter as Auntie Ree. She entered as Queen Aretha, *the* original diva. At the time, Whitney was the biggest music star in the world and didn't realize that Aretha felt that she had something to prove. Aretha came with her game face. Whitney was acting like a furry puppy dog. Aretha was like a boxer staring down her opponent. Of course, the song was about two women competing for the same man, so Aretha was clearly in character. I was as sweet as pie to her. If I hadn't been, she would have squashed me like a bug. She also appreciated that I wanted to produce this Diane Warren song—'It Isn't, It Wasn't, It Ain't Never Gonna Be'—in a Teddy Riley, New Jack Swing mode, the new R-and-B style that was sweeping through the neighborhood. Aretha dug the groove and hit it hard. But she also stayed extremely aloof and gave Whitney little love. In fact, Aretha was so tough that she herself thought she might have overdone it. A couple of days after, she called me to ask whether I thought she should call Whitney to apologize. I thought it was a good idea. I never asked Aretha whether she actually made that call—it was none of my business—but I do know that the climate between the two women was frosty for quite some time.

"The James Brown and Elton John duets were entirely different stories. James came to my studio in Northern California expecting to find Aretha there. 'The Queen don't fly,' I told him. 'Wouldn't it be something for the King and Queen to be singing in the same studio?' he asked. 'We'd be so good together that after the session we'd have to get married.' Elton would have also preferred to do his vocal in the same room as Aretha. But he kindly agreed to record to the Aretha vocal track I had prerecorded in Detroit. Elton did his part in LA."

In the midst of ongoing power struggles and difficult professional relationships, one of Aretha's closest personal relationships ended with the passing of Cecil Franklin, the brother she adored. On December 26, 1989, Cecil died from lung cancer. He was forty-nine.

"I was the one who called to tell Aretha to hurry to the hospital," said Ruth Bowen. "I'd been talking to Earline, who told me that he was only hours away from dying. I knew Aretha would want to tell him good-bye. When she didn't arrive in time, it broke her heart. His death was one of the most difficult things Aretha has had to endure. She calls him her greatest fan and greatest friend— and she wasn't wrong. My relationship with Aretha has always been strong but confrontational. But Cecil's relationship was smooth. He stood between her and the world of business. If for a period of time she was able to stay on a steady course, it was because of Cecil. Without him, her world would change. There wasn't anyone—me included—who she could trust the way she trusted her brother. In fact, she would never really hire another manager—just different agents, like me and Dick Alen, to book her gigs. If she was largely unmanageable even when Cecil was alive, she became hopelessly unmanageable after he was gone. With Cecil by her side, you had a chance to get her to do what was reasonable and right. But without Cecil, and by managing herself, she became completely impossible."

"This period when we lost Carolyn, Big Mama, and Cecil in the span of two years was crushing," said Erma. "For a long time afterward, Aretha walked around in a fog."

Nearly a decade later, Aretha still had a difficult time discussing these deaths. As we worked on *From These Roots* together, she struggled to voice her feelings about the passing of her siblings and grandmother. For long periods, she could do little more than wipe the tears from her eyes. I offered sympathy, and together we sat in silence. Finally came the day when she began to speak of the ordeals. In her mind, though, she had reversed the chronology; she had Big Mama dying after Cecil when, in fact, Rachel Franklin had died in late 1988, a year before her grandson. When I gently pointed this out, Aretha grew furious. She informed me that in the matter of the deaths of her loved ones, she hardly needed correction. I checked again with Erma and Earline, my original sources for the information. I also obtained the death certificate. The facts confirmed what I had told Aretha, yet Aretha remained adamant. In her published book, she has Cecil dying before her grandmother, mistakenly stating that Big Mama passed in 1990.

"Aretha is a woman who suffers mightily," said Erma, "but doesn't like to show it. I'm not sure why. I can't express to you the pain she experienced after we lost Cecil. It really was incalculable. But rather than mourn, she tends to turn the hurt to anger. I can understand that. We lost our mother, we lost our dad, we lost our sister Carolyn, we lost our grandmother, and now we lost our beloved brother. It's too much loss. It's so hard to grieve. When we turn that grief on ourselves, it's too much to bear. We can try to pray it away or sing it away. Praying and singing helps. And I'm sure praying and singing are part of Aretha's way of coping with all these deaths. Unfortunately, though, so is rage. It may be uncomfortable or even unbearable for others, but Aretha's emotional survival has a lot to do with plain old anger. If she's feeling afraid or lost or terribly sad, there's a good chance she'll take it out on you."

"I made it a point to call Aretha," said Luther Vandross, "because I knew how close she was to Cecil and I wanted to express my sympathy. I remember telling her how concerned I was about her. She took offense. She thought that I was implying that she might have a nervous breakdown or fall apart. I wasn't saying that at all. I was merely voicing my concern. She got on her high horse and went off on a tirade, saying that the world saw her as weak and fragile and she wasn't weak or fragile at all. God knows that I agreed with that. Aretha's strong as steel. When I tried to explain that I only wanted to know if she needed anything, there was no consoling her. She grew angry at me when all I was trying to do was comfort her. It was a bizarre call. It made me understand that Aretha just doesn't want to seem vulnerable. Maybe she really is afraid of falling apart, so if anyone even remotely approaches the subject, she blows up. It was a long time before I called her again."

"I actually think Aretha enjoyed her feuds with Luther," said Ruth Bowen. "It gave a spark to her life that was becoming increasingly boring. After all, she was out there in the suburbs with not that much to do. She did little traveling and was becoming increasingly withdrawn. If she could get into a verbal catfight with a big star like Luther, why not? I think she saw that as fun. If you haven't had a falling-out with Aretha, you haven't lived. Falling-outs are her specialty."

32. PARTY THERAPY

W e all have our own ways of dealing with our depression, our mood swings, and our tough times," said Erma shortly after Cecil's death. "Aretha's way is to give parties. Every year she throws herself a big birthday party. She'll rent a ballroom in a swanky hotel and invite everybody who's anybody in Detroit. The planning takes her mind off what's bothering her. She takes it upon herself to get the entertainment, the caterers, the whole bit. She'll spend weeks picking out her dress. If she's on speaking terms with me, my kids, and our cousin Brenda, we'll be invited and usually have a great time. Then during the year she has a number of smaller parties at her house. Some of those can be last-minute ideas on her part and don't always come off so well. I think she throws them because she knows if she invites the press, she'll get her picture in the papers. I don't blame her for that. Stars need to remain highly visible."

In the late eighties, photographer Paul Natkin was assigned by *InStyle* magazine to cover a Christmas party that Aretha was hosting at her Bloomfield Hills home. He was told that Aretha was doing the cooking herself and that the Detroit Pistons basketball team as well as the Temptations, the Motown singing group, would be on hand. When Natkin arrived, he saw two big catering trucks in the driveway. Aretha had changed her mind about cooking. It also turned out that the Pistons were in LA that night playing the Lakers, and the only entertainer was one of the lesser-known former Temptations, who sang to a karaoke machine. The biggest stars were a few local TV anchors. According to Natkin, Aretha spent the entire evening sitting in a chair, her purse on her lap, her hands on the purse, with a security guard standing directly behind her.

Still, there were extraordinarily happy moments for Aretha in the nineties. In a few years, the Democrats would be back in power, and invitations to the White House would be forthcoming. Unlike Ray Charles, who had unapologetically sung for Presidents Reagan and George H. Bush, Aretha, with her deep roots in the Democratic Party, declined such performances.

"At the start of the decade," said her booking agent Dick Alen, "she was making anywhere from two to five million a year. She was still playing big theaters and could tour behind all her hits. The usual mix were, of course, all her Atlantic hits from the sixties and seventies and then her Arista hits—'Freeway' and 'I Knew You Were Waiting'—from the eighties. She could have made three or four times that much had she flown. She wouldn't play west of the Rockies. She didn't want to drive that far, and a bus ride over the mountains made her uneasy. She continued to ignore her international markets—Europe, Asia, Latin America—where she could have earned a fortune. And of course, there were the ongoing cancellations, most of which went unexplained. Given all that, it's a testimony to her staying power as an artist that she earned as much as she did."

"In the early nineties she called me to discuss her new record," said Arif Mardin. "I was always eager to work with Aretha and delighted to entertain whatever ideas she might have. We had a long and happy history together. I found her to be a positive person—the new album was always going to be her biggest—and I respected her determination to realize another top-ten hit. This time, though, I wasn't sure she was on the right track. Her notion was to do all originals—an 'Aretha Franklin sings Aretha Franklin.' She sent me some songs, and several had some charm, but I'm afraid I didn't hear any hits. In the most tactful terms possible, I told her what I knew Clive Davis had to be telling her—that it might be best to include songs by proven hit makers. There was silence on the other end of the phone. Then she thanked me for my time, and years passed before I heard from her again. Next year, when the album came out—the one with the unfortunate title *What You See Is What You Sweat*—I noted that Burt Bacharach had written and produced two of the songs; Pic Conley, a hot producer at that time, was responsible for another two; and of the ten or so Aretha originals she had sent me, only two were included. It was clear that Clive had prevailed."

Clive also kept her on the charts, if just barely. One of the Bacharach songs, "Ever Changing Times," with a shadow background vocal by Michael McDonald, crept into the top-twenty R&B listings. But neither it nor anything else on the album crossed over.

Oliver Leiber, who coproduced one of the tracks, "Mary Goes Round," went to Detroit for the recording session.

"We were called in by Clive Davis," said Oliver, "because my cowriter Elliot Wolff and I were the flavor of the month. We had both produced and written hits for Paula Abdul—Elliot did 'Straight Up' and 'Cold Hearted' and I did 'The Way That You Love Me,' 'Forever Your Girl,' and 'Opposites Attract.' So Elliot and I got together, turned out some demos, and sent them to Clive. My understanding was that he was basically telling Aretha what songs to sing. When he sent her our 'Mary Goes Round,' she had no objections, and, just like that, we were on our way. The other understanding, of course, was that working with Aretha meant doing so in her playground. Her playground was United Sound in Detroit, which was great because I knew that George Clinton had cut much of his Funkadelic stuff in that very studio. Elliot and I couldn't have been any more excited.

"I wish I could say the same for Aretha. She wasn't hostile but she certainly wasn't warm. She lived up to her diva reputation—haughty and cold. From the get-go she made it plain that she was there to do a job and wanted it done quickly. As she blew through her vocals, a process that probably took a couple of hours, she chain-smoked Kool cigarettes. Even as she sang, smoke billowed out of her mouth. As far as the song itself went, her heart wasn't in it. She seemed far more interested in the fried chicken that her assistant was cooking up in the kitchen. We got the notion that once that chicken was fried, our session was over. So we worked in a hurry.

"She had learned the melody and knew the groove and could certainly sing the thing down, but there were certain runs and little licks that were sung in the demo that both Elliot and I thought would add flair. Elliot made the suggestion in the mildest manner possible. 'No, baby,' she said, 'it's okay the way it is,' and never bothered to try it our way. Her only suggestion—well, really her demand—was that we use her son Teddy on guitar. We plugged him in. He was fine, but what he played didn't match the mood of the song and ultimately was not used.

"At the end of the day, the chicken was cooked and so were we. Even though we were listed as producers, we really only produced the instrumental track. We didn't produce her vocals; we were merely there to record her vocals. I'm not sure anyone really produces an Aretha vocal. She has a strong notion of what she will and will not sing—and God help the poor soul who tries to convince her otherwise. We certainly felt the honor of working with the great Aretha Franklin. But she remained a distant character, an imperious queen."

In the winter of 1990, press reports about the Mahalia Jackson fiasco began to appear. A *Jet* headline read "New York Magistrate Rules Aretha Should Pay $230,000 for Backing Out on Play." Producer Ashton Spring was quoted as saying that "the show had been scheduled to open in Cleveland in July 1984, but never got off the ground because Ms. Franklin failed to appear at rehearsals for the musical."

That summer, Aretha did not fail to appear at a program in Detroit honoring Nelson Mandela, who had been released from his South African prison in February.

Aretha stayed home for the remainder of the summer, with the exception of a notable concert at New York's Radio City Music Hall.

In the *New York Times,* Jon Pareles wrote, "Ms. Franklin managed a few sublime, cascading vocal phrases...But saddled with schlock ballads and gussied up with an unnecessary orchestra—does 'Respect' really need violins?—she remains as frustrating as she is matchless." He wrote that "Ever Changing Times" sounded like "a Whitney Houston reject." Sitting in that cavernous auditorium, I had the opposite reaction. I leaped to my feet at the end of her stirring rendition of the song, one of the best of Bacharach and Carole Bayer Sager's collaborations.

That same summer of 1990 marked a major tragedy for American music. On August 13, during a freak windstorm, Curtis Mayfield was struck by a light tower at an outdoor concert at Wingate Field in Brooklyn, leaving him paralyzed from the waist down.

"Aretha and I were close to Curtis—all the Franklins were—and the news was just awful," said Erma. "For some time, he and Aretha had been talking about doing a new record together. When you think of Aretha's greatest producers, only two of them were singers—Luther and Curtis. That's why I think the material she sang under the auspices of those two artists has such a special flavor. I was hoping that Curtis, in spite of the terrible blow, might be able to sing again. It took several years, but my hope came true, and he and my sister did work together again."

The new year began on a happy note. In January 1991, Wayne State University, in Detroit, gave Aretha an honorary doctorate degree.

"Not having graduated high school, this was a tremendous day for her," said Erma. "Because Carolyn, Cecil, and I all had higher educations, Aretha suffered with a bit of a complex. She was just as smart as the rest of us, and she was always an avid reader and astute student of the cultural and political scene. She had no reason to feel intellectually inferior, but quitting school in your teens does something to your attitude. I think she was always trying to compensate for feeling less-than. That's why this degree from Wayne State was right on time. It gave her confidence a boost."

In March, Reverend James Cleveland died in Los Angeles. He was fifty-nine. Aretha did not make it to his funeral at the Shrine Auditorium in Los Angeles but released a statement that said, "He had the single greatest influence on gospel music to this date... James was my earliest musical influence and musical mentor in my formative years."

Two weeks later, she sang at the Detroit funeral of Anthony Riggs, who was murdered after returning home from the Persian Gulf War.

"My sister was always engaged in acts of kindness and charity that went unreported," said Erma. "She and I would be watching the late news. There'd be a story about a woman who lost her home in a fire, and the next thing you know, Aretha was on the phone to the news station getting the woman's number. The next day she'd send her a check for thirty thousand dollars."

In June, she was back in her father's church singing at the funeral of David Ruffin, dead at fifty. She spoke of David with the same admiration with which she spoke of Sam Cooke, Marvin Gaye, Smokey Robinson, Levi Stubbs, and Dennis Edwards, placing him in the highest category of soul singer.

"This was a lonely period for Aretha," said Ruth Bowen. "Mentors and friends were dying all around her. Romantically, she and Willie Wilkerson were always off and on, but more off than on. She was definitely on the prowl for a man, something of a lifelong preoccupation of Aretha's. Unlike other women, though, Aretha didn't have to worry about letting the world know that she was in the market for a new man. All she had to do was call *Jet,* and they put the announcement on the cover."

In fact, the August 19 cover story on Aretha declared that "Aretha Franklin, who says she's ripe for romance, is wealthy, willing and waiting for Mr. Right who won't 'take me for granted.' 'I love men,' she said, stressing she is interested in only one relationship at a time. 'The kind of men I am talking about don't have to come from the entertainment world. They don't have to be celebrities, either. They just have to be men who are not intimidated by my success. I engage in girl talk with other celebrated women and they all agree that the intimidating factor keeps men from making romantic overtures.'"

Aretha went on to explicate the lyrics from a song she wrote for her upcoming album, *What You See Is What You Sweat,* called "You Can't Take Me for Granted."

"It's a personal testimony, a song I wrote with someone in mind, a six foot bronze brother with multi-charms—but no names, please. The lyric is saying 'Your picture's in my locket but I'm not in your back pocket.' So, yes, there's definitely a story there."

It's not a story, though, that Aretha has ever shared with her public.

"There's only one real story about Aretha and men after she and Glynn divorced, and that's Willie Wilkerson," said Ruth Bowen. "Willie proved to be a good and loyal friend to the lady. He became the escort she could count on. All her other fantasy love affairs never amounted to anything."

"Because Willie's a secure guy," said Erma, "he didn't mind if Aretha went off on her side trips. He didn't care what she said in the press. It wasn't that Aretha was his only lady friend. But because I believe he truly loves her and didn't have an image to maintain, he allowed her to give the public whatever impression she wanted to give. He couldn't have cared less, and I'm not sure the public cared either. They certainly didn't care as much as Aretha thought they did."

The public didn't seem to care much for *What You See Is What*

You Sweat—it was her weakest-selling album for Arista. Even her duet with Luther Vandross, "Doctor's Orders," their final collaboration, failed to make a dent in the marketplace.

"By then I had lost track of all the times Aretha had promised never to speak to me again," said Luther. "She was always imagining insults that I had inflicted on her. If I came to perform in Detroit, she would demand tickets for twenty-four of her best friends, and if I provided twelve, I was suddenly in the doghouse. It was a draining friendship, to say the least. In the end, though, I couldn't stay mad at Aretha because she is, after all, Aretha. So when she asked for another 'Jump to It'–style jam, 'Doctor's Orders' was what I came up with. It isn't among the favorite things I've done. I consider it trifling. And of course it wasn't helped by the fact that Aretha refused to leave Detroit to let me produce her vocal where I wanted to produce it—in a studio in LA or New York, where I could do the best job. Her voice was beginning to show signs of age. All voices fray. Recording older voices requires extra-special care. With Aretha, though, that care can't be applied because she won't recognize that there's been even the slightest bit of deterioration."

In 1991, the careers of Aretha and Luther were moving in different directions. His latest album, *Power of Love,* maintained his bestselling status, while Aretha hadn't enjoyed a number-one hit since she had recorded with George Michael, five years before.

When she played Radio City again in September, *New York Times* critic Stephen Holden wrote, "The singer has long aspired to a Las Vegas style of showmanship that seriously undermines what she does best, which is to perform unadorned, gospel-flavored pop with the passion and spontaneity of a church singer. Echoes of that passion invariably find their way onto her records, even a scatter-shot concoction like her newest album, 'What You See Is What You Sweat.'"

Ever mindful of maintaining a high public profile, in November Aretha appeared on the TV sitcom *Murphy Brown,* looking considerably heavier than she did in the photos accompanying her current album. At the piano, she sang "Natural Woman" while Candice Bergen sang the background parts.

Aretha's tradition of throwing herself birthday parties continued in March 1992, when she turned fifty. In a Detroit hotel ballroom, the Duke Ellington Orchestra, led by Duke's son Mercer, entertained. Among the two hundred guests were members of the Detroit Pistons, several local broadcasters, and her older half brother Vaughn.

"Aretha and I became much closer after Cecil died," said Vaughn. "I'd come to Detroit for certain parties and was always grateful to be included. Aretha might get blue sometimes, but these social occasions never failed to perk her up. She also began calling me to help her arrange her travel and keep her business affairs in order. The calls became more frequent in the nineties when she was having some problems with the IRS. I had retired from a long military career in 1974, when I was forty. Afterwards I had lived in the South, where I worked for the postal service. When Aretha asked me to help her I was already in my sixties and contemplating a calm retirement. Show business held no appeal for me. At the same time, because of the great love I had for the mother that Aretha and I shared, I saw my duty. Because I'm basically a trained soldier used to regimentation, it wasn't easy. The soldier's life is about discipline. The artist's life is about mood. Mood determines whether you're going to play a concert or cancel it. Mood determines whether you're going to stick to your recording schedule or ignore it. This was a new world for me, with new rules. I had to learn to bend with the breeze and go with the flow. This was not my style, and for many years I found myself in an uncomfortable position. I found it unpleasant to be put in a position where I had to apologize for Aretha's mercurial moods. The money part was also not easily understood. My sister made a great deal but always needed a great deal more. I understood her relationship to money when I noticed that when she left her dressing room for the stage, she always took her purse with her. That purse stayed with her onstage for as long as she sang. She carried the cash to pay those who worked for her. I tried to get her to do this by check so she could have a receipt. But there were no receipts. She paid cash on the barrelhead."

"Nearly every Aretha gig that I booked," said Dick Alen of the William Morris Agency, "required that of her total fee, she had to have twenty-five thousand in cash before she went onstage. That was the money she used to make her payroll. She deducted no taxes and made no records. I'd beg her to implement some system of documentation, but she refused. I knew that eventually there'd be hell to pay from the IRS."

"For all the money complications," said Vaughn, "her mood changed the minute that Bill Clinton came on the scene. It was more than the fact that, like us, he was a Democrat. He was also a music man, a saxophonist himself, and someone who loved rhythm and blues. Aretha figured she'd be hearing from him in no time. And she did. She worked for [his campaign], and once he was elected, he never forgot her. He put her back on that throne. He helped keep her in the newspapers. He gave her the props she deserved."

In the summer of 1992, fifty-year-old Aretha Franklin sang the national anthem at the Democratic National Convention that nominated Bill Clinton. That same summer, while her Arista album sales sagged, *Amazing Grace,* cut on Atlantic twenty-one years earlier, was certified double platinum.

"I remember calling her with that wonderful news," said Jerry Wexler. "I knew that she was increasingly having a hard time selling records and that piece of news would warm her heart. Of course she was happy. We reminisced for a while and I was feeling good vibes coming my way. That gave me the courage to suggest that maybe we should go back in the studio and cut a classic album, either all blues or all jazz, something for the ages. That suggestion killed our conversation. 'Oh, no,' she said, 'Clive has Babyface and L. A. Reid writing for me. You know who they are, don't you, Jerry?' Of course I knew. They'd just done Whitney's 'I'm Your Baby Tonight.' But when, in the most diplomatic way possible, I asked Aretha whether she thought their material might be a bit young for her, she took great offense. That set off another long period of silence when, in her view, I became persona non grata."

That summer she traveled to New York to perform at the Friars Club roast of Clive Davis at the Waldorf Astoria. Among the performers were Dionne Warwick, Kenny G, and Barry Manilow. Aretha insisted that she go last. Then came the shocker: She came out wearing a tutu and started twirling about with a troupe from the City Center Ballet Company.

"When she told me what she was going to do," said Ruth Bowen, "I couldn't believe it. I wanted to tell her that she'd look ridiculous—and she did. But it was another one of those times when Aretha's sense of reality was off. In her mind, she looked graceful and demure. But to the world, she looked like a dancing hippo. And the thing that killed me most was her reasoning for doing it. She said it was out of respect for Clive!"

In *The Soundtrack of My Life,* Davis's autobiography, he wrote, diplomatically, "She went through pirouettes and dancing with very impressive agility."

"Mr. Davis was the one man she seemed to respect above all others," said Vaughn. "She felt that because he had knowledge of and access to all the current hit writers and hit producers, she couldn't afford to alienate him. At the same time, I often heard her tell him that she was also going to record her own compositions. She didn't need his approval for that. That was a given."

"Including songs she had written on each album was a way to guarantee extra income," said Dick Alen. "You could hardly blame her for that."

"I think if she had focused more or been open to collaborate more, Aretha might have added to that short list of hit songs that she wrote," said Billy Preston. "But if I ask the average Aretha fan to name one song she wrote after leaving Atlantic in the seventies, I'll get a blank stare. Same with Ray Charles. What did he write after 'What'd I Say'? You can't tell me because that was his last self-penned hit."

"I wouldn't call my sister lazy," said Vaughn, "because every year she does travel and play a certain amount of dates. But when she's home she can lack a certain discipline. Coming out of the military, discipline is my second nature. With Aretha, though, she has to fight the tendency to just hang around the house for weeks at a time, sitting on the couch and doing nothing but watching TV and eating. A couple of times I tried to say something about how those habits can be debilitating, but she bit my head off—so I never opened my mouth again."

The idea of singing a duet with the great Teddy Pendergrass, then in a wheelchair, was enough to get Aretha off the couch and onto the stage at the Mann Music Center in Philadelphia.

For decades Erma Franklin had lived with the notion that her musical gifts were largely underappreciated. So it was particularly cheering when, in November of 1992, her career was briefly revived: her version of "Piece of My Heart," featured in a new European commercial for Levi's jeans, was released in England. It sold 100,000 in the UK alone and was played on the Continent as well. Due to its widespread popularity, Erma was asked to shoot a video.

"I loved it all," she told me, "and was excited to be back in the public eye—even if the public was Great Britain rather than America. The English have such a deep appreciation of our music that I couldn't help but be flattered by the attention. I received a couple of lucrative offers to appear in London. They requested that Aretha and I do a concert together. Millions were being offered. I had long ago accepted and empathized with my sister's fear of flying and told the promoters that she would never agree. The promoters countered with a half dozen first-class tickets on a luxury liner. For a while Aretha considered it but never made the commitment. Then the deadline passed and so did the opportunity. I had no illusions that it would have resuscitated my long-dormant public profile. I just thought it would have been fun. Basically, though, I continued to derive great satisfaction from my work at Boysville, then the largest child-care agency in Michigan. To see the rehabilitation of children who had been neglected, delinquent, and often abused was a beautiful thing. At this point in my life, even if I could have had a recording or concert career, I'm not sure I would have chosen to do so. I was so grateful to God that I had survived the crazy emotions of an earlier life in show business and continued to pray that my sister could keep surviving as well."

The survival of Aretha's career, both artistically and commercially, was indeed nothing short of remarkable. Just when you suspected that she was on an irreversible downward slide, she seemed to find a way to get back up. Given her status as one of the great singers of the century, opportunities came her way. When filmmaker Spike Lee sought a grand conclusion to his 1992 film *Malcolm X,* he turned to Aretha. Aretha reached out to Arif Mardin, and his arrangement of Donny Hathaway's "Someday We'll All Be Free" put her back in the same down-home churchy mode of *Amazing Grace,* her classic gospel album. As she sang the song over the credits of Spike Lee's film, the irony was inescapable: the story of one of Islam's most famous converts is set to a Christian-sounding anthem.

As her vocal interpretations continued to soar, her financial situation hit rock bottom. At the end of the year, the IRS put a $225,000 tax lien on Aretha's home in Bloomfield Hills due to a dispute over her 1991 taxes. "While she hasn't been accused of a crime," wrote *Jet,* "the lien represents the amount the legendary singer would have to pay the government if she sold the property."

"Actually the IRS might have been doing us a favor by initiating those actions," said Vaughn, "because, in response, Aretha would go to work. If she were inactive a long period of time, only something scary like a letter from the government would get her going. That made her realize that, win or lose, she needed to be out there earning money. I wasn't privy to the details about her tax problems, and maybe she was being unfairly singled out, but I do know that weeks after she got the IRS bill, she was on the phone with Ruth Bowen or Dick Alen looking for some bookings."

For all her money problems, Aretha did not hesitate to work for free if it involved honoring an artist she respected. In December, for example, she appeared at the Kennedy Center Honors in tribute to jazz vibraphonist Lionel Hampton.

"I have a rule about supporting Republicans," Aretha explained, "and Lionel was a lifelong Republican. But when it came to Hamp, I broke my rule, because my dad loved him. We all did. Hamp had worshipped at New Bethel, and during a concert in Detroit, where Daddy had taken me and Erma, Hamp asked us onstage to do a little dance while he played behind us. Outside of church, that was probably my first time on a public stage. So I had to break party lines and honor the great Lionel Hampton and forgive the fact that he voted for the wrong party."

A month later, Aretha was back with the right party, performing at several of Bill Clinton's inaugural events.

"I saw how my sister is in her element when she appears at these galas with presidents and princes," said Vaughn. "She really does become a queen and relates to them on an equal level. It was fascinating to see these foreign dignitaries responding to her like she was just as important and impressive as them. That's when I first understood that Aretha is genuine royalty."

Her singing in the nation's capital garnered positive reviews, but her wardrobe did not. Animal rights activists complained about her full-length Russian sable coat.

Time magazine titled the article "Respect? Fur-get It." Reportedly, PETA sympathizers Alec Baldwin and Chrissie Hynde were outraged that Aretha had worn fur. A small furor followed.

"Aretha heard about the controversy and asked me to find the articles criticizing her," said Vaughn. "I didn't want to do it. You know what the queen does when the messenger brings [bad] news.

I pretended like I couldn't find the clippings but she wouldn't accept the explanation. So I did what was asked of me. Fortunately, she didn't take it out on me—but she did carry on for a good thirty minutes about who the hell are they to criticize what she wears. She wanted to know how many cows were slaughtered to make their leather shoes and what about the diamonds they wore— didn't they come from those South African mines where workers were treated like slaves? She was livid."

Aretha wrote a brief defense in *Vanity Fair*. "We're all using a lot of leather with respect to our shoes and handbags and things like that, so come on, let's be for real."

In April of 1993, her public relations were lifted somewhat by her Fox television special *Aretha Franklin: Duets*. The concert, a benefit for the Gay Men's Health Crisis, took place at New York City's Nederlander Theater. Bonnie Raitt, Elton John, Rod Stewart, and Gloria Estefan performed. Dustin Hoffman and Robert De Niro gave spoken tributes. Other than a warm and winsome duet with Smokey Robinson on his hit song "Just to See Her," I found it a dull and schmaltzy show-business affair.

Jon Pareles in the *New York Times* saw it differently: "Perhaps by adding competition, 'Duets' brought out Ms. Franklin's improvisational genius. She can summon the agility of jazz, the pain of the blues, the sultriness of pop and the fervor of gospel, and while her voice is smokier now than it was in her 1960s heyday, she has all the range she needs."

In *Vanity Fair,* James T. Jones IV, describing the unfortunate dance sequence in which the singer's voluminous breasts were on the very edge of full exposure, wrote, "Others were left speechless by a surreal ballet sequence in which Aretha, in a tutu, attempted pirouettes."

The next morning, nationally syndicated columnist Liz Smith went on the attack, writing, "She [Aretha] must know she's too bosomy to wear such clothing, but clearly she just doesn't care what we think, and that attitude is what separates mere stars from true divas."

Deeply wounded, Aretha fired back in a statement to Smith that she issued to the press: "How dare you be so presumptuous as to presume you could know my attitude with respect to anything other than music...Obviously I have enough of what it takes to wear a bustier and I haven't had any complaints; I'm sure if you could you would...When you get to be a noted and respected fashion editor please let us all know."

"Like all women, Aretha is highly sensitive to insensitive criticism," said Erma. "Also like many women, when she looks in the mirror, she sees what she wants to see. She wants to see someone who's a lot thinner than she is, and she wants to see someone — herself thirty years ago — who had a dream of being a ballet dancer. She also had a dream of being an opera singer. Aretha's not one to give up dreams, and for that I have to admire her. We don't always make the best choices, but when we stop dreaming, all those choices go away."

Emboldened by her Liz Smith counterattack, Aretha renewed her vow to conquer her fear of flying. She was actually on the verge of boarding a plane for the short flight from Toronto to Detroit when, at the last minute, she panicked and chartered a bus to drive her home.

"I really thought that this time Ree was going to do it," said Erma. "She was so determined. And, God bless her, she really tried, but fear got the best of her. My opinion is that she never got to the bottom of that fear. It's all about control. Aretha needs to feel in control. Riding on her bus, she can tell the driver to go faster or slow down. She can tell him to change routes or to pull over at a rest stop. On the plane she feels completely out of control — and that's the one feeling she can't tolerate."

Aretha felt that she could exert control over one vitally important thing—her career. Having influenced the latest crop of hit makers, she saw no reason why she herself couldn't realize more commercial success.

The fall of 1993 marked her thirteenth year at Arista, which was roughly the same amount of time she had spent at Atlantic. Going back to her signing at Columbia, thirty-three years earlier, the goal had never changed: cut a hit. At age fifty-one, she was convinced that she could be as popular as hot stars like Madonna, Janet Jackson, Mariah Carey, and Paula Abdul.

"Aretha used to say that it's all about getting the right track and the right producer," said Erma. "She'd hear Janet Jackson do that 'Rhythm Nation' or Madonna do her 'Vogue' and say, 'Hey, I invented this rhythm nation. I started this vogue. If I had gotten those songs, I could have turned them into even bigger hits.' It was my sister's competitive side that sustained her and gave her the strength to get back out there and trade blows with this new young crop. The only problem was this concept they called imaging. After MTV, you had to have videos—and your look was almost as important as your song. Tina Turner excelled at imaging because, even though she's actually a couple of years older than Aretha, Tina stayed in shape. Aretha didn't, and she paid the price."

"My sister told me she was just too tired to cut an entire new album," said Vaughn. "But she was willing to record three new singles that would be part of a greatest-hits package."

Those singles and their producers were, as usual, picked by Clive Davis. His first choice was a production group called the C + C Music Factory. In 1990, its members had released an album of their own, *Gonna Make You Sweat,* which sold over five million copies and contained four singles that got to number one on the dance charts, including the title cut, "Gonna Make You Sweat (Everybody Dance Now)," and "Things That Make You Go Hmmm." The style was an unapologetic and infectious throwback to straight-up seventies disco. Despite her previous lamentations about the restrictions of disco, Aretha went with Clive's recommendation and put her vocals atop a C + C dance track called "A Deeper Love." Aretha gave it a shot, singing with what feels like determined—as opposed to natural—effort. The single was played in the clubs but didn't make a dent on the charts. It came and went quickly.

She had a far more comfortable rapport with the team of Babyface, L. A. Reid, and Daryl Simmons, who wrote in the kicked-back R&B groove that echoed old-school masters Marvin Gaye and Curtis Mayfield.

"Willing to Forgive," a Babyface/Simmons song, allowed Aretha room to breathe and time to tell the story. It lopes along with the kind of sassy strut that's far more suitable to Aretha's persona than the frantic dance demands of "A Deeper Love." The same is true of "Honey," a sultry ballad that Aretha could have sung in the sixties. "Willing to Forgive" proved popular, a top-five R&B hit.

With these three new songs attached to Aretha's first greatest-hits package, the album wound up going platinum, a testimony to the strength of her previous hits on the label—from "Jump to It" to "Freeway of Love" to "I Knew You Were Waiting (for Me)"—and to Clive Davis's phenomenal ability to keep an aging classic artist current.

"If you put Aretha's Atlantic material next to her Arista stuff, there's no comparison," said Jerry Wexler. "Artistically, Atlantic wins, hands down. But if you count up the money we made with Aretha as opposed to Clive, Clive is the clear winner. What makes his victory even more remarkable is the fact that he had to market her when she was clearly past her prime. And yet he still found a way to present and package her in products that sold big-time. Incredible."

"I'll go to my grave longing for the great Aretha Franklin albums she could have made," said Carmen McRae, "instead of the schlock she kept turning out. I remember talking to Shirley Horn about this very thing. Sarah Vaughan had just died and I was recording a tribute to her. Shirley, a great jazz singer herself, was playing piano. 'You know who should really be doing this tribute to Sarah, Shirley?' I asked. 'You're thinking of Aretha, aren't you?' said Shirley. I was. 'Well, forget about it, Carmen, because she'll be chasing after hit songs long after you and I are dead and gone.' 'Well, ain't that a shame,' I said. 'Not really,' said Shirley, 'not if she finds something as good as "Dr. Feelgood." ' "

Aretha also participated in what some considered a less than stellar marketing trend meant to keep older singers on the charts— a full duets album. This time, the artist was seventy-eight-year-old Frank Sinatra. The first of his two *Duets* albums was a crafty exercise in musical salesmanship. It was an enormous success—the only Sinatra album to sell over three million copies—but artistically, it was nothing more than a curiosity. His pairing with Aretha, "What Now My Love," serves as a case in point.

They're singing in different studios at different times and, unsurprisingly, sometimes sound like they're singing different songs. After Aretha's grandiose introduction, the band breaks into a straight-ahead jazz groove with Aretha shadowing Sinatra. The shadow doesn't match the master, and both masters—Aretha and Frank—sound relieved when the song is finally sung.

Phil Ramone, the record's producer, saw the pairing as a triumph.

"I took the completed track to Detroit," he told me. "Frank's vocal was already on there, and Aretha was excited about singing the song with Sinatra. She got to the studio early and was completely prepared. She knew that I had worked with Frank many times before and wanted me to know how much she admired his artistry. 'Why don't you tell him?' I said. 'How?' she asked. 'Before you start singing, just put a message on tape.' She hesitated briefly and then did just that, openly and sincerely telling Frank how much he meant to her and how much he had taught her about phrasing, intonation, and dynamics. Of course we didn't include it on the record itself, but Frank got to hear Aretha's beautiful spoken tribute. Then we went to work on her vocals. She already had all her ideas mapped out, and, needless to say, they were brilliant."

In 1994, Aretha returned to form and classic rhythm and blues by participating in the album *A Tribute to Curtis Mayfield*. She hired her longtime associate Arif Mardin to arrange and produce May-field's magnificent "The Makings of You."

"She wanted me to leave lots of space at the end for a long vamp," said Mardin. "Because she so deeply admired Curtis's genius for infusing R-and-B motifs with jazz flavoring and jazz voicings, she wanted to conclude her interpretation with a sequence of scat singing. Aretha is justifiably celebrated for the fusing of gospel and R-and-B, but I think her scatting has been overlooked. To my mind, she's the first and best singer to execute what I call soul scatting. That's where you hear her uncanny ability to improvise over the chord changes as a jazz musician but one rooted in the great soul blues tradition of Sam Cooke and Little Willie John."

The recording that appeared on the album—along with contributions by, among others, Steve Winwood, Bruce Springsteen, Lenny Kravitz, Whitney Houston, and Eric Clapton—is memorable for Aretha's relaxed approach. Her rapport with Curtis's material, so evident in *Sparkle*, is as strong as ever. But it is her remarkable appearance on Donnie Simpson's *Video Soul* television program that demands repeated viewing on YouTube.

Simpson traveled to her home in Detroit, where he sat beside her. Aretha was at the grand piano. When he begged her to sing "The Makings of You," she wasn't sure whether she knew the chords. She asked him to sing the first few notes. That was all she needed. After a few seconds spent searching for the right voicing, she found the song on piano and, accompanying herself, gave *the* definitive reading. The casualness of the moment made it that much more moving. Soaring high and moaning low, she located the sweet spot that defines Curtis's genius for merging the optimism of divine faith with the poignancy of earthy love. In her divine earthiness, Aretha was the perfect instrument of Curtis's song.

"I don't care what they say about Aretha," said Billy Preston. "She can be hiding out in her house in Detroit for years. She can go decades without taking a plane or flying off to Europe. She can cancel half her gigs and infuriate every producer and promoter in the country. She can sing all kinds of jive-ass songs that are beneath her. She can go into her diva act and turn off the world. But on any given night, when that lady sits down at the piano and gets her body and soul all over some righteous song, she'll scare the shit out of you. And you'll know—you'll swear—that she's still the best fuckin' singer this fucked-up country has ever produced."

33. A ROSE

When I met Aretha in 1994 and we started the long collaboration that led to the publication of her autobiography *From These Roots,* one of the first things she showed me was an article she had clipped from *Billboard.* It was the Chart Beat column by Fred Bronson from May 14 of that year, and it said, "By debuting on the Hot 100 at No. 88 with 'Willing to Forgive,' Aretha Franklin extends her chart span to 33 years and three months. Rob Durkee of 'America's Top 40' notes that hers is the longest chart span for any female artist, beating Tina Turner's 33 years and two months."

For Aretha, this was evidence that her career had not, as one naysayer had hinted, peaked several years before. She was certain that her fifties would be her strongest years, and that her sixties would be stronger still.

A high point of her fifties was certainly her appearance on the Grammy broadcast in March, where she received a lifetime achievement award. That summer, she was invited to President Bill Clinton's party on the White House lawn. Wearing an alarmingly low-cut white dress and long white gloves, she sang a somewhat overwrought "Natural Woman" and a slightly underwhelming "Say a Little Prayer." While in Washington, she also performed for the Black Caucus at the Kennedy Center before hosting her own black-tie affair for two hundred guests.

When, later that summer, *Jet* reported that Janet Jackson had broken Aretha's record of fourteen gold singles by a female solo artist, Vaughn told me that he was asked by his sister to double-check the figures. Aretha thought that the count had been weighted in Janet's favor.

"When it turned out that the count was accurate," said Vaughn, "the topic was dropped and never brought up again. I knew this was part of Aretha's competitive nature, something that I respect. Without that drive she would never have gotten to the top. I also respected how she was driven to rid herself of her bad habits. I saw her give up her thirty-five-year-old habit of heavy cigarette smoking. She went cold turkey and never smoked again. Back in the early seventies, she did the same thing with liquor—she simply gave it up. She's an iron-willed woman in many areas. I know she wishes that the willpower could be applied to overeating, the one habit that's hardest of all to break."

In November, she played Carnegie Hall and talked about how she had sworn off cigarettes and was managing her weight with a combination of "Slim Fast and young men." I was bothered by her cover versions of over-the-top ballads—Mariah Carey's "Hero" and Whitney Houston's "Greatest Love of All"—but agreed with Stephen Holden's observation in the *New York Times* that "Ms. Franklin's concerts are notoriously uneven, but on Thursday she was in fine voice and high spirits."

Another November article, this one by Aretha scholar David Nathan in *Billboard,* argued that Franklin, Gladys Knight, and Patti LaBelle were continuing to appeal to new generations of record buyers. There was mention of how Aretha's twenty-five-week chart run with "Willing to Forgive" was spurring interest in her *Greatest Hits* album. Jean Riggins, senior VP of black music for Arista, admitted that "breaking Franklin's 'Willing to Forgive' was a major challenge. We had all the classic ingredients: a great artist, a great producer, a great song and a great time working the record.

But with classic artists like Aretha, it happens on a record-by-record basis. We didn't deliver 'A Deeper Love' all the way although it was a very big club record…Early on, we experienced a lot of resistance from radio. We felt that 'Willing to Forgive' was a take-no-prisoners record and a lot of people were surprised when it went top five."

That winter, along with Kirk Douglas, Morton Gould, Pete Seeger, and Harold Prince, Aretha received the Kennedy Center Honors award. Her escort to the celebratory dinner was Renauld White, high-fashion model and an actor on the daytime soap *The Guiding Light,* one of Aretha's favorite programs. During the telecast, Patti LaBelle and the Four Tops sang in Aretha's honor.

Not everything she received was an honor. Saks Fifth Avenue served her with a lawsuit for her long overdue bills amounting to over $262,000 for purchases including sables and shoes.

"My sister needs to turn over her money management to a professional," said Erma, "but she won't give up the control. She overspends and then loses track of the bills. Because she doesn't trust anyone to pay those bills, they pile up and overwhelm her. Because she's Aretha Franklin, she's extended unlimited credit all the time, but when her creditors see that she's four or five months in arrears, they lose patience. I've worked as an administrator in an office for years, and so has our cousin Brenda. Either one of us could have easily put Aretha's affairs in order. But you can't tell her that. You can't tell her anything."

To counter the negative publicity and keep herself in front of her core audience, that spring Aretha invited *Ebony* to her home for a long interview. Once again she presented herself as a down-home diva in a cover story entitled "Aretha Talks About Men, Marriage, Music and Motherhood." She also talked about releasing a cooking video, an upcoming *Live at Carnegie Hall* album, and a record she was making with her sons for a label that she was starting up—World Class Records. Those projects never materialized. She spoke of producing a black fairy tale as a feature film as well as a biopic about her own life in which she would star—two more unrealized ventures. On quitting smoking, she said, "I'd rather be overweight a few pounds and work on that than on my way to cancer." She noted that being free of tobacco had given her her high notes back. Men were discussed, including Renauld White, with whom she said she was "close, very close." The general thrust of the article was that she didn't have a care in the world.

Aretha and I planned to complete the interviews for her book by the end of 1995. I estimated that I would need no more than six months to finish the interviewing process. In the end, it took years. Dozens of interviews were postponed or canceled. When we did meet, we often spent as much time listening to music as talking. The music gave us both great pleasure. Her preferences, like mine, were always gospel, R&B, and jazz. In each genre, she celebrated the classics with deep knowledge and true passion. We spent hours listening to, among many others, Albertina Walker, Rance Allen, Nancy Wilson, Andy Bey, Candi Staton, and Betty Carter. At the same time, because she was planning her new record, she studied producers sent her way by Clive Davis. She read the trades carefully and knew who was hot and who was not. She was familiar with everyone from Aaron Hall to R. Kelly. Although highly opinionated, when it came to the current crop of writer/producers, she deferred to Clive. She talked often about receiving private lessons from an opera instructor and of her intention to begin studying classical piano at Juilliard in New York.

Shortly thereafter she told other interviewers about her aspirations to sing bel canto and learn Chopin sonatas. She had, in fact, hired an opera coach and would soon insert a couple of Italian arias into her repertoire. But Juilliard remained a distant dream. She never enrolled at the school.

Our interviews, when they finally took place, were restricted to ninety minutes. Our collaboration agreement gave her the right to end the sessions whenever she felt the questioning was not to her liking. She would also cancel concerts at the drop of a hat. Her agent, Dick Alen, told me that once she had insisted on leaving North Carolina the day before a booking because of a forest fire some two hundred miles away. Even though weather reports had indicated otherwise, she was afraid that the fire would change course and head in her direction.

"There's the fearless Aretha," said Erma, "and then there's the fearful Aretha. The fearless Aretha will sing any material in any venue. Put her on television before a worldwide audience of millions and she doesn't flinch. She's as comfortable there as if she were singing in your living room. The problem is getting her there. It's beyond a fear of flying. She canceled several bus trips to California because she doesn't want to ride over the Rockies. She's afraid of the mountain roads."

Aretha made a point, however, not to cancel her commitment to what turned out to be one of the year's most successful record projects. Along with Whitney Houston, Brandy, Patti LaBelle, Chaka Khan, Faith Evans, and Toni Braxton, Aretha sang on Babyface's soundtrack for *Waiting to Exhale,* a number-one Arista album that would eventually sell over nine million copies. There were several individual hits—Whitney's "Exhale (Shoos Shoop)," Toni Braxton's "Let It Flow," Brandy's "Sittin' Up in My Room," and Mary J. Blige's "Not Gon' Cry." Aretha's reading of "It Hurts Like Hell," a poignant Babyface ballad, was effective and eventually released as the album's sixth single, but it never achieved hit status. Yet in the *Washington Post,* Geoffrey Himes wrote, "The album's peak moment belongs to Aretha Franklin, who makes us hear in every note what the title of [the song] is talking about."

In 1996 the Queen traveled to Toronto to catch Diahann Carroll playing the lead in a new staging of *Sunset Boulevard.*

"She didn't realize it wasn't going to be freezing," said Erma, "so she ordered up a mink coat from one of the better department stores. Because the coat was so enormous, she decided it required a ticket of its own. She and her coat sat together on the front row. It was hysterical."

"My sister likes to go out and make a splash," said Vaughn. "She knows how to have a good time at shows and parties and celebrations. At the same time she makes sure that the press is around to take her picture. She realizes the importance of staying in the public eye. Like most of these stars, she's afraid if she's out of the spotlight for too long the fans will forget her."

That summer she was photographed making a grand entrance to the Kennedy Center's twenty-fifth anniversary gala in Washington, DC. Her escort was Arthur Mitchell, founding director of the Dance Theater of Harlem.

A few weeks later, while we were working on her autobiography, she asked me to meet her in New York, where she was playing Carnegie Hall as part of the JVC Jazz Festival. I jumped at the chance. This was the twentieth Aretha concert I had attended in recent years, and, although always eager to hear her sing, I was a little skeptical. Lately her performances had been perfunctory. But on this night she was on fire. In the *New York Times,* Jon Pareles wrote, "If anyone had forgotten, she proved herself yet again as one of America's greatest vocal improvisers." Thirty years after she wrote and recorded "Dr. Feelgood," she sang the song with almost frightening conviction. I was thrilled to hear her sounding so good. The vitality was back.

That same vitality was evident at a free outdoor concert in Chicago's Grant Park. The occasion was the opening of the Democratic National Convention at which Bill Clinton would be nominated for a second term.

She kept working the press, kept up appearances, kept projecting plans, kept vowing to overcome her fear of flying. All that was evident in the October cover story of *Jet* in which she discussed her memoir in progress before mentioning a Julia Child–style cooking video that, alas, never materialized. She also cited the antianxiety tapes she'd been listening to and the "fearless" classes she had attended.

"You have to admire her for trying," said Ruth Bowen. "She's always trying. She's always trying to get back on planes, always trying to lose weight, always trying to manage her money and figure out how to manage a relationship with a man. It's good to try. But if you're gonna succeed, you have to understand yourself. You have to look deep into yourself and figure out what makes you fail. Why do I have so many fears? Why am I a compulsive eater? Why do I wind up chasing off all these men? Aretha does not want to look at herself. She doesn't want to critique herself. She doesn't know how to do that. She can't take criticism either from without or from within. The result is that nothing changes for her. The world keeps knocking on her door because the world wants to hear her sing. That will never change. But neither will she, because she's the hardest-headed woman since Eve ate the apple. What it comes down to is this: no one can tell Aretha shit."

"In the sixties and seventies I could tell Aretha a few things," said Jerry Wexler, "because I was helping her put together hit records on Atlantic. When the hits stopped, she stopped listening. In the eighties and nineties, Clive could tell her a few things, because she was having hits with him. As long as the hits keep coming, you can talk to her. When the hits stop, so does the communication."

In 1996, communication between Aretha and Clive was excellent. He recommended a new group of hot producers, including Sean "Puffy" Combs, Jermaine Dupri, Dallas Austin, and Daryl Simmons. Aretha added Michael Powell, who had produced a slew of hits for Anita Baker, and also her old friend Narada Michael Walden.

"When she cut her new multi-deal with Arista in the mid-nineties," said Ruth Bowen, "she wanted the press release to emphasize how much creative freedom she was given. She wanted the public to know that she was free to sing her own songs and produce her own records. For years Aretha had been seeing herself as a great lady mogul and she insisted that now was the time. But, in truth, if you look at that album she made after signing her new Arista contract—the one called *A Rose Is Still a Rose*—she only produced one song: 'The Woman,' a song she wrote. Everything else was done by outside producers. And the one hit on the record, the title cut, didn't come from Aretha but from Lauryn Hill. It was Lauryn's song and Lauryn's production. Lauryn even came to Detroit to do it."

Along with Wyclef Jean and Pras Michel, Hill was a member of the Fugees, a hip-hop/R&B crossover sensation. Their 1996 *The Score,* with the massive hit "Killing Me Softly with His Song," a sweet echo of Roberta Flack's 1973 version, was one of the biggest albums of the year. A couple of years before Hill's worldwide solo smash *The Miseducation of Lauryn Hill,* she had started writing and producing independently of her fellow Fugees.

"A Rose Is Still a Rose" works flawlessly on several levels. The twenty-two-year-old writer/producer gives the fifty-five-year-old singer/diva a text she deeply understands. Wisely, Hill also gives Aretha the role of the narrator, an older woman giving advice to the young girl wounded by love. "Listen, dear," says Aretha in her spoken introduction, "I realize you've been hurt deeply...because I've been there." Then unexpectedly the prelude takes a spiritual turn when the singer adds, "But regardless...we're all precious in His sight." The tale is told from the perspective of a believer. The villain is quickly identified as someone with whom Aretha is familiar: the two-timing man who with his "sticky game...steals her honey and forgets her." But God's grace is bountiful, and beauty comes from within. "Baby girl," sings Aretha, "you hold the power." As an anthem celebrating self-esteem, it's the most interesting lyric Aretha has sung since "Respect." With its Fugees-fueled track of loping funk, it's also her best single in decades.

Although "Rose" was the only hit from the album—it reached number twenty-six on the pop charts—the rest of the record is relaxed and satisfying. The songs and productions are geared to make Aretha sound authentic as opposed to young. There is far less desperation—*I'll sing anything for a hit*—than had characterized her earlier Arista records. She takes to the overarching theme of great loss in love with obvious sympathy. The one caveat, though, is that the top of Aretha's voice, once a marvel, is now marred by shrillness.

During the making of the album, Aretha invited me to write liner notes and watch her record a few of the vocals at the Vanguard Recording Complex in Oak Park in suburban Detroit. We met in the early afternoon, and Aretha, dressed in a casual tracksuit, went to work immediately. There were no live musicians. She was singing to a completed music track, her main method of recording since she had moved to Detroit some fourteen years earlier. She worked quickly and efficiently. The producer was out of town, so it was just Aretha and an engineer. She listened to the playbacks with studied scrutiny that seemed neither gratuitous nor excessive. At the same time, when the engineer asked if she wanted to sing a passage over, one in which she sounded especially shrill, she asked him what the point would be. Wisely, he retreated and withdrew the question. I thought of Erma's observation that when Aretha looks in the mirror, she sees a different person than we do. It was obvious that when Aretha listens to her voice, she hears it differently than we do.

"When these young guys tell me, 'I produced Aretha,'" said Ruth Bowen, "I have to laugh because they didn't really produce Aretha. They gave her a song to sing. They gave her a track and then they got the hell out of her way. Jerry Wexler and Luther Vandross were probably the last men alive who had the balls to even make suggestions about how she should sing. Clive could suggest—or even demand—that she work with a certain producer, but none of those guys would dare tell her how to sing."

In this same period—the midnineties—I asked Ray Charles, who had also struggled with the idea of being produced by others, if he thought that singers like himself and Aretha ever benefited from advice in terms of vocal performance.

"What the fuck are these so-called producers gonna tell us?" asked Ray, whose cockiness as a singer matched Aretha's. "Maybe they've come up with a new twist on an old rhythm. Maybe they've got some groove that the kids are dancing to. Maybe they've got a little catchphrase that's caught on with the cool set. All that's fine. Give us the new groove and give us the new catchphrase. But please, don't tell me or Aretha Franklin or Gladys Knight or Lou Rawls how to sing this shit. We been singing before these producers were sperm squirts inside their daddies' dicks. We made a ton of money singing—not just singing, but fighting to sing in our style. It's our style that got us the attention and sold the records that made us famous. So you tell me, who's more qualified to tell us how to express this style on a record—us, the people who invented the style, or you, a producer who's twenty-five years old and has two or three little hits to your name?

"Now don't get me wrong—those two or three little hits mean something, especially for older artists like me and Aretha who still wanna make that money. But here's how I work it. When my friend Quincy Jones said he had this producer who could help me make money, I said, 'Fine, Q, send me the tracks. If I can feel the songs, I'll sing 'em. I'll learn the songs from the tracks. I'll let the producer fix up the music the way he wants it. But when it comes time to put on my vocal, I don't want no suggestions. Matter of fact, I don't even want the fuckin' producer in the same building as me.'"

Humility, however, did characterize one superb veteran soul singer, the man who had been so significant in turning around Aretha's midseventies sales slump at Atlantic: Curtis Mayfield. After his traumatic accident in 1990, Mayfield returned to the studio for one last album, the remarkable *New World Order.* It was released in 1996, three years before his death, at age fifty-seven. In order to generate enough breath to sing, Curtis recorded from a supine position, filling up his lungs, and he was able to articulate only a single line at a time. The process took months. To vocalize while flat on your back is no small feat, but to do so while you express undying optimism and hope is a singular achievement.

The most moving moment comes in a song cowritten by Curtis, produced by Narada Michael Walden, and featuring Aretha— "Back to Living Again." In heartbreakingly beautiful falsetto, Curtis sings the first four minutes of the song alone. His is a gentle story in which sweetness struggles with bitterness, righteousness with recklessness. His mantra is simple: "If you're feeling inferior, make yourself superior." His faith in healing is undiminished. And in the final seconds it is Aretha, in full gospel mode, who underlines the message with a sequence of magnificent exhortations. She pushes Curtis, the writer of "Keep on Pushing," as she urges, "Right on, Mayfield!... Go ahead, Mayfield!," sharing her strength with the creative giant whose *Sparkle* remains one of the great glories of her career.

Forever in favor with the Democratic Party that the Franklin family had unswervingly supported ever since C.L. settled in Detroit in 1946, Aretha performed at Clinton's second inauguration in January 1997.

"I never doubted Aretha's political convictions," said Ruth Bowen. "Her liberalism is strong and genuine. She was happy to back the party that we both believed served our people best. But she was also miffed that she didn't receive enough publicity as a result of her appearance. That winter, there was very little written about her. Well, if a month or so goes by and Aretha doesn't see her name in a magazine or the trade papers, she'll pick up the phone, call a reporter, and make some news. That's her way of staying in front of the public. The only problem is that most of the news she gives out is bullshit."

An example would be a *Billboard* article that ran in the spring. Aretha spoke about the activities of her self-owned Crown Productions. She had acquired the dramatic rights to Marshall Frady's biography of Jesse Jackson and was planning to produce a bio on her longtime friend. She also discussed her World Class Records and the soon-to-be-released disc by the New Bethel Church Choir. But nothing came of either the Jackson movie or the gospel production.

She did do a gospel show on her own—Aretha Franklin's

Gospel Crusade for AIDS—at Avery Fisher Hall in New York City to open the JVC Jazz Festival in June. I came as her guest and was overwhelmed. In recent performances, the top of her voice had been sounding uncertain. But not on this night. Backed by the New Jersey Mass Choir, she sang songs from *Amazing Grace,* revitalized by the sacred material from her 1972 masterpiece. Sitting next to me, an elderly woman who had come from Detroit to hear Aretha said, "The Holy Ghost got her and ain't letting her go."

During this New York trip, she told the press that she was determined to enroll at Juilliard to study classical music.

To strengthen her commitment, she told *Billboard* that she had, in fact, been accepted at Juilliard and would be matriculating in the fall. "She'll have little time to buy school supplies before September, however; Franklin is busy recording a new version of 'Respect' for the movie *Blues Brothers 2000* in which she reprises her role as a restaurant owner."

The new "Respect" was, in fact, recorded, but her commitment to Juilliard remained unrealized. Come September, she got sidetracked, dropped the idea, and never enrolled.

While Aretha and I were in the middle of interviews for her autobiography, another memoir was published that caught her attention: Gladys Knight's *Between Each Line of Pain and Glory.* Erma spoke about Aretha's dissatisfaction with the book and how her sister complained that Gladys unfairly trashed her. In the memoir, Knight cites several instances when Aretha snubbed her. According to Gladys, one time at the Grammys, the two women passed each other in the hall. When Gladys said hello, Aretha kept on walking, not bothering to acknowledge her. Aretha claimed that never happened. Gladys, in turn, claimed it happened all the time.

"Aretha's always had problems with her female contemporaries," said Erma. "Her fantasy is that they would all disappear and she and she alone would be the only singer. Her fantasy is to eliminate the competition. By not acknowledging them—whether it's

Gladys or Mavis or even younger artists like Natalie or Whitney — in her mind, she's making them go away."

Another publication angered Aretha: *How I Got Over: Clara Ward and the World-Famous Ward Singers,* by Willa Ward-Royster. An eyewitness to the long affair, Willa spent many pages documenting the twenty-four-year relationship between C. L. Franklin and her sister Clara.

Aretha told Erma that she didn't believe Willa and was convinced she'd inserted that section only to sell books and generate publicity. It didn't matter that Temple University Press was a purely academic concern not interested in mass marketing. Aretha was certain that Willa would show up on *Oprah* and that the text was nothing but an attempt to slander her father. Willa never appeared on *Oprah,* and the book got practically no notice.

Small dramas aside, Aretha was always able to rise to the dramatic occasion where her voice was needed. This was, in fact, the period of her life when she seemed to take on the role of America's national funeral singer.

Coleman Young was a much revered figure in American politics, the first black man to be elected as mayor of Detroit, where he served for five terms and twenty years. He and Aretha had enjoyed a cordial relationship. She had endorsed his campaigns from the start. When he died, at the end of November 1997, she sang "The Impossible Dream" at his funeral.

In the aftermath of the death of Princess Diana — killed in Paris on August 31 of that year — producers were putting together a tribute album, and they asked, among others, Barbra Streisand, Paul McCartney, Whitney Houston, Sinead O'Conner, Diana Ross, and Aretha to contribute. Due to time constraints, most of the artists simply turned in performances they had already released, such as Streisand's "Evergreen" and Ross's "Missing You." Moved by the tragic loss of the young mother, Aretha went to a studio with a Baptist church choir and sang the old hymn "I'll Fly Away," easily the most affecting performance on the double CD.

"I was proud of Aretha for doing that," said Erma. "She could have just as easily sent in something from *Amazing Grace* or *One Lord, One Faith, One Baptism*. But she didn't. She cared enough to take the time to do something wholly original. We all can be self-involved, and Aretha is no different. But then there are times when she'll go out of her way to do something completely kind and giving."

No doubt Aretha often expressed a charitable spirit. At the same time, her hunger for a hit never dissipated. She told the press that she was certain *A Rose Is Still a Rose* was a smash.

Billboard agreed, calling the early 1998 release "a sleek, jeep-styled cruiser that matches her with Lauryn Hill of the Fugees. It's an absolutely electric union that results in Franklin's strongest, most instantly pop-viable single in eons."

A week later, the trade paper ran a feature on Aretha, who enthused, "I'm cooking, and my voice is at an all-time high—the clarity, the range, everything." Addressing the fact that six years earlier, *What You See Is What You Sweat* had been a major sales disappointment, Aretha spoke with rare self-criticism. "I know the last album wasn't as good as it should have been. The public lets you know that, and you have to take the advice to reinvest yourself for modern times."

She acknowledged that her career needed a boost—and *A Rose Is Still a Rose* would provide it. Sales were robust and the reviews strong. Robert Christgau, a tough critic, wrote in the *Village Voice* that "at its heart is Aretha Franklin's voice. Its power is so ineffable that no one has ever satisfactorily described it in words."

Rolling Stone called it "an extraordinary piece of work... it renders [Aretha] legendary and contemporary all at once."

But beyond the album or its one hit single, another event, completely unplanned, would do far more to reinforce Aretha's iconic status on the world stage. Aretha's brother Vaughn came to call this the Great Event. It would happen in New York City at Radio City Music Hall during the fortieth annual Grammy Awards, where she was set to sing "Respect" with Dan Aykroyd and the Blues

Brothers, a preview of her appearance in the upcoming *Blues Brothers 2000*.

She sang the song that she had sung thousands of times before. Even if the performance was somewhat uninspired, the crowd loved it. Then she went to her dressing room, believing that the evening was over. But the evening had just begun. The Great Event was at hand.

34. *VINCERÒ*

Aretha invited me to the Grammy activities in New York in February 1998, thinking we might have time to do some interviews for the book. We didn't. She was understandably preoccupied with the events at hand.

The week kicked off at a dinner at Le Cirque 2000, the posh Madison Avenue restaurant at the Palace Hotel. Aretha, an avid reader of *Gourmet* magazine, was excited about visiting the establishment celebrated for haute cuisine. Curious about the chef's approach to beef, fowl, and fish, she ordered several main courses. When the food arrived and she was not completely satisfied with the tastes, she opened her purse and fished out an economy-size bottle of Lawry's seasoned salt that she generously sprinkled on the food. Her brother Vaughn, sensing the waiter's disapproval, leaned over to me and whispered, "I've seen chefs come out of the kitchen and tell her to put that Lawry's away, but she doesn't care. She does this all the time. And I think she's right. I think this food is underseasoned."

The next night, at a MusiCares charity event with Luciano Pavarotti present, she sang "Nessun Dorma," the famous aria from Puccini's *Turandot*. With the help of her opera coach, she had been practicing the piece at home for several months, singing to a tape of the full orchestration. Her rendition, while hardly conventional, was greeted with a standing ovation.

"Opera purists may take issue with your liberties," Pavarotti told her afterward, "but I loved your interpretation. Puccini has great soul but you made his soul even greater. Will you do me the honor of coming to my home in Modena, where we can record together?"

When Aretha explained that she didn't fly, Pavarotti said, "I have a private jet and a pilot who makes flying in the plane more soothing than taking a bubble bath. I will dispatch the jet for you and you alone, my dear Miss Franklin."

Aretha expressed gratitude and said she might just take him up on his offer. She invited him to Detroit for one of her homemade soul-food dinners.

"Nothing would please me more," he said, "but I am in terrible pain. You see, I am preparing for hip surgery. But the moment I recover, I am instructing my pilot to head for Detroit and, afterwards, we will head back to Italy."

Aretha was charmed, Pavarotti was charmed, and the evening, according to Aretha, was a triumph.

Three days later, on the evening of February 25, it was Grammy time. On the stage of Radio City Music Hall, Aretha was scheduled to sing "Respect." Some thirty minutes later, Pavarotti was set to sing the same aria Aretha had sung at MusiCares, "Nessun Dorma."

After "Respect," Aretha returned to her dressing room, where producer Ken Ehrlich was waiting for her. Ehrlich told her that the ailing Pavarotti had canceled at the last minute. Was there any way in the world that Aretha could step in and take his place? Naturally Aretha wanted to know the details. Would the orchestra be playing the same arrangement she had used at MusiCares? No. It was a different arrangement and a much larger orchestra—sixty-five pieces, plus a twenty-voice choir. Did Ehrlich have a tape of the arrangement? Did he know if it was in Aretha's key? He answered yes to both questions. But hearing the first few notes, Aretha realized it was not in her key. She asked him exactly when the piece was scheduled to be performed. Ehrlich looked at his watch. Less than twenty minutes from then. The assumption—given that it was a strange arrangement and written in an uncomfortable key—was that Aretha couldn't and wouldn't do it.

Yet, after thinking about the situation for less than twenty seconds, she nodded her head. "I'll do it," she said. With that, she asked that everyone leave the dressing room so she could concentrate on the tape.

Twenty minutes later, introduced by Sting, who explained the last-minute nature of the performance, Aretha stepped back out onstage. Wearing a red brocade dress with mink cuffs and a mink collar, she appeared calm, as if she had been rehearsing this moment for hours on end. The Puccini aria, written for a man, is all about determination. A suitor is determined to win the hand of a princess by solving a riddle. The culmination of the aria comes with a repetition of the word *Vincerò*, "I will win." The text suited the singer. Aretha was determined to win. She had everything going for her—her fine-tuned sense of pitch, her still relatively enormous range, her unshakable confidence, and the fact that she had been carefully studying this piece for months. That studying had convinced her; if she could interpret Hoagy Carmichael and Johnny Mercer's "Skylark" as a twenty-one-year-old—and she had, magnificently—then she could certainly interpret Puccini at age fifty-six. Grand opera—at least Puccini's brand of grand opera—shared many of the same elements as melodies from the Great American Songbook.

"When I heard Aretha sing 'Nessun Dorma' that night," said Jerry Wexler, "I thought of the one night I spent with Frank Sinatra discussing music. Sinatra adored Puccini and was convinced that all the great American tunesmiths—Irving Berlin, Jerome Kern, and especially George Gershwin—came out of Puccini. He was surprised that more jazz musicians hadn't taken Puccini melodies and used them as the basis of improvisation. Well, Aretha understood exactly what Sinatra had understood—you didn't have to sing Puccini literally. She could use her own stylistic devices—and no one employs more of those devices than Aretha—in sculpting his songs according to her own vocal vision. That night, everyone saw that Aretha had a helluva vision. The top of her voice might have been a little rough, but the bottom was all syrup and molasses. The bottom was beautiful. She swooped down to the bottom of those passages with great elasticity. Mainly, though, it was the feeling that got her over. She wasn't afraid of the aria. She owned it, claimed it, and made it her own. After she hit that last note, the crowd jumped to its feet and started hooting and hollering, celebrating what was undeniable—she had pulled it off!"

There were other surprises at the Grammys. During Bob Dylan's performance, a shirtless man with *Soy Bomb* written across his chest had jumped onstage; Ol' Dirty Bastard had jumped onstage while Shawn Colvin was speaking. Barbra Streisand canceled her duet performance with Celine Dion. Yet the evening will be remembered as the night that Aretha took on Puccini. For the most part, the reaction was positive.

Billboard's headline read "The Grammys: Big Wins, Big Buzz." The article noted, "Apparently, an artist doesn't even need to be nominated in order to bask in the retail afterglow of the Grammys. Soul legend Aretha Franklin appears poised to enjoy a rush of consumer interest after simply performing on the show."

A week later, Fred Bronson's Chart Beat column in *Billboard* put Aretha's achievement in historical perspective. "'A Rose Is Still a Rose,' new at No. 43, is the first Franklin single to chart since 'Willing to Forgive' peaked at No. 26 in 1994. It's only the third Franklin chart entry in the '90s, but it does extend the superstar chart span to 37 years and two weeks." Bronson pointed out that Franklin's span on Arista was now over seventeen years, longer than her chart history on Columbia (seven years) and Atlantic (ten years).

As an artist battling to stay current in the ever-changing, ever-fickle American pop music market, Aretha had demonstrated tremendous resilience. But the Grammy performance and the release

of *A Rose Is Still a Rose* would prove to be her last significant commercial moment—at least as of this writing. Because of the success
of her "Nessun Dorma" performance, there was also the possibility
of singing with symphony orchestras.

"We were all certain," said Erma, "that Aretha's opera success
would move her career in a new and exciting direction."

"Offers from classical-music venues started rolling in," said
Vaughn. "They wanted Aretha to sing some of those arias in
famous concert halls across the country—and Europe as well. It
opened up a whole new world, and for a while it looked like Aretha
would go down that path. But it never really happened. She likes to
be in complete control of her concerts, down to the last detail. I
understand that. I understand why, coming in to Boston or Cleveland to sing with their symphony orchestras, she's not comfortable
being under the direction of some distinguished conductor or
famous maestro. She wants to be the director and the maestro. She
wants to run the show, and, after all these years in the business, isn't
she entitled to?"

"There's a precedent for the career redirection that Aretha
might have adopted after her Grammys triumph," said Jerry Wexler. "Sarah Vaughan had played symphony dates for years. The
New York Philharmonic, for example, might play Mahler for the
first half, then after intermission, Sarah would come out and, with
the strings soaring behind her, she'd sing Gershwin's 'Summer-
time,' Sondheim's 'Send in the Clowns,' and another half dozen
classic melodies. Aretha was perfectly positioned to play this circuit. The opening was there."

"Everyone was excited about the idea of Aretha performing
with classical symphonies," said Ruth Bowen. "It was the obvious
next move. And it also suited her style. She could become an even
greater diva. She could wear fabulous jewels and fabulous furs and
gain even greater status. She could go where no other rhythm-and-
blues singer had ever gone and conquer a whole new world. What's
more, the audience was affluent, and the fees would be large. And
yet I knew it wouldn't happen—at least not on a grand scale. These

dates are locked in long in advance—often more than a year. Aretha doesn't like to plan that far away. She's also been known to cancel at the last minute. In the classical world, that's a no-no. But what ultimately made it unworkable was the fact that Aretha would not be entirely in charge. Maybe it's true of all of us aging dames, but the older Aretha gets, the greater her fear that she won't be in charge—and the greater her need that she has to be in charge."

There was, in fact, a period when Aretha discussed a new paradigm of performing. Vaughn and Ruth Bowen weren't entirely wrong that her controlling nature interfered with the plans. But it was more than that; it was the success of "A Rose Is Still a Rose" that convinced Aretha that she could compete with the Janet Jacksons and the Madonnas. She spoke of an even more elaborate self-contained show, with dancers and rappers and a full gospel choir. She vowed to lose at least sixty pounds and realize her dream of not only studying classical piano at Juilliard but getting in shape and performing her own form of ballet.

Aretha proudly gave me a copy of the March 21 issue of *Billboard* in which statistician Fred Bronson's article gave her something to smile about:

"'Rose' is Franklin's 96th r&b chart entry, the second-highest total in history (James Brown has 118). It's also her 52nd top 10 hit. The only artists with more are Brown (58) and Louis Jordan (54)."

In the spring, Aretha kept her visibility high by appearing on VH1's *Divas Live* concert in New York that raised more than $750,000 for the network's campaign to restore school-music programs. An energized Aretha sang "Chain of Fools" with Mariah Carey, and then, with the choir—consisting of Mariah, Carole King, Celine Dion, Gloria Estefan, and Shania Twain—she did "Natural Woman." Aretha sang the first and last choruses, and although she finally shared the mic, she was adamant on doing the long and extended last vamps alone. Carole King, the song's composer, failed to get any solo time, but that seemed to be okay with Carole. Long ago, it had become Aretha's song, and on this night, Aretha was reestablishing that fact.

In May she was back on the cover of *Jet*. She complained about the lack of offers of movie roles. In other areas, she was upbeat: she'd committed to losing weight; she was thrilled with the success of "Rose" and *Divas Live;* and she was in love. When asked for specifics, she called him her Mystery Man. "[He's] a cutie," said Aretha. "He's not in the industry. It doesn't matter what age he is."

When I read the article to Ruth Bowen at the time, she said, "It doesn't matter what age he is because he doesn't exist. If he were real, she'd let us know. She was hardly shy talking about Ted White or Dennis Edwards or Glynn Turman or Willie Wilkerson. Why suddenly is she getting so secretive about naming some man she's dating? Who is she protecting? Most men would be proud of the fact that they're dating the Queen of Soul. They'd want the world to know. But, mind you, for a long time now, this was when Aretha started getting strange. In order to have something to say, she just made up shit."

In June, *Time* listed her as one of the most influential people of the twentieth century.

In July, *Billboard* reported the *Rose* album had sold 292,000 units and the single — "A Rose Is Still a Rose" — had gone gold.

In August, *Ebony* ran another major profile on Aretha, a puff piece. "These days she is radiant with the glow of love," the reporter wrote, "but she is reluctant to identify the object of her affection."

She was not at all hesitant, though, to identify herself once again with the Mrs. Murphy role in *Blues Brothers*. She revived that character from the original film, this time singing "Respect" in the sequel that starred Dan Aykroyd and John Goodman, who took Belushi's place.

Her profile remained high and her career news remained positive. But then, at the start of the new year, Aretha suffered a major public relations setback in her hometown that sent her into a rage.

35. DAMAGE CONTROL

During my long conversations with Erma, she told me she
was concerned that her sister's charitable heart was not fully
understood or appreciated.

"Most people don't realize how much she's done, not merely
for her family but for people in need," Erma said. "I can't tell you
how many times over the years there'd be stories about families
who lost everything due to a storm or illness. Aretha would ask me
to get money to them anonymously. She just wanted to help. She
didn't care about the attention or the credit."

At the same time, she invited *Jet* magazine to a holiday party
she hosted in the auditorium of Detroit's Henry Ford Hospital that,
according to the magazine, "had hundreds of patients and staffers
dancing in their seats."

"For the next twenty minutes or so," Aretha told the patients,
"nobody here is going to be sick."

That was Christmas. Two months later, in February 1999, a
published report revealed another side of her character. The front-
page story from the *Detroit Free Press* carried the headline "Why
Doesn't Aretha Pay Her Bills?" The exposé went deep into Aretha's
finances, claiming that in the past ten years, more than thirty

lawsuits had been filed against her for nonpayment of bills. Virtually all her creditors were Detroit merchants and professionals. One of the more critical accusations came from Dean Pitcairn, owner of a limousine service. He insisted that Aretha tried to burn him. "I think it was the type of thing where [Franklin and her lawyers] felt if they prolonged it long enough, we would forget about them. It just made me mad because everyone thinks she's a big hero, and she doesn't think twice about stepping on little people." Pitcairn won a settlement of $1,500.

The list of other creditors—plumbers, florists, caterers—was long.

Harvey Tennen, a former judge and attorney who had represented Aretha in the past, explained that her economic woes were linked to her personal woes, especially the passing of her father and brother. Tennen also said that Aretha struggled with trusting others, thus taking on the burden of self-management.

"The truth of the matter," said Erma in response to the story, "is that this was pure karma. For years we'd been telling Aretha to get an accountant or a bookkeeper and give him or her the authority to pay bills. We've been telling her that she needs to be put on a budget because she never balances what she spends against what she earns. But every time we'd make suggestions, she'd fly into a fury and stop talking to us. We'd be frozen out for months at a time, simply for saying what was evidently true—that she requires help in the all-important area of money management."

Aretha's reaction to the *Free Press* article was immediate. She was infuriated and indignant. She told Erma that she planned to organize a boycott against the paper. Within a few days, she issued a statement and was quick to say that it was written by her and her alone.

"With respect to a front-page story that ran in a local paper, it is clearly, in my opinion and in the opinion of many others, a malicious and vicious attempt to discredit me by reprinting old, warmed-over news that local people knew about 15 years ago to have a cumulative effect with the general public. There was nothing new

about it. It certainly didn't deserve front-page or national attention, but I take responsibility for the handful of suits brought by a
small fraction out of the 99.9% of people who are paid responsibly
and in a timely way. There are many happy creditors who have my
business accounts. As reported in the said article, not one is owed
anything today and I have no knowledge nor do my representatives
have any knowledge of any suits with the state of Michigan. And
liens are not suits and cannot be construed as suits. They are
demands for payment with which we are all familiar. Due to my
travel and performance schedule and a lack of a secretary in place
during that period of time, that small fraction of people, less than
0.1% of the people with whom I do business, who were not paid,
utilized their option to sue. That is not uncommon. Celebrities are
sued every day for a number of reasons. And sometimes, some people just want their 15 minutes of fame and some people resent having to wait for payment. Others are legitimate. I am very sorry that
it had to come to the suit status, however, this was not intentional.
I intended no malice, no disrespect, and no lack of concern for the
working people and small businesses of Detroit. I have never purchased any goods or services without the intention of paying my
bills in a timely and responsible manner."

Undaunted by the bad press, Aretha threw herself a gala fifty-
seventh birthday party in March at the Atrium Gardens in Southfield, Michigan. Mayor Dennis Archer attended, along with a slew
of local celebrities. Chaka Khan and Nnenna Freelon performed.

"We were all excited when Aretha told us that Prince Rainier
had personally invited her to a command performance in Monaco,"
Erma remembered. "It was going to be a gala occasion in the
springtime, and my sister had her heart set on performing. After
Monaco, she was planning to spend time in Paris, a city she loved
dearly and hadn't visited for nearly thirty years. We were all hoping
that the lure of such a glamorous trip would finally motivate her to
come to terms with her fear of flying. She tried her best, just as she
had tried in the past. But, just like the past, when it came time to
step on the plane, Aretha was nowhere to be found."

She did step on the private bus—the only means of transporta-
tion in which she could control the schedule—to go down to
Washington, DC, in May, where she sang at the White House
Correspondents' Association's annual dinner and, according to the
New York Times, was paid $55,000. On the way to the event, she
talked about a new album she was planning. She was going to call
it *The Queen of Duets* and model it after Sinatra's successful duet
ventures. Soon after that, she told *Billboard* that the record was in
the works, but, like so many other Aretha-proclaimed projects, it was
never realized.

Despite all the starts and stops that had characterized her recent
career, her iconic status in American music never faltered. In fact,
it grew. When, for example, VH1 listed the one hundred greatest
women in rock and roll, Aretha was in the number-one position.

"I didn't even know that Aretha sang rock and roll," said Ruth
Bowen. "I thought she was an R-and-B singer, or a jazz singer, or
a gospel singer. When did the world start seeing her as a rock-
and-roller?"

Her private bus carried her to the Hamptons on Long Island,
New York, for a two-week summer vacation. During her stay, she
cohosted a fund-raiser for the Children's Academy of Harlem and
also threw a party at a grand mansion that once belonged to Henry
Ford. Guests included Christie Brinkley, Lloyd Price, Geoffrey
Holder, Freddie Jackson, and Star Jones.

The honors were unceasing. In September, she was back at the
White House, where President Clinton awarded her the National
Medal of Arts.

She viewed the publication of her autobiography on which we
had worked as another laudatory moment. *Aretha: From These Roots*
was finally published in the fall of 1999, some five years after we
had started it. Although she barred me—and everyone else—from
the final editing process, my name appeared on the cover as her
collaborator.

Aretha was invited to be the only guest on a segment of Oprah
Winfrey's hour-long TV show. Before she accepted the invitation,

though, she had two demands—that the women in the audience wear fancy dresses or gowns, and that the men wear suits or tuxes.

During the interview, Aretha was defensive about what she had not included in her book. She was anything but open and at times even combative. It was an awkward exchange. Afterward, the publisher's publicist said to me, "Aretha came off as so protective and private that the average reader is not going to want to read the book."

From These Roots appeared on the *New York Times* bestseller list for one week and then fell off. Sales were so weak that plans for a paperback reprint were scrapped. Reviews were largely negative, and there were no foreign editions. The main complaint was that Aretha revealed little.

"Why bother to write a book," said Ruth Bowen, "if you're not going to give it up? Aretha's book read like one long press release. To those who know her well, her lack of candor was nothing new. But why broadcast that kind of self-serving puff piece to the world? By trying to protect her image, all she did was damage it."

Yet as time went on, Aretha characterized her book as a commercial and critical triumph. In all our many encounters after its publication, she spoke of the work and its reception in glowing terms and considered it the one and only true chronicle of her life.

Part Five

THE LIONESS
IN WINTER

36. WHAT ARETHA WANTS

As the twentieth century came to an end, Aretha Franklin, approaching sixty, had established herself as one of America's most profoundly admired and influential singers. She had forged a trajectory that had carried her from gospel to jazz to pop to rhythm and blues and then back again. Having mastered each of these genres, she had learned to effectively bend and blend them with unforced naturalness. She was a jazzy gospel singer and a gospel-like jazz singer, a pop-wise soul singer and a soulful pop singer. Somewhere along the way, she was labeled a pioneer rock-and-roller, and, for good measure, she began performing operatic arias.

Her early years at Columbia had been hit or miss. At Atlantic she gained superstardom. For the rest of her career she tenaciously fought to retain that status. The struggle was great. A weaker artist would have wilted, and after a historic run of R&B, pop, and gospel hits in the late sixties and early seventies, she faced a drought. She came back with *Sparkle,* only to face another drought during the age of disco. She came back again in the eighties with her hits on Arista, and then faced a deeper drought in the nineties. Yet by the end of that decade, she was on the charts once again, and, with her triumphant "Nessun Dorma" performance at the Grammys, she returned to the spotlight and stood at the very center of our musical culture.

"You may not like all the stuff she did to stay popular," said her old producer Jerry Wexler. "You may be bothered by cracks in her voice and the lapses of taste when it came to material. There was a lot of cheesy shit. But in the end, you got to give it to her. The woman is fuckin' fierce. In a half dozen different epochs of music, she managed to stay in the middle of the mix. She isn't a Miles Davis, who kept breaking through barriers and never stopped innovating. And she isn't a Duke Ellington or a Marvin Gaye, who never stopped writing brilliantly. She chiefly became an interpreter and an adapter of very diverse material. She studied the *Billboard* charts and, for over forty years, found a way to stay on those charts. That's one hell of an accomplishment."

But beginning in 2000 and continuing for the next thirteen years, she would not realize another commercial success of any consequence. Her public appearances would be less frequent and her recordings far fewer. According to her closest relatives, her moods would darken as her emotional volatility intensified.

Her family would also observe her falling into a long one-sided fantasy affair with Tavis Smiley, the well-respected broadcast journalist who, while friendly with Aretha, had not the slightest interest in a romantic relationship. Yet Aretha spoke of their having a major love affair, had even titled an album after the imagined affair's demise.

"When it comes to men," Ruth Bowen told me, "Aretha's always been able to delude herself. But these days she's so far over the top, it's crazy."

The one project that hardly seemed delusional—her duets album—kept coming up whenever I spoke with her. During one of our conversations, she asked me to write liner notes and promised that a track listing would be forthcoming.

In March 2000, *Billboard* reported, "Aretha's long-awaited 'Duets' LP is set to drop June 20. Final song lineup is still being determined but one confirmed track is the Grammy-nominated duet with Mary J. Blige, 'Don't Waste Your Time.'"

That song had been included on Blige's 1999 *Mary* album, a project that in some ways took its marketing cue from Aretha. Moving to the right of hard-core hip-hop, Mary J., like Aretha, collaborated with Elton John and Lauryn Hill in addition to doing a Diane Warren ballad, "Give Me You," featuring Eric Clapton.

"Aretha had these grandiose plans to record with the great artists of our time," said Ruth Bowen. "She was talking about everyone from Julio Iglesias to Tony Bennett to R. Kelly. I thought it was the right move, and I presume Clive Davis felt the same. But then came Aretha's demands and her schedule changes and her cancellations and God knows what else. The record didn't have a chance. It fell apart in the planning stage because Aretha refused to have anyone help her with the planning. Her control thing was getting worse by the day."

If she couldn't control the production and release of her duets album, at least she could control her birthday parties.

"She loved those parties," said her brother Vaughn, "and loved to fuss over all the details. They were always in Detroit and she always had her choice of entertainers. She always liked having the local TV stars. That's because she watched the news every night and got a kick out of seeing the news-anchor personalities at the party. For her fifty-eighth birthday party at the Town Center Atrium Garden in Southfield, Mayor Dennis Archer showed up and so did Lloyd Price. She had Rose Royce playing 'Car Wash' and Pete Escovedo playing cool Latin jazz."

That summer she was back at the JVC Jazz Festival, where she had her problems. The *New York Times* headline was "What Aretha Wants and Needs, She Doesn't Always Get." Reviewer Ben Ratliff wrote, "By the third request to her band to lower its volume, Aretha Franklin wasn't kidding around. She fixed her eyes on her bandleader and got an ovation from the crowd when she asked him, specifically, to fix the problem. But the evening had already lost so much momentum that there was virtually no way Saturday night's concert at Avery Fisher Hall…was going to end up very satisfying."

Whether it was the muddled sound mix or a bloated band

playing out of tune, all evening long, Aretha struggled to find her form. The tried-and-true medley of her hits—"Respect," "Think," "Ain't No Way"—felt gratuitous and uninspired. She sang "Nessun Dorma," by now part of her repertoire, with surprising indifference. For me, the only moving moment came when she went to the piano to accompany herself on Leon Russell's "A Song for You," sung for Johnnie Taylor, the recently deceased R&B titan whom she had known since the fifties, when they traveled the same gospel circuit.

While she generously paid tribute to the fallen colleagues from her early years, it would take little to rekindle her spirit of rivalry. That November, for example, she became enraged when Natalie Cole's recently released autobiography, *Angel on My Shoulder,* described how Aretha had snubbed Cole: "She would get upset if I was on the same TV show with her, and she would walk out of the room if I walked in. That really hurt." When Aretha read those words, she called me to say that she was furious. She claimed that no such thing had ever happened and wanted to write a rebuttal. I pointed out that Natalie's next lines read "Thankfully, that's changed. Aretha and I are now friends." Ultimately Aretha dropped the idea of defending herself.

Some months later, when she sang on a live recording with James Carter at a famed Detroit jazz club, Natalie was in the audience cheering her on. However, Aretha's performances were excluded from the album, *Live at Baker's Keyboard Lounge.* When I asked Ahmet Ertegun, Aretha's great friend and executive producer of Carter's Atlantic album, why, he said, "I was able to use my influence to get Aretha to come to the club and sing. As usual, she sang magnificently. But when it came to the business negotiations, things got complicated and I had to bow out."

During the winter of 2000, the business of booking Aretha faced serious challenges. According to Dick Alen, her agent at William Morris, this was a period when the demand for Aretha had slowed down considerably. "It had been three or four years since her last studio album," said Alen. "She had no new product out there and the offers weren't what they used to be. Fortunately, VH One came up with an idea to honor her on a *Divas Live* program. That saved the day. It kept Aretha in the spotlight during a period that otherwise was pretty dark."

Billed as a tribute to Aretha, the show from New York's Radio City Music Hall was broadcast in April 2001. A benefit for VH1's Save the Music Foundation, the program featured everyone from jazz trumpeter Clark Terry to Mary J. Blige to Kid Rock to Bishop Paul Morton of the Greater St. Stephen Full Gospel Baptist Church Ministries. Aretha was in high spirits, especially doing her witty musical dialogue with Stevie Wonder.

"Aretha loved the *Divas Live* shows and they did her a world of good," Erma told me. "We were getting along well when I came over to her house to congratulate her on her TV performance. The reviews were all great. I was used to seeing Aretha's house in disorder. That was just her way. But when I got there, it was far worse than I had ever seen. It was chaos. She still hadn't unpacked from her last trip two weeks before. Opened suitcases with clothes falling out were everywhere. Plastic bags from the dry cleaners were piled up on the floor. Dishes were piled in the sink. Aretha said she had to fire her housekeeper. I didn't ask why. Aretha has always had problems trusting housekeepers. I wasn't going to say a word until I looked under the coffee table in the living room and, stuck between old copies of *Vogue* magazine, spotted a royalty check for twenty thousand dollars. 'Aretha,' I said. 'You need to get better organized. You're about to lose a big check.' 'What check?' she asked. When I pointed it out, she bent down, picked it up, stuffed it in her purse, and asked me who I was to criticize her. 'I'll have you know that I'm extremely well organized,' she said. After that she wouldn't talk to me for weeks."

In August 2001, Erma was diagnosed with cancer. It was her daughter, Sabrina, and cousin Brenda who told Aretha.

"Aretha became furious," Sabrina told me. "She flew off the

handle and said that my mother's doctors were incompetent and
didn't know what they were talking about. She kept saying, 'Don't
call me with bad news like this. I just don't want to hear it. I don't
believe it, not for a minute.' I knew that, when it came to her own
life, Aretha lived in great denial. But this was different. This was a
matter of applying her denial to the physical condition of someone
else. It was almost as if her rejection would make the cancer diagnosis go away. Aretha had suffered the loss of her dad, her sister
Carolyn, and her brother Cecil. She simply didn't want to deal
with the prospect of losing her sister Erma.

"When Aretha could no longer deny the accuracy of the prog-
nosis, she called my mother often but was reluctant to visit. After a
few months, though, she did stop by with tons of groceries. She'd
stay and cook lavish dinners. By then Mom didn't have much appetite but she appreciated Aretha's effort. Their rift was finally healed
and their disagreements and misunderstandings all behind them.
They talked warmly and laughed freely. Those visits did my mother
a world of good. As Mom grew sicker, Aretha showed up more
frequently. She also paid Eva Greene, my mother's neighbor and
closest friend, to move in and care for Mom. Aretha would send
my mother beautiful fresh flowers—Gerbera daisies—to brighten
her room, along with fresh fruit baskets, CDs, magazines, and all
sorts of goodies she thought would help her sister's spirit. My view
of the Erma-Aretha relationship was this: It was highly complicated. Their history had definitely been marked by intense sibling
rivalry. But in the end, they loved and understood each other on
the deepest level. Everyone knew not to get in the middle of their
disagreements because the sisters would eventually work things
out. When my mother passed on September seventh, 2002, some
fourteen months after the diagnosis, she and Aretha were certainly
at peace with one another, and that was beautiful."

Aretha's grief intensified with the death of her brother Vaughn
nine weeks later. His passing was another crushing blow.

"The more people Aretha lost," said her sister-in-law Earline,
"the less people she trusted. That's when she became more control-

ling. That's also when her weight got out of control. Fear had her wanting to control everyone and everything, but the one thing she couldn't control was her appetite. And the more anxious she became, the more she ate."

Her mood wasn't helped when, in November of 2001, the *Detroit Free Press* reported that Aretha had sued the tabloid the *Star* "for a story last year describing her as an out-of-control drunk." The report was indeed false. Aretha had not had a drink since the early seventies. According to Aretha, the tabloid settled with her out of court and issued an apology.

"That vicious and untrue article put Aretha in an understandably terrible mood," said Ruth Bowen. "You combine that with Erma getting so sick and passing away so quickly, you can imagine how down she was. Then in November one of her big houses in the Detroit burbs burned to the ground. She hadn't lived in that one for years, but she kept all sorts of clothes and records stored there. Everything went up in flames."

In January 2003, the *Detroit Free Press* reported that Franklin wouldn't cooperate with investigators looking into the fire but that she relented after being subpoenaed.

"Aretha hates any publicity that's not completely positive, and this fire story darkened her mood," said Ruth Bowen. "No one ever discovered the cause of the blaze, but the papers made it sound like there was funny business when there wasn't. I told Ree to forget the whole thing and just concentrate on recording a new record. It had been six years since *A Rose Is Still a Rose*. By then L. A. Reid had taken over Arista and was hungry for some Aretha product. Given how she was struggling, though, I couldn't imagine what kind of record she wanted to make. But count on Aretha to act like nothing was wrong. In the midst of her misery, she called her new album *So Damn Happy*."

37. OLDIES BUT GOODIES

O ne of the most attractive aspects of Aretha's public persona was her unabashed nostalgia. She had passionate fondness for the music of her youth and deep regard for her contemporaries who performed that music with such singular style.

In 2003, Aretha agreed to cohost an installment of *American Soundtrack,* a PBS series of concert shows produced by WGED in Pittsburgh. It was basically an oldies show geared to the aging-baby-boomer market. Her cohost would be Lou Rawls and the other entertainers included her former boyfriend Dennis Edwards as well as Gloria Gaynor and Mary Wilson.

"Ree loves old school," said Ruth Bowen. "She has great appreciation of her contemporaries and is rightfully proud of the rich lineage of rhythm and blues that she's so much a part of. But she's also said that she never wants to go out on the oldies circuit. She agreed to do it because the money was right and also because she wanted to sing with Lou."

The Aretha/Lou Rawls duet, "At Last," is a rereading of the classic long associated with Etta James. Excited by Lou's ultra-relaxed presence and nuanced gospel shadings, Aretha tells the audience, "Sounds like the Pilgrim Travelers to me." The reference is to the fifties gospel group with whom Rawls originally sang. Aretha is in fine form, turning in one of her great performances of the 2000s.

"The show made her happy," said Ruth. "It did her good to reconnect to so many of the soul stars she came up with. But the next day she was on the phone telling me that she had no intention of being typecast as an aging diva. In fact, she was going to do a hip-hop record. 'Oh no, you're not,' I said. 'Just watch me' was her reply."

That record—*So Damn Happy*—would more accurately be called hip-hop-influenced. Troy Taylor cowrote and produced three of the tracks, including the first single, "The Only Thing Missin'."

"I had been writing songs with Mary J. Blige," said Taylor, "originally designed for her reunion album with Puffy Combs. At the last minute, Mary thought Puffy was being too controlling, so she withdrew from the project. Around the same time L. A. Reid, looking for a cutting-edge R-and-B album for Aretha, called to see if I was willing. Was I! Mary was thrilled to have Aretha do the songs. In fact, Mary sings background on one of them—'Holdin' On.' We recorded in Aretha's living room, where she had set up a studio. I've produced a lot of legends, including Patti LaBelle and Ron Isley, and I like to think I come prepared and confident. But my preparation was nothing compared to Aretha's. When I looked at the lyric sheet on the piano I saw that she had made all sorts of notations, where she would twist the melody this way or that. She had a complete vision of how to sing the song. So when it came time to lay down the vocals, she pulled it off in one or two takes. When I suggested that she scat, she jumped right into it. I've always considered Aretha one of the dopest scatters, and she proved me right. Later I learned that she had recently lost some dear family members, but you'd never know it by her demeanor at those sessions. She was the complete professional. And as far as critics claiming that her voice was off, I strongly disagree. She could—and did—reach any note she wanted to reach."

Gordon Chambers, who cowrote "The Only Thing Missin'" and cowrote and produced "Ain't No Way," had much the same reaction.

"When I arrived at her home studio in Detroit," said Chambers, "she was at the piano practicing. I discovered that she not only learns the song by listening to the tapes, but she actually works out the song on piano. That's how she's able to Aretha-ize it. In her golden era, she may have sung more full-out from her chest and was now singing more from her head, but she knew how to make that adjustment flawlessly. I was a little reluctant to make any suggestions whatsoever, but at one point I gathered my courage and said, 'That last verse was great but I'd love to hear you sing it again.' She looked me up and down in a school principal–diva way and said, 'I don't know what you think is wrong with that verse but I'll do it again.' The second time she sang it with more fire. 'It was good before,' she said, 'but now it's better.' That was her way of saying I had good ears.

"She was also extremely gracious. I heard stories about eating collard greens with Aunt Ree Ree in the kitchen. But this was strictly gourmet. She had a beautiful spread of all sorts of exotic foods, including Middle Eastern fare. She made us all feel welcome. After the album came out, I went to see her at Radio City. My mother was with me that night, and when Aretha asked me to stand and introduced me to the audience, that meant the world to me. No other artist had treated me with such respect."

Burt Bacharach also produced one of the album cuts — "Falling Out of Love," a song he wrote with Jed and Jerry Leiber.

"I actually wrote three or four songs that she recorded in that period," Bacharach told me. "My idea was to write the arrangement in LA and cut the track before going to Detroit to produce the vocal. On 'Falling Out of Love,' the only song that made it on that record, I played the arrangement for her over the phone. I wrote it in G. 'It's too low, Burt,' she said. 'I think it's right in your ballpark, Aretha.' 'Well, please try it a minor third higher.' 'I'm afraid that'll be too high,' I gently pushed back. With that, she took the phone over to the piano and started playing it a minor third higher. She was absolutely right. It sounded better. When I arrived in Detroit, she invited me to her home studio and said, 'The background singers are all set.' 'The arrangement doesn't call for background singers,' I said. 'Oh, you'll love the background parts.' And I did. Aretha wrote extremely tasteful and beautifully harmonious backgrounds.

"The only minor disagreement we had involved interpretation. Because these were all new songs, I encouraged her to sing the melodies as written, at least in the opening verses and chorus. After that she could introduce whatever variations she liked. For the most part she was accommodating. But because Aretha is both a flawless singer and a brilliant interpretative artist, it's difficult for her not to put on her own spin. In the end, her spins usually improved the original material."

The first single, "The Only Thing Missin'," released in the summer of 2003, was well received. "Aretha Franklin sounds more natural than she has in years," Jon Pareles said in the *New York Times*.

In *Billboard*, Fred Bronson wrote, "The four-year, nine-month gap between Aretha Franklin's most recent hit ('Here We Go Again' in 1998) and...'The Only Thing Missin'' is by far the longest break in her extensive r&b singles chart history."

"I was still amazed that after Erma and Vaughn's deaths," said Ruth Bowen, "Aretha could call her record *So Damn Happy*. But that's her way of coping—pretending that sadness and suffering don't really exist. It works for her most of the time, but then, before the release of the record, when Luther Vandross fell so sick, she couldn't keep up the façade. She couldn't go around saying that she was still 'so damn happy.' Luther's tragedy hit her really hard. For all their dueling-diva dramas, she was crazy about him."

On April 16, 2003, Luther suffered a near-fatal stroke in his apartment in midtown Manhattan. A month later, Aretha held a candlelight vigil and prayer service at the Little Rock Baptist Church in Detroit, recruiting the Four Tops and the Ebenezer Mass Choir. On several occasions, she held private prayer vigils in her home in Bloomfield Hills.

"Her intentions were all good," said Ruth Bowen. "It was as though by praying long and hard, she could get God Himself to save Luther's life. She figured that if God was gonna listen to anyone, He'd listen to Aretha. But unfortunately, Luther got worse. And despite all this 'so damn happy' business, no one was sadder than Aretha."

Sadness briefly turned to delight in July when, during a concert in Atlanta, she was joined onstage by ex-boyfriend Dennis Edwards, who transposed the Temptations' "My Girl" into "My Queen."

On one of her favorite stages—New York City's Radio City Music Hall—she gave an especially lackluster performance. It felt like the same-old-same-old to me. Only a medley of some of her earliest material on Columbia, including a stirring "Skylark" and "Try a Little Tenderness," seemed to challenge her enormous interpretative gifts. She spent a great deal of time complaining about the sound system. After the concert she told me that she had regrets about missing that afternoon's rehearsal. "My agents and publicists are pushing me in too many directions at once," she said.

She had no regrets, though, about the laudatory profile in *Jet* in which she exclaimed that her new beau, whom she refused to name, "is making me so damn happy." She also discussed, without details, the upbeat careers of her sons Kecalf, Eddie, and Teddy. "Eddie is going to be recording soon and I will record him on my own label." She also mentioned plans to open her own booking agency, Crown Booking, to handle her own dates as well as other artists', like her sons'.

"I knew that Crown Booking was a dig at Queen Booking, my agency that for so many years had been helping Aretha get more and more money," said Ruth Bowen. "She was mad at me because I couldn't get her the astronomical fees she was asking for. She thought she could get Janet Jackson or Michael Jackson or

Madonna money. But of course that was ridiculous. As for starting her own booking agency, that was more of her delusional thinking. She couldn't even balance her own checking account. How the hell was she gonna run a booking business? Naturally it never happened. She wound up going back to Dick Alen at William Morris, the only man in America patient enough to put up with her bullshit."

"This is a big breakthrough," Aretha told me when we spoke in early 2004. "I've made up my mind to come to California this summer! Do you realize that I haven't sung on the West Coast for over twenty years?"

"Are you flying?"

"I wish," she said. "We're going on my bus, and we're going to take our time getting there."

After our pleasant conversation, I called Ruth Bowen for a reality check. Was Aretha really riding across the country? "She's been wanting to play LA for years," said Ruth, "but she always winds up canceling. The thought of that long bus ride is too much for her. She also hates the idea of riding through the Rockies. One time she agreed to go the southern route, through Texas and New Mexico, but then she heard weather reports about impending storms and changed her mind. But this time she sounds like she's sticking to her guns. She's booked for two nights at the Greek Theater. But that's way off in September. I wouldn't be surprised if she cancels."

That spring, Aretha spoke to *Ebony* about breaking up with her boyfriend, but, as usual, she would not name him. "I cannot believe that I was this naïve and gullible at this point in my life," she said. "When you love somebody, it's sometimes kind of hard to see everything that you need to see. It's a lot easier when you're not emotionally involved." She went on to make three vows: "I'm going to lose weight, get more organized, and I'm going to leave these bullshit men alone."

In this same period she was treated for an allergic reaction to antibiotics at Detroit's Sinai-Grace Hospital. She made a point of telling the press that Clive Davis had sent flowers.

"I can't tell you all the times that Aretha had broken off communication with Clive," said Ruth Bowen. "It was always about money demands. She wanted crazy advances that he wouldn't pay. But ultimately, they'd always get back together because she's got the prestige and he's got the clout. To be frank, they're like two aging queens basking in each other's glory. Aretha is the Queen of Soul and Clive is the Queen of Pop Radio. They fawn over each other to where it's sickening. They never get tired of kissing each other's behind. If you read what Aretha says about Clive in her album acknowledgments it's always, 'The epitome of a great record man, the very urbane and esteemed Clive Davis.' Clive eats that shit up. And she just loves how he escorts her to his fancy-shmancy Grammy parties."

The death of another old friend affected her mightily. Knowing I was close to Ray Charles, Aretha called me after he passed, on June 10, 2004. She wanted to know where to send flowers. She talked lovingly of the time she brought him to the stage of the Fillmore West to sing "Spirit in the Dark." In her statement to the press she spoke of his courage and confidence:

"He had a broad scope of music and could deliver it with savoir faire, no matter what genre it was in. His courage also stands out to me as much as his musicology, how he had the courage to go on after his mother died by the time he was fifteen. I'll also remember his level of confidence. He was confident on every level as a writer, as a producer, as a singer. He also had a charitable soul."

Aretha's own charitable soul was evident when she sang a benefit for the Southwest Women Working Together in Chicago, an organization formed to help women and children victimized by domestic violence.

She also made good on the promise to take that long bus trip to

California. She sold out the Greek Theater in Los Angeles on September 17 and 18. In attendance were both Clive Davis and Tavis Smiley, who the day before had interviewed her for his television show. This encounter perpetuated Aretha's one-sided infatuation with Smiley.

"She went around saying how they were an item," said Earline. "She even implied that they'd get married. But everyone who knew the real story understood that Tavis respected her as an artist and that was it. He wasn't about to be Aretha's boy toy. He's just not that guy. But she went on for years acting like—or, better yet, *pretending* like it was this torrid affair. Believe me, it wasn't."

The opening-night concert itself was a disappointment. She started strong, reaching back to her Columbia days for a soaring "Try a Little Tenderness." But from there it was downhill. There was a perfunctory medley of her hits and strangely ineffective hip-hop-ish choreography from a dance troupe. Her great weight had her looking sluggish, and the once glorious top range of her voice was gone. Teddy Richards, her talented son with Ted White, was, as he had been since 1984, her featured guitarist.

"It took her forever to get back to Detroit," said Ruth Bowen, "because she didn't like driving more than a few hundred miles a day. She told me that she was so exhausted from the trip she was taking off the rest of the year. When she did get home, I think she must have had another falling-out with Clive because she started telling me about her Aretha's Records, her own label where finally no one could tell her what to do. 'But Aretha,' I said, 'no one's been telling you what to do for the last twenty-five years. What the hell are you talking about?' That's when she decided she wasn't talking to me again."

On March 26, 2005, Gail Mitchell reported in *Billboard* that Aretha was planning a June release "for her still-untitled album." It was all set to be on Aretha's Records with guests Faith Hill, Dennis Edwards, and gospel singer Smokie Norful. The record never came out.

In June she appeared at Madison Square Garden, headlining a show for the twenty-second annual McDonald's Gospelfest.

"It's time to renew those gospel roots," she told me. "I'm bringing in Joe Ligon from the Mighty Clouds of Joy," the same Ligon who sang on her self-produced *One Lord, One Faith, One Baptism* back in 1987.

The highlight was her version of "Amazing Grace," a hymn that never failed to excite her boldest creative instincts.

Then in July, along with Alicia Keys, Patti Austin, and Patti LaBelle, Aretha sang at Luther Vandross's funeral at New York's Riverside Church. He had died at age fifty-three. She later wrote that "he was so earthy and down. But as down and earthy as he was, he was just as classy and elegant. And the most beautiful part was that he was real and not plastic. He was very much the gentleman. I just enjoyed him being the superb vocalist and person that he was. 'Get It Right' is my opening song to this day. Real friendships are rare. He was full of fun, humor, and wit. We didn't have to spend a lot of time together to know that we were friends. We knew that."

"I felt the need to do more gospel," Aretha told me after the death of Luther. "I've always felt that need and I always will. But losing all these beautiful people who were so close to me, well, I needed to express my feelings in the songs that had comforted me ever since I was a little girl."

In July, at a revival at Detroit's Greater Emmanuel Church, Aretha did just that. Along with the Spiritual QCs, Beverly Crawford, and Candi Staton, she sang the old church songs that brought back happy memories of traveling with her dad as a teenager.

"I was especially happy to see Candi," said Aretha. "I knew her long before she had her pop hit with 'Young Hearts Run Free' in the seventies. I knew her when she was in the Jewel Gospel Singers and I'd go see them sing at the Apollo. Back then she was calling herself Cassietta and she was one of the best. So to share a pulpit with her again at this mature time of our lives was a beautiful blessing."

That sacred/secular switch, repeatedly turned off and on

throughout Aretha's career, was heavily employed in 2005. Shortly after the Detroit gospel fete, she scatted on the remix of "I Gotta Make It," a self-determination anthem by young R&B heartthrob Trey Songz, who sang in the R. Kelly mode of seductive soul. As she had done on Lauryn Hill's "A Rose Is Still a Rose," Aretha played the part of the sagacious matriarch, doling out advice to a younger generation.

Switching tracks again, she paid homage to an older generation in her soaring tribute to the great matriarch of the civil rights movement Rosa Parks, who died on October 24, 2005. She was the first woman to lie in state in the rotunda of the Capitol in Washington, DC, after which her casket was returned to Detroit, where for two days it remained in view at the city's Museum of African American Culture. Thousands of people walked by in tribute. Then, on November 2, at Detroit's Greater Grace Temple, her funeral was held in the city where she had lived since the sixties.

The seven-hour, twenty-eight-minute service was broadcast on CNN. The rhetoric was extravagant. Tributes were offered by, among others, then-senators Hillary Clinton and Barack Obama and ministers Jesse Jackson, Al Sharpton, Louis Farrakhan, and T. D. Jakes. The emotional high point, though, wasn't spoken but musical — Aretha's inspired treatment of "The Impossible Dream," the syrupy ballad from the Broadway musical *Man of La Mancha* magically transformed into a sacred hymn.

In that same month, Aretha traveled to Washington, DC, where she overlooked party differences and accepted the Presidential Medal of Freedom from George W. Bush. Among the others honored were Carol Burnett, Alan Greenspan, Muhammad Ali, Andy Griffith, Paul Harvey, and Jack Nicklaus.

Like Aretha, Lou Rawls was a singer who had followed the road from gospel to R&B to jazz and pop. When he died, in January

2006, Aretha felt that his contributions were woefully underrated. "He'd begun in the church," she told me, "and then spread out to the world. He had his hits but he was bigger than that. He covered all the bases. He was a giant."

In June, upon the passing of her longtime arranger Arif Mardin, she celebrated his great talent, saying, "What arrangers Nelson Riddle and Billy May did for Sinatra, Arif did for me. He was the best of the best."

Learning of James Brown's death that December, she argued that he was every bit as important as Duke Ellington, calling him "the most exciting and thrilling R-and-B male performer of all time."

It was a string of difficult passings, and the loss of her colleagues was taking its toll. In considering her own mortality, she began telling friends that her next major project would be producing a Broadway show from her autobiography *Aretha: From These Roots*. Over the next several years she would hold auditions in Detroit and Los Angeles. She'd throw out names to the press of women who might play her—everyone from Jennifer Hudson to Halle Berry—but plans never got off the drawing board. Investors were never found. At one point, she said that instead of a musical, her life story would be turned into a feature film. When she was asked about a script, she said it would be based strictly upon her book and that she would have total control over every aspect of the movie. But nothing ever materialized.

"R&B is alive and well," she told *Jet* in June 2007. In the article she listed the current artists she admired most—Erykah Badu, Jill Scott, Soulchild, Ne-Yo, Chris Brown, Mary J, Trey Songz, Anthony Hamilton, Gerald Levert, and Nelly.

She saw no reason why she couldn't be as popular as the performers she named. She put the blame for her faltering sales on Arista. All year, she had been privately complaining that Arista was not promoting her properly and owed her money long past due. That winter she went public, telling the *New York Times* that *Jewels in the Crown,* a compilation of previously released duets, would be her last album on Arista. She and Clive Davis had fallen out. "It's over," she told Jon Pareles. "You might as well say it's over." Clive demurred: "The lawyers say that there are cuts owned. I don't know that for a fact. I have not gotten into that. She and I, we've had a long relationship."

She announced the launching of her own label, Aretha's Records, and said that her first album, *A Woman Falling Out of Love,* was already complete. All she lacked was a distributor. She also said that she had selected the title "because it happens to be true. It was based on a relationship that I had, and it just didn't happen for a number of reasons." Her close relatives told me that this was simply Aretha inventing high romantic drama around her platonic relationship with Tavis Smiley.

As she had been doing for the past decade, she declared her intention to enroll at Juilliard to study classical piano, another plan that would remain unrealized.

Jet put her on the cover to discuss her weight, which had dramatically increased. She blamed it on giving up smoking in 1992 and vowed to diet. When asked whether she was backing Hillary Clinton or Barack Obama for the Democratic nomination, she had praise for them both and remained undecided.

In the winter of 2008, she rode her tour bus to the West Coast, where she appeared at LA's Nokia Theater. Then it was back on the bus to New York.

The Radio City Music Hall show came two days before her sixty-sixth birthday on Easter Sunday. To my ears, she sounded uninspired and tentative. After singing "Respect," she asked her musical director H. B. Barnum to help her with a strap that had come undone on one of her shoes. The result was that Barnum was literally kneeling at Aretha's feet.

"I didn't mind," he told me afterward. "After all, she *is* the Queen."

The next number was her rendition of Keyshia Cole's "I Remember," at the time a huge hip-hop/R&B hit. To help her with the song, she enlisted Ali Ollie Woodson. A lead singer powerful enough to be put in the same category as his Temptations predecessors David Ruffin and Dennis Edwards, Woodson told me, "When Aretha couldn't get hold of Dennis, she'd call me. Naturally I took that as a compliment because Dennis is one of the greats, but when I asked Aretha if I might have a slot on her show and maybe sing a couple of songs on my own, she took offense. She said I should be satisfied singing the bridge of Keyshia Cole's song. I knew better than to argue with the Queen, so I didn't."

"One day out of the blue the phone rings and it's Aretha Franklin," Keyshia Cole told me. "I was amazed. Like every young singer, I see her as the ultimate. She told me how much she liked my 'I Remember' and wanted me to write a song just as good for her. I was more than willing. I told her that the reason 'I Remember' worked so well was because it came out of a personal experience of mine. If she wanted me to custom-tailor such a song for her, I'd have to know what she was going through—personally. That made her clam up. 'If I tell you that, you'll have to give me the publishing on the song.' 'I don't mind,' I said. 'Well, I'll have to get back to you.' She never did. Later, someone who's known her for years said that Aretha never reveals anything personal about herself. He called her the ice queen who never melts."

Aretha's collaboration with Keyshia Cole was never realized, but she did enjoy a successful duet with Mary J. Blige. In March, Aretha and Mary won a Grammy for their gospel duet "Never Gonna Break My Faith" from *Jewels in the Crown*.

But Aretha was miffed when on the Grammy telecast Beyoncé introduced Tina as "the Queen," a title Aretha jealously guarded as her own. Her statement to the press was strangely ambiguous: "I am not sure whose toes I may have stepped on or whose ego I may have bruised between the Grammy writers and Beyoncé. However, I dismissed it as a cheap shot for controversy. In addition to that, I thank the Grammys and the voting academy for my twentieth Grammy and love to Beyoncé anyway."

More bad press came during that same month of March — news reports that her home in Detroit was facing foreclosure. Aretha quickly called *Jet* to set the matter straight.

"This is not even the home where I live," she said. "If you listen to the news it sounded as if I was going to lose the house and tomorrow I would be out on the street corner selling pencils and pies on the corner . . . I went down and paid everything. This whole thing was much ado about nothing. They got the cart way ahead of the horse. Everything is fine now."

That summer her friend and most important producer, Jerry Wexler, died at ninety-one. His children planned his memorial in New York City for a time when they knew Aretha would be in Manhattan. As it turned out, her hotel was less than a mile from the service. On the day before the tribute, I called her several times, leaving messages to remind her of the time and place. Yet she failed to make an appearance. A few weeks later, when I asked what happened, she claimed not to have known about the memorial

Although she didn't show up for Jerry, that November she showed up in a big way in *Rolling Stone*. The magazine ran a feature about the one hundred greatest singers of the rock era, naming Aretha number one. For the next several years, she projected that honor on a big screen at all her concerts.

That same winter she released a lackluster and painfully overwrought Christmas album that she both produced and arranged. She used the opportunity to take a shot at her old mentors, writing in the liner notes, "I am thrilled to record the first Christmas LP of my career, and it is so unfortunate that John Hammond, Jerry Wexler, and Clive Davis never put this on the front burner because it is everything that I wanted it to be and more."

The album, distributed by Rhino, the Warner division responsible for her Atlantic reissues, received little notice in the press and sold poorly.

"Poor sales never bother Aretha," Earline told me. "She'll tell you that the record was really a big hit but the distributor, wanting to hide her royalties, is giving out false figures. Or she'll simply ignore the failure and move on to the next thing. Because Aretha is who she is—one of the great personalities in all American culture—the next thing keeps getting bigger and bigger. And in 2009, nothing was bigger than the inauguration of the first black president in American history."

38. A WOMAN FALLING
OUT OF LOVE

Given her unchallenged status as a singer of historic importance and as the artist whose "Respect" resonated with the
generation who broke through the barriers of racial discrimination, Aretha was, unsurprisingly, invited to sing at the inauguration of Barack Obama on January 20, 2009. In answer to the first
question any woman receiving such an invitation would ask herself—
What am I going to wear?—she surprised her critics, who have often
accused her of garish taste. She chose a tasteful gray outfit topped
off by a gray felt hat that became the day's most discussed fashion
item. After perusing the websites of Europe's storied designers,
Aretha found the perfect hat in Detroit. Its creator, Luke Song, a
thirty-six-year-old born in Seoul, Korea, had built a reputation
among the city's highly discriminating African American church
ladies. The chapeau is built around an oversize gray bow tilted on
its side.

Writing about her fashion choice for *Newsweek*, Aretha
observed, "They had to work on it a little bit, because I wanted it
edged in tiny rhinestones. And the bow was on the left side, but I
wanted it on the right. I have a favorite side...the right. I just think

it photographs better. The mistake I made was that I was looking at famous designers worldwide for something that ended up being right down the street."

The story was seen as another victory for downtrodden Detroit, a city that over the years Aretha had championed with relentless loyalty.

That freezing day in January she received higher marks for fashion than singing. In talking to the women on *The View,* she said she was displeased with her performance—"It was just too cold out there to sing," she said. When, four years later at Obama's second inauguration, Beyoncé caused a minor stir by lip-synching, Aretha was understanding, remarking, "I thought it was really funny, but she did a beautiful job with the pre-record...next time I'll probably do the same."

That winter, while promoting her Christmas album and discussing her upcoming new pop record, *A Woman Falling Out of Love,* she granted a series of interviews, including one to Rashod Ollison, entertainment writer for the *Virginian-Pilot* and an astute music critic. As Aretha approached her sixty-eighth birthday, I asked Ollison to explain his feelings about her.

"Besides my mother's, Aretha's voice is among the first I remember hearing," he wrote me. "My parents played her records constantly. The authority of her sound, especially in the way she sang gospel, anchored me. It still does. There are never any traces of self-pity in Aretha's music, even when the song is sad and she's pleading for a man's return. She always communicated a sense of transcendence, something she learned from the church, of course, but also from the salty blues of Dinah Washington.

"But in my interviews with her, and in the many I've read and seen on TV, Aretha's aloofness and slight condescension were always off-putting. She came off as petty, too. The palpably insecure woman, obsessed with staying relevant despite her towering legacy, is so strikingly different from the indomitable persona she conveys in her music.

"As a culture critic, part of my job is peeling back the layers, scraping away the glitter that sometimes deludes and mystifies fans. Aretha is gloriously complex, a musical genius, and there seems to be a lot of intriguing darkness and mystery behind the legacy. That isn't surprising.

"Like so many artists with such huge talent, there's often a disconnect inside. Perhaps it's necessary. Something within must remain childlike and wide-eyed in order for the art to be pure and adventurous. Who knows? But in Aretha's case, especially in the last 20 years or so—maybe longer—there hasn't been much adventure musically. [She] seems to be shoehorning her enormous gift into trite productions and trends. In concerts these days, she often coasts. It's unreasonable to expect her to sound the way she did in 1967, or perform with the same vitality. (I must note that her contemporary Gladys Knight, whom Aretha has shaded many times in interviews, holds up amazingly well onstage these days, sounding almost the way she did in 1973, if not better.) Aretha's lack of musical engagement onstage, exacerbated by the booming Vegas-style arrangements, never fails to disappoint."

Aretha's longtime booking agent, adviser, and friend Ruth Bowen died in May 2009. In my last interview with her, she said, "I love that girl and always will. Never did meet anyone who needed a mother as bad as Aretha did. And maybe, at least for a while, I served that role. But only a mother could put up with Aretha's fits and changing moods. I couldn't. And only a mother could love those cheesy shows she kept putting on. When she asked me what I thought, I couldn't lie. I had to tell her, 'Get a big-time producer. Get someone who knows how to stage a show. Quit trying to control everyone and everything. Quit trying to do all this shit by yourself. Admit your limitations. We all got 'em, even a genius like you.' But everything I said fell on deaf ears. She didn't want to hear it, and that's why, for all the love between us, we kept falling out."

That summer Aretha sang at both the Hollywood Bowl, where she paid tribute to Michael Jackson, whose recent death had shocked the world, and Radio City Music Hall. During these performances, she resorted to what Jerry Wexler used to call "over-souling"— too heavy on the melisma, overwrought emotionality, musicality overwhelmed by theatricality.

The year 2010 began quietly. She spent the winter in Detroit, drifting in and out of the studio. The recording of the *Woman Falling Out of Love* album was slow going. She took months to select songs and cultivate the tracks. She was still estranged from Clive Davis and determined to remain free of any major label. This time she would be not only her own producer, but her own record executive as well. No second opinions, no interference.

At one point she played a version of the record for executives from Rhino Records, the Warner division that controlled the Atlantic catalog and a logical candidate to distribute her album.

"The president of the label and I were called from LA," said Cheryl Pawelski, then head of A&R for Rhino, "for a private meeting at the Trump International Hotel in New York. We were excited at the possibility of bringing out a new Aretha record. We waited downstairs in the lobby for quite a while before being ferried upstairs, where Aretha had an entire floor to herself. Her suite was sweltering. Apparently she doesn't like air-conditioning. It was also filled with huge flower arrangements sent by Elton John and Mariah Carey for her recent birthday. She was quite cordial. As we listened to the record, she ate breakfast. I commented that the pianist on three of the tracks was superb and I suspected the player was Aretha herself. She was pleased that I had identified her correctly. As a whole, though, the record didn't work for me. There were multiple producers and multiple genres. It was all over the map and far from remarkable. Naturally I didn't express my opinion. Nor was my opinion sought. After the last track was played, we congratulated her, thanked her for her time, and left. When we learned that she was demanding an advance of a million dollars, we quickly passed. Even if the album had been great, the price would be high.

But for a record as disconnected as this one, I felt the price was unrealistic."

In July, Aretha appeared in Philadelphia along with, improbably enough, former secretary of state Condoleezza Rice, who had been trained as a concert pianist. Ms. Rice played various selections by Mozart, and, in closing the show, Aretha sang a medley of her hits.

That same summer she shot a humorous commercial for Snickers candy bar that played off her grand diva image. Of the four teenage boys riding in a car, two are ravenously hungry to the point that they transform into short-tempered divas, played by Aretha and Liza Minnelli.

Then in the fall of 2010, everything changed. Aretha fell seriously ill. Excruciating stomach pain led her to cancel all engagements. Tests were conducted. Major surgery was required. In December, the *National Enquirer* ran a headline that said "Aretha Franklin, 6 Months to Live! Her Pancreatic Cancer Battle." Later, Aretha denied any dire diagnosis while refusing to name the ailment.

Aretha had long lived with the contradictory attitude of wanting great attention while insisting on absolute privacy. At this point, her obsession for privacy overwhelmed everything else. She insisted that not a single word about the nature of her sickness be spoken by anyone close to her. She would not entertain one question regarding her malady. Beyond saying that she was sick, her handlers were forbidden to offer even the smallest detail. When cousin Brenda suggested that Aretha might go public with her diagnosis as a way to encourage others to seek treatment, she bristled. "You are confused," she said. "There's nothing that wrong with me." Once again denial set in—this time stronger than ever.

"That's just Aretha's way," said her sister-in-law Earline. "She'll never change. It doesn't matter that many public figures afflicted with physical diseases discuss it openly and use it as an opportunity to bring awareness of these maladies. Aretha reacts the opposite way. She shuts down completely. When she was dealing with alcohol in the sixties and seventies, she wouldn't say a word about it.

Same thing with her mysterious stomach ailments in 2010. I got the feeling that she felt if the facts about her sickness got out there, it would harm her career."

"After her big operation that winter," said niece Sabrina, "those closest to her spent an enormous amount of time in the hospital with her. She appreciated that—but then she didn't. Once she got home, she became moodier than ever. If you inadvertently said the wrong word to her, she might turn on you and not speak to you for weeks. That was certainly the case with me and my cousin Brenda. She also turned on people who had worked with her for years. She was firing longtime employees for reasons no one understood. Naturally, after major surgery, you're in a vulnerable emotional state. But with Aretha it was far more than that. It was as though she was chasing away the people who loved her most."

"I've known Ree my entire life," a longtime member of New Bethel, the church founded by Aretha's father, told me. "When I read that article in the National Enquirer, I didn't believe that cancer was going to kill her—not for a minute. If anyone's strong enough to scare away cancer, it's Aretha. If I were cancer, I wouldn't mess with that girl. I'd get out of there."

A month after the operation, Aretha's resilience was in full evidence. She began a concentrated campaign to assure her public that she was healthy and would soon be ready to work.

Not surprisingly, her first interview was given to Jet, the always loyal weekly that spoke directly to the black community. In a January 2011 interview headlined "The Lord Will Bring Me Through," Aretha sounded both determined and optimistic. She thanked her fans for their support and Stevie Wonder for being there when she emerged from surgery. She called the operation "highly successful." "I feel great," she said, adding, "I am putting Aretha first. We will put Ree together first. This is Aretha's time to do whatever it is that I need to do."

In February, looking dramatically thinner, she appeared in a videotape played after the Grammys honored her with a musical tribute by Jennifer Hudson, Christina Aguilera, Yolanda Adams, Florence Welch, and Martina McBride singing Aretha's hits.

In March, she appeared on the cover of *Jet*. Dressed in a long pink chiffon gown adorned with strands of cultured pearls, the Queen was back in charge. The headline read "It's a New Chapter in My Life." She refused to discuss the nature of her illness or operation. She spoke of her new healthy diet and her weight loss of twenty-five pounds. Included were pictures of Aretha with her sons Eddie, Teddy, and Kecalf plus niece Sabrina Owens, cousin Brenda Corbett, and Willie Wilkerson.

Later that month Aretha invited Wendy Williams to Detroit, where the talk-show host conducted an interview, decorously referring to her as "Miss Franklin," in a hotel dining room over high tea. Again avoiding all specifics about her health history, she joked about her former weight, saying, "I was just too fat for words." But when Williams suggested that, like most women, Aretha could be gullible and "get stupid falling in love," Aretha took umbrage, countering that Wendy might be gullible and get stupid, but not her. They went on to discuss possible casting for the biopic based on *From These Roots*. When Aretha suggested that Wendy help finance the film, the talk-show host backed off.

A Woman Falling Out of Love, after being rejected by Rhino, was released on May 1 under the banner of Aretha's Records. According to Dick Alen, who was still advising Aretha on business and bookings, Walmart had advanced her the million dollars she had long sought. That gave the chain the exclusive right to sell the record in their stores and on their website for a full month before it was available on iTunes.

"Aretha got her wish," said Alen. "She was in charge of virtually every aspect of the record. But unfortunately she wound up doing everything she could to mess up the deal. She delivered it months late and even then sent in a bad master that had to be redone. The record got no traction. The public ignored it, it didn't sell, and that was virtually the end of the short, unhappy life of Aretha's Records."

Writing for *Rolling Stone,* Will Hermes offered one of the more generous reviews: "The good news is that Aretha Franklin, who just turned 69, is recording, and that her magnificent instrument, though thinning a bit, retains plenty of its power and agility."

I loved her rendition of B.B. King's "Sweet Sixteen," a song, she told me, "that reminded me of teen years in Detroit when my father would go see B.B. in the clubs and play his records in our home. It felt great to get back to those blues."

But the rest of the record is sadly lacking. There's an unsatisfying mix of saccharine ballads: "The Way We Were," a strained duet with Ron Isley; "Theme from a Summer's Place"; and Aretha's self-penned overwrought "How Long I've Been Waiting." There's lightweight gospel: "Faithful," featuring Karen Clark Sheard, and "His Eye Is on the Sparrow," sung by her son Eddie. And there's a bizarrely histrionic redo of "My Country 'Tis of Thee," the anthem she sang at the 2008 inauguration of President Barack Obama.

On May 9, she gave her first concert since falling sick some eight months earlier. The venue was the Chicago Theater.

Attending the concert, I was struck by Aretha's resurgent energy. She sang a blistering version of "Sweet Sixteen" that made the entire evening worthwhile. Her requisite medley of hits—"Ain't No Way," "Chain of Fools," "Baby, I Love You"—felt fresh. She sang as though she was grateful to be alive. In the *Chicago Tribune,* Bob Gendron wrote, "She treated notes like putty, shortening and lengthening them at will, slipping in gritty moans before transitioning to climactic finishes." It was good to see Aretha up to her old tricks.

In her dressing room after the show, she was keen to discuss the biopic of *From These Roots* with me. "If Halle Berry doesn't have the confidence to portray me in my movie," she said, "there are plenty of actresses dying to play the role. We're moving ahead with the project and continuing the auditions."

"She keeps talking about that movie as if it's a done deal," said

Dick Alen, who was also at the Chicago concert. "As far as I know, there isn't a single studio or investor that has put up a dime. It's another one of Aretha's fantasy projects."

When it came to a real movie project—Alan Elliott's attempt to release Sydney Pollack's magnificent film of the *Amazing Grace* church performance from 1971—Aretha was less than cooperative.

"Because I'm convinced that this is the premier film of American popular music," Elliott told me, "I committed myself to do all I could to bring it to the public. Over the course of five long years I tried to engage Aretha. When I offered her half of the profits, she said she'd rather have a million-dollar advance. When I put together a group of financiers and offered her a million dollars, she wanted that—plus half the profits. In the course of negotiations, her demands kept increasing. She went from a million to three, then four, then five. At some point she hit me with a frivolous lawsuit demanding that I stop the imminent release of the film when, in fact, no release date had been set. The suit also claimed I had been profiting off her name when, in truth, I had remortgaged my house twice to keep this film project alive. I still cling to the hope that one day we will come to terms and this movie, a brilliant representation of her genius, sees the light of day." As of this writing, the master reels are still sitting on a warehouse shelf.

She kept a light schedule of touring in the summer of 2011, playing the Toronto Jazz Festival as well as Wolf Trap, outside Washington, DC. In spite of poor record sales and some negative reviews, she stayed focused on performing and getting back in form.

That form was challenged when, in August, *Billboard* reported that composer Norman West had filed suit against Aretha for her failure to sign a royalty agreement for the song "Put It Back Together Again" that he had written for *A Woman Falling Out of Love*. West claimed that he went to court only after he could not resolve the matter privately.

Aretha was incensed and issued a public statement: "To say the least, I am extremely disappointed that Norman West had the unmitigated gall to file a lawsuit against Springtime Publishing, Inc., considering how I've personally assisted and advised him over the past fifteen years.

"I've helped Norman West make a name for himself in the music industry, earn a living and in the past I've used several of his songs on my CDs, which resulted in other artists performing and recording his compositions."

When I recently called West to see if the matter had been resolved, he had no comment.

In September, Aretha appeared with Tony Bennett on his *Duets II* CD, joining him on the song "How Do You Keep the Music Playing?"

In October, she sang "Precious Lord" at the dedication of the Dr. Martin Luther King Memorial in Washington.

That same month, the *New York Times* reported that Aretha was the wedding singer at a high-society marriage between same-sex couple Bill White and Bryan Eure held at the Four Seasons restaurant in Manhattan. Three months later, on January 6, 2012, came her surprise announcement to the Associated Press that she would be marrying Willie Wilkerson in the summer. She mentioned asking Smokey Robinson, Stevie Wonder, and gospel singer Karen Clark Sheard to perform at the wedding. She rejected the idea of a wedding planner, saying, "There is no way in the world anyone else could plan my wedding other than myself."

"The singer admits to 'an intimate affair' with a fellow celebrity in the past," the AP reported, quoting Aretha as saying, "He was one of America's late-night talk-show hosts. At this point I'm thrilled it didn't [work], and what I was looking for was already here. We're very compatible, and he supports me and I support him a lot, and he has given me specialized attention that I don't think I've received from anyone else. I receive a lot of male attention, but Will is more special than all the rest."

According to sister-in-law Earline, Aretha fabricated the story. "God bless Aretha," said Earline, "but when she feels she's been out of the news for too long, she finds a way to get back in. This wedding story was something she just made up. When Will read about it, he was furious. He's a great guy and has been a loyal friend, but he has other women besides Aretha. He had no intention of marrying her and never asked her. As far as that old story about her and Tavis Smiley, well, that was another Aretha invention that she couldn't let go of."

Two weeks later Aretha's publicist Tracey Jordan issued this statement:

"Regretfully, To Our Friends and Supporters: Will and I have decided we were moving a little too fast, and there were a number of things that had not been thought through thoroughly. There will be no wedding at this time. We will not comment on it any further because of the very personal and sensitive nature of it."

The misunderstanding behind them, Willie and Aretha repaired their relationship, and once again he was seen at her side at a number of public events. Aretha continued to maximize her press appearances, assuring one and all that her reign, now in its sixth decade, was in no danger of ending.

39. THE ONCE AND FUTURE QUEEN

When Whitney Houston died in Los Angeles on February 11, 2012, Aretha issued a statement: "I just can't talk about it now. It's so stunning and unbelievable. I couldn't believe what I was reading coming across the TV screen. My heart goes out to Cissy, her daughter Bobbi Kris, her family and Bobby." Two days later, at a private concert in Charlotte, North Carolina, she called Whitney "one of the greatest singers who ever stood before a microphone." In an interview with Al Roker shortly before Houston's funeral, Aretha remembered meeting a ten-year-old Whitney. "I said, 'Oh, this little girl can sing! Okay, Cissy's baby can sing!'"

Aretha played Radio City Music Hall in New York the night before Whitney's funeral in nearby Newark, New Jersey. During the concert, Aretha sang two songs associated with Whitney—"I Will Always Love You" and "The Greatest Love of All." There was great strain in her voice as she tried to negotiate the demanding ballads, but there was also great feeling.

Expected to sing at Whitney's memorial service held at the

New Hope Baptist Church, Aretha failed to appear. According to Tracey Jordan, she was beset by muscle spasms and leg cramps.

"It wasn't that she didn't care about Whitney," said her cousin Brenda Corbett. "She cared deeply. But the pressure of her recent shows was taking its toll and the health concerns were real. She did all she could to honor Whitney. In every concert for the next year she'd sit at the piano and accompany herself to 'I Will Always Love You.' It was always a heartfelt tribute."

Aretha wrote generous tributes following the deaths of colleagues Etta James, Don Cornelius, Donna Summer, and Dick Clark.

"She took these deaths hard," said her sister-in-law Earline. "They seemed to be coming one after the other. But Ree has her own way of dealing with dark news. She goes out and creates some good news of her own."

She made sure the press was there when she threw herself the customary gala birthday party in March—her seventieth—this year at the Helmsley Park Lane Hotel in Manhattan, where Clive Davis sat at her table. "I've re-signed with Clive," she told a reporter, making up with the man who forged her comeback in the eighties and was now chief creative officer at Sony Records. Over the next months, reports indicated that, working with producers Kenny "Babyface" Edmunds and Nate "Danja" Hills, she would cover songs associated with the great pop divas of the past, a typically high-gloss commercial Clive Davis project. As of this writing, though, production has not begun.

"I've been singing background with my cousin for some forty-two years," Brenda told me, "and I still don't know—record from record or concert from concert—where she's going to hire me or fire me. Months will go by when she cuts off all communication with me. She's furious with me and I never know why. Then she'll call and we're back together like nothing has happened. The same is true with her relationships with Sabrina, Earline, and Earline's daughter, Tiffany. This isn't just a pattern with family members. It also applies to longtime employees. She fired H. B. Barnum, her musical director for decades and a man who had been loyal to her in the most difficult situations. When I asked her why she said, 'He didn't visit or call me when I was in the hospital.' 'But Aretha,' I said, 'he did call and send flowers and cards and could not have been more concerned.' She didn't want to hear about it. H. B. Barnum was gone—and that was it."

In April, Aretha fired William Morris Endeavor, switching over to ICM for booking and management. In addition, she continued her pattern of firing and rehiring two separate publicists, Gwendolyn Quinn and Tracey Jordan.

She also continued to call reporters with tidbits about her biopic, the latest one casting Audra McDonald, the celebrated Broadway singer with an operatic voice, in the lead role. Yet there was no script, no director, no studio deal.

In June she attended a forty-thousand-dollar-a-plate fund-raising dinner for President Obama's reelection campaign at the home of Sarah Jessica Parker before heading out on the bus to New Orleans to play the Essence Music Festival. "Ms. Franklin's set was a deflation," wrote Ben Ratliff in the *New York Times,* "full of awkward silences."

Later that month, at the Nokia Theater in Los Angeles, I attended her surprisingly abbreviated concert. She sounded winded and looked alarmingly unsteady. When we spoke afterward, she said she wasn't feeling well and couldn't wait to get back to Detroit, though she was dreading the long bus ride. She also mentioned her desire to return to Hollywood and become a television personality. Reuters reported that "Queen of Soul Aretha Franklin said on Saturday that she is interested in joining 'American Idol' as a judge, just days after Jennifer Lopez and Steven Tyler declared they have ended their judging roles on the Fox show."

In the following weeks, she kept putting out hints in the press, describing herself as the ideal judge. The invitation, though, never arrived.

She spent the winter at home in Detroit. In March 2013, at age seventy-one, she traveled to New York. I was in the audience at the Performing Arts Center in Newark for Aretha's Saturday-night concert.

The New Jersey crowd was an even mix of black and white, the average age somewhere between fifty-five and seventy. The place was packed with Aretha fans prepared to love her. Newark's then-mayor, Corey Booker, gave a flowery, heart-warming introduction, describing how when he was a child, Aretha's voice had connected him to the divine. He said her songs were the core of our collective consciousness. When he called her to the stage, it was with great emotion and high anticipation. But Aretha was nowhere to be found. Forty minutes passed before she appeared.

She came out wearing a white mink coat that she quickly removed and dropped to the floor. Willie Wilkerson picked up the fur and carried it off to the wings. Her sleeveless glittery silver gown was far from flattering. She had regained considerable weight in the past few months. With a big band blaring behind her, she sang a medley of a few of her hits—"Baby, I Love You," "Think," "Natural Woman." The top of her voice was frayed but her middle and lower range strong. Her singing lacked emotional commitment until she attacked B.B. King's "Sweet Sixteen." Early in this traditional twelve-bar blues, she caught the Holy Ghost. She performed the miracle that only the greatest of R&B artists can realize—the union of the secular and the sacred, the marriage of heaven and earth—as she broke into a little church dance, not caring that her bra straps were slipping and her gown askew. I remembered how B.B. had worshipped at the sanctuary where her dad shouted the good news. She mentioned her glory days at the Atlantic studios in midtown Manhattan during the golden age of soul before singing "Ain't No Way," her cousin Brenda hitting the high notes behind her. And then, after this short twenty-minute set, she left the stage, saying she'd be right back. During the ten-minute interlude, the band vamped on Marvin Gaye's "Got to Get It Up" while the audience stirred restlessly.

The second half of her show began with Aretha telling an

interminable shaggy-dog story—a tired old joke about a talking canine—that was not in the least funny. The audience groaned. I wondered why the show included this bit of humor. But, as always, this was Aretha's show—planned, produced, and realized according to her own lights. She sang a couple of more hits—"The House That Jack Built" and "Call Me"—before moving to the piano, where she accompanied herself to "I Will Always Love You," the tribute to Whitney Houston. She sang the song slowly, exquisitely, turning the sentimental ballad into a gospel dirge. She dedicated "Make Them Hear You," from the musical *Ragtime,* to Mayor Booker, who apparently had left the building. Her choice of a Broadway-style inspirational song reminded me that fifty-three years earlier, during her first recording session for Columbia in 1960, she had sung a similar semi-inspirational number—"Are You Sure," from the musical *The Unsinkable Molly Brown.* In trying to please a mainstream audience by covering mainstream genres, the seventy-one-year-old Aretha was hardly different than the eighteen-year-old Aretha.

Before concluding with the inevitable "Respect," she broke into "It's About Time for a Miracle," the kind of up-tempo church stomper her idol Clara Ward brought into jazz cabarets and Vegas lounges back in the fifties when Aretha was a preteen singing at her father's gospel shows.

The show was short. She sang for barely forty-five minutes. In a few instances, she was inspired. Even when her voice was tired, I marveled at the creativity of her phrasing. She read the material with her usual mixture of cunning and intelligence. The production itself took away from her singing. The slide projections on a screen in the back of the stage—showing a number of family pictures, plus the issue of *Rolling Stone* trumpeting her as the number-one singer of all time—looked like something out of a junior-high-school graduation party.

And yet her fans, loyal to a fault, gave her a standing ovation. They sensed that she had done her best—and I believe she had.

Later she spoke of her plans to tour extensively in the coming summer. But those plans were canceled when her medical condition deteriorated and she was forced into treatment. She remained adamant in refusing to reveal the nature of her disease to the public.

Her adamancy never diminished. She returned to the stage at the end of 2013 to play a casino in Detroit. She sang for merely thirty minutes, but she did sing. She scheduled concerts for Radio City Music Hall the following January and spoke to the press about her new album, in which she would cover songs associated with other divas and work under the supervision of Clive Davis with producers Babyface and André 3000. One had to respect her tenacity and courage in the face of a life-threatening disease.

As I watched these truncated appearances, I felt sadness—she was but a shadow of her former self—but also deep admiration for her sheer willpower. At the same time I kept thinking of what I wanted her to do:

I wanted her to realize a concert with only a superb jazz trio behind her as she sings George Gershwin and Cole Porter and the blues ballads of Percy Mayfield.

I wanted her to sit at the piano and accompany herself as she revisits her best songs and the songs of Thomas A. Dorsey and James Cleveland and Curtis Mayfield.

I wanted her to put her performing and recording career in the hands of producers noted for impeccable taste, musical restraint, and unfettered imagination.

I wanted her to give up the notion of having to stay current by working with music executives whose obsession for sales trumps concern for lasting quality or musical integrity.

In short, I wanted her to be a different kind of artist—and a different kind of woman—than who she is.

I remind myself that my job is not only to tell her story but to understand and accept her for who she is.

And who is that?

Who is Aretha Franklin?

★   ★   ★

She is the third of four extraordinarily bright and gifted children born to extraordinary parents—her mother a gifted singer, her father a gifted preacher.

She is a child who watches her mother leave the family as her father, a charismatic figure in the socially and politically progressive wing of the black church, galvanizes his power and status.

She is a child who, while still vulnerable and young, learns of her mother's death and seeks motherly love from a number of women who are romantically involved with her dad.

Although all her siblings demonstrate precocious talent, she is the young woman with the golden voice, her father's favorite, and, while barely a teen, a featured part of his gospel services that earn him—and her—a reputation among African American churchgoers.

She is the young woman who, while still a teen, has two children of her own.

She is the young woman who, while still a teen, is urged by her father to enter mainstream show business and sign with the world's biggest record company.

She is the young woman who, in her early twenties, marries a man known as a gentleman pimp and allows him to run her career and her life with a forceful hand.

Frustrated by her semi-success on her first label, she switches labels and achieves superstardom with a series of records unparalleled in the history of American music.

She is the superstar who becomes the musical voice of the civil rights movement, a cultural icon—all this before she turns thirty.

In a Los Angeles church, she is the rhythm-and-blues and jazz singer who looks back to her childhood and records what is universally regarded as the greatest album in the history of gospel.

Amid the confusion of a frenetic personal and professional life, she is crowned the Queen of Soul as she struggles with alcohol and depression.

As Queen of Soul, she leaves her native Detroit and moves to

Los Angeles, where she is frustrated by her inability to realize domestic happiness and produce or star in films.

In the second half of the seventies, as her long run of hits comes to an end, the Queen stumbles again, this time in her effort to reinvent herself as a disco diva.

With a new label and a new mentor, the Queen refuses to relinquish her crown, achieving commercial success with a new label and a series of dance-oriented producers in the post-disco era.

In the eighties she suffers the tragic death of her beloved father in addition to the demise of two of her beloved siblings. She leaves Hollywood and her unrealized film career to return to the affluent suburbs of Detroit, where she will live for the rest of her life.

In her fifties, sixties, and seventies, she focuses on staying musically current. She seeks out younger producers as well as duet partners, and the hits that result, although not comparable to her earlier creative triumphs, are enough to keep her in the public eye.

In her fifties, sixties, and seventies, the accolades never stop. She wins every honor and award imaginable. As her iconic status builds, her reign remains unchallenged; the Queen is a permanent fixture of our popular culture.

In her fifties, sixties, and seventies, without the help of her father and brother — her two most trusted advisers — and without an ongoing romantic relationship, she becomes more afraid. The Queen will not step on an airplane. The Queen will not ride a bus through thunderstorms or over high mountain passes. The Queen deals with fear through control. The Queen becomes overwhelmed by fear and obsessed with control.

When she becomes seriously sick, the Queen fears that the public will learn the nature of her disease and thus dismiss her as irrelevant. So she does her best to control the press. When she is out of the news for too long, the Queen fears that the public will forget her and so she circulates stories — about love affairs, marriages, or biopic movies — that keep her name alive.

Afraid of losing her money, the Queen carries her purse with her onstage, where she can see it at all times.

In her troubled mind, control is the antidote to fear. She hires, fires, and rehires a battery of publicists, booking agents, and managers because, when all is said and done, she cannot relinquish control. Thus she starts her own record label, becoming her own producer and marketing manager.

When these operations fail, she deflects the blame. Self-scrutiny is not her way. Her methods of denial have been perfected over a lifetime. Finally, when she has no choice and turns to others for help, help is always there. She is, after all, our once and future Queen. In the annals of our magnificent music, there is only one Queen of Soul.

The Queen is the ultimate survivor, a symbol of strength. She fights off physical ailments. She fights off depression. With steely determination, she keeps moving forward, no matter what.

Today I imagine her walking through her sprawling home in the woodsy suburbs of Detroit. There is the ever-present larger-than-life photograph of her father, young and vibrant, reminding her of the spiritual community where her artistry was born. I see her looking at the pictures of her beloved siblings—Erma, Cecil, Carolyn, Vaughn—all gone. Memories absorb her. In her own fashion, she passes over bad memories and replaces them with good ones. In looking for comfort, she walks over to the grand piano, sits on the stool, and runs her fingers over the keys. Then she closes her eyes and sings. The comfort comes. She hears her voice as clean and clear. Her voice may be shakier with age, but it is immortal, deeply and perfectly her own.

ACKNOWLEDGMENTS

Roberta Ritz and Aaron Cohen toiled mightily to provide critical research. I am deeply grateful to them both.

Gratitude to Michael Pietsch, my superb editor John Parsley, my superb agent David Vigliano, Malin von Euler-Hogan, my many interviewees—especially Earline Franklin, Brenda Corbett, and Sabrina Owens—as well as Dick Alen and Alan Elliott.

Much love to my family—Roberta, Alison, Jessica, Charlotte, the Nins, James, Isaac, Henry, Jim, Esther, Elizabeth, and all nieces and nephews.

Much love to my dear friends Alan Eisenstock, Harry Weinger, Herb Powell, and everyone in the Tuesday-morning crew.

Thanks to David Freeland, whose work with Ruth Bowen greatly deepened my understanding of her complex and brilliant personality.

Thank you, Jesus.

NOTES

1. Father and Daughter

Interviews

Bobby "Blue" Bland, Jesse Jackson, Marvin Gaye, James Cleveland, Carolyn Franklin, B.B. King, Cecil Franklin, Erma Franklin, Ruth Bowen

Books

Franklin and Ritz, *Aretha: From These Roots*
Heilbut, *The Fan Who Knew Too Much*

2. Instability

Interviews

Cecil Franklin, Anna Gordy, Smokey Robinson, Buddy Guy, Erma Franklin, Carolyn Franklin, James Cleveland

3. Mothers and Fathers

Interviews

Ruth Bowen, Erma Franklin, Billy Preston, James Cleveland, B.B. King, Cecil Franklin

Books

Salvatore, *Singing in a Strange Land*
Ward-Royster and Rose, *How I Got Over*

4. The Sex Circus

Interviews

Ray Charles, Billy Preston, Ruth Bowen, Etta James, Jerry Wexler, Carl Bean, Vaughn Franklin, Erma Franklin, Cecil Franklin, Carolyn Franklin, James Cleveland, Johnnie Taylor

Books

Wexler and Ritz, *Rhythm and the Blues*

5. The Blood

Interviews

Jerry Wexler, Carolyn Franklin, Cecil Franklin, James Cleveland, John Hammond, Brenda Corbett, Erma Franklin

Recordings

Songs of Faith, Chess Records, 1956

Articles

"Blast on Gospel Singers' Style Pits Baker Against Clara Ward," *Chicago Defender,* November 26, 1955

"Disc by Detroit Minister on Top," *Chicago Defender,* October 20, 1956

Books

Salvatore, *Singing in a Strange Land*

6. Moving On Up

Interviews

James Cleveland, Ray Charles, Oscar Peterson, Erma Franklin, Johnnie Taylor, Cecil Franklin, Carolyn Franklin

7. The Biggest and Best

Interviews

Cecil Franklin, Phil Moore, Major Holley, Jerry Wexler, John Hammond, Harvey Fuqua, Carolyn Franklin, Carmen McRae

Recordings

Aretha, Columbia, 1961

Articles

Review of "Love Is the Only Thing" and "Today I Sing the Blues," *Billboard,* September 26, 1960

Review of "Won't Be Long" and "Right Now," *Billboard,* December 26, 1960

Jack Maher, "Aretha Franklin Debs at Vanguard," *Billboard,* October 17, 1960

8. Gentleman Pimp

Interviews

Erma Franklin, Carolyn Franklin, Bettye LaVette, Etta James, Cecil Franklin, Harvey Fuqua, Joe Newman, Quincy Jones

Recordings

The Electrifying Aretha Franklin, Columbia, 1962

Articles

New York Beat, *Jet,* May 4, 1961

Franklin named top new-star female vocalist, *Down Beat,* August 3, 1961

"From Gospel to Jazz Is Not Disrespect for the Lord," *New York Amsterdam News,* August 26, 1961

Books

LaVette and Ritz, *A Woman Like Me*

9. Water, Water Everywhere

Interviews

Carolyn Franklin, Erma Franklin, Bobby Scott, Jerry Wexler, Phil Walden,
   Cecil Franklin, Etta James, Sarah Vaughan

Recordings

The Tender, the Moving, the Swinging Aretha Franklin, Columbia, 1962
Laughing on the Outside, Columbia, 1963
Unforgettable: A Tribute to Dinah Washington, Columbia, 1964

Articles

Jack Maher, "Newport '62 a Swinging Affair," *Billboard,* July 21, 1962
Review of "Just for a Thrill" and "Try a Little Tenderness," *Billboard,* August 11,
   1962
People Are Talking About, *Jet,* November, 29, 1962
People Are Talking About, *Jet,* June 13, 1963

Books

Kelley, *Thelonious Monk*
Freeman, *Otis!*
Cohodas, *Queen*

10. What a Difference a Day Makes

Interviews

Etta James, Ruth Bowen, Erma Franklin, John Hammond, Clyde Otis

Recordings

Unforgettable: A Tribute to Dinah Washington, Columbia, 1964

Articles

"The Swingin' Aretha," *Ebony,* March 1964

11. Fools

Interviews

Clyde Otis, Jerry Wexler, John Hammond, Carolyn Franklin, Cecil Franklin,
   Erma Franklin

Recordings

Runnin' Out of Fools, Columbia, 1964

Articles

Roger Scott, Nashville Scene, *Billboard,* May 29, 1965

12. Never Loved

Interviews

Jerry Wexler, Jimmy Johnson, Ruth Bowen, Erma Franklin, Carolyn Franklin,
   Roger Hawkins, Dan Penn, Rick Hall, Tommy Dowd, Cecil Franklin, Luther
   Vandross

Recordings
I Never Loved a Man the Way I Love You, Atlantic, 1967

Articles
Franklin signs exclusive contract with Atlantic, reported in *Billboard*, December 3, 1966

Books
Wexler and Ritz, *Rhythm and the Blues*

13. Keep Rolling

Interviews
Carmen McRae, Jerry Wexler, Earline Franklin, Cecil Franklin, Ray Charles, Ruth Bowen, Erma Franklin, Carolyn Franklin, Joe South, Nat Hentoff

Recordings
I Never Loved a Man the Way I Love You, Atlantic, 1967
Aretha Arrives, Atlantic, 1967

Articles
Franklin recovering from broken arm, reported in *Jet*, May 18, 1967
Franklin appears at tribute to her father, reported in *Time*, June 29, 1967

14. Natural

Interviews
Jerry Wexler, Arif Mardin, Carolyn Franklin, Erma Franklin, Ruth Bowen

Recordings
Lady Soul, Atlantic, 1968

Articles
Franklin recuperating from eye injury, reported in *Jet*, December 14, 1967
C. Higgins, reported in People Are Talking About, *Jet*, December 28, 1967

15. Year of Years

Interviews
Carolyn Franklin, Jerry Wexler, Cecil Franklin, Arif Mardin, Tommy Dowd, David Newman, Erma Franklin, Ruth Bowen, Carmen McRae

Recordings
Lady Soul, Atlantic, 1968
Aretha Now, 1968
Aretha Franklin: Soul '69, Atlantic, 1969
Aretha in Paris, Atlantic, 1968
Aretha's Gold, Atlantic, 1969

Articles
"Unsound Thing Happened to Aretha at the Forum," *Billboard*, February 3, 1968
"Atlantic Signs Aretha to New Long-Term Pact," *Billboard*, May 4, 1968
Franklin signs new long-term pact with Atlantic, reported in *Jet*, May 9, 1968
"Lady Soul Singing It Like It Is," *Time*, June 28, 1968
Ed Ochs, "From Sermons on Sunday to All-Day Success," *Billboard*, July 13, 1968
C. Higgins, People Are Talking About, *Jet*, August 22, 1968

Ed Ochs, "Soul Sauce," *Billboard,* October 12, 1968
Franklin arraigned in traffic court for reckless driving and an expired driver's
  license, reported in *Jet,* December 12, 1968

16. High Maintenance
Interviews
Dennis Edwards, Erma Franklin, Carolyn Franklin, Jerry Wexler, Cecil Franklin, Brenda Corbett, Ruth Bowen

Recordings
Aretha Now, Atlantic, 1968
This Girl's in Love with You, Atlantic, 1970
Spirit in the Dark, Atlantic, 1970

Articles
Franklin asked to write Carolyn Franklin's liner notes, reported in *Jet,* April 3,
  1969
Ed Ochs, Plans for "Soul Bowl '69," reported in *Billboard,* May 17, 1969
C. Higgins, Franklin's whereabouts a mystery, reported in People Are Talking
  About, *Jet,* July 10, 1969
Franklin's stay in Ford Hospital, reported in *Jet,* July 24, 1969
"Aretha Franklin Fined $50," *New York Times,* July 26, 1969
"Aretha Franklin Forfeits Bond; Pays $50 Fine," *Jet,* August 7, 1969

17. Spirit
Interviews
Carolyn Franklin, Jerry Wexler, Cecil Franklin, Earline Franklin, Joel Dorn,
  Ruth Bowen, Erma Franklin, Stan Getz, Billy Preston

Recordings
*Aretha Franklin: Rare and Unreleased Recordings from the Golden Reign of the Queen of
  Soul,* Rhino, 2007
Spirit in the Dark, Atlantic, 1970
Young, Gifted, and Black, Atlantic, 1972

Articles
"Sam Cooke's Brother, Charles, Is Shot in Detroit," *Jet,* January 15, 1970
"Aretha Falls Ill in St. Louis; Is Treated in New York," *Jet,* July 16, 1970
C. Higgins, Franklin back from European tour, reported in People Are Talking
  About, *Jet,* September 15, 1970
"Aretha Says She'll Go Angela's Bond If Permitted," *Jet,* December 3, 1970
C. Higgins, Franklin family forming charitable foundation, reported in People
  Are Talking About, *Jet,* December 24, 1970

18. Right Reverend
Interviews
Carolyn Franklin, Erma Franklin, Ruth Bowen, Cecil Franklin, Jerry Wexler,
  Billy Preston, Brenda Corbett, Claude Nobs

Recordings
Young, Gifted, and Black, Atlantic, 1972
Let Me in Your Life, Atlantic, 1974

Articles

"Aretha Denies Being Told Not to Perform to Aid Angela Davis," *Jet,* May 27, 1971

Ian Dove, review of Franklin's Apollo Theater Concert, *Billboard,* June 12, 1971

"Soul Queen Fumes Over Treatment by Italian Cops," *Jet,* July 15, 1971

"Aretha Ignores Critics; Resets South African Tour, January, 1972," *Jet,* July 29, 1971

Don Heckman, "Spell on Audience Is Cast at Garden by Aretha Franklin," *New York Times,* October 24, 1971

Charles L. Sanders, "Aretha: A Close-Up Look at Sister Superstar," *Ebony,* December 1971

Books

Pleasants, *The Great American Popular Singers*

19. Amazing

Interviews

Jerry Wexler, James Cleveland, Marvin Gaye, Cecil Franklin, Carolyn Franklin, Carmen McRae, Billy Preston

Recordings

Aretha Franklin: Rare and Unreleased Recordings from the Golden Reign of the Queen of Soul, Rhino, 2007

Spirit in the Dark, Atlantic, 1970

Young, Gifted, and Black, Atlantic, 1972

Amazing Grace, Atlantic, 1972

Books

Cohen, *Amazing Grace*

20. Hey

Interviews

Billy Preston, Cecil Franklin, Jerry Wexler, Erma Franklin, Ruth Bowen

Recordings

Aretha Franklin: Rare and Unreleased Recordings from the Golden Reign of the Queen of Soul, Rhino, 2007

Aretha Franklin: Soul '69, Atlantic, 1969

Hey Now Hey (The Other Side of the Sky), Atlantic, 1973

Amazing Grace, Atlantic, 1972

Articles

"Jackson PUSHes On," *Time,* January 3, 1972

M. Cordell Thompson, "Aretha Is Rocking Steady Now," *Jet,* March 9, 1972

Lynn Van Matre, review of Franklin's concert at Chicago's Arie Theater, *Chicago Tribune,* June 12, 1972

"Aretha to Entertain Inmates Here," *Chicago Tribune,* June 12, 1972

Franklin's diet and exercise regimen, reported in *Jet,* August 24, 1972

Books

Jones, *Q: The Autobiography of Quincy Jones*

21. Shop Around

Interviews

Ruth Bowen, Cecil Franklin, Jerry Wexler, Earline Franklin, Erma Franklin, Norman Dugger, Gene Page, Brenda Corbett

Recordings

Amazing Grace, Atlantic, 1972
Hey Now Hey (The Other Side of the Sky), Atlantic, 1973
Let Me in Your Life, Atlantic, 1974
With Everything I Feel in Me, Atlantic, 1974
You, Atlantic, 1975

Articles

Franklin and Ken Cunningham scouting locations for a film, reported in *Jet,* October 12, 1972
"Aretha Franklin's 'Mini Meals' Diet Helps Shed Pounds," *Jet,* March 29, 1973
"Aretha Buries Rumors About 'Going Crazy,' " *Jet,* April 12, 1973
William Earl Berry, rumor that Franklin has seminude scene in film, reported in People Are Talking About, *Jet,* April 12, 1973
Franklin's surprise Easter visit to Canaan Baptist Church in Harlem, reported in New York Beat, *Jet,* May 17, 1973
Franklin returns from yacht cruise, reported in New York Beat, *Jet,* January 31, 1974
Franklin's stellar performance at the Auditorium Theater, Chicago, reported in *Jet,* March 21, 1974
John Rockwell, "Aretha Franklin Opens at the Apollo," *New York Times,* March 10, 1974
Ken Cunningham writing a script, reported in *Jet,* March 28, 1974
M. Cordell Thompson, "A Visit with Aretha Franklin," *Jet,* May 2, 1974
"First Lady of Talent Booking," *Ebony,* June 1974
"The New Aretha," *Ebony,* October 1974
Schooling of Franklin's sons Clarence and Edward, reported in *Jet,* June 9, 1975
Review of concert at Westchester Premier Theater, *Billboard,* June 14, 1975
Franklin back in New York, reported in New York Beat, *Jet,* September 25, 1975

22. The Spark

Interviews

Ruth Bowen, Carolyn Franklin, Cecil Franklin, Erma Franklin, Jerry Wexler, Natalie Cole, Jeffrey Kruger

Recordings

Sparkle, Atlantic, 1976
Sweet Passion, Atlantic, 1977

Articles

Bob Lucas, "Looking Ahead with Aretha Franklin," *Jet,* February 26, 1976
Ken Cunningham aiming for a filmmaking career, reported in New York Beat, *Jet,* April 22, 1976
Ace Burgess, "Aretha Franklin's Hidden Asset: Her Brother Cecil," *Jet,* July 15, 1976
"Aretha Franklin, Her Soul Mate End Their Love Match," *Jet,* August 12, 1976
"Still on a Throne, Aretha Loses Weight, Looks Ahead," *Jet,* June 23, 1977

Geoff Brow, Franklin going out with Glynn Turman, reported in People Are
Talking About, *Jet,* July 28, 1977
"Aretha Franklin's Soulmate Upset About Romance Rumors," *Jet,* July 28,
1976
"Is There Room at the Top for Big Three of Song?," *Jet,* September 15, 1977
Aretha to perform in England, reported in *Jet,* October 22, 1977
"U.K. Pact Flap Axes Aretha Gig," *Billboard,* December 3, 1977
Photo of Franklin and Glynn Turman in *Jet,* December 29, 1977
Review criticizes Aretha's show in Paris, *Billboard,* January 21, 1978

Books
Cole and Ritz, *Love Brought Me Back*

23. Fairy-Tale Princess

Interviews
Carolyn Franklin, Erma Franklin, Cecil Franklin, Jerry Wexler

Recordings
Sweet Passion, Atlantic, 1977
Sparkle, Atlantic, 1976
Almighty Fire, Atlantic, 1978

Articles
"A Fabulous Party—Until Somebody Stole the Doves," *Jet,* May 11, 1978
Full-page self-promotional ad in *Variety,* June 20, 1978
"Aretha and Glynn," *Ebony,* July 1978
Jean Williams, "Los Angeles Aretha Fete a Puzzler," *Billboard,* July 22, 1978

24. The Hustle

Interviews
Cecil Franklin, Ahmet Ertegun, Ruth Bowen, Carolyn Franklin, Jerry Wexler

Recordings
La Diva, Atlantic, 1979

Articles
"Aretha Adopts New Lifestyle with New Family," *Jet,* January 25, 1979
Jean Williams's review of Franklin's concert at Harrah's Lake Tahoe, *Billboard,*
February 10, 1979
Photo with Jimmy and Rosalynn Carter, *Jet,* March 29, 1979

25. Daddy's Little Girl

Interviews
Carolyn Franklin, Erma Franklin, Cecil Franklin, Ruth Bowen, Arif Mardin

Recordings
Aretha, Arista, 1980

Articles
Review of performance at Kool Jazz Festival, New Jersey, reported in *Billboard,*
August 25, 1979
Franklin appears at a benefit concert for C. L. Franklin in Detroit, reported in
Jet, April 17, 1980

Jean Williams, Franklin's questionable costumes, reported in Counterpoint, *Billboard*, July 26, 1980

Franklin's weight loss, in *Jet*, November 15, 1980

Franklin's contract worth $9 million, reported in *Ebony*, January 1981

Robert Palmer, "Aretha Franklin, with Feeling and Fireworks," *New York Times*, February 27, 1981

Franklin rates her top men, reported in *Ebony*, 1981

26. Back on Track

Interviews

Arif Mardin, Cecil Franklin, Luther Vandross, Erma Franklin, Carolyn Franklin

Recordings

Love All the Hurt Away, Arista, 1981

Jump to It, Arista, 1982

Articles

Stephen Holden, review of *Love All the Hurt Away*, *New York Times*, October 11, 1981

Julie Chenault, "Aretha Franklin Tells Why Weight Doesn't Worry Her Anymore," *Jet*, September 17, 1981

Review of *Jump to It*, *Billboard*, July 31, 1982

Nelson George, review of Franklin at Superfest, *Billboard*, September 25, 1982

Franklin comments on her father's health, reported in *Jet*, August 9, 1982

Dissolution of Franklin-Turman marriage, reported in Celebrity Beat, *Jet*, August 23, 1982

27. Home

Interviews

Carolyn Franklin, Cecil Franklin, Ruth Bowen, Erma Franklin

Recordings

Jump to It, Arista, 1982

Articles

"Aretha Franklin Sponsors 2nd Annual Artist's Ball to Benefit Comatose Dad," *Jet*, November 7, 1983

Franklin to sue Arista, reported in *Jet*, November 21, 1983

28. Our Father

Interviews

Earline Franklin, Erma Franklin, Carolyn Franklin, Ruth Bowen, Cecil Franklin, Narada Michael Walden, Luther Vandross, Jerry Wexler

Recordings

Who's Zoomin' Who?, Arista, 1985

Articles

Gary Graff, "Aretha Franklin: The Queen of Soul Decides 'It's Time to Get Back to It,'" *Chicago Tribune*, February 24, 1985

Franklin's fear of flying over, reported in *Jet*, February 25, 1985

Paul Grein, "Freeway of Love" tops charts, reported in Chart Beat, *Billboard*, August 3, 1985

Nelson George, success of *Who's Zoomin' Who?*, reported in Rhythm and the Blues, *Billboard*, December 7, 1985

29. Diva-fication

Interviews
Jerry Wexler, Erma Franklin, Carolyn Franklin, Ray Charles, Luther Vandross, Brenda Corbett, Cecil Franklin, Ruth Bowen, Dick Alen

Recordings
Aretha, Arista, 1986

Articles
Jon Pareles, review of *Aretha*, *New York Times*, November 2, 1986
Nelson George, Franklin doesn't travel by plane, reported in Rhythm and the Blues, *Billboard*, July 19, 1986

Books
Richards and Fox, *Life*

30. In the Storm Too Long

Interviews
Cecil Franklin, Brenda Corbett, James Cleveland, Erma Franklin, Ruth Bowen, Ahmet Ertegun

Recordings
One Lord, One Faith, One Baptism, Arista, 1987

Articles
John Rockwell, review of *One Lord, One Faith, One Baptism*, *New York Times*, December 13, 1987
Photo of Franklin at annual masquerade ball, in *Jet*, August 22, 1988

Books
Bego, *Aretha Franklin*

31. The Mixture As Before

Interviews
Ruth Bowen, Jerry Wexler, Erma Franklin, Luther Vandross

Recordings
Through the Storm, Arista, 1989

Books
Franklin and Ritz, *Aretha: From These Roots*

32. Party Therapy

Interviews
Erma Franklin, Dick Alen, Arif Mardin, Oliver Leiber, Ruth Bowen, Vaughn Franklin, Jerry Wexler, Carmen McRae, Phil Ramone

Recordings
What You Gon Is What You Sweat, Arista, 1991
Amazing Grace, Atlantic, 1972

Aretha Franklin Greatest Hits 1980–1994, Arista, 1994
"What Now My Love," on *Duets,* Frank Sinatra, Capitol, 1993
"The Makings of You," on *A Tribute to Curtis Mayfield,* various artists, Warner Brothers, 1994

Articles

"New York Magistrate Rules Aretha Should Pay $230,000 for Backing Out on Play," *Jet,* February 19, 1990

Jon Pareles, "The Unpredictable Aretha Franklin," *New York Times,* August 11, 1990

"Aretha Franklin Talks About Men in Her Life and Sings Songs About Them," *Jet,* August 19, 1991

Stephen Holden, "Aretha Franklin Almost Turns a Concert into a Fashion Show," *New York Times,* September 16, 1991

"IRS Puts $225,000 Tax Lien on Aretha Franklin's Home," *Jet,* December 14, 1992

Ginia Bellafante, "Respect? Fur-get It," *Time,* February 1, 1993

Jon Pareles, "Aretha Franklin in Stellar Company and on Her Own," *New York Times,* April 29, 1993

"Aretha Blasts Columnist Over Quips About Gown," *Jet,* May 31, 1993

Books

Franklin and Ritz, *Aretha: From These Roots*
Davis and DeCurtis, *The Soundtrack of My Life*

33. A Rose

Interviews

Vaughn Franklin, Erma Franklin, Ruth Bowen, Ray Charles, Jerry Wexler

Recordings

"It Hurts Like Hell," on *Waiting to Exhale: Original Soundtrack Album,* various artists, Arista, 1995

A Rose Is Still a Rose, Arista, 1998

"I'll Fly Away," on *Diana: Princess of Wales Tribute,* various artists, Sony Records, 1997

What You See Is What You Sweat, Arista, 1991

Articles

Fred Bronson, Chart Beat, *Billboard,* May 14, 1994

Janet Jackson beats Franklin's record for gold singles, reported in *Jet,* August 29, 1994

Stephen Holden, "Playful Aretha Franklin Plumbs Roots of Soul," *New York Times,* November 5, 1994

David Nathan, "Veteran Divas Find New Audiences," *Billboard,* November 19, 1994

Laura B. Randolph, "Aretha Talks About Men, Marriage, Music and Motherhood," *Ebony,* April 1995

Geoffrey Himes, review of "It Hurts Like Hell" from *Exhale* soundtrack, *Washington Post,* November 29, 1995

Photo with Arthur Mitchell at Kennedy Center, in *Jet,* May 27, 1996

Jon Pareles, "Soaring on Passion, Rooted in Gospel," *New York Times,* June 28, 1996

Clarence Waldron, "Aretha Franklin Still Gets R-E-S-P-E-C-T," *Jet,* October 7, 1996

J. R. Reynolds, Rhythm and the Blues, *Billboard,* April 26, 1998

Larry Flick, review of *A Rose Is Still a Rose, Billboard*, February 7, 1998

Fred Bronson, Chart Beat, *Billboard,* February 14, 1998

Robert Christgau, review of *A Rose Is Still a Rose, Village Voice,* March 17, 1998

Review of *A Rose Is Still a Rose, Rolling Stone*, March 19, 1998

Books

Franklin and Ritz, *Aretha: From These Roots*

Knight, *Between Each Line*

Ward-Royster and Rose, *How I Got Over*

34. *Vincerò*

Interviews

Vaughn Franklin, Jerry Wexler, Eric Keil, Ruth Bowen

Recordings

"Respect," on *Blues Brothers 2000,* Universal Records, 1998

"Nessun Dorma," on *Jewels in the Crown: All-Star Duets with the Queen,* Arista, 2007

Articles

Larry Flick, "The Grammys: Big Wins, Big Buzz," *Billboard,* March 7, 1998

Fred Bronson, Chart Beat, *Billboard,* March 14, 1998

Fred Bronson, Chart Beat, *Billboard,* March 21, 1998

Clarence Waldron, "Aretha Franklin Talks About Being a Diva," *Jet,* May 18, 1998

Franklin listed as one of the most influential people of the twentieth century, *Time,* June 8, 1998

"Arista's Record Year," *Billboard,* July 25, 1998

Lynn Norment, "Aretha Roars Back and Gets R-E-S-P-E-C-T," *Ebony,* August 1998

35. Damage Control

Interviews

Erma Franklin, Ruth Bowen

Articles

"Why Doesn't Aretha Pay Her Bills?," *Detroit Free Press*, February 15, 1999

"Franklin Calls Story on Alleged Financial Woes 'Malicious and Vicious,'" *Jet,* March 8, 1999

Franklin performs at the White House Correspondents' Association dinner, reported in *New York Times,* May 3, 1999

Gail Mitchell, "Aretha Pairs Up for Set of Duets and Turns Author," *Billboard,* July 29, 1999

Aretha: From These Roots on *New York Times* bestseller list (hardcover nonfiction), September 24, 1999

Books
Franklin and Ritz, *Aretha: From These Roots*

36. What Aretha Wants
Interviews
Jerry Wexler, Ruth Bowen, Dick Alen, Ahmet Ertegun, Erma Franklin, Sabrina Owens, Earline Franklin

Recordings
Jewels in the Crown: All-Star Duets with the Queen, Arista, 2007
A Woman Falling Out of Love, Aretha's Records, 2011

Articles
Gail Mitchell, review of the *Duets* album, Rhythm and the Blues, *Billboard*, March 25, 2000
Ben Ratliff, "What Aretha Wants and Needs She Doesn't Always Get," *New York Times*, June 26, 2000
Franklin suing *Star* for article disparaging her, reported in *Detroit Free Press*, November 29, 2001

Books
Cole and Diehl, *Angel on My Shoulder*

37. Oldies but Goodies
Interviews
Ruth Bowen, Troy Taylor, Gordon Chambers, Burt Bacharach, Earline Franklin

Articles
Jon Pareles, review of "The Only Thing Missin'," *New York Times*, June 29, 2003
Fred Bronson, "Missing No More," *Billboard*, July 19, 2003
Clarence Waldron, "Aretha Franklin Returns with Soulful CD, 'So Damn Happy,'" *Jet*, September 29, 2003
"The Queen Still Reigns," *Ebony*, March 2004
Clarence Waldron, "Queen of Soul Aretha Franklin Proclaims Today's New R&B Royalty," *Jet*, June 25, 2007
Jon Pareles, "The Queen of Soul Takes Control," *New York Times*, November 4, 2007
Clarence Waldron, "Life on the Road Forces the Queen of Soul to Find a New Strategy in Her Battle with Weight," *Jet*, November 19, 2007
"Aretha Franklin Refuses to Share Her Royal Title," *Jet*, March 3, 2008
Franklin named greatest singer of the rock era, reported in *Rolling Stone*, November 2008
"Diva's Duet," *Jet*, August 23, 2010

Recordings
Jewels in the Crown: All-Star Duets with the Queen, Arista, 2007
So Damn Happy, Arista, 2003
This Christmas, Rhino, 2009
A Woman Falling Out of Love, Aretha's Records, 2011

Books

Franklin and Ritz, *Aretha: From These Roots*

38. A Woman Falling Out of Love

Interviews

Rashod Ollison, Ruth Bowen, Cheryl Pawelski, Earline Franklin

Recordings

A Woman Falling Out of Love, Aretha's Records, 2011

Articles

Franklin discusses her inauguration hat, reported in *Newsweek,* March 12, 2012

"Aretha Franklin Cancer," *National Enquirer,* December 8, 2010

Patricia Shipp, "Aretha Cancer Tragedy," *National Enquirer,* December 20, 2010

Clarence Waldron, "Aretha Franklin: The Lord Will Bring Me Through," *Jet,* January 10, 2011

"It's a New Chapter in My Life," *Jet,* March 7, 2011

Will Hermes, review of *A Woman Falling Out of Love, Rolling Stone,* May 26, 2011

Composer Norman West sues Franklin, reported in *Billboard,* August 2, 2011

Franklin sings at same-sex wedding, reported in *New York Times,* October 20, 2011

Franklin announces she is marrying Willie Wilkerson, reported by the Associated Press, January 6, 2012

Books

Franklin and Ritz, *Aretha: From These Roots*

39. The Once and Future Queen

Interviews

Earline Franklin, Brenda Corbett

Articles

Ben Ratliff, review of the Essence Music Festival, *New York Times,* July 9, 2012

Franklin interested in being *American Idol* judge, reported by Reuters, July 15, 2012

BIBLIOGRAPHY

Bego, Mark. *Aretha Franklin: The Queen of Soul.* New York: Da Capo, 1989.

Boyer, Clarence, and Lloyd Yearwood. *How Sweet the Sound: The Golden Age of Gospel.* Washington, DC: Elliott and Clark, 1995.

Branch, Taylor. *At Canaan's Edge: America in the King Years, 1965–1968.* New York: Simon and Schuster, 2006.

Carpenter, Bill. *Uncloudy Days: The Gospel Music Encyclopedia.* San Francisco: Backbeat Books, 2005.

Charles, Ray, and David Ritz. *Brother Ray.* New York: Dial Press, 1978.

Cohen, Aaron. *Amazing Grace.* New York: Continuum, 2011.

Cohodas, Nadine. *Queen: The Life and Music of Dinah Washington.* New York: Pantheon, 2004.

Cole, Natalie, with David Ritz. *Love Brought Me Back: A Journey of Loss and Gain.* New York: Simon and Schuster, 2010.

Cole, Natalie, with Digby Diehl. *Angel on My Shoulder.* New York: Grand Central Publishing, 2000.

Davis, Clive, with Anthony DeCurtis. *The Soundtrack of My Life.* New York: Simon and Schuster, 2012.

Dobkin, Matt. *I Never Loved a Man the Way I Love You: Aretha Franklin, Respect, and the Making of a Soul Music Masterpiece.* New York: St. Martin's, 2004.

Farley, Charles. *Soul of the Man: Bobby "Blue" Bland.* Jackson: University Press of Mississippi, 2011.

Franklin, Aretha, and David Ritz. *Aretha: From These Roots.* New York: Villard, 1999.

Franklin, Rev. C. L. *Give Me This Mountain: Life History and Selected Sermons.* Edited by Jeff Todd Tilton. Urbana: University of Illinois Press, 1989.

Freeman, Scott. *Otis!* New York: St. Martin's, 2001.

Heilbut, Anthony. *The Fan Who Knew Too Much: Aretha Franklin, the Rise of the Soap Opera, Children of the Gospel Church, and Other Meditations.* New York: Knopf, 2012.

———. *The Gospel Sound: Good News and Bad Times.* New York: Simon and Schuster, 1975.

James, Etta, and David Ritz. *Rage to Survive.* New York: Villard, 1995.

Jones, Quincy. *Q: The Autobiography of Quincy Jones.* New York: Doubleday, 2001.

Kelley, Robin D. G. *Thelonious Monk: The Life and Times of an American Original.* New York: Free Press, 2009.

King, B.B., with David Ritz. *Blues All Around Me: The Autobiography of B.B. King.* New York: Avon Books, 1996.

Knight, Gladys. *Between Each Line of Pain and Glory: My Life Story.* New York: Hyperion, 1997.

LaVette, Bettye, with David Ritz. *A Woman Like Me.* New York: Blue Rider Press, 2013.

Pleasants, Henry. *The Great American Popular Singers.* New York: Simon and Schuster, 1974.

Prial, Dunstan. *The Producer: John Hammond and the Soul of American Music.* New York: Farrar, Straus and Giroux, 2006.

Richards, Keith, with James Fox. *Life.* Boston: Little, Brown, 2010.

Ritz, David. *Divided Soul: The Life of Marvin Gaye.* New York: McGraw-Hill, 1985.

Robinson, Smokey, with David Ritz. *Smokey: Inside My Life.* New York: McGraw-Hill, 1989.

Salvatore, Nick. *Singing in a Strange Land: C. L. Franklin, the Black Church, and the Transformation of America.* Boston: Little, Brown, 2005.

Schwerin, Jules. *Got to Tell It: Mahalia Jackson, Queen of Gospel.* New York: Oxford University Press, 1992.

Seymour, Craig. *Luther: The Life and Longing of Luther Vandross.* New York: Harper-Collins, 1994.

Ward-Royster, Willa, as told to Toni Rose. *How I Got Over: Clara Ward and the World-Famous Ward Singers.* Philadelphia: Temple University Press, 1997.

Wexler, Jerry, and David Ritz. *Rhythm and the Blues: A Life in American Music.* New York: Knopf, 1993.

SELECTED DISCOGRAPHY*

Albums on Chess Records
  Songs of Faith (1956)

Albums on Columbia Records
  Aretha (1961)
  The Electrifying Aretha Franklin (1962)
  The Tender, the Moving, the Swinging Aretha Franklin (1962)
  Laughing on the Outside (1963)
  Unforgettable: A Tribute to Dinah Washington (1964)
  Runnin' Out of Fools (1964)
  Yeah!!! In Person with Her Quartet (1965)
  Soul Sister (1965)
  Take It Like You Give It (1967)
  Aretha Franklin's Greatest Hits (1967)
  Take a Look (1967)
  Aretha Franklin's Greatest Hits Vol. II (1968)
  Soft and Beautiful (1969)
  Today I Sing the Blues (1969)
  In the Beginning: The World of Aretha Franklin 1960–1967 (1972)
  Aretha: The First 12 Sides (1972)
  Aretha Franklin: Legendary Queen of Soul (1981)
  The Queen in Waiting: The Columbia Years 1960–1965 (2002)
  Take a Look: Aretha Franklin Complete on Columbia (2011, box set; includes
    DVD *Aretha '64! Live on The Steve Allen Show*)

Albums on Atlantic Records
  I Never Loved a Man the Way I Love You (1967)
  Aretha Arrives (1967)
  Lady Soul (1968)

*Compiled by Roberta Ritz

Aretha Now (1968)
Aretha in Paris (1968)
Aretha Franklin: Soul '69 (1969)
Aretha's Gold (1969)
This Girl's in Love with You (1970)
Spirit in the Dark (1970)
Aretha Live at Fillmore West (1971)
Young, Gifted, and Black (1972)
Amazing Grace (1972, two-record set)
Hey Now Hey (The Other Side of the Sky) (1973)
Let Me in Your Life (1974)
With Everything I Feel in Me (1974)
You (1975)
Sparkle (1976)
Sweet Passion (1977)
Almighty Fire (1978)
La Diva (1979)
Aretha's Jazz (1984)
Aretha Franklin: 30 Greatest Hits (1986, two-record set)
Amazing Grace: The Complete Recordings (1999, two-disc set)

Albums on Arista Records

Aretha (1980)
Love All the Hurt Away (1981)
Jump to It (1982)
Get It Right (1983)
Who's Zoomin' Who? (1985)
Aretha (1986)
One Lord, One Faith, One Baptism (1987, two-record set)
Through the Storm (1989)
What You See Is What You Sweat (1991)
Aretha Franklin Greatest Hits 1980–1994 (1994)
A Rose Is Still a Rose (1998)
So Damn Happy (2003)
Jewels in the Crown: All-Star Duets with the Queen (2007)
Knew You Were Waiting: The Best of Aretha Franklin 1980–1988 (2012)

Albums on Aretha's Records

A Woman Falling Out of Love (2011)

Albums on Rhino Records

Aretha Franklin: Queen of Soul: The Atlantic Recordings (1992, box set)
*Aretha Franklin: Rare and Unreleased Recordings from the Golden Reign
of the Queen of Soul* (2007, two-disc set)
Oh Me Oh My: Aretha Live in Philly, 1972 (2008)
This Christmas (2009)

Appearances on Other Albums

"Until You Come Back to Me (That's What I'm Gonna Do)." Johnny Carson, *Here's Johnny: Magic Moments from the 'Tonight Show'* (Casablanca Records, 1974)

"Think." *The Blues Brothers: Original Soundtrack Recording,* various artists (Atlantic, 1980)

"Sisters Are Doin' It for Themselves." Eurythmics, *Be Yourself Tonight* (RCA, 1985)

"Someday We'll All Be Free." *Malcolm X: Music from the Motion Picture Soundtrack,* various artists (Qwest, 1992)

"O Christmas Tree." *A Very Special Christmas 2,* various artists (A&M Records, 1992)

"What Now My Love." Frank Sinatra, *Duets* (Capitol, 1993)

"A Deeper Love." *Sister Act 2: Back in the Habit—Songs from the Original Motion Picture Soundtrack,* various artists (Hollywood Records, 1993)

"Respect." *Grammy's Greatest Moments Volume II,* various artists (Atlantic, 1994)

"Bridge Over Troubled Water." *Grammy's Greatest Moments Volume III,* various artists (Atlantic, 1994)

"The Makings of You." *A Tribute to Curtis Mayfield,* various artists (Warner Brothers Records, 1994)

"You've Got a Friend." *Tapestry Revisited: A Tribute to Carole King,* various artists (Atlantic, 1995)

"It Hurts Like Hell." *Waiting to Exhale: Original Soundtrack Album,* various artists (Arista, 1995)

"Jumpin' Jack Flash." *Jumpin' Jack Flash: Original Movie Soundtrack,* various artists (Musicrama, 1995)

"I'll Fly Away." *Diana: Princess of Wales Tribute,* various artists (Sony, 1997, two-disc set)

"Respect." *Blues Brothers 2000: Original Motion Picture Soundtrack,* various artists (Universal, 1998)

"Chain of Fools," "A Natural Woman," "Testimony." *VH1 Divas Live,* various artists (Sony, 1998)

"Don't Waste Your Time." Mary J. Blige, *Mary* (MCA Records, 1999)

"Ain't No Way." *Ali: Original Soundtrack* (Interscope, 2001)

"Respect." *Forrest Gump: The Soundtrack—Special Collectors' Edition* (Sony, 2001, two-disc set)

"A House Is Not a Home." *So Amazing: An All-Star Tribute to Luther Vandross,* various artists (J Records, 2005)

"Message from Aretha," "Gotta Make It (Remix)." Trey Songz, *I Gotta Make It* (Atlantic, 2005)

"Never Gonna Break My Faith." *Bobby* (motion picture soundtrack), various artists (Island Def Jam, 2006)

"How Do You Keep the Music Playing?" Tony Bennett, *Duets II* (Columbia, 2011)

Selected Albums by Rev. C. L. Franklin

Hannah the Ideal Mother (Atlanta International, 2006)
The Best of Rev. C. L. Franklin (Jewel Records, 2010)

Albums by Erma Franklin

Super Soul Sister (Brunswick Records, 2003)
Piece of Her Heart: The Epic and Shout Years (Shout Records, 2009)

Albums by Carolyn Franklin

Baby Dynamite! (RCA, 1969)
Sister Soul: The Best of the RCA Years 1969–1976 (Ace Records, 2006)

SELECTED VIDEOGRAPHY AND FILMOGRAPHY*

Videography

Aretha Franklin Live at Park West
(*Image Entertainment*, 1985)

The Blues Brothers (Collectors' Edition)
(*Universal*, 1998)
"Think" [1980]

The Blues Brothers 2000
(*Universal*, 1998)
"Respect"

VH1 Divas Live
(*Sony*, 1998)
"Chain of Fools"
"Natural Woman"

Eurythmics: Greatest Hits
(*BMG*, 2000)
"Sisters Are Doin' It for Themselves"

25 Years of Hits: Arista Records 25th Anniversary
(*Sunset Home Visual Entertainment*, 2000)
"I Knew You Were Waiting (For Me)," "It Hurts Like Hell," and
    "Freeway of Love"
[medley]

Note: Dates in brackets indicate original release of material.
*Compiled by Roberta Ritz

Ladies and Gentlemen: The Best of George Michael
(*Sony*, 2000)
"I Knew You Were Waiting (For Me)"

Rhythm, Love and Soul
(*SHOUT! RECORDS*, 2003)
"Respect"
"At Last"
"Freeway of Love"

More Rhythm, Love and Soul
(*SHOUT! RECORDS*, 2003)
"Chain of Fools"

This Is Tom Jones
(*Time Life*, 2007, three-disc set)
"I Say a Little Prayer" [1970]
"The Party's Over" [1970]

Take a Look: Aretha Franklin Complete on Columbia
(*Columbia*, 2011, box set)
Includes DVD *Aretha '64! Live on The Steve Allen Show*
"Lover Come Back to Me" [1964]
"Rock-a-Bye Your Baby with a Dixie Melody" [1964]
"Won't Be Long" [1964]
"Skylark" [1964]
"Evil Gal Blues" [1964]

Aretha Franklin: Live in Paris [1977]
(*Hudson Street*, 2011)

Tony Bennett: Duets II — The Great Performances
(*Sony*, 2012)
"How Do You Keep the Music Playing?"

Filmography

The Blues Brothers
(*Universal*, 1980)

The Blues Brothers 2000
(*Universal*, 1998)

The Zen of Bennett
(*Columbia*, 2012)
[documentary]

INDEX

Note: The abbreviation AF refers to Aretha Franklin.

115, 172, 185; funeral of, 18, 185–86,
260; political views of, 196
Knight, Gladys: AF's relationship with, 298,
422–23; AF's vocal impression of, 304;
and Ray Charles, 236; continued appeal
of, 412, 465; and Martin Luther King's
funeral, 186; memoir of, 422; and PUSH
Expo, 269; singing style of, 72, 420
Kruger, Jeffrey, 299–300, 304, 326

LaBelle, Patti, 412, 413, 415, 449, 456
LaVette, Bettye, 7, 92–94, 96–97, 104
Lee, Peggy, 37, 66, 191, 272
Leiber, Jerry, 7, 243, 309, 450
Lieberson, Goddard, 90–91, 106, 127–28,
129, 132, 135
Ligon, Joe, 375, 376, 456
Little Richard, 260, 306, 359–60
Lynn, Cheryl, 336, 370

Madonna, 385, 406, 431, 453
Malcolm X, 137, 258
Manilow, Barry, 313, 400
Mardin, Arif: as AF's arranger, 4, 177–78,
179, 187, 188, 196, 199, 250; as AF's
producer, 323–25, 329, 331, 334, 384,
391–92, 402, 409; as coproducer of AF,
210, 211, 233, 248, 284; death of, 458
Mathis, Johnny, 65, 77, 127
Mayfield, Curtis: accident of, 394, 420; as
AF's producer, 254, 287–91, 294, 295,
296, 305–6, 337, 338, 394, 409, 421; and
Carolyn Franklin, 286–89, 295; and
Erma Franklin, 180, 287, 288–89, 394;
and Donny Hathaway, 222; and message
songs, 130; recordings of, 290, 407,
420–21, 479; tribute album to, 408–9
Mayfield, Percy, 187, 306, 479
McCartney, Paul, 214, 423
McCoy, Van, 131, 171, 283, 309, 320, 361
McFarland, Leslie, 101, 102
McPhatter, Clyde, 65, 147
McRae, Carmen, 72, 88–89, 121, 164,
199, 257, 361–62, 407–8
Mercer, Johnny, 113, 428
Mersey, Bob: as AF's producer, 98,
105–7, 112, 116, 117, 122, 124, 125,
132, 135; and Barbra Streisand, 131

Michael, George, 366, 368, 397
Miller, Marcus, 332, 336, 337, 343–44
Miller, Mitch, 106, 112
Mingus, Charles, 66, 72
Minnelli, Liza, 22–23, 181, 278, 467
Moman, Chips, 146, 153, 154, 156, 215
Monk, Thelonious, 43, 71, 105, 107–8
Moore, Lola, 34–35, 36, 52–53
Moore, Phil, 78–80, 81
Morales, Pancho, 235, 248

Nathan, David, 272–73, 412
Newman, David "Fathead," 187–88, 199
Newman, Joe, 102–3, 188
Nixon, Richard, 162, 199, 217, 258,
265, 280

Obama, Barack, 457, 459, 463, 464,
470, 476
Oldham, Spooner, 146, 153, 169, 179, 196
Otis, Clyde: as AF's producer, 127, 128,
129–39, 150; on Dinah Washington,
124, 134; and Ted White, 147
Owens, Sabrina, 10, 99, 232, 445–46,
468, 469, 475

Palmer, Robert, 325, 327–28
Pareles, Jon, 369, 394, 404, 416, 451, 459
Parker, Charlie, 32, 54, 80, 188
Parrish, Avery, 43, 264
Pavarotti, Luciano, 426–27
Penn, Dan, 154, 156, 215
Peterson, Oscar, 42, 66, 80, 105, 107
Phillips, Esther, 104, 111, 191, 264
Pickett, Wilson, 146, 147, 150, 177, 381
Pollack, Sydney, 249, 252, 256, 471
Porter, Cole, 306, 479
Powell, Michael, 372, 417
Presley, Elvis, 102, 123
Preston, Billy: on AF's church, 38; and
AF's gospel album, 257; and AF's live
performances, 235, 236, 237; on AF's
piano playing, 409–10; and AF's
recordings, 264; and AF's songwriting,
400; James Cleveland as mentor to, 6,
228; on C. L. Franklin, 41; on gospel
circuit, 46, 47; on Mahalia Jackson, 260
Price, Lloyd, 83, 99, 167, 208, 436, 443

Prysock, Arthur, 42, 188
Purdie, Bernard, 235, 242–43, 248, 249, 250, 252

Radcliffe, Jimmy, 221–22
Rainey, Chuck, 248, 249, 250
Ratliff, Ben, 443, 476
Rawls, Lou, 189, 420, 448–49, 457–58
Reagan, Ronald, 326, 349, 360, 391
Redding, Otis: AF as influence on, 107; AF recording "Respect," 151, 153, 161–62, 177, 196, 325; AF recording songs of, 324; death of, 176–77; manager of, 193; recording for Atlantic, 146, 147, 148, 149
Reese, Della, 67, 77–78, 89, 261
Reid, L. A., 399, 407, 447, 449
Richards, Keith, 332, 366–67, 368, 372
Richards, Teddy White (Aretha's third son): and AF's Arista records, 344, 393; and AF's concerts, 455; AF's pregnancy, 102, 118; birth of, 122; career of, 452; in press, 469; and Ted White's family, 205
Riggins, Jean, 412–13
Robinson, Smokey: AF recording songs of, 187, 188; AF's duets with, 340, 404; on AF's talent, 31; and AF's wedding, 472; autobiography of, 4, 7; and Cecil Franklin, 71, 72, 77, 349, 372–73; and Franklin family, 4; recordings of, 77, 104, 133, 322, 357, 395; and Rock and Roll Hall of Fame, 372–73; and Mary Wells, 89–90
Rockwell, John, 278, 377
Rodgers, Nile, 295, 308–9
Rodgers and Hammerstein, 113, 117, 250
Rollins, Sonny, 72, 107
Ross, Diana: AF's relationship with, 268, 298, 299, 328; AF's vocal impression of, 261, 304; childhood in Detroit, 29; costumes of, 325; portrayal of Billie Holiday, 268, 294, 309; and Princes Diana tribute album, 423; recordings of, 237, 332, 357; singing style of, 72, 160; in Supremes, 291; Luther Vandross on, 335
Ruffin, David, 201, 309, 379, 395, 460

Rushing, Jimmy, 107, 188
Russell, Leon, 272, 444

Sager, Carole Bayer, 331, 332, 394
Salvatore, Nick, 22, 59, 110, 115
Sam and Dave, 146, 148, 164, 191, 223, 332
Scott, Bobby, 106, 116–18, 121
Scott, Little Jimmy, 7, 37, 182
Seeger, Pete, 136, 413
Shannon, Ronnie, 151, 159, 169, 183
Sheard, Karen Clark, 470, 472
Simmons, Daryl, 407, 417
Simon, Paul, 139, 226
Simone, Nina, 97, 228
Sinatra, Frank: AF compared to, 124; AF's admiration for, 112–13, 131; AF's duets with, 408; AF singing songs of, 182, 221; introduction of AF at Academy Awards, 209–10, 281; on Puccini, 428; recordings of, 100, 106, 127, 220, 436, 458
Singleton, Raynoma, 70, 93
Sledge, Percy, 147, 150
Smiley, Tavis, 7, 455, 459, 473
Smith, Bessie, 161, 163, 293–94
Sondheim, Stephen, 263, 430
Songz, Trey, 457, 458
South, Joe, 169–70, 176, 178
Spann, Pervis "the Blues Man," 163, 224
Springfield, Dusty, 203, 214
Springsteen, Bruce, 357, 385, 409
Staples, Mavis: AF performing songs of, 282; and AF's gospel album, 375, 376–77; AF's relationship with, 298, 423; AF's vocal impression of, 304; and Ray Charles, 236; and C. L. Franklin's death, 317; singing style of, 72
Staples, Pops, 178, 317
Staton, Candi, 414, 456
Staton, Dakota, 72, 103
Stewart, Jim, 146, 148–49, 150
Stoller, Mike, 7, 309
Streisand, Barbra: and Academy Awards, 209–10; AF compared to, 127, 128, 130–31; as Broadway star, 222; canceled Grammy performance of, 429; and Columbia Records, 91, 98, 126, 191, 209, 268; and Barry Gibb,

266–67, 269, 270, 271, 272–73, 278, 283–84, 288, 289, 417, 419, 461; AF's relationship with, 9, 89, 148–49, 158–59, 169, 175–76, 180–81, 189, 193–94, 306–7, 311, 312, 357–58, 399–400; on AF's relationship with father, 59; on AF's singing style, 55, 84, 466; on AF's talent, 121; and Dick Alen, 359; and Atlantic Records, 145–49, 150, 157, 171, 287, 296, 381; autobiography of, 4; and LaVern Baker, 57; and Bert Berns, 168; and Ray Charles, 236–37; on Eric Clapton, 179–80; and King Curtis, 242; on Clive Davis, 365; death of, 461; on Lamont Dozier, 294–95; on gospel music, 49; and John Hammond, 81; and Donny Hathaway, 222; Etta James on, 101; and Curtis Mayfield, 288, 291; on Sam Moore, 223; on Clyde Otis, 134; on Keith Richards, 367; and Rock and Roll Hall of Fame, 372, 373; on Narada Michael Walden, 368–69; and Ted White, 147–48, 160, 193, 198
White, Barry, 282, 283, 303
White, Ted (husband): AF's divorce from, 204, 213–14, 218–19; as AF's manager, 44–45, 96–97, 100, 109, 111, 113, 117–18, 121–22, 123, 127–28, 131, 132–33, 134–35, 136, 138, 150–55, 156, 157, 159, 163, 165, 174, 175, 179, 183, 189–90, 193, 195, 196–97, 198, 275; AF's marriage to, 93, 94, 96, 101–2, 111, 118, 131–32, 134–35, 136, 140–41, 152, 156, 158, 159–60, 162, 163, 166, 171, 172, 173, 174, 175, 178, 180, 181, 182, 185, 194, 201, 244, 245, 254, 302, 432, 455,

480; alcohol consumption of, 154, 165, 173, 254; Ruth Bowen on, 166, 181; and domestic violence, 8, 162, 174, 191, 192; and Rick Hall, 154–56; LaVette on, 92–94, 96; as pimp, 93, 94, 95, 96, 480; relationship to C. L. Franklin, 139; relationship with Dinah Washington, 26, 44–45, 94, 119; and shooting of Charles Cooke, 218–19; and *Time* magazine story, 191, 192; and Jerry Wexler, 147–48, 156–57, 167, 168, 169
Wilkerson, Willie, AF's relationship with, 368, 380, 395, 396, 432, 469, 472, 473, 477
Wilkins, Ernie, 117, 187
Williams, Andy, 91, 98, 106, 181
Williams, Jaspar, 352, 375
Williams, Jean, 305, 325
Williams, Joe, 118, 188, 272
Wilson, Flip, 236, 261
Wilson, Jackie, 70, 90, 92, 96, 348, 372
Wilson, Mary, 291, 448
Wilson, Nancy, 89, 90, 97, 124, 191, 414
Winfrey, Oprah, 363, 436–37
Wolff, Elliot, 392–93
Womack, Bobby, 68, 176, 264, 272, 306
Wonder, Stevie: AF recording songs of, 239, 272, 273; AF's musical dialogue with, 324, 445; AF's relationship with, 468; and AF's wedding, 472; and Ruth Bowen, 280; and King Curtis, 242; singing style of, 103, 312, 333; and tribute concert for C. L. Franklin, 243

Young, Andrew, 344–45
Young, Lester, 54, 106, 116, 225